REPLIES

TO

"ESSAYS AND REVIEWS."

BY THE

I. REV. E. M. GOULBURN, D.D.
II. REV. H. J. ROSE, B.D.
III. REV. C. A. HEURTLEY, D.D.
IV. REV. W. J. IRONS, D.D.
V. REV. G. RORISON, M.A.
VI. REV. A. W. HADDAN, B.D.
VII. REV. CHR. WORDSWORTH, D.D.

WITH A PREFACE

BY THE LORD BISHOP OF OXFORD;

And Letters

FROM THE RADCLIFFE OBSERVER AND THE READER IN GEOLOGY IN THE UNIVERSITY OF OXFORD.

NEW YORK:
D. APPLETON AND COMPANY,
443 & 445 BROADWAY.
M.DCCC.LXII.

ADVERTISEMENT.

It is necessary to state that the seven Essays contained in this volume have, like those Essays to which they are replies, been "written in entire independence of each other, without concert or comparison."

Each author was, individually, requested by the Publishers to write an Essay on a subject named, with the especial object of replying to a given Essay in the volume of "Essays and Reviews."

For the selection of writers, and for the choice of subject assigned to each, the Publishers are responsible. Beyond this, each writer was free to exercise his own judgment in the mode of treatment of the Essay: nor was he guided in any way by what others had written, or were writing, for the same volume.

This course of proceeding was not adopted without due consideration. It was thought, firstly, that as the "Essays and Reviews" professed to be written independently of each other and without concert among the Authors, so ought the "Replies;" otherwise, it might be objected that the latter volume was written under advantages which did not belong to the former, and therefore be refused the possession of the same weight as that volume. Secondly, that the Authors, unfettered by suggestions from Publishers or Editor, would be enabled to treat their subjects more thoroughly, to write more freely, and so more convincingly.

In most cases, the Publishers are well aware that such a course would be attended with danger, but in this case they have such full confidence in the several writers that they believe a supervision beyond that of the ordinary details attendant in passing works through the press would have been needless. They feel fully assured that all the main arguments are such as would be subscribed by all the writers, while on unimportant and avowedly open questions any discrepancies, if there should be such, might be reasonably allowed in a volume written on the plan thus adopted.

The Publishers take this opportunity of tendering their thanks to the several writers who so readily accepted the task imposed on them.

To the Bishop of Oxford, not only for the Preface, but for advice and assistance also in making the necessary arrangements for producing such a volume.

To the Radcliffe Observer, and the Reader in Geology in the University of Oxford, they are also indebted for two valuable letters. They insert them in the volume because, although unreasonably, the "Essays and Reviews" obtained the title of "The Oxford Essays." In the volume itself it will be seen that the writers are selected partly from Oxford and partly from Cambridge, as was the case in the volume to which it is hoped the present will be found to be a satisfactory and convincing reply.

OXFORD,
January 1, 1862.

CONTENTS.

PAGE

Preface. 7

By the Lord Bishop of Oxford.

I. *The Education of the World* . . . 15

By the Rev. E. M. Goulburn, D.D., late Head Master of Rugby School; Prebendary of St. Paul's; Chaplain in Ordinary to the Queen, &c.

II. *Bunsen, the Critical School, and Dr. Williams* 60

By the Rev. H. J. Rose, B.D., Rector of Houghton Conquest, Bedfordshire.

III. *Miracles* 125

By the Rev. C. A. Heurtley, D.D., Canon of Christ Church, and Margaret Professor of Divinity in the University of Oxford.

IV. *The Idea of the National Church* . . 177

By the Rev. W. J. Irons, D.D., Prebendary of St. Paul's, and Vicar of Brompton, Middlesex.

V. *The Creative Week* 242

By the Rev. G. Rorison, M.A., Incumbent of Peterhead, Diocese of Aberdeen.

PAGE

VI. *Rationalism* 299

By the Rev. A. W. HADDAN, B.D., Rector of Barton-on-the-Heath, Warwickshire.

VII. *On the Interpretation of Scripture* 350

By the Rev. CHR. WORDSWORTH, D.D., Canon of Westminster; Proctor in Convocation, &c.

Appendix.

I. LETTER from the Rev. ROBERT MAIN, M.A., Pembroke College, Radcliffe Observer 425

II. LETTER from JOHN PHILLIPS, M.A., Magdalen College, Reader in Geology in the University of Oxford . . 436

PREFACE.

The volume which is here placed in the reader's hands seems to me to need neither preface nor recommendation. The importance of its subject, the gravity of the occasion which has called it forth, the weighty names in the catalogue of its writers, all combine to demand for it the full attention which preface or recommendation might solicit for an ordinary volume. Nevertheless, yielding to the request of those who had combined to produce it, I had promised to contribute a preface to it; and having done so, I desired to enter at some length into the general subject towards which these several essays converge, and to the mode in which it had been dealt with here.

Diocesan engagements compelled me to postpone my work to an approaching period of comparative leisure. But at this moment my contribution is called for, and rather than delay the publication of the work, I have resolved to furnish it at once, reduced to the narrowest dimensions; and even before I have been able myself to read any of the following Essays.

It is then of the general object only of the work that I can speak. As to which let me say,—first, that its object is not so much to reply directly to error, as to establish truth, and so to remove the foundations on which error rests; secondly, that the publication of this volume is no admission that new or powerful arguments against the truth have rendered necessary new arguments in its defence. Rather, the re-statement of old truths of which it consists is a declaration that the fresh-varnished objections which have called it forth are neither new nor profound. Further, there is no allowance here that the views which have called it forth are open questions or fair subjects for discussion between Christians, still less between Church of England men. Its scope is to shew that the objections to which it refers are old objections, the urging of which must of necessity, with our limited faculties, be possible against all revelation; and that, as such, they have been often put forth, repeatedly answered. Such difficulties are to be set at rest in any mind rather by strengthening the deep foundations of the faith than by the labored refutation of every separate, captious, and casuistic objection in which repugnance to all fixed belief of dogmas, as having been directly communicated by God to man, is wont to vent itself.

That such objections to revelation should appear in this day, and should clothe themselves in the fresh garb which they have assumed, will not seem strange to thoughtful minds. Not, indeed, that it is other than a very narrow philosophy which would conceive of them as a mere reaction from recently renewed assertions of the pre-eminent importance of dogmatic truth and of primitive Christian practice, or even from the excesses and evils which have, as they always do, attended on and disfigured this revival of the truth. To attempt to account for these phenomena by such a solution as this, is to fix the eye upon the nearest headland round which the stream of time and thought is sweeping, not daring to look further; and so to deal with all beyond that nearest prospect as if it were not. No; this movement of the human mind has been far too wide-spread, and connects itself with far too general conditions, to be capable of so narrow a solution. Much more true is the explanation, which sees in it the first stealing over the sky of the lurid lights which shall be shed profusely around the great Antichrist. For these difficulties gather their strength from a spirit of lawless rejection of all authority, from a daring claim for the unassisted human intellect to be able to discover, measure, and explain all things. The rejection of the faith, which in the last age assumed the coarse and vulgar features of an open atheism, which soon destroyed itself in its own multiplying difficulties, intellectual, moral, civil, and political, has robed itself now in more decent garments, and exhibits to the world the old deceit with far more comely features. For the rejection of all fixed faith, all definite relation, and all certain truth, which is intolerable to man as a naked atheism, is endurable, and even seductive, when veiled in the more decent half-concealment of pantheism. The human soul in its greatness and in its weakness crying after God, cannot bear to be told that God is nowhere, but can be cajoled by the artful concealment of the same lie under the assertion that God is everywhere, for that everything is God. The dull horror of annihilation is got rid of by the notion of an absorption into the infinite, which promises to the spirit an unlimited expansion of its powers, with the misty hope of retained individual consciousness. Nor in this system is all former belief to be cast away at the rude assault of an avowed infidelity; on the contrary, it is to be treated with the utmost tenderness. It is not even stated to be false; in a certain sense it, too, is allowed to be true; for there is nothing which is wholly true or wholly false. It is but one phase of the true—an imperfect, childish, almost infantine phase, if you will; to be cherished in remembrance like the ornaments or the delights of childhood, only not to be rested in by men; to be put away and looked back upon, as early forms which, as soon as the Spirit which had of old breathed through them revealed itself in rosy light, dissolved, like the frost-work of the morning beneath the full sunlight of noon. On this theory, the facts of the Bible may be false, its morals deceptive, its philosophy narrow, its doctrines mere shadows cast by the acting of the human mind in its day of lesser light: and yet, on the other hand, it is not to be scorned; it is to be loved, and honoured, and revered as a marvellous record of the God-enlightened man in his infancy, in the comparative obscurity of his intellect, in his youthful struggles, and reachings forth after the truth; only it is not to fetter his now ripened humanity. The man is not to be swathed in the comeliest bands of his infancy.

Thus no prejudice is to be shocked, no holy feeling rudely wounded, no old truth professedly surrendered. Rather, mighty revelations are to be looked for amidst the glowing feelings with which the past is fondly recognised and the future eagerly expected. Thus the pride of man's heart is flattered to the utmost; thus the old whisper, "Ye shall be as gods," disguises itself in newest utterances; thus in the universal twilight all the fixed outlines of revealed truth are confounded;

the forms of Christianity are dissolved into nothingness, and the good deposit of the faith evaporated into a temporary intellectual myth, which has played its part, done its work, and may be permitted quietly to disappear amongst the venerable shadows of the past.

Such a state of the human mind may be traced with more or less distinctness, during this century, everywhere in Christendom. It may be seen speculating in German metaphysics, fluttering in French literature, blaspheming in American spiritualism; or it may come, as it has come amongst ourselves, with dainty step and faded garments, borrowed from one school or another of stronger unbelievers, as it was supposed that our less prepared minds could endure the revelation.

The conflict between such a system and all true Christianity must be certain and complete. For, disguise it as you will, it is simple unbelief. Pantheism is but a tricked-out Atheism. The dissolution of Revelation is the denial of God.

With such a wide-spread current of thought, then, the strong foundations of Church-of-England faith came rudely in contact. Her simple retention of the primitive forms of the Apostolic Church; her Ministry, and her Sacraments; her firm hold of primitive truth; her Creeds; her Scriptures; her Formularies; her Catechism; and her Articles; all of these were alike at variance with the new rationalistic unbelief. The struggles and strifes of the last thirty years have been the inevitable consequence. The passionate re-assertion of the old truths, with all the evils which have waited on that passion, as well as all the immeasurable good which has been the fruit of the re-assertion,—all of these have been themselves the consequence of the widely-acting influence to which the human mind has of late been subjected. Short-sighted men have looked at these things with their narrow range, and believed that the scepticism which on the one side has been evolved in the struggle, was the fruit of that energetic assertion of the truth which was itself but one consequence of the unbelief with which it was striving.

As well might they believe that the causes of the existence of some naked promontory, which has had its sharp and rocky point defined by the great current it has long breasted, or of that mighty ocean-like flow which sweeps against it, are to be found in the boisterous waves which roar down the lower stream, and fleck with foam the agitated waters of its troubled bosom.

Two distinct courses seem to me to be required by such a state of things.

First, the distinct, solemn, and if need be, severe, decision of authority that assertions such as these cannot be put forward as possibly true, or even advanced as admitting of question, by honest men, who are bound by voluntary obligations to teach the Christian revelation as the truth of God.

I put this necessity first, from the full conviction, that if such matters are admitted by us to be open questions amongst men under such obligations, we shall leave to the next generation the fatal legacy of an universal scepticism, amidst, an undistinguishable confusion of all possible landmarks between truth and falsehood.

To say this, be it observed, is to evince no fear of argument against our faith though the freest, or of enquiry into it though the most daring. From these, Christianity has nothing to dread. In their issue these do but manifest the truth. The roughest wind sweeps the sky the most speedily, and shews forth the soonest the unclouded sun in all his splendour. It is not, therefore, because believers in Revelation fear enquiry, that authority is bound to interfere. But it is to prevent the very idea of truth, as truth, dying out amongst us. For so indeed it must do, if once it be permitted to our clergy solemnly to engage to teach as the truth of God a certain set of doctrines, and at the same time freely to discuss whether they are true or false. First, then, and even before argument, our disorders need the firm, unflinching action of authority.

Secondly, we need the calm, comprehensive, scholar-like declaration of positive truth upon all the matters in dispute, by which the shallowness, and the passion, and the ignorance of the new system of unbelief may be thoroughly displayed.

That this volume may in some measure, at least, fulfil these conditions, is the endeavour of its writers, and the hope of him who ventures now to commend it to the prayers of the Church, and the study of its readers.

S. O.

CUDDESDON PALACE,
Dec. 1861.

THE EDUCATION OF THE WORLD.

"*The Education of the World.*" *By* FREDERICK TEMPLE, D. D., *Chaplain in Ordinary to the Queen; Head Master of Rugby School; Chaplain to the Earl of Denbigh. The Second Edition.* (*London: John W. Parker and Son, West Strand.* 1860.)

"*The Education of the Human Race.*" *From the German of* GOTTHOLD EPHRAIM LESSING. (*London: Smith, Elder, and Co.* 1858.)

> "How charming is Divine Philosophy!
> Not harsh and crabbèd, as dull fools suppose;
> But musical as is Apollo's lute."

WE quite echo back these words of our great bard. Divine philosophy is charming in its every shape;—not only that discovery of precious moral truth in ancient myths which, judging from the context, Milton seems to have had principally in his thoughts, but any true theory of the dealings of God with man to which the words "divine philosophy" might be suitably appropriated. If we can at all get a glimpse into the significance of the Scheme of Grace, as God has been unfolding it from the primitive prediction of the Seed of the woman until now, this glimpse cannot fail to be attractive and cheering,—as attractive and cheering (though perhaps as much obstructed) as that which the pilgrim gains, at interstices between tangled boughs, of the spires and pinnacles of the city to which his steps are bent. But just as in physical science the true philosopher will never form theories independently of the facts of nature; just as his crude guesses will be originated, modified, enlarged by those facts, in some cases retracted and thrown aside in obedience to them; just as all natural philosophy consists in being led by the hand of nature into natural truth,—so the divine philosopher will never draw up his scheme independently of the truths of Holy Scripture, (which are in theology what the facts are in nature;) his theories will not only be started, but corrected, by those truths, and will be safe, and sound, and valuable, just so far as in forming them he has been led by the hand of God's Word.

We have before us two essays on the education of the human race, and the slightest glance at either of them shews that the author means the religious or spiritual education which God is conferring upon man. We shall attempt to clear the ground for our criticism by pointing out the senses in which man may be truly said either to have received from God, or to be receiving, a spiritual education.

I. First, there can be no doubt that man (or rather that portion of the human race which is under the divine economy, and which we think, with Dr. Temple, may not unfairly be regarded as a representative of the whole race*) is receiving an education in time for eternity. Earth is the school in which God's people are being trained for heaven. This is clearly implied in the well-known passage, 1 Cor. xiii. 9, &c. We are children at present, conceiving darkly, reasoning uncertainly, and expressing ourselves imperfectly; but hereafter we shall come to the full maturity of our

* "*If the Christian Church be taken as the representative of mankind*, it is easy to see that the general law observable in the development of the individual may also be found in the development of the Church."—*Essays and Reviews*, p. 40.

We do not see that the hypothesis can be quarrelled with. Though in one important sense the world and the Church are opposed to one another, yet, under another aspect, regenerate humanity is surely a sample of the whole. "Of His own will begat He us with the word of truth, that *we should be a kind of first-fruits of His creatures.*" (James i. 18.)

powers, knowing no longer in the way of discovery, but intuitively, "even as also we are known," and no longer needing to express things divine by figures and images drawn from things earthly. Take the dawning intelligence and the limited experience of a little child, not yet emancipated from the restraints of the nursery, and contrast them with the large research of a Columbus, the sagacious investigations of a Bacon, and the profound discoveries of a Newton, and you have then, if the Scripture analogy be correct, some idea of the proportion which our present mental and spiritual faculties will bear to our attainments hereafter. The analogy at once teaches us this, that just as there are many truths, quite on a level with a man's understanding, which cannot be at all explained to a child with its present capacities, and others which can only be explained very imperfectly, by illustrations drawn from its own narrow circle of ideas and associations; so there are some spiritual truths altogether out of our reach in our present condition, and others which can be conveyed to us only through the imperfect medium of earthly relations and human language. All man's insight into divine truth is and must be, as its essential condition, "through a glass," and all his knowledge in a riddle, (ἐν αἰνίγματι.) He can only see, not the object itself, but an image of it reflected in a mirror, whose surface is never quite true or quite smooth; he can only know heavenly things by comparisons with earthly, (which comparisons must break down somewhere,) not by conversancy with the realities. And the moral lesson to be learnt from this education of the human race would be, that our heavenly Father intends for us, by our present condition of existence, a discipline of humility of mind; and that, therefore, having once seen our way to faith in God's Word, (and abundant light is supplied to us for this purpose,) we must thenceforth acquiesce devoutly in the difficulties and obscurities which beset some of its statements, remembering that, if we could see through all entanglements, faith would cease to be faith, and become sight. This theory of man's education humbles his reason, instead of exalting it, and pours contempt upon his utmost mental progress, instead of magnifying it as the maturity of his powers.

II. But there is another sense in which we may speak of the education of man,—a sense more definitely recognising the race as one creature, and so more nearly approaching Dr. Temple's theory of "a colossal man, whose life reaches from the creation to the day of judgment."

We are told that God's ancient Church received from Him a preparatory discipline to fit it for the reception of the Gospel:—"The Law," says the Apostle, "was our schoolmaster to bring us unto Christ." While the economy of the Law was running its course, God's child (His Church) was under "tutors and governors," "in bondage under the rudiments of the world." But the fulness of the time came, when the One great Master, to whose class-room the pedagogue had but conducted* the learner, appeared upon earth. He taught the truth, which made men free; and, hearing this truth, the heir was emancipated from the restraints of childhood, and entered upon his inheritance. This education, therefore, was terminated, not by the end of the world, or the day of judgment, but by the first coming of Christ.

Now, guiding ourselves by this clue, a most interesting theory might be drawn out of the education of the world, the outline of which, at all events, would be correct. Such a theory has been attempted in a little work, which has been many years before the public, but which perhaps is less extensively known than it deserves.† We can here only find space for the most rapid sketch of the argument. Before the Saviour appeared upon earth, it was necessary that men should be prepared to appreciate the blessings and the truth

* Persons acquainted only with the English version of the Holy Scriptures will need to be warned that the word translated 'schoolmaster' in the passage referred to, properly denotes, not the actual instructor, but a domestic employed to take charge of children and see them safe to school. Christ is our rabbi, at whose feet we sit, to receive the truth which makes us free; and the Law is the domestic who "brought us unto" Him.

† The Philosophy of the Plan of Salvation: a Book for the Times.

which He would reveal; otherwise they would never have intelligently received the Gospel. No mind could apprehend Christianity, which was not first well grounded in certain elementary religious ideas, which had been corrupted in the Fall, and further depraved in that frightful result of the Fall, the degeneracy of idol worship. In restoring these ideas to the mind of man, and forming there certain new ones, which were necessary to the intelligent reception of the Gospel, God determined to act on His usual principle (which runs through all His dispensations) of using men for the instruction of men. One man, however, would not suffice for so great a work as the preparatory initiation of the human mind into elementary religious ideas. He would not live long enough; and, while he did live, could not make his influence felt widely enough. God therefore must raise up *a nation of teachers;* must thoroughly imbue them with the elementary ideas, and then finally disseminate them, in the order of His Providence, and cause them to come in contact with the mind of other nations. This, accordingly, was the plan which He adopted. He first prepares the Israelites for His purpose, riveting them together by a common parentage felt to have the sacredness of caste in it, by a common worship, distinct altogether from that of other nations, by the long oppression under which they groaned in a strange country, and by the miraculous deliverance from Egypt, which came to them just as their minds were in a high state of excitement and susceptibility. This is the account which we should be inclined to give of that "extraordinary toughness of nature" * in the Jew, upon which Dr. Temple comments, so far indeed as the result was brought about by natural causes, and not chiefly due to the special interference of God, who for His own purposes has endowed their nationality with extraordinary vital powers. Israel having by these means become a strongly marked and firmly united people, with

* "The people whose extraordinary toughness of nature has enabled it to outlive Egyptian Pharaohs, and Assyrian kings, and Roman Cæsars, and Mussulman caliphs," &c.—*Essay on the Education of the World*, p. 14.

the most exclusive sympathies and antipathies, then commenced the throwing into their minds those religious conceptions with which, in long process of time, and by varied discipline, their whole souls were to be imbued. First was communicated, as the original ground of all religious thought, the personality, and existence of God, altogether independently of His attributes, which were afterwards to be revealed. If a man does not believe that God exists, or that a personal God exists, there is no basis for religion to stand upon in that man's mind. The first name, therefore, under which God made Himself known to the people whom He was training as the religious teachers of the world, was "I am,"—leaving all besides to subsequent development, "I am that I am."

Next followed the covenant relationship in which God condescended to stand to them, (for the idea of absolute God is bleak and dreary, however sublime,—chilling rather than attractive to the heart): "And God said moreover unto Moses, Thus shalt thou say unto the children of Israel, The Lord *God of your fathers, the God of Abraham, the God of Isaac, and the God of Jacob*, hath sent me unto you: this is my name for ever, and this is my memorial unto all generations." * This personal God, so related to them, was then shewn by the miracles which preceded and attended the Exodus, to be mightier than all the gods of the Egyptians; or, to use the words of Lessing, (Sect. 12,) "Through the miracles, with which He led them out of Egypt and planted them in Canaan, He testified of Himself to them as a God mightier than any other god." Thus the Israelitish mind got as far as these three ideas—personality, covenant relationship, Almighty power. The moral attributes had next to be impressed upon it. And this was done by the promulgation of the Law, both moral and ceremonial. The Ten Commandments, revealing, as they did, the will of God as regards man's conduct, proclaimed His holiness. But the people being still in the infancy of religious knowledge, the

* Exod. iii. 15.

same lesson was taught in another way by external observances and an appeal to the senses. The notion of moral purity was developed in their mind, and connected with the thought of God, by the ceremonial distinctions between clean and unclean beasts, and the use of the former class only in sacrifice,—by the separation of the priests from the people, of the holy of holies from the holy place, and of that from the court of the tabernacle, and by the ceremonial washings and sprinklings which both sacrifices and priests and worshippers had to undergo. The justice of God, which exacted the forfeiture of life as the desert of sin, and at the same time the possibility of transferring the penalty to an innocent victim, which constitutes the idea of atonement, would be taught by the sin-offerings, with which the worshipper was supposed to identify himself by laying his hands on the victim. In short, all the observances of the Mosaic ritual would be to the Jew like so many pictures in a child's primer, by which rough but lively ideas are conveyed to the child of objects which it never yet saw.

The unity and spirituality of God, enforced so often by positive precepts and minor punishments, were the truths which the national mind found it most difficult to master. Has the propensity to Pantheism,—to the recognising something divine in every object of the world of nature,—so entirely ceased among Christians of the nineteenth century, who live under the ripest experience of the "colossal man," that we shall be surprised to find a similar propensity somewhat tenaciously rooted in the minds of a people always stiff-necked, and uncircumcised in heart and ears? Is no tendency manifested now-a-days in any part of the Christian Church to lean unduly upon objects of sense and external aids in religious worship? Well,—tendencies similar to these in principle were to be sternly corrected in those who were to be the appointed religious teachers of the human race. When less severe discipline had failed, God smote them with a stroke so heavy, that the smart of it taught them this, the lesson of His unity and spirituality, effectually, and printed it in ineffaceable characters upon their minds. The Babylonish captivity cured them altogether of idol worship; while the dispersion which accompanied it answered another great end,—*it brought the Jews into contact with the Gentile mind, and thus put God's trained masters into communication with their scholars.* It domesticated many of them in different parts of the heathen world, made them learn Gentile tongues, and enabled them to introduce into those tongues the ideas which they themselves had imbibed. The Septuagint translation of the Old Testament Scriptures enshrined for ever the religious ideas of the Jews in the language which, through the Macedonian conquest, had spread itself over the whole civilized world.

This design of God's providence in the dispersion of the Jews, is implied in the strongest way, if we cannot say that it is expressed, in the Holy Scriptures of the New Testament. The day on which the new dispensation was solemnly inaugurated under the auspices of the Holy Spirit, found Jews at Jerusalem out of every nation under heaven,—"Parthians, and Medes, and Elamites, and the dwellers in Mesopotamia, and in Judæa, and Cappadocia, in Pontus, and Asia, Phrygia, and Pamphylia, in Egypt, and in the parts of Libya about Cyrene, and strangers of Rome, Jews and proselytes, Cretes and Arabians." And we know from other parts of the Acts of the Apostles that large bodies of proselytes were found in all the chief cities of the ancient world,—Jews by religion, Gentiles by birth,—who, as having affinities with both, acted as a ready-made bridge by which the truths of the Gospel might pass over from one to the other. Does not the existence of these proselytes argue that the Jews had leavened very considerably the religious mind of the Gentiles in the various countries of their dispersion? They had leavened it by the diffusion of those fundamental religious ideas—such as the personality and unity of God, holiness, the atonement, the inseparable union of morality with religion—which are necessary to the acceptance and appreciation of Christianity. And thus the intellect of the human race may be said to have been matured for the reception of the Gospel.

In the fulness of the Time* came the great Teacher, to impart the knowledge of the Truth (or, in other words, of Himself) which should make men free. He lifted from off their necks the yoke of the ceremonial Law, which neither that generation to which He came, nor their fathers, were able to bear. He relieved them sensibly of the burden of unforgiven sin, cancelling in His Blood the records of the accusing conscience, and the handwriting of the moral law, "which was contrary to us." He relieved them also of the oppressive tyranny of sin by His grace, which communicated a new spring of energy to their wills, and brought into operation motives which, if they existed before, were never before so powerfully elicited. But in speaking of this liberty wherewith Christ made us free, it is observable how carefully both our Lord and His Apostles guard themselves against the notion of its being lawless, or emancipated from moral restraints. He promises to give rest to those who come to Him, but the rest consists not in the absence of a yoke and burden, but in its light pressure: "Take *My* yoke upon you . . . . and ye shall find rest unto your souls. *For My yoke is easy, and My burden is light.*" The freedom which He bestows is a freedom from the service of sin.† It is an obedience from the heart to a form of doctrine; it is

* Dr. Temple's Essay is said to have grown out of a sermon (preached before the University) on "the fulness of the Time."

We have attempted (in a humble way) to shew how, when our Lord appeared, *the Church* of God was prepared for His appearance by the gradual discipline of foregone dispensations. The subject, however, may be looked at in another light; and the "fulness of the times" may be considered in reference to *the desperately corrupt state of the world* at large, which called for some direct Divine interference. See a masterly sermon by Dr. Robertson the historian, (1759,) "On the Situation of the World at the Time of Christ's Appearance," in which it is shewn how "the political, moral, religious, and domestic state of the world at that time" were all eminently suitable to the great event. The sermon is now, unfortunately, one of those rare pieces which is only to be found in old collections of tracts.

† See John viii. 32, 34, 36.

a service of God.* The Christian has a law, and a law by which he will be judged; although indeed it is a law of liberty.† And St. Paul, when shewing how he adapted his ministry to those whom he approached with it, and how to the Gentiles who were without (revealed) law he became as without law, retracts the very word *ἄνομος*, ('lawless,') lest it should be misunderstood: "Being *not* without law to God, but under the law to Christ." He was, even as an apostle, under a law, although indeed it was "the law of the Spirit of life."‡ Thus the Bible gives no sanction to the idea that the present state of the Christian is one of emancipation from law, though no doubt we are exempt from obedience to the ceremonial rules imposed by the old economy.

Even to this exemption we do not find that the original Jewish converts, or even the original Apostles, easily accommodated themselves. The Jewish mind had yet need of further training, (even after the descent of the Holy Ghost,) before it burst the shell of ritual restraints. The liberty of the Church from ceremonial bondage, and its essential Catholicity, are gradually developed in the Acts of the Apostles. St. Peter is reconciled to this part of the Divine plan by a vision, and a voice from heaven, and a providential circumstance, and an intimation of the Holy Ghost; and yet afterwards recalcitrates, and needs to be publicly expostulated with by a colleague.§ The first Christian Council solemnly decides for all time the question that circumcision is not necessary for Gentile converts. St. Paul's preaching and influence at length, under the blessing of God, brought about that full and free expansion of religious thought which had been so long unfolding by various agencies. But it was only an expansion which refused to be cramped any longer within the narrow limits of the Mosaic law; not one, like that affected by moral Rationalists, which feels itself narrowed by creeds and formularies of doctrine. With deference to Dr. Temple,

* Rom. vi. 17, 22.
† James i. 25, and ii. 12.
‡ Rom. viii. 2.
§ Acts x. 11, 13, 17, 20; Gal. ii. 14.

who tells us that "there are no creeds in the New Testament, and hardly any laws of Church government," we think that 1 Tim. iii. 16 sounds remarkably like a creed, and that "the form of sound words" * which Timothy is exhorted to hold fast, must have been something of the kind; and we should be at a loss to define the contents of the pastoral Epistles, if we might not say that they contained the laws of primitive Church government.

In concluding this sketch, we may venture to suppose that the signal for the final emancipation of religious thought from the bondage of the Mosaic law was given by God's own hand, when Jerusalem and the Temple were demolished, and Judaism had no more a local habitation upon earth.

And shall we say that after this period all further religious development of the mind of the Church ceased? We think that the intimations of Holy Scripture, if not its express declarations, lead us to an opposite conclusion. We have seen that even after the day of Pentecost an Apostle had something of religious truth yet to learn. We have seen that even the presence of the Holy Spirit, in His miraculous gifts, did not supersede the necessity for the sentence of a Christian Council. And certain it is, that the Apostolic age, when it passed away, left the Church founded in the earth, and nothing more; that its full organization had yet to be given it, its battlements had yet to be constructed. Accordingly, as Dr. Temple says, "the Church's whole energy was taken up, in the first six centuries of her existence, in the creation of a theology." Heresies (that is, deviations from the faith taught by the Apostles and embodied in their writings) sprang up, and made it necessary that the truth should be, not indeed revealed anew, but re-stated, and cleared by definition and illustration. This was done by Œcumenical Councils; and we have the results of the process in our Creeds. In the decisions of these Councils, forms of expression and technical terms of theology are

* 2 Tim. i. 13.

of course introduced, which are not found in the Holy Scriptures, (for if the bare Scriptural expressions had sufficed for the refutation of heresy, where would have been the need of a conciliar determination?) but it is remarkable how the first four Councils found their conclusions on the uniform and continuous belief of the Church from the beginning, shewing that they did not presume to add anything to primitive truth, but merely to vindicate and clear it of those parasitical errors which threatened its existence. In short, divine truth, having been cast into the seed-plot of human minds, was constantly springing up with certain accretions which came from the vice of soil, which accretions had to be removed as they arose; and thus each of the four great Councils, if in one sense an expositor of the Word of God, was in another sense a reformer, bringing things back to the primitive model of belief. They sought perfection of theology, not in the developments of future ages, but in what had been received in the past.*

And shall we say that, since the decisions of the Œcumenical Councils, the science of theology has received no further accessions? None, we think, similarly authenticated. We should attach the greatest deference now-a-days to the decisions of an Œcumenical Council, if such could be gathered, which should have a sufficient occasion and object, should be impartially constituted, and should found its decisions entirely on Holy Writ, as interpreted by primitive antiquity. But at the same time we fully concede that, in the absence of such Councils, and without the sanction which they would lend, the evolution of divine truth in the human mind is always going on.

On this head we quote Mr. Archer Butler's letter in reply to Mr. Newman's "Theory of Development." Nowhere else shall we find words at once more succinct and more exhaustive of the subject:—

* Mr. Archer Butler describes the functions of the early Councils with admirable terseness as well as clearness, when he says, (Development, p. 224,) "The function of the early Councils was . . . to define *received* doctrine, *to elucidate obscured* doctrine, *to condemn false* doctrine. But it was *not* to *reveal new* doctrine."

"I have no disposition to conceal or question that theological knowledge is capable of a real movement, in time, a true successive history, through the legitimate application of human reason. This movement may probably be regarded as taking place in two principal ways:—

"The first is the process of *logical development of primitive truth* into its consequences, connexions, and applications." [An instance of what the author means by logical development, is thus given in a former part of the work: "When we have learned, on the infallible authority of inspiration, that the Lord Jesus Christ is Himself very God, and when we have learned from the same authority the tremendous fact of His Atoning Sacrifice, we could collect (even were Scripture silent) the priceless *value* of the atonement thus made; the wondrous *humiliation* therein involved; the unspeakable *love* it exhibited; the mysteriously awful *guilt* of sin, which would again reflect a gloomy light upon the equally mysterious eternity of *punishment*."]

"The *second* is, *positive discovery*. Members of the English Church—which (by a strange dispensation of Providence) has, since its lapse into 'heresy,' done more to benefit Christianity in this way than all others put together—will not find much difficulty in conceiving many classes of these precious gifts of God to His Church, conveyed through the ministration of human sagacity. Such are—

"1. Unexpected confirmations or *illustrations of revealed doctrine* from new sources; as from unobserved applications or collations of Holy Scripture; or from profound investigations of natural religion, and the philosophy of morals, as in some parts of the researches of Bishop Warburton.

"2. New proofs in support of *the evidences of religion;* such as the conception and complete establishment of the analogical argument by Bishop Butler, or the invention and exquisite application of the test of undesigned coincidence by Paley.

"3. Discoveries regarding *the form and circumstances of the Revelation itself;* such as those of Bishops Lowth and Jebb on the remarkable structure of the poetical and sententious parts of Holy Writ.

"4. Discoveries of *divine laws* in the government of the Church and world, so far as the same may lawfully be collected by observation and theory.

"5. Discoveries, through events disclosing the *meaning of prophecy*, or correcting erroneous interpretations of Scripture."

To these we may add what perhaps the learned and highly-gifted writer intended to classify under the third head:—

Accessions to the stock of knowledge, already possessed by the world, of the languages in which the Holy Scriptures were written.

While upon this point, we cannot avoid quoting the weighty testimony of one who (great as Mr. Archer Butler was) was greater than he, to "the possibility of a real movement of theological knowledge in time, through the *legitimate* application of human reason." It is a grand passage, and will well repay perusal:—

"As it is owned, the whole scheme of Scripture is not yet understood; so, if it ever comes to be understood, *before the restitution of all things*, and without miraculous interpositions; it must be in the same way as natural knowledge is come at, by the continuance and progress of learning and of liberty; and by particular persons attending to, comparing and pursuing, intimations scattered up and down it, which are overlooked and disregarded by the generality of the world. For this is the way, in which all improvements are made; by thoughtful men's tracing on obscure hints, as it were, dropped us by nature accidentally, or which seem to come into our minds by chance. *Nor is it at all incredible, that a book, which has been so long in the possession of mankind, should contain many truths as yet undiscovered.* For all the same phenomena, and the same faculties of investigation, from which such great discoveries in natural knowledge have been made in the present and last age, were equally in the possession of mankind, several thousand years before. And possibly it might be intended, that events, as they come to pass, should open and ascertain the meaning of several parts of Scripture."—*Butler's Analogy of Natural and Revealed Religion*, book ii. ch. 3.

It will be seen that both Mr. Archer Butler and his illustrious namesake quite admit a certain progress of the human mind on theological subjects by "the legitimate application of reason." How can such a progress be questioned? Would there be any room at all for the science of theology, if the illustration, elucidation, interpretation, application, enforcement of the sacred Books had been stereotyped at the time they were given? Does not the Church's ordinance* of preaching, which is to endure for all time, assume that the human mind is to be brought in contact with the Word of God, and to deal with it in the way of explanation, enforcement, and so forth? And if a good sermon of a single preacher, composed with the ordinary help of God's spirit, often throws real light on the Word of God, can the ministers of the whole Church of Christ from the beginning, (thousands of them men of the profoundest erudition as well as the deepest piety,) have failed to do a great deal, not indeed in the way of revealing any new thing, but of unfolding and illustrating what has been revealed? It may be greatly questioned whether any truth in the world can be fully appreciated by the human mind, when it is freshly lodged there. It must first be studied and discussed,—must pass through the various stages of questioning, controversy, advocacy, before it can gain a real and influential hold. In this respect, of course, later ages of the Church have an advantage over earlier ones. The truth has been more maturely considered, filtered through a larger variety of human minds, devout and indevout; and if, on the one hand, it has gained certain accretions from the process, on the other its bearings and significance are now more fully understood.

It is, however, most important to remark that between this progress of the mind of the Church, and the progress, which Dr. Temple brings into comparison with it, of the individual mind, there is one very striking difference, which he has wholly overlooked. The education of the individual is carried on by substantive accessions of knowledge, and the rudiments are swallowed up and lost as the knowledge grows. But *the education (if we are to call it so) of the Church is all*

* An ordinance which surely must not be narrowed to oral addresses made in a church, but must include also religious instruction by books, &c.

wrapped up in the rudiments;—it is simply an expansion of "the faith once delivered to the saints." Revelation stands not at the end, but at the beginning, of the Church's career. The highest degree of knowledge is communicated to the Church in the first instance; all that follows is merely a full development of the import of that knowledge. IN INDIVIDUAL EDUCATION, THE MORE ADVANCED SCIENCE EMBRACES THE RUDIMENT; BUT IN THE EDUCATION OF THE CHURCH, THE RUDIMENT (WHICH IS REVELATION) EMBRACES THE MORE ADVANCED KNOWLEDGE. He that is perfectly master of a language, so as to speak and write fluently in it, forgets his rules of grammar; they remain with him only in the shape of "a permanent result." But when the Council of Constantinople condemned the Macedonian heresy, it by no means superseded, but simply unfolded, and brought out more clearly into the general consciousness of Christendom, the import of that great precept, "Grieve not the Holy Spirit of God," and of that comfortable benediction, "The grace of the Lord Jesus Christ, and the love of God, and the communion of the Holy Ghost, be with you all." The man who can read Greek has outgrown his English spelling-book. But the "colossal man" (or, as we should prefer to put it, the Church of the latter days) can never outgrow Scripture; all she can do is to appropriate more thoroughly the nourishment of divine truth contained in it, and to "grow thereby."

We conceive that the above theory of the education of the world, although not in all its parts explicitly Scriptural, yet holds all along to the clue which Scripture furnishes. For,—

1. Scripture speaks of the law as pædagogic,—a discipline of childhood, "to bring us unto Christ."

2. Scripture speaks of a Church synod, after the first promulgation of Christian truth, for the determination of questions vitally affecting the interests of the Church.

3. Scripture provides a ministry of teaching and preaching among uninspired men.

We shall now proceed to examine the first of the "Essays and Reviews" under the light thus gained.

Very early one of the fallacies which pervades it is made to appear. The writer having told us (what doubtless may be admitted) that the long lapse of time since the creation of man must have a purpose, and that "each moment of time, as it passes, is taken up into the time that follows in the shape of permanent results," goes on to assert that not only does knowledge receive continually a fresh accession, but also "the discipline of manners, of temper, of thought, of feeling, is transmitted from generation to generation, and at each transmission there is an imperceptible but unfailing increase." (p. 4.) What, precisely, does the learned Essayist mean by this "discipline of manners, temper, thought, and feeling," which is always on the increase? Does he allude to the humanizing influences of civilization, which certainly gild and varnish the surface of society, while they leave the vices of the human heart untouched? It may be conceded to him that these influences do secure an improvement in manner, and to a certain extent in temper, round off many a sharp angle, and restrain many an impetuous sally, which might end in provocation and mischief. We are not quite sure, however, that civilization has been regularly and steadily progressive among men. In the more prominent nations of the world it has had its day, has run its course, and then has collapsed and become effete. But granted that we could trace in it (as regards mankind in general) any regular progression, surely Dr. Temple does not mean to represent this as a divine education, either of the Church or of the world. Yet the thought is constantly obtruded upon us, as we read his Essay, that he is confusing the progress of the species by civilization, with the progress of the Church in divine knowledge.

But will he say that by discipline of manners, temper, thought, and feeling, he means a *moral advance* of the human species, or of the professing Church? Then surely this is contrary to all the facts of experience as to the anticipations of man's moral career which Holy Scripture would lead us to form. With Dr. Temple, we suppose that the long succession of time exists for a great purpose. A mighty drama is developing its plot upon the earth, which shall issue, if the Scripture be true, not in the moral improvement of the species, but in the glory of God, by the final salvation of His true people from the present evil world. So far from the moral improvement of the species being gradually worked out, as this drama proceeds, the fallen will of man, instigated by external evil agency, is everywhere counterworking God, and continually being overruled by His good Providence to His own greater glory. And what we have to expect, as time goes on, is that both evil and good will draw to a head together; that if on one side of us the lights will be brighter, on the other the shadows will be darker, until the Righteous One and the Evil One in personal manifestation confront one another on the stage of the earth. Such is the history of the race which Scripture leads us to expect. But putting out of sight the intimations of Scripture, are any traces of moral progress visible in the history of the world? To take only the histories of Rome and Greece, to which Dr. Temple more than once refers, is not the picture which they present one of moral degeneracy rather than of moral improvement? What had become of the stern integrity and primitive simplicity of the ancient Romans in the last days of the Empire? Did the public virtue and patriotism of Greece stand higher in the days of Aristides or in the days of Philopœmen? And to turn to the history of the Church of God, were the Jews of Manasseh's day better or worse than those of David's? Was the spirit of true religion more developed among the Pharisees and Sadducees of our Lord's time,* than among the

* Dr. Temple admits further on, that "it is undeniable that, in the time of our Lord, the Sadducees had lost all depth of spiritual feeling, while the Pharisees had succeeded in converting the Mosaic system into so mischievous an idolatry of forms, that St. Paul does not hesitate to call the law the strength of sin."—(p. 10.)

little band who, in obedience to the edict of Cyrus, sought again their country, and rebuilt, amidst manifold oppositions, their temple? Has even Christianity eradicated the vices of the human species? We cannot think it, when we remember the monstrosities of the French Revolution, and the rampant tyranny which the three worst passions of the human heart (vanity, ferocity, and lust) then exercised among a people moving in the first rank of civilization, and who had been for centuries nominally Christian. Quite as much then, we suspect, as in the antediluvian world, was there to be seen upon earth "brutal violence and a prevailing plague of wickedness." Surely these and similar instances prove that whatever development of human resources, and of the natural powers of the mind, may attend the lapse of time, there has not been in the species generally any moral or spiritual progress; and that man, if (under certain circumstances) restrained by law and softened by civilization, is still fundamentally what he became in the moment of his fall, "earthly, sensual, devilish."

Or again, can it be anyhow made to appear that from the days when man first began to make his own nature, relations, and duties a subject of study, *moral science has been steadily advancing?* A simple comparison of the moral philosophy of Cicero with that of Plato, will shew that any such theory must be utterly baseless. Plato embodied the Socratic teaching on moral subjects; and never in after ages was there any heathen teacher of moral truth at all approaching to Socrates.

What then, precisely, *is* the progress of the species to which our Essayist refers? Great as his abilities unquestionably are, we cannot but think that his Essay is pervaded by confusion of thought, and that in its most fundamental idea. There is the Scriptural assertion, (certain, because Scriptural,) that the ancient Church was disciplined by the Law for the reception of Christ. There is the patent fact, that the civilization of a single people advances (at least up to a certain point) and brings in its train certain humanizing influences. There is the old remark, so beautifully embodied in the first *Pensée* of Pascal, that in respect of knowledge and research we enter into the possession of the stores which our ancestors have accumulated, and have a wider range of prospect than they, because, being mounted higher, we can see further. There is the admitted fact, that explanations and illustrations of God's Word are multiplied and varied "through the legitimate application of human reason," as time goes on. Finally, there is all around us in the present age, when "men run to and fro and knowledge is increased," a rapid movement of mind, which continually throws up new ideas to the surface; a jewel here and there, and a great deal of rubbish. The learned Essayist has, as far as we can see, mingled all these sorts of progress together, and elicited from them the idea of a "discipline of manners, of temper, of thought, of feeling, transmitted from generation to generation," which, we are persuaded, has no existence but in his own mind. This we hold to be the *πρῶτον ψεῦδος* of the whole Essay. But to proceed.

The divine training of mankind, he tells us, has three stages. In the individual, "first come rules, then examples, then principles." In the species, "first comes the Law, then the Son of Man, then the gift of the Spirit." The sins of the antediluvian world (like those of a child before he is sent to school) were those of violent temper and animal appetites :—

> "The education of this early race may strictly be said to begin when it was formed into the various masses out of which the nations of the earth have sprung. The world, as it were, went to school, and was broken up into classes."—(p. 7.)

The classes, as it appears from a subsequent part of the Essay, were four :—the Roman class, in which the will was disciplined; the Greek class, which cultivated the reason and taste of the race; the Asiatic class, in which was developed the idea of immortality; and the

Hebrew or highest class, in which the conscience was trained.

Now, independently of the puerility of detail into which the illustration is allowed to run, we must here object to Dr. Temple that, letting go of the Scriptural clue which might have guided him to a right theory, he thereby throws the divine agency in the education of man entirely into the background. The great Parent, Master, and Guide of the world's youth is as much as possible hidden away from our eyes. Where and how does it appear that Rome, Greece, Asia, were in any sense *religious* educators of the human race? That they contributed much to the education of the *human mind*, (and in the way which Dr. Temple eloquently and beautifully states,) no one will be disposed to deny. That the mind of the human race has been, and ever will be, applied to religion, sometimes with evil and sometimes with good results, must be also universally admitted. But from these premises we can never collect that the discipline bestowed by Rome, and Greece, and Asia, was a discipline in divine truth. *It gave nothing beyond simple mental development.* A soil is formed by the fall and decomposition of decayed leaves, by accidental deposits of manure, or by some alluvial residuum; and when it is formed, an agriculturist throws a fence round it, and sows seed in it, and rears plants; but *we do not speak of the agencies which acted upon and prepared the soil, as either seeds or sowers.* Why could not our Essayist have followed where Scripture points the way, and have told us that, man having proved a disobedient and prodigal son, his heavenly Father for awhile left him to pursue his own devices, (as parents will sometimes allow wilful and truant children to run riot and injure themselves,) that the hopeless disorder into which his nature had fallen might be proved to himself,—and not until this was becoming apparent by the wide-spread and deepening corruption of idolatry, did God take in hand the education of the species, (an education which was of the nature of a recovery,) by founding a nation of teachers, and throwing

His revealed truth like seed into that nation's mind? As it is, there is a painful ignoring of any truth divinely communicated or revealed; and the impression left is, that the mental culture, for which the race is indebted to Greece and Rome, is a thing the same in kind with the special discipline in truth and holiness which has been the prerogative of the Church of God.

Moreover, in describing this gradual discipline, as it took effect upon the ancient Church, while much that he says is true and forcible, Dr. Temple drops altogether the idea that the discipline was *preparatory for Christ.* The Law, according to him, was a schoolmaster to bring men—not to Christ, but—to that period of the age of humanity when the world was ripe for example. Not a word of the ceremonial Law, darkly prefiguring Christ. Not a word of the moral Law, convicting and condemning, and, by doing so, creating a feeling of moral need which only Christ could meet; but simply an expansion of religious thought, paving the way for its further expansion under the Gospel,—a weaning from idolatry, and a discipline in chastity of morals and spirituality of conception. All true, no doubt, and important in its place; but we become (and surely not without reason) impatient of the little prominence given to the revealed Object of faith, and of Christ being represented rather *as a stage in the human mind, than as the One Centre of hope, and aspiration, and devout desire.*

Having conducted his colossal man through the period of childhood, the Essayist next notices his youth:—

"The tutors and governors," he says, (that is, Greece, Rome, Asia, and more especially Israel,) "had done their work. It was time that the second teacher of the human race should begin his labor. The second teacher is Example. . . . The youth can appreciate a character, though he cannot yet appreciate a principle. . . . He instinctively copies those whom he admires, and in doing so imbibes whatever gives the colour to their character."

Dr. Temple states very forcibly the power of example in the youth of the individual, and then goes on to draw out the analogy in this respect between the individual and the species :—

> "The second stage of the education of man was the presence of our Lord upon earth. . . . Our Lord was the Example of mankind, and there can be no other example in the same sense. But the whole period from the closing of the Old Testament to the close of the New, was the period of the world's youth—the age of examples."

Surely, it is very questionable whether the generations which lived between the close of the Old Testament and that of the New, were peculiarly susceptible to example more than men of the present day. Dr. Temple himself, perhaps, would hardly have said so, had not the exigencies of his theory demanded it of him. At all events, what proof can be given that it was so? For our own part, we believe that the influence of example is now as potent with men in general as it ever was. The most profitable and the most popular of all religious works are the biographies of saints and eminent Christians; nor do we believe that any period of the Church has been left destitute of such testimony to divine truth, and the indwelling of the Spirit, as example furnishes. As God has illustrated His truth by *the variety of minds* brought to bear upon it, so He has also confirmed it in the Church's experience by *the variety of hearts* in which its sanctifying power has been recognised. His saints have, no doubt, adapted themselves to the circumstances and manners of their own time; but in all essential graces they have been one with the saints of the world's youth, and have all taken up the cross and followed the great Exemplar. Indeed, Dr. Temple recognises this when he says :— "Saints had gone before [our Lord] and saints have been given since; . . . there were never, at any time, examples wanting to teach either the chosen people or any other." But his theory demanded that the age of our Lord should be represented as the age of examples;

and accordingly the facts of the case, if admitted, must be glossed over.

But there are graver charges which lie against this part of the Essay than that of an analogy which, when examined, will hardly hold water.

When we are reviewing, as Dr. Temple professes to be reviewing, the great scheme of God's dealings with man; and when we remember that Christ is the key and corner-stone of all those dealings; we must say that the position assigned to our Lord in the theory of the Essayist is totally inadequate. For what does this position amount to? In the course of the world's history there has been an age of examples; and Christ, as the Example of examples, stands at the head of that age. Now it is true, no doubt, that the atoning work of our Blessed Lord, *in its objective character*, it did not come within the province of the Essayist to notice. He is writing upon the sanctification, not on the justification, of man; he is treating of the work which has to be done upon the human mind, and does not profess to go higher. It is man's education, not God's provision for his salvation, which is in question. But granting this, (and in fairness it ought to be granted,) should the *subjective bearings of Christ's Atonement* have been wholly ignored in an Essay tracing the theory of the education of the human race? Was it not a step in man's education, which at least deserved notice, when God threw into his mind that new and most powerful of all motives, the love of a crucified Saviour, and wholly altered his conceptions of virtue by giving to the passive graces of character,—submission, resignation, humility, meekness, poverty of spirit,—a lustre which they never had before? But no; the theory is rigidly to confine itself to an imaginary natural progression of the species, analogous to the growth of the individual, and cannot easily make room for supernatural interferences on the part of God. In these omissions of the first Essayist we perceive with sorrow the germs of those frightful errors which, stated positively, disfigure the other parts of this unhappy book.

But worse remains behind in this section of the Essay. The Essayist is explaining how our Blessed Lord came in the fulness of time, "just when the world was fitted to feel the power of His presence." And on this point he says,—"Had His revelation been delayed till now, assuredly it would have been hard for us to recognise His divinity; for the faculty of faith has turned inwards, and *cannot now accept any outer manifestations of the truth of God.*" In plain words, the world has now become too wise to accept miracles as the credentials of a message from God. Surely this statement is both unphilosophical and unscriptural. Whatever marvels natural science may have discovered, the laws of the mind have not altered. And can it be disputed that it *is* a law of the mind to expect that a divine message will be accredited by miracles, and to demand such credentials from a person claiming to come with a new message to the world? We believe instinctively that the effect will be commensurate with the cause, and that the work will bear some proportion to the nature of the agent. We expect from irrational creatures actions on a level with their capacity,—the display of appetites and passions, and occasionally the sagacities of instinct. From men, in like manner, we expect what we know humanity to be competent to. *From God, on the same principle, we expect (when the occasion worthy of them arises) actions exceeding human power.* Constituted as we are, we shall never outgrow this expectation, any more than we can outgrow any other law of the mind. It is true indeed that the expectation may *take degenerate or superstitious shapes*, that it may form its conclusions with undue precipitation, and so mislead us. The tendency to expect from a Divine Being an evidence of supernatural power, has often prompted men to credit too hastily the professed supernatural, or to accept as God's work that which is the devil's. These are perversions of the instinct which shew that it needs regulation. But dispense with the instinct we cannot. It is another instinct of the mind, which may be depraved, but of which we can never rid ourselves, to infer a general truth for particular instances. Hasty inductions are very foolish and very unscientific, and have been the fruitful parents of error. *But no one on this account throws over the principle of induction altogether as a means of arriving at truth.* A man of well-disciplined mind may say that it wants regulation, and that it must be exercised with discrimination; but he will never say that we can do without it. So with the tendency to expect supernatural events as credentials of a divine message. We may rest too much on the supernatural events. They may not be the most important credentials, and in the absence of others, (such as teaching which approves itself to the moral sense,) they may be altogether unsatisfactory and inconclusive. But to reject the supernatural altogether as a credential is to strain the mind awry out of its natural constitution; to cut ourselves off altogether from one means of access to divine truth; to shut one door by which God's revelations reach us.

Nor is the position of the Essayist more Scriptural than it is philosophical. Our Blessed Lord more than once rests His claims on His miracles: "If I do not the works of My Father, believe Me not. But if I do, though ye believe not Me, believe the works: that ye may know, and believe, that the Father is in Me, and I in Hm." * Does our Essayist mean to tell us that He rested His claim on a ground which did not really bear it out? which would not have even seemed to bear it out, had His generation been more enlightened? Could our Lord have expressly sanctioned a view of things which has no foundation in truth? If "outer manifestations of the truth of God" are to an advanced and disciplined intellect unsatisfactory and inconclusive, would Christ (whose province surely it was to raise the tone of the popular mind) have appealed to them? Would it not have been far worthier of Him in that case to come with no other credentials than that of a doctrine which went home to man's heart, and to have said, "Believe Me on this ground; for on no other

* See also John xiv. 10, 11; Matt. xi. 4, 5.

ought a messenger of God to be received and believed?" To use such language would have been quite in the genius of an ancient philosopher; it is altogether language which might have been held by Socrates, and very nearly approaches to much of the language which Socrates actually did hold:—"If what I say does not carry with it the convictions of your reason, I would not have you believe it, even were it attested by a sign from heaven." But our Lord *did not* use such language. He referred to the signs from heaven as rendering the people inexcusable for not believing. ("If I had not done among them the works which none other man did, they had not had sin.") And yet our Essayist implies that "the works which none other man did," would not have secured credit for Christ as a divine ambassador from the men of this generation, because, forsooth, "faith has now turned inwards and cannot accept any outer manifestations of the truth of God." Dr. Temple, we are sure, is an earnest and devout Christian, who would shrink sensitively from shaking in any mind the evidences of Christianity. Has he considered what is the real scope and significance of this unfortunate sentence of his Essay? It has been admirably shewn by Davison* that "the vindication of our faith rests upon an accumulated and concurrent evidence," derived not from one but from many sources, —"miracles, fulfilment of prophecy, the sanctity of our Lord's doctrine, His character as expressed in His life, the triumphant propagation of His religion without arms, eloquence, or learning, and its singular adaptation to the nature and condition of man." Our Lord Himself seems to have rested the evidence on three main supports:—I. Miracles.† II. Purity of doctrine, re-echoed by the moral sense; "If I had not come and *spoken unto them*, they had not had sin." III. Prophecy; "Search the Scriptures; for in them ye think ye have eternal life: and they are they which testify of Me." "Had ye believed Moses, ye would have believed Me: for he wrote of Me." No. I. perhaps

* Discourses on Prophecy, i. † See the passages just referred to.

might be called an appeal to the senses; No. II. to the conscience; No. III. to the understanding. No doubt, one age will attach greater weight to one of these branches of evidence, another to another. No doubt, also the present generations of men, being to a certain extent familiarized with scientific marvels and having gained a considerable power over nature, would be impressed by miracles in a less lively way than men of former times, when the material laws which govern the universe had not been discovered. But is it wise, or is it reverent, to knock away any one of the fair columns, on which the Lord Himself has rested the truth of His holy religion, on the pretext, that the superior enlightenment of the nineteenth century enables us to dispense with it? The argument for Christianity being essentially cumulative, is it charitable to weak brethren (to take the lowest ground) to destroy its cumulative force? Yet this is really what Dr. Temple's argument in the above passage goes to.

Besides our Lord, (though in a scale far inferior to Him,) the Essayist enumerates certain other examples vouchsafed to the human creature when in a state of adolescence. Greece and Rome, who were in the former period teachers of classes, ("giving us the fruits of their discipline,") now appear as associates, and "give us the companionship of their bloom." The early Church was another associate, "an earnest, heavenly-minded friend, whose saintly aspect was a revelation in itself."

As regards the placing Greece and Rome in the same category with the early Church, (that is, with our Lord's immediate followers,) we find here another instance of that confusion of thought, by which the mental and social development of mankind—his arts, his learning, his civilization—is made part of his religious progress. Dr. Temple writes an exquisite passage (the gem of his Essay, quite worthy of being preserved in a commonplace-book) on the distinguishing excellence of classical literature, the *freshness* of its grace. We thank him for a noble piece of writing; but how is it *ad rem?* What has the mere cultivation of taste (to which, of course, classical literature has very largely contributed) to do with the very serious subject on which we are engaged, "God's education of the human race?" That the classics have contributed much to the civilization of man will not be denied. But are not civilization and the progress of the Church somewhat sharply distinguished in Scripture, which surely is a sign that the two should be kept asunder as separate subjects of thought? We commend to Dr. Temple's notice the pregnant fact, that in the earliest extant history of mankind it is stated that *arts, both ornamental and useful*, (and arts are the great medium of civilization,) *took their rise in the family of Cain.* In the line of Seth we find none of this mental and social development. Is he not mixing up in his theory the mental and material progress of the world, with the spiritual progress of the Church, two things which God has kept carefully distinct?

As regards the early (i. e. the Apostolical) Church, he strives to make out (as his theory requires of him) that it presents to us example chiefly, to the exclusion of doctrine and precept. It has left us, he says, little beyond examples. "The New Testament is almost entirely occupied with two lives, the life of our Lord and the life of the early Church." As for the Epistles, they are only "the fruit of the current history." Doubtless, all the books of the New Testament (and the same might be said of most of those of the Old) were written *on special occasions;* but who will deny that principles both of doctrine and duty, which disentangle themselves from and rise very much above the occasion, are continually being thrown out by the sacred writers? Who will deny that the mind of the Spirit, though legislating primarily for the occasion, contemplates beforehand and provides for the future emergencies of the Church? Is there no warning against future error in the reproof of the Blessed Virgin by our Lord? or in His assertion that "he who hears God's word, and keeps it, the same is His mother?" or in His severe censure of St. Peter? or in St. Paul's withstanding St. Peter to the face?

Great part of the Scriptures are no doubt narratives; but the narrative is only the vehicle of doctrine and precept, which are always more readily received in a concrete than in the abstract form. No writing, however eloquent and ingenious, (and Dr. Temple's is both,) will ever successfully gloss over the fact that the New Testament *does* contain the principles of all Christian doctrine and duty; nor would any one (*εἰ μὴ θέσιν διαφυλάττων*) ignore the usual definition of the Epistles as doctrinal books.

We now come to the last stage of the Essayist's theory:—

> "The susceptibility of youth to the impression of society wears off at last. The age of reflection begins. From the storehouse of his youthful experience the man begins to draw the principles of his life. The spirit or conscience comes to full strength and assumes the throne intended for him in the soul. As an accredited judge, invested with full powers, he sits in the tribunal of our inner kingdom, decides upon the past, and legislates upon the future, without appeal except to himself. He decides not by what is beautiful, or noble, or soul-inspiring, but by what is right. Gradually he frames his code of laws, revising, adding, abrogating, as a wider and deeper experience gives him clearer light. He is the third great teacher and the last."—(p. 31.)

In this last stage of his progress the individual learns, we are told, by "the growth of his inner powers and the accumulation of experience," by "reflection," by "the mistakes both of himself and others," and by "contradiction." Though free from outward restraint, he is still under an internal law, "a voice which speaks within the conscience, and carries the understanding along with it." If his previous education have not given him the control over his will, he must acquire it by a self-imposed discipline, which with weak persons assumes the shape of a regular external law. Then passing (as his wont is), from the moral to the intellectual, from the discipline of the will to that of the mind, Dr. Temple tells us that persons of mature age, who really think for themselves, are often obliged to put a temporary restraint on their intellects, and finding their speculations (specially if they turn on practical subjects) bewildering and unsatisfactory, "finally take refuge in a refusal to think any more on the particular questions." Some, on the other hand, are always forming theories on insufficient grounds, and are "as little able to be content in having no judgment at all, as those who accept judgments at second hand." Then, finally, even the matured intellect of the full-grown man does not altogether break with the associations of childhood :—

> "He can give no better reason very often for much that he does every day of his life than that his father did it before him; and provided the custom is not a bad one, the reason is valid. And he likes to go to the same church. He likes to use the same prayers. He likes to keep up the same festivities. There are limits to all this. But no man is quite free from the influence; and it is in many cases, perhaps in most, an influence of the highest moral value."—(p. 39.)

Analogous to this, we are then told, is the last stage in the education of the human race, so far as it has yet gone. Since the Apostles' days, the Church has been left to herself to work out, *by her natural faculties*, the principles of her own action. Her doctrines were evolved, partly by reflection on her past experience, and by formularizing the thoughts embodied in the record of the Church of the Apostles, partly by perpetual collision with every variety of opinion. (This corresponds to the growth of the individual's inner powers by "reflection," "contradiction," and "the mistakes both of himself and others.") But "before this process was completed, a flood of new and undisciplined races poured into Europe," and "necessitated a return to the dominion of outward law." The papacy of the middle ages was "neither more nor less than the old schoolmaster (Judaism) come back to bring some new scholars to Christ." (This corresponds to the self-discipline which the grown man, who has imperfectly acquired self-control, is obliged to impose upon himself.) Then came the Reformation, when the yoke of mediæval discipline was shaken off. Its great lesson was—not, as one would imagine, the power of God's pure Word over the human heart, and of the simplicity of primitive religion, but—the lesson of toleration. Men then began to see, and have ever since seen more clearly, that "there are insoluble problems upon which even revelation throws no light." "The tendency of toleration is to modify the early dogmatism by substituting the spirit for the letter, and practical religion for precise definitions of truth." (This corresponds to that state of mind of the individual in which, finding speculations bewildering and unsatisfactory, he refuses to think any more on the questions which trouble him, and contents himself with so much of truth as he finds necessary for his spiritual life.) Some definitions of truth, however, seem to be necessary, as a point without the world of religious opinion, from which the lever may be applied to move the world. Accordingly, the post-Reformation Church looks for these definitions in the volume of Holy Scripture. In this connexion we find the passage to which so much objection has been made. We will not trust ourselves to represent its meaning in our own words. It runs thus:—

"In learning this new lesson, Christendom needed a firm spot on which she might stand, and has found it in the Bible. Had the Bible been drawn up in precise statements of faith, or detailed precepts of conduct, we should have had no alternative but either permanent subjection to an outer law, or loss of the highest instrument of self-education. But the Bible, from its very form, is exactly adapted to our present want. It is a history; even the doctrinal points of it are cast in a historical form, and are best studied by considering them as records of the time at which they were written, and as conveying to us the highest and greatest religious life at that time. Hence we use the Bible—some consciously, some unconsciously—not to override, but to evoke the voice of conscience. When conscience and the Bible appear to differ, the pious Christian immediately concludes that he has not really understood the Bible. Hence, too, while the interpretation of the Bible varies slightly from age to age, it varies always in one direction. The schoolmen found purgatory in it. Later students found enough to condemn Galileo. Not long ago it would have been held to condemn geology, and there are still many who so interpret it. The current is all one way—it evidently points to the identification of the Bible with the voice of conscience. The Bible, in fact, is hindered by its form from exercising a despotism over the human spirit; if it could do that, it would become an outer law at once; but its form is so admirably adapted to our need, that it wins from us all the reverence of a supreme authority, and yet imposes on us no yoke of subjection. This it does by virtue of the principle of private judgment, which puts conscience between us and the Bible, making conscience the supreme interpreter, whom it may be a duty to enlighten, but whom it can never be a duty to disobey."—(pp. 44, 45.)

The advance of toleration, however, is not entirely progressive. It is apt to be retarded by a strong inclination, in all Protestant countries, to "go back, in every detail of life, to the practices of early times." (This corresponds to the love which grown people often manifest for the customs and associations of their home, —a feeling of great moral value, though accompanied perhaps with something of narrowness.) Still toleration is progressing in the main, (though, like the tide, it has refluent waves,) and gains gradually upon the mind of the race. Then our author (somewhat inconsecutively it appears to us) springs from toleration to the subject of Biblical interpretation. That interpretation, he thinks, we must expect to be greatly modified. Nor need we fear such modification. We should welcome all discoveries which really throw light on the Scripture, however rudely they may jar with preconceived notions. This is the age of thought: "clear thought is valuable above everything else, excepting only godliness;" and to exert it upon Scripture and elicit original results is the great task and vocation of the age. That we should address ourselves to the task candidly and fearlessly, is the practical exhortation with which the Essay is wound up.

Dr. Temple appears to mean by toleration something distinct from what commonly goes by the name. Most people would define toleration as the allowing to others the free exercise of their religion. Dr. Temple seems to identify it, as far as we can catch the thread of his argument, with *a free interpretation of doctrines and articles of faith.* The two things, however, by no means go together. If we might admit that at the Reformation, toleration, in the ordinary and popular sense, first dawned as an idea upon the mind of the Church, (which yet a person thinking of Servetus and Joan Bocher might be disposed to doubt,) *surely the Reformation had no conceivable sympathies with laxity or indefiniteness of doctrine.* Only let a person read the elaborate Confessions of Faith of the Protestant Churches, and we are persuaded he will come to the conclusion that sharp and austere definition of doctrine (and not the reverse) was the genius of the Reformation. Indeed, the second article of the Solemn League and Covenant * alone is enough by itself to raise a question how far, *in any sense of the word*, toleration made its appearance with the Reformation. Our modern latitudinarians (we do not mean to include Dr. Temple under this designation, though we are compelled to apply it to some of his coadjutors) wish to extract from the carcase of religion the hard skeleton of definite doctrine, (upon which the whole structure is built,) and to leave only the pliable and soft parts, ("practical religion," "the spirit instead of the letter,") which are constantly in a transition state, like the flesh and blood of the animal frame. But they will not find among the Reformers, either English or foreign, any sympathies with such a design. The post-Reformation

* "That we shall in like manner, without respect of persons, endeavour the extirpation of popery, prelacy, (that is, church-government by archbishops, bishops, their chancellors, and commissaries, deans, deans and chapters, archdeacons, and all other ecclesiastical officers depending on that hierarchy,) superstition, heresy, schism, profaneness, and whatsoever shall be found to be contrary to sound doctrine, and the power of godliness, lest we partake in other men's sins, and thereby be in danger to receive of their plagues; and that the Lord may be one, and His name one, in the three kingdoms."

creeds are generally quite as hard in outline as the Athanasian. And we may confidently assert that the Reformers were right in building their systems on the framework of creeds. Without such framework, religion is apt to collapse and corrupt, as a body of flesh from which the bones should be withdrawn.

We have been accustomed to think that the Christian is under the twofold guidance of the Spirit and Word of God,—distinguished and yet combined in that admirable collect for St. John's Day:—"Merciful Lord, we beseech Thee to cast Thy bright beams of light" (the Spirit) "upon Thy Church, that it being enlightened by the doctrine of" (the Word) "Thy blessed Apostle and Evangelist St. John, may so walk in the light of Thy truth, that it may at length attain to the light of everlasting light; through Jesus Christ our Lord." But in the education of the individual, the learner being emancipated from all restraints when he has reached mature age, it did not suit Dr. Temple's theory to notice these external guides; his "colossal man" must be left to guide himself when he comes to years of discretion. Accordingly, in the last section of the Essay, the guidance of the Holy Spirit is entirely ignored, as far as explicit statement goes; and were it not for the capital letter in the sentence, "The human race was left to itself, to be guided by the teaching of the Spirit within," and for the slight intimation, "*Whatever assistance* the Church is to receive in working out her own principles of action, is to be through her natural faculties, and not in spite of them," we might say of the author what the Ephesian disciples, who had received only John's baptism, said of themselves, "He hath not so much as heard whether there be any Holy Ghost."

Dr. Temple, no doubt, will say that in virtue of His indwelling in the faithful, he regards the Spirit of God as identified with the spirit of man. But we cannot help thinking that a far more explicit recognition of the Holy Spirit's personality, and a far more constant reference to His agency, might have been made without the smallest interference with the plan of the Essay; nor, indeed, can we think that the office of the blessed Comforter is at all exhausted, or even adequately represented, by saying that the Church is now to guide herself, not by external rule, but by the application of principles to the varying exigencies of her position.

The guidance of the Word, however, being more extrinsic than that of the Holy Spirit, some attempt must be made to surmount the obstacles which it seems to throw in the way of the theory. And the attempt is made in the passage quoted at length above. We find it exceedingly hard to trace the exact connexion of thought between the sentences of which this passage is composed. We *suppose* it to be something of this kind:—"The Bible is indeed external to the mind of man; but then it is very elastic, and, as the history of its interpretation shews, accommodates itself very readily to the mind of man. So that the Bible promises at some future, but not distant, time, to resolve into enlightened reason, and leave the spirit of man the sole arbiter of its own duties." We think Dr. Temple is here confounding the conscience of man with his understanding, and the preceptive character of the Bible with its aspect as a history of certain miraculous events. Had he confined his remarks to *the preceptive part* of the New Testament, every one would of course admit that it is a book of principles rather than rules, and that the adjustment of those principles *is* left to the individual conscience, under the direction of the Holy Spirit of God. It is also most true (and most important truth) that this guidance of the Holy Spirit is in the New Testament itself thrown very much more into the foreground than any written document; that, under the present economy, it is "the anointing from the Holy One which teacheth all things," and "the law of the Spirit of life" (not a law graven on tables) which presides in the human spirit. Had Dr. Temple said this, he would have said what not only does not admit of dispute, but also what appears to us to suit his argument quite as well as the gravely questionable things which he has said. But, as the paragraph stands, he has mixed up *the record of miraculous facts in* Scripture, *which are in the sphere of man's understanding*,* (not in that of conscience,) with its precepts, *which are in the sphere of his conscience and not of his understanding;* thereby producing a sad confusion of thought. He alludes to certain narratives of Scripture which, in consequence of modern discoveries in natural science, are now understood in a manner different from that in which people once accepted them. This is a matter for the understanding, surely, and not at all in the sphere of the conscience. Researches into nature shew that the miracle in Joshua and the Mosaic cosmogony have been misunderstood, and that we must correct our apprehensions of the meaning of these passages. Well, what then? Argal, says Dr. Temple, "The current is all one way,—it evidently points to the identification of the Bible with the voice of *conscience.*" We confess we cannot catch the connexion between the premises and the conclusion. We should have drawn the conclusion somewhat in this fashion:— "The current is all one way,—it evidently points to a general recognition of the truth that the interpretation of Scripture is one thing, and the true sense another." If there be *any* connexion between the premises and the conclusion, we avow ourselves unable to trace it, except in this most offensive form, (which we believe Dr. Temple would repudiate as earnestly as ourselves):—"Geological and astronomical discoveries have proved the Bible *wrong* on points of natural philosophy. It does not much matter, however; for the true Word of God is not co-extensive with the Bible, but only contained in it; that portion only of the Bible is the true Word which is recognised by the moral sense or verifying faculty. So that the current is all one way,—we are gradually knocking away from the framework of our

* We have said above (p. 42) that miracles may be called "an appeal to *the senses.*" But of course the understanding must operate upon the notices of the senses, in order that the evidence derived from a miracle may be appreciated.

belief those portions of the Bible which the conscience cannot assimilate; histories we may doubt or give up, only retaining their moral; much more may we give up cosmogonies; the only residuum we need leave is that portion of the sacred volume to which our verifying faculty saith 'Yea;' so that at length the Bible resolves itself into the voice of conscience." This gives the passage in question a certain logical sequence, and also a melancholy coherence with the avowed sentiments of other Essayists. If Dr. Temple meant this, why did he not say it explicitly? But we will not believe he did mean it. Of the two alternatives open to him, illogical writing and the reduction of God's Word to the square measure of man's conscience, we joyfully accept for him the former. And we take his Essay as a solemn warning of the dreadfully unsafe statements into which a very good and very able man may be driven, who will ride an ingenious and plausible analogy to death, even when at every turn it breaks down under him afresh.

We turn, with something of a sense of relief, to notice Lessing's treatise on the "Education of the Human Race," which, perhaps, may have suggested Dr. Temple's. If so, we think that the original conception of Lessing (although parts of it are far more extravagant than anything to be found in the first Essay) has materially suffered in clearness and power from Dr. Temple's method of treatment. Our readers shall judge. The German author begins with this fundamental statement:—

> "That which education is to the individual, revelation is to the race.
>
> "Education is revelation coming to the individual man; and revelation is education which has come, and is yet coming, to the human race.'"—(Sects. 1, 2.)

Revelation, it will be observed, *and revelation exclusively*, is, according to Lessing, the educator of the race. He does not, with Dr. Temple assign a class to Greece, and a class to Rome, and a class to Asia, recognising them as teachers, and thus putting them on a level with revelation. He supposes, indeed, that when "in captivity under the wise Persians," the doctrine of the Mosaic Law respecting the unity and spirituality of God, and its hints and allusions in regard to the doctrine of immortality, were developed in the consciousness of the Jews by their contact with the Gentile mind. But he knows nothing of any educator save God in revelation, nor of any other persons as educated by Him, save the people of His covenant. The other nations of the earth, he thinks, were left without education by the Universal Father, in consequence of which,—

> "the most part had remained far behind the chosen people. Only a few had got before them. And this, too, takes place with children who are allowed to grow up left to themselves; many remain quite raw; some educate themselves even to an astonishing degree.
>
> "But as these more fortunate few prove nothing against the use and the necessity of education, so the few heathen nations, who even appear to have made a start in the knowledge of God before the chosen people, prove nothing against a revelation. The child of education begins with slow yet sure footsteps; it is late in overtaking many a more happily organized child of nature; but it *does* overtake it; and thenceforth can never be distanced by it again."—(Sect. 21.)

So far we think the German has the advantage of the Englishman, inasmuch as he gives revelation a far more exclusive prerogative.

At the outset of Lessing's Essay he makes the following startling assertion, of which, if we cannot agree with it in its present form, we may at all events say that we wish all the assertions of our seven Essayists were as explicit, and presented as clear an outline to the understanding:—

> "Education gives to man nothing which he might not educe out of himself; it gives him that which he might educe out of himself, only quicker and more easily. IN THE SAME WAY, TOO, REVELATION GIVES NOTHING TO THE HUMAN SPECIES WHICH THE HUMAN REASON LEFT TO ITSELF MIGHT NOT ATTAIN: ONLY

IT HAS GIVEN, AND STILL GIVES TO IT, THE MOST IMPORTANT OF THESE THINGS EARLIER."—(Sect. 4.)

It immediately rises to the mind of the reader that there are doctrines of revelation (such as those of the Atonement and the Trinity) which never could be attained by the human reason, and are plainly altogether out of its reach. The German theologian is prepared for this, and carries his theory through with a boldness which, at all events, is perfectly consistent. He thinks the doctrines of the Atonement and the Trinity *may be ultimately reached by the human reason;* and he believes the great end of God's training of the human race to be *the recognition by reason of all the truths of revelation.* But he shall speak for himself:—

"As we by this time can dispense with the Old Testament, in reference to the doctrine of the unity of God, and as we are by degrees beginning also to be less dependent on the New Testament, in reference to the immortality of the soul: might there not in this book also be other truths of the same sort prefigured, mirrored as it were, which we are to marvel at, as revelations, exactly so long as until the time shall come when reason shall have learned to educe them out of its other demonstrated truths, and bind them up with them?

"For instance, the doctrine of the Trinity. How if this doctrine should at last, after endless errors right and left, only bring men on the road to recognise that God cannot possibly be One in the sense in which finite things are one, that even His unity must be a transcendental unity, which does not exclude a sort of plurality? Must not God at least have the most perfect conception of Himself, i. e. a conception in which is found everything which is in Him? But would everything be found in it which is in Him, if a mere conception, a mere possibility, were found even of his necessary reality, as well as of His other qualities? This possibility exhausts the being of His other qualities. Does it that of His necessary reality? I think not. Consequently, God can either have no perfect conception of Himself at all, or this perfect conception is just as necessarily real (i. e. actually existent) as He Himself is. Certainly the image of myself in the mirror is nothing but an empty representation of me, because it only has that of me upon the surface of which beams of light fall. But now if this image had everything, everything without exception, which I have myself, would it then still be a mere empty representation, or not rather a true reduplication of myself? When I believe that I recognise in God a similar reduplication, I perhaps do not so much err, as that my language is insufficient for my ideas: and so much at least remains forever incontrovertible, that they who wish to make the idea thereof popular for comprehension, could scarcely have expressed themselves more intelligibly and suitably than by giving the name of a Son through whom God testifies of Himself from eternity.

"And the doctrine of Original Sin. How, if at last, everything were to convince us, that man standing on the highest and lowest step of his humanity, is not so entirely master of his actions as to be *able* to obey moral laws?

"And the doctrine of the Son's satisfaction. How, if at last, all compelled us to assume that God, in spite of that original incapacity of man, chose rather to give him moral laws, and forgive him all transgressions in consideration of His Son, i. e. in consideration of the self-existent total of all His own perfections, compared with which, and in which, all imperfections of the individual disappear, than *not* to give him those laws, and then to exclude him from all moral blessedness, which cannot be conceived of without moral laws."—(Sects. 72—75.)

How far this attempt at an explanation of them really clears up the doctrines in question, or even modifies their difficulty to the mind, we leave to metaphysicians to determine. To ourselves, it seems to let in so little light on these abstruse subjects, that we much prefer to fall back upon "what is written," that is, upon the divine authority; and we cannot but think that, in respect of such profound verities, our blessed Lord encourages us to do so, when in answer to one who asked in reference to the doctrine of regeneration, "How can these things be?" He replied, "Verily, verily, I say unto thee, We speak that we do know, and testify that we have seen; and ye receive not our witness. If I have told you earthly things, and ye believe not, how shall ye believe, if I tell you of heavenly things? And no man hath ascended up to heaven, but He that came down from heaven, even the Son of man which is in heaven." At all events, it must strike every reader of Lessing's treatise as an objection to his theory, that if no further advanced towards that end than it is at present, the human reason will take an enormous time in fully recognising these abstruse truths of revelation. This objection is anticipated by the writer, and is disposed of, unless we misunderstand him, by the very extraordinary hypothesis that each individual may perhaps live more than once upon the earth, and come back again to acquire new light on divine truth by a fresh pilgrimage in a more advanced stage of thought. But, again, we would not have the reader trust our own representation of the meaning:—

"Go thine inscrutable way, Eternal Providence! Only let me not despair in Thee because of this inscrutableness. Let me not despair in Thee, even if Thy steps appear to me to be going back. It is not true that the shortest line is always straight.

"Thou hast on Thine eternal way so much to carry on together, so much to do! so many side steps to take! And what if it were as good as proved that the vast slow wheel, which brings mankind nearer to this perfection, is only put in motion by smaller, swifter wheels, each of which contributes its own individual unit thereto?

"It is so! The very same way by which the race reaches its perfection, must every individual man—one sooner, another later—have travelled over. Have travelled over in one and the same life? Can he have been, in one and the self-same life, a sensual Jew and a spiritual Christian? Can he in the self-same life have overtaken both?

"Surely not that! *But why should not every individual man have existed more than once upon this world?*

"Is this hypothesis so laughable merely because it is the oldest? Because the human understanding, before the sophistries of the Schools had dissipated and debilitated it, lighted upon it at once?

"Why may not even I have already performed those steps of my perfecting which merely temporal penalties and rewards can bring man to?

"And, once more, why not all those steps, to perform which the views of eternal rewards so powerfully assist us?

"Why should I not come back as often as I am capable of acquiring fresh knowledge, fresh expertness? Do I bring away so much from once, that there is nothing to repay the trouble of coming back?

"Is this a reason against it? Or, because I forget that I have been here already? Happy is it for me that I do forget. The recollection of my former condition would permit me to make only a bad use of the present. And that which even I must forget *now*, is that necessarily forgotten forever?

"Or is it a reason against the hypothesis that so much time would have been lost to me? Lost?—And how much then should I miss?—Is not a whole eternity mine?"—(Sects. 91—100.)

Do these extravagances—this revival of the doctrine of Pythagoras in the nineteenth century of the Christian era—spring (as we believe many modern errors in theology do) from a morbid hankering after the novel and the startling? Why could not Lessing have been content to say *that the full revelation of these subjects to the human reason is probably reserved for a future state of existence?* To be sure, this has been said a thousand times before in sermons and religious books. But because it is a very old idea, is it therefore a false one? For our own part, we do not feel sure that Lessing's theory, apart from its absurd extravagances, is fundamentally wrong. We should be quite prepared to accept it, if only he would not disfigure it by insisting that the reason of man may become competent *in this condition of existence* to recognise all the truths of revelation. Why should we doubt that it will recognise these truths *in that other land beyond the grave?* That the Atonement was necessary in the nature of things, and not a mere arbitrary arrangement of the divine will; that the divine nature necessarily embraces a tri-personality, just as the human nature necessarily involves a body, soul, and spirit, few thinking persons will be disposed to deny. But whether *we can see into* the necessity for the Atonement, or into the essential constitution of the divine nature, *while we are in the body*, we take the liberty (notwithstanding all metaphysical explanations) to doubt. Humours hang about our reason, and a cloudy atmosphere, which intercepts and refracts the rays of divine truth. But we entirely believe that a better condition of the intellect is in store for us, when we shall see no longer "in a mirror enigmatically," but face to face, and know no longer partially, but "as we are known."

We have only to add, that Lessing's essay, with all its wild fancies, will well repay the perusal of thoughtful persons, and that side by side with theories flagrantly unsound, the author throws out hints well worthy of being preserved and digested. This we suspect (from our very narrow acquaintance with it) to be the genius of German theology,—three or four diamonds in a heap of rubbish, several beautiful and valuable thoughts lying hid in a mass of writing and a tangle of talk. Of the latter fault, however, the little treatise of Lessing now before us is certainly not guilty. It is (even severely) terse, and may be read through in a quarter of an hour.

We have noticed it here not only for its intrinsic interest, but because we think Dr. Temple's mind must, in the composition of his Essay, have travelled along a similar line of thought. And we much regret that he has confounded with this a line of thought which appears to us distinct—that of the merely intellectual progress of the human species, thus producing an entanglement between the Church and the world, between the advance of civilization and the development of religious truth, which exceedingly perplexes those who desire to follow his argument.

In conclusion, may the writer of these pages be allowed to express the hope that the controversy which the seven Essays have roused, will be conducted by those opposed to them not only calmly and temperately, but with a candid acknowledgment of those truths after which the Essayists are groping, and with which their very serious errors are weighted? Mere denials and protests do little or nothing; we must seek to disentangle the truth which they are misrepresenting, and to set it forth, if possible, free of their perversions.

We do not fear the storm with all its bluster, even

though it seems that some of the fundamental articles of faith, nay, the principle of theism itself, is perilled. Persuaded as we are that our own Church is the palladium both of Scripture truth and Apostolic order, we believe that the special providence of God watches over her, and that Christ Himself is in the tempest-tossed bark. He can and will overrule this mass of error and contradiction for good. Indeed, may it not be said that, except through the antagonism of opposing error, truth can never be thoroughly appreciated or developed in its full proportions in the human mind? Truth learned by rote, as children learn the Catechism, is *not* appreciated, nor even understood. But truth, which has been beset round about by heresies, and perplexed by grave questionings, and which at length has emerged, with its ground cleared and its limits well defined, this becomes a valuable acquisition, in which the mind may take a just and intelligent delight.

Only let us never for a moment drop the clue to all religious truth which the Word of God lends to us. Holding fast to it, we shall find our way with safety and ease through every labyrinth, however dark and intricate, and shall emerge into that sunlight of "clear thought" on subjects of religion, which Dr. Temple tells us is "valuable above all things, excepting only godliness."

BUNSEN, THE CRITICAL SCHOOL, AND DR. WILLIAMS.

It will scarcely be denied by any man of pure and elevated mind, that the highest object to which our faculties can be directed, is the attainment of religious truth. Our natural longings after immortality, our instinctive apprehensions of the mysterious presence of Him in whom we live, and move, and have our being, unite to persuade us that all questions are of inferior moment to the great question, whether He has made any revelation of Himself by which we may be guided in our search after this truth; and if we are convinced that He has not left Himself without witness in the world, then the true interpretation of that revelation must be, to every pure mind and holy spirit, the greatest problem on which his energies can be employed. I think, however, that it will also be generally conceded, that these questions in the present day are almost limited to the enquiry into the evidence for the truth of the Bible, and the true principles on which it ought to be interpreted. If that book is not derived from direct revelation, no other source of revelation will create much discussion among the men of our own age and nation. Of these two great questions,—the truth of the Bible and its interpretation,—it is difficult to say which is the most important. The enquiry into the truth of the document is prior indeed in order, but when once fairly decided in the mind, its work is done; while the interpretation of the word that has been revealed will give a deepening interest to our studies to the end of life. Nay, the very means employed in the investigation of the true meaning of Scripture by those who have had any success in interpreting it, is worthy the attention of all who believe in its divine origin. It is, therefore, always a source of gratification to learn any particulars concerning the lives of men who have devoted themselves entirely to the study of Scripture, or have attained to distinction by writings connected with sacred studies.

The late Baron Bunsen may be said to have been a person of this class. He has written many works connected with sacred literature, and his name has so long been before the public, that a general interest is felt among those, who have not had leisure or an opportunity to study deeply the subjects to which his attention has been directed, to know something definite about the value of his researches and the results to which he has attained. The expectations of this portion of the public must have been highly raised, when they learned that Dr. Williams had undertaken the very task which they desired to see performed. He is a man of reputation as a scholar, who obtained high academical distinctions, and is in a position of eminence as Vice-Principal of a College for the Education of the Clergy. These circumstances would seem to offer a sufficient guarantee to his readers that the information he would present to them would be of the most trustworthy character, and that matters of such deep and overwhelming importance, as the truth and the interpretation of Scripture, would be treated in a manner suitable to their great value and dignity. But they who opened this Essay with such expectations would soon be inclined to close it with feelings of sorrow and disappointment. They could not fail, however slight their acquaintance might be with the subject, to perceive that the tone in which these great questions are treated is, for the most part, that of one who plays with them as if they were subjects for the exercise of ingenuity, rather than questions on which it is of vital importance to us to hold truth rather than error. They would find that Baron Bunsen receives almost as high a meed of praise for missing what his reviewer believes to be the true explanation of Scripture as for discovering it, and that although Dr. Williams vaunts the greatness of the Baron's exploits in sacred literature, he very carefully abstains from committing himself in general to the conclusions of this great authority. Indeed, the Essay is so written, that while Dr. Williams would persuade his readers that Baron Bunsen is immeasurably superior to those English divines who maintain old-fashioned opinions on Scripture truth and prophecy, he generally expresses himself in such a manner that he cannot be charged with holding the opinions he reports. As an instance of this mode of writing, we may cite the passage where Bunsen's opinion on the antiquity of the human race is reported. It is said in p. 54 that

> "He could not have vindicated the unity of mankind if he had not asked for a vast extension of time, whether his petition for twenty thousand years be granted or not."

Now certainly it is a matter of deep importance in regard to the foundations of our faith, whether the Bible is to be esteemed a trustworthy history even in its chronology; and it is, to say the least, surprising to see it treated as a matter of indifference, whether it is wholly wrong in its account of the origin of man or not.* But this is the manner in which great questions appear to be treated in this Essay; and in the present instance it will be observed that while the twenty thousand years are rather unceremoniously disposed of, Baron Bunsen alone is left responsible even for the "large extension of time." If Dr. Williams were charged on the strength of this passage with maintaining that the Hebrew text of the Bible contains a manifestly false account of the origin of man, he might re-

* It may easily be shewn that the Bible chronology is scarcely elastic at all. For a proof of this assertion it will be sufficient to refer to Clinton's Scripture Chronology in the third volume of his *Fasti Hellenici.*

ply that he has only asserted that Bunsen could not maintain the unity of mankind on this hypothesis. He might say that with Bunsen's standing point this was impossible, but that he has not asserted that it cannot be maintained at all. Indeed, after sketching out some arguments in favour of this view of Baron Bunsen, through rather more than a page, he ends with the favourite refuge of reviewers in distress, who are desirous to praise, but not inclined to follow the author they are reviewing, by assuring us that "*his theories are at least suggestive.*" The real question which we desire to investigate is this—are they *true?* And when an author is put forth as a great luminary to the world, it may be interesting to speculative students to know that his theories are suggestive, but to the great mass of readers the real question must be their truth or falsehood! In the same manner we find the highest praise bestowed on Bunsen for his masterly exposition of a prophecy, where the reviewer declines to follow his explanation.* Again, Bunsen has exerted all his ingenuity to persuade us that the latter portion of the prophecies of Isaiah were written by Baruch, and his reviewer, in praising the ingenuity of his arguments, assures us that "most readers of the argument for the identity will feel inclined to assent;" but he takes care to assure us that the argument does not convince *him*, for he adds immediately,—

> "But a doubt may occur, whether many an unnamed disciple of the prophetic school may not have burnt with kindred zeal, and used diction not peculiar to any one; while such a doubt may be strengthened by the confidence with which our critic ascribes a recasting of Job, and of parts of other books, to the same favorite Baruch."—(p. 75.)

The fact is, that the rashness of Baron Bunsen, in hazarding conjectures as to the authorship of the books of Scripture, has found little favour with the better class even of rationalist divines in Germany; and his

* "Still the general analogy of Scripture . . . may permit us to think the oldest interpretation the truest."—(p. 73.)

English reviewer, though he immediately hazards a conjecture far more rash, has given us a quiet hint that the German author has put more upon Baruch than his evidence will warrant. It certainly surprises one—and if the subject were less sacred it would amuse a reader not a little—to see with what pertinacity Bunsen is exhibited as a great discoverer and an admirable guide, not for leading us to truth, but for his ingenuity in dressing up error so as almost to persuade men to accept it for truth. We can only remark that, however strange it may appear to us, this seems to be the way of Dr. Williams. Every writer has his own way, and this appears to be his way. We who differ from him *toto cœlo*, can have no objection to his removing with one hand the praise he has just bestowed with the other, except that it rather appears likely to mislead the ignorant. They will remember the praise, and forget the dissent, which is so delicately hinted. To those who are able to read Bunsen in his own language, or are well acquainted with the subjects he discusses, such observations are quite superfluous. But it is clear that although there is a certain parade of learning in this Essay, it cannot be intended for learned readers, or if it be intended for them, the author is very slenderly acquainted with that which men of learning would require. He can scarcely imagine that any persons capable of investigating the reading and the proper translation of a difficult passage in Scripture, can do anything but smile when he pronounces an opinion upon it *ex cathedrâ*, and ventures to attribute improper motives to those who take a different view. They will naturally ask how he has acquired a right to pronounce so peremptorily on questions which the greatest Hebrew philologers have considered to involve very great difficulties. It is therefore to be presumed, from this and other reasons, that Dr. Williams intends rather to dazzle the minds of those who are called 'general readers,' than to address his observations to those who are capable of discussing these questions. An opinion somewhat similar to this is expressed in a very learned periodical, of which the first number has just appeared, in a German review of the "Essays and Reviews," * where we find in p. 173 the following observation:—

> "For all who know Bunsen's 'Biblical Researches,' Dr. Williams says nothing new; and those who do not coincide with Bunsen's notions on certain prophetical portions of Isaiah, will still less be likely to be converted to them by the reasons alleged by his reviewer. If they [these authors] had taken into consideration the history of the Jews, and the history of Jewish interpretation of Scripture, they would have seen clearly why Saadias Gaon and the Rabbis who follow him—from whom certain men of our own day, and among them Dr. Williams, derive their dogmatic views—gave up *on paper* the original interpretation of the 53rd chapter of Isaiah."

The writer then proceeds to adduce other instances of a class of criticism, which could have no weight with persons who are acquainted with the Bible in the original.

It is clear that the writer views, as I do, the Essay of Dr. Williams as addressed rather *ad populum* than *ad clerum*; and it is on this account that I deplore the tone in which it is written. If Dr. Williams believes that it is for the interest of man, and likely to promote the advancement of religious truth, that the everlasting contests which have been carried on in Germany about the genuineness of the Scriptures and the truth of their main facts should be imported into our English literature, and occupy a large share of our attention, he has a right to introduce them to any extent he may desire, by writings addressed to those who are capable of investigating the questions thus brought forward: the fair discussion of Scripture difficulties will not endanger the cause of truth, and we, who believe that the truth is with those who are opposed to Dr. Williams,

* *Deutsche Vierteljahrschrift für Englisch-Theologische Forschung und Kritik; herausgegeben von Dr. M. Heidenheim*, (in London). No. I. March 31, 1861. This is a critical journal and review printed at Leipzig, and published at Gotha, by Perthes, but conducted by Germans living in England.

cannot fear the fullest discussion of Scripture questions: but if any man addresses to those who have neither the leisure, nor always the acquirements, necessary to the prosecution of such enquiries, the most peremptory decisions on questions which have exercised the greatest philologers, and accompanies them with gross insinuations against those who differ from him; if he represents the state of opinion in Germany, and the course of prophetic exegesis in general, with the utmost unfairness, and attempts by such representations to bias the opinions of his readers, we may fear that he is likely to cause many, who are but slightly acquainted with these subjects, to make shipwreck of their faith. This is the *only* ground of fear. We have no fear that the truth of Scripture, which has borne for more than a thousand years the battle and the strife of man, will succumb under a puny attack like this. It has survived the assaults of Celsus and Porphyry, of Bayle and Voltaire, of Gibbon and Hume, and it is not very likely that it will fall by the hands of Bunsen and Dr. Williams. It is the unfair representations, the partial and the one-sided views of this Essay, announced *ex cathedrâ*, and coupled with contemptuous insinuations against those who hold the ancient opinions, which render it worth while to spend a moment in answering it. They may deceive the unlearned and the superficial, but there is really nothing in the Essay itself which adds a new argument to the old conditions of the great problem, or would give the smallest uneasiness to those who really know the history of Scripture criticism in Germany and England. These accusations may appear to be expressed in strong language, but if they can be substantiated they will shew that, however learned Dr. Williams may be, however capable of writing a trustworthy treatise on Scripture, the Essay he has ventured to publish in this volume is worthless as a guide to truth, and altogether unworthy of his reputation and his position. It is a very legitimate subject of enquiry to ascertain generally, whether the representations of this Essay, or Review, are trustworthy or not, and to that enquiry I now propose to devote my attention.

It deals with vast questions and it abounds in very strong assertions concerning them, and in the most peremptory decisions about matters of vital importance as to Scripture truth and Scripture interpretation. The question before us is—What is the value of these assertions and decisions? Before we enter on the great point,—the truth of Scripture and the true method of interpreting it,—as Baron Bunsen was the peg on which this Essay was suspended, it would be uncourteous not to make a few remarks on his life and labours.

Entirely opposed, as I have always been, to the opinions of Baron Bunsen, I have no wish to detract from his merit or to diminish his legitimate reputation. I believe that few persons will be disposed to deny his abilities and acquirements, although during the time he was in great favour with the sovereigns of Prussia and of England, it is probable that the adulation of his followers may have given exaggerated notions of both. Such leisure as was afforded by a life of high diplomatic employments was eagerly devoted to literature, and I believe that he had a very earnest spirit with regard to religion. But, unhappily, these high qualifications were combined with other habits of mind, which neutralized their value, and rendered his Biblical researches unsound and mischievous. He appears to have been self-confident in the extreme, and rash in speculation, almost beyond the example of his countrymen. The adulation of his friends and followers increased his self-confidence, gave license to his spirit of speculation, and thus he announced his decisions with a degree of dogmatism which contrasted very strongly with the argumentative support on which they rested. He was born and educated in Germany at a season when the religious faith of the country had been almost overwhelmed by the torrent of unbridled rationalism, and even the lamp of religious feeling burnt very feebly. It seems to me to have been a dreary time, but Dr. Williams appears to consider it a time of glorious light and knowledge.

After a few incivilities about England, with some remarks on the language of pulpits and platforms, he speaks thus of the close of the last century and the beginning of the present :—

"But in Germany there has been a pathway streaming with light, from Eichhorn to Ewald, aided by the poetical penetration of Herder and the philological researches of Gesenius, throughout which the value of the moral element in prophecy has been progressively raised, and that of the directly predictive, whether secular or Messianic, has been lowered. Even the conservatism of Jahn amongst Romanists, and of Hengstenberg amongst Protestants, is free and rational compared to what is often in this country required with denunciation, but seldom defended by argument.

"To this inheritance of opinion Baron Bunsen succeeds."—(pp. 66, 67.)

This was, unhappily for him, the case. He was trained in sacred philology at a period when the divine authority of Scripture was daily undermined by professors and divines, and we cannot wonder if the seed thus sown should have produced very bitter fruit. That Baron Bunsen did not give up his devotional feelings and his earnestness in religion is not to be ascribed to the teaching of the period in which he was educated, but to the more religious frame of mind with which it had pleased God to endow him. And in considering this portion of his character we must never forget the difference between the German and the English mind. The paradise of the German appears to consist in unlimited license of speculation, while the practical element is the prevailing characteristic of the English: and thus it often happens that a German will not cast off a certain phase of faith when he has demolished every ground which an Englishman would deem a rational and logical foundation for holding it. We ought not, therefore, to be surprised at finding that, after denying the genuineness of half of the books in the Bible, and treating a very large portion of its history as mere idle tales or legendary myths, Baron Bunsen, to the very end of his life, had a great love for devotional hymns, framed upon a very different hypothesis, and addressed to a very different state of mind. I have heard, on the authority of private friends, that in his last hours he was cheered and supported by the words of the old German hymn, "Jesu, meine Zuversicht," *—"Jesus, my trust." The same explanation will solve the discrepancy which Dr. Williams finds between the *Gesang und Gebetbuch* of Baron Bunsen and his criticisms:—"Either reverence or deference may have prevented him from bringing his prayers into entire harmony with his criticisms." (P. 91.) The truth is he was better than his principles: he was not in flesh and blood what he was upon paper. Dr. Williams, however, evidently rests his claim to celebrity on the brilliancy of his Biblical researches. My own belief is that although some ingenious suggestions in the Liturgical portion of Baron Bunsen's "Hippolytus and his Age" may be referred to hereafter, his name will be unknown in Biblical criticism twenty years hence. But on this point the opinions of Dr. Williams and myself are wholly unimportant: it is one of those questions which posterity alone can decide, and to which the words of a writer familiar to Dr. Williams exactly apply,—

Ἁμέραι δ' ἐπίλοιποι, Μάρτυρες σοφώτατοι.

And indeed, this Essay on Bunsen has brought forward in the strongest manner other questions, compared with which, the reputation of any man, however eminent, is insignificant. The truth and the interpretation of Scripture are discussed in a manner which must leave an impression on the minds of those who have not leisure or opportunity to study deeply such questions, that their faith is founded on ignorance and misappre-

* The hymn is found in Bunsen's collection of Prayers and Hymns, 1833, among those whose commencement is changed. It is there No. 497, and begins, "Guter Hirte, willst du nicht." But many of the German hymns have a commencement nearly similar.

hension; and thus a general spirit of scepticism is likely to be promoted. Now this impression I believe to be promoted by a series of misrepresentations of the most unfair and one-sided character; and I therefore proceed to point out some of the most striking of these misrepresentations.

It may be convenient briefly to state the nature of the misrepresentations to which I advert, and the order in which I propose to consider them.

1. The state of opinion as to the Scriptures among the learned men of Germany.

If we are to believe Dr. Williams, the researches of the German critical school have disproved the genuineness of a very large portion of the Bible, and entirely deprived the prophecies, except in one or two doubtful cases, of any direct Messianic prediction. And Baron Bunsen, accepting this state of the question,* is highly praised by Dr. Williams for endeavouring on this hypothesis to shew that the doctrine of the Bible contains divine truths.

I propose to shew that this is utterly at variance with fact; that whatever currency such opinions may have had some years ago in Germany, they are repelled by the most distinguished men of that nation, and that they are gradually dying away.

2. The second great misrepresentation with which

* This is of course a mere general statement of Bunsen's views. In fact, he agrees in details with no writer of eminence whatever, but simply considers himself at liberty to assign any date to any book in the Bible, to explain any part of it as legendary or parabolical, and to correct its authors on all questions in the most arbitrary manner. Thus, the fall of man is not a narrative of a real event, but a history of the fall of man as it appears in the contemplation of the Divine Mind, the serpent being the symbol of man's perverted understanding, his reason separated from his conscience; the Pentateuch is a late book with a few ancient documents; an universal deluge is a simple impossibility; Jonah is a legendary tale; the song of Hannah was not hers, but the song of the mother of Saul on her son's elevation to the kingdom, &c. It would be easy to multiply these instances to any extent, but it is needless—as needless as to refute such gratuitous assertions and suppositions in detail. Were every one of them proved impossible, their author would have been ready the next day with another list, just as gratuitous, just as unfounded, and just as absurd.

I charge Dr. Williams relates to the interpretation of prophecy in our country.

Dr. Williams asserts that as men have become more learned, each writer on the prophecies has detracted something from the extent of literal prognostication; which means in plain language, that the belief in Messianic predictions has gradually ceased in England.

I propose, in the second place, to examine this statement.

3. I then propose to examine in detail the misrepresentations of Dr. Williams in regard to particular passages of Scripture.

The first and greatest misrepresentation on which I would remark occurs in a passage which has just been quoted, but it pervades also the whole Essay. It is the attempt to insinuate, rather than to assert, that the opinion of the genuineness of the Old Testament and a very large part of the New has been universally given up by the scholars of Germany, and that they have proved that it cannot be maintained. The contemptuous language with which an opposite view is treated may be judged of by the following specimen.

After an enumeration of all the triumphs of philology over prophecy, by which only a few doubtful passages are left to testify of the Messiah and one of the final fall of Jerusalem, and a declaration that even these few cases are likely to melt, "if not already melted, in the crucible of searching enquiry," the author proceeds thus:—

> "If our German had ignored all that the masters of philology have proved on these subjects, his countrymen would have raised a storm of ridicule, at which he must have drowned himself in the Neckar.
>
> "Great then is Baron Bunsen's merit, in accepting frankly the belief of scholars, and yet not despairing of Hebrew prophecy as a witness to the kingdom of God."—(p. 70.)

We may think it a happy thing for Baron Bunsen that the miserable trash which rationalism often sends forth for enlightened philology, did not rob him altogether of his faith in Christ; but if the principles of these philologers were erroneous, it is no "merit" that he was led astray by them, nor does it much mend the matter that he has made some awkward attempts to patch up the cause he supposes them to have damaged, by introducing a new source of confusion. But the representation here given of the state of sacred philology is so utterly unlike the reality, that one wonders how any person of the acquirements and knowledge of Dr. Williams could venture to bring it forward. It must be supposed, by those who read it without the means of correcting the statements by an enquiry into German criticism, that the philologists of Germany have made the spuriousness of the books of the Old Testament so apparent, and have so confuted the older notions about prophecy, that no man, who had any regard for his reputation as a scholar, would venture to maintain the antiquity and genuineness of the Pentateuch, or express a belief in the existence of prophecies which in former ages were appealed to in proof of the great truths of Christianity. In short, that if a man maintained that Moses wrote the Pentateuch or Isaiah prophesied of Christ, he would be met by "a storm of ridicule" under which life would be intolerable. I fear, if all who venture, notwithstanding the sneers of Dr. Williams, to maintain these opinions, were to follow his prescription, the channel of the Neckar would soon be choked up. It is perfectly true that for a considerable period these subjects have been debated with the utmost freedom in Germany, and that at the beginning of the present century these opinions were, upon the whole, in the ascendant,—even then, however, not without opposition, although that opposition was feeble. But the result of the discussion has been of a very different character from that which Dr. Williams would lead his readers to believe. The defenders of the old opinions are now more than maintaining their ground against the impugners of the truth of Scripture. Have Keil, and Havernick, Hengstenberg and Delitzsch,

Lange and his coadjutors in his *Biblewerk*, Tholuck and Lechler, with many others of similar powers, found it necessary to "drown themselves in the Neckar," or to hide their heads in privacy? It is easy enough to make such an assertion in the pages of a volume addressed to general readers in England, but if the assertion had been made in Berlin, it would probably have raised so great "a storm of ridicule," that the author would have been glad to find himself at Lampeter again. The tide has turned, and although some writers of great philological attainments, like Ewald and Hupfeld, maintain the rationalist opinions with all the violence which seems a natural inheritance of rationalism, yet the prevailing tone is conservative, and that in a degree which is constantly increasing.* It would be supposed also, that in what Dr. Williams calls a "destructive" process, the rationalist authorities were in agreement, or at least, not in direct contradiction to each other, in regard to the arguments on which they found their system. But when you examine their opinions, you find that they seem to agree in nothing except a determination to reject the theory of the truth of Scripture. No matter what hypothesis is set up in its place, that hypothesis is altogether tabooed. And the consequence is that their theories are often, not only divergent, but contradictory and mutually destructive. There are among these writers three who have done considerable service in certain departments of Hebrew philology, I mean Gesenius, Ewald, and Hupfeld, and I am very glad to avail myself of the fruit of their labours, but when they begin to reason on the books of Scripture, I find it necessary to watch every assertion with the utmost vigilance, almost every step. When a theory is at stake, assertions are constantly made of the occurrence or non-occurrence of words, which the use of a Concordance proves to be groundless. Such accusa-

* It is a significant fact that the clever and eloquent sermons of L. Harms, who assails the rationalists continually, and gives them no quarter, have been eagerly listened to by crowds, and created an unexampled sensation throughout the kingdom of Hanover.

tions are not to be lightly made, and therefore I invite any person who doubts its truth, to examine the list of words brought forward by Gesenius and Hartmann* in order to prove Deuteronomy later than the rest of the Pentateuch: he will find that six of the ten instances do occur where they are said not to be found. Or let him examine the phrases said to be peculiar to the Elohist in Genesis,† and he will find them in passages where the name Jehovah occurs. These are minor points in the great conflict of opinion, but they serve to shew how these opinions are supported. But if we ask in what conclusion do these critics agree, it would be difficult to find any position maintained by one which is not destroyed by the rest. I must anticipate an objection which will at once rise to the mind of a reader of these lines. If these men differ so entirely in these minor matters, is not their agreement in one conclusion, viz., that the old belief in the genuineness of Scripture is untenable, a very strong argument in its favor? It might have some weight in the general argument, if it rested on other and independent grounds, but when that agreement is founded on arguments which each new hypothesis destroys, it appears to me that its value is nothing. Perhaps this may be best illustrated by an example. If a person is enquiring into the age of the Pentateuch, he would naturally read what Gesenius has said concerning the age of the Hebrew language. He has laid it down as a rule that the language of the prose writers in the greater part of the Bible is identical with that of the Pentateuch in its prose, and of the poets with that of the poetical parts of the Pentateuch, such as, e. g. the

* See Gesenius, *Geschichte der Hebraischen Sprache und Schrift*, p. 32, (1815;) and Hartmann, *Historisch-Kritische Forschungen, &c., über die Funf Bücher Mosis*, p. 660, (1831.)

* See Gramberg, *Libri Geneseos secundum fontes rite dignoscendos adumbratio nova.* (Leipzig, 1828.) Some of these incorrect statements are repeated in the last Introduction to the Scriptures published in Germany. See Dr. Bleek's *Einleitung in das Alte Testament, &c.*, p. 249. (Berlin, 1860.) This is only one of the many instances which might be given of arguments repeated in the most careless way by one writer after another.

blessings of Jacob and of Moses. He assures us that with the Captivity a new epoch of the language begins. Gramberg tells us that some of the books of the Pentateuch were written at the conclusion of the Captivity, and Von Bohlen declares it altogether to be a production of the age of Josiah. It is true, they all agree in rejecting the Mosaic origin of the Pentateuch, but then the enquiry remains, why they reject it. There may be prejudices against its Mosaic origin, as well as prejudices in its favour, and if men are determined at all events to reject it, one can understand why they differ when they begin to frame hypotheses to suit the facts. But if they are led by these enquiries to reject it, any two out of these three base their rejection of it on grounds overthrown by the third. Again, the Song of Solomon is declared by Gesenius to have been written at a time when the Hebrew language had been altered by an admixture of Chaldaic forms and phrases. Suppose, with this decision fresh in our minds, we take up one of the latest publications by a great authority on the Semitic dialects,—I mean Ernest Renan,—who handles all Scripture matters as freely as our Essayists could wish, we are assured that the Song of Solomon cannot have been written later than towards the end of the tenth century before Christ! The stream of light, of which Dr. Williams speaks in such glowing terms as having illuminated Germany from the time of Eichhorn and Gesenius, does not appear to shine with all the brightness which he proclaims, even upon purely philological questions. I am not taking obscure writers of small tracts, but acknowledged leaders and men of eminence. Indeed, Gesenius is the highest name among the philologers of the critical school; and Ernest Renan stands very high among the Semitic scholars of the present day. But the fact is, that each book of the Pentateuch, and the whole work itself, is hunted up and down the four centuries between the time of David and the Captivity, till the heart and the mind are wearied alike with fruitless enquiries and hypotheses which have no foundation. Sometimes it is written about the time of the Captivity, then it cannot be later than David; sometimes it is written before, sometimes after the division of the kingdoms. And the only conclusion left for the mind is to wonder whether it was ever written at all! The everlasting differences on these subjects pervading the lecture-rooms of Germany, must have wearied many a noble mind and earnest spirit, that panted after truth and found only husks like these. One such spirit* has expressed the loathing with which he was at last driven to regard such enquiries. He found, as he tells us, that "one day St. Matthew and the Gospel of the Hebrews were up, the next day St. Luke, and then an original Gospel; and the fourth day St. Mark; one day Deuteronomy was a late book, the next it was an early one," and so forth; and at last he felt that he could gain no nourishment for his soul in a perpetual round of self-destructive hypotheses, and changed his course.† It might be supposed, from the rounded periods and positive statements of Dr. Williams, that this critical school has run a triumphant course in Germany, but unfortunately for this supposition, this school is daily losing its influence.

There is a spirit of infidelity spread abroad among the middle classes in Germany which the writings of this school have helped to foster, but there is also a large and increasing number of zealous Christians; and the hold of rationalism on those who acknowledge a revelation is daily relaxing. There is also an altered tone in the rationalist works themselves. The latest Introduction to the Old Testament which I have seen is that of Dr. Bleek,‡ who handles all these questions with the utmost freedom, and decides in many cases against the old opinions. He assigns the Pentateuch in its present form to the time of David, and is against the

* Vilmar, now Professor of Theology at Marburg. *Die Theologie der Thatsachen wider die Theologie der Rhetorik* is the title of his work.

† Vilmar, p. 15.

‡ This work is posthumous. Its title is *Einleitung in das Alte Testament von Friedrich Bleek. Herausgegeben von J. F. Bleek und Ad. Kamphausen, &c.* (1860.) A. Kamphausen was a coadjutor of Bunsen in his *Bibelwerk*. See the *Vorerinnerungen* to the *Bibelwerk*, p. cxxv.

genuineness of Daniel. But his tone is altogether different from that of the critical school in the day of Gesenius and his followers. His admissions are such as would have been treated with scorn in the palmy days of rationalism; and he speaks with reverence of the prophets, as receiving revelations from God and being the interpreters between God and man: and when he controverts the positions of Hengstenberg or other writers of orthodox opinions, he does it with courtesy. It is true the gift of evil-speaking which appeared to be pre-eminently the prerogative of rationalist writers, has not entirely departed, and the mantle of former critics has fallen on Ewald and Hupfeld. The name of Hengstenberg appears to excite a degree of positive fury in Hupfeld; and in the preface to his Commentary on the Psalms he openly declares that he considers it a duty to drag Hengstenberg forward wherever he can accuse him of error. He says of Hengstenberg that he is trying to "*insinuate his poison into our blood*," which is no doubt very becoming language for a great rationalist, but would be thought rude in a Christian divine. But perhaps if Hengstenberg and the anti-critical reactionary school, as he calls it, are so displeasing to him, Ewald and the rationalists are quite to his taste. Not at all, I am sorry to say,—for in the same preface he complains that Ewald has pursued him for many years "with peculiar fury," (*mit besondern wuth*,) simply because in reviewing some of Ewald's critical essays in Hebrew, Hupfeld had hinted that he wanted more knowledge of the language. These two men, Ewald and Hupfeld are mentioned here, because they appear to be the only two of the rationalist school whose observations on Hebrew philology are really worth considering. And as they seem to be rather discordant, the happy family of rationalism has some chance of breaking up altogether before long.

Where every man has—not his psalm and his doctrine—but a theory about every book in Holy Writ, where it happens that every two or three years the order in which these books were written is infallibly discovered and as infallibly refuted, it would, of course, be impossible to specify each opinion even on one book; but it may be convenient to exhibit to the English public a glimpse or two of that clear stream of light which has been shed on sacred literature by the scholars of Germany. Let us take for example Genesis, as that was the book on which rationalist criticism for some time bestowed its most particular attention.

It was very early observed that two names for God in the Book of Genesis were used in a peculiar manner; that passages occurred in which *Elohim* was the predominant, if not the only word used, while in other passages *Jehovah* predominated or appeared to be used exclusively. On this foundation it is almost impossible to enumerate the various theories which have been formed. Eichhorn endeavoured to shew that these different portions of the book proceeded from two different and independent writers. But when once this notion was fairly launched there was no end to the modifications it underwent. Every few months a new theory, which of course superseded all the former ones, made its appearance, and professed to solve all the difficulties, only just to make room for another more pretentious system. Ilgen imagined two *Elohists* and one *Jehovist*. Gramberg modified the hypothesis one way, Hartmann another, Ewald a third, and so forth till the world was weary of these endless suppositions.* About this time it was almost assumed as an axiom that it was absurd to imagine that a book could be written in the time of Moses, as the means of writing books were not discovered at that early period, and a number of auxiliary arguments of the same kind were pressed into the service. The result of these discussions has been that the hypothesis of a number of independent fragments is generally looked upon with disfavour, and the prevailing tone is in favour of what is called the *Urkun-*

* This representation will be found, with circumstantial details, in Keil's edition of Hävernick's *Spezielle Einleitung in den Pentateuch*. It coincides with the results of a more elaborate enquiry which I made into these theories some years ago.

den-hypothese, or theory of one original document receiving additions during the lapse of time in successive editions. The objections raised against the probability of the means of writing being found in the time of Moses are, I suppose, now generally given up. At least so Bleek, a rationalist himself, informs us. These are his words: "That the art of writing (*schriftstellerei*) existed among the Hebrews in the time of Moses, according to our present indications, cannot be a matter of doubt."

I suppose that in the palmy days of rationalism any divine who ventured to maintain this proposition would have been met with such "a storm of ridicule," that he would have been glad "to drown himself in the Neckar;" and therefore, when I hear of the unpopularity of opinions which I believe to be true, I am willing to hope that further discussion will only prove their truth.

I find that it is now acknowledged that some of the most telling arguments against the Mosaic origin of the Pentateuch must be given up: and I find also from Nitzsch's "Academical Lectures" that it cannot any longer be maintained that the demonology and angelology of the Jews was learned at Babylon. This was another point on which the assertions of the rationalists were most positive. Indeed, this belief of the Babylonian origin of these notions was one of the great arguments on which reliance was placed to prove the late composition of the Pentateuch. If my readers ask who Nitzsch is, I must refer them to Bunsen's "Signs of the Times," (p. 406 in the translation,) where he is said to be "the man who is almost universally throughout Germany considered as the first of Evangelical theologians;" so that we are not quoting an obscure writer, but the man who occupies "the most distinguished post" in the Prussian Church, i. e. Provost of Berlin.

The examples which have here been given relate for the most part to the Pentateuch, because that is one of the chief battle-grounds of the critical school, and it serves as well as any other portion of Scripture to shew how much darkness is mixed with "the stream of light" from Eichhorn and Gesenius to the present day. In fact, the philological and linguistic collections and criticisms of Gesenius and Hupfeld are highly valuable, although their conclusions even on these subjects must be received with caution. But it is self-evident that a man may be extremely useful in illustrating *the language* of Scripture who would be a very unsafe guide in unravelling the difficulties of its history, or reasoning upon the genuineness of its books. But it is to be remarked that the contradictions I have brought forward are chiefly contradictions on the very subject on which alone these men would be entitled to speak with any authority,—I mean the determination of date and authorship from the language of a book. One more remark shall be made on this subject, and then I leave it to the reader's own judgment. If Jerome is to be condemned, as Dr. Williams would lead us to believe, for what he considers an absurd dictum on prophecy, we might quote numberless absurdities from these critics of the most flagrant kind. Did Jerome ever patronize so preposterous a notion as that the name *Noah* was derived from the Latin *no*, or *ναῦς*, (!) as Von Bohlen gravely conjectures?* or did the best abused of the Fathers ever propose such drivelling absurdities as that the story of Æsop, as a great writer of fables, possibly arose from some report of Solomon's apologues about the *Hyssop* on the wall, (!) as Hitzig suggests in the preface to his translation of the Book of Proverbs?

These circumstances, to which a great deal more of the same kind might be added, will afford a considerable source of modification, to say the least, to the assertions of Dr. Williams about the state of Biblical criticism in Germany. They shew that the impression which any reader of his Essay would inevitably derive from it on this subject is entirely erroneous. Whether he has wilfully and intentionally misled those who can-

* Von Bohlen on Genesis, vol. ii. p. 106, Eng. Tr.

not check his statements, can only be known by himself and by Him Who searches the heart, and to Whom he stands or falls.

But if this Essay gives a false impression with regard to the state of Biblical criticism in Germany, its representation of the progress of opinion in England as to prophecy is still more plainly unjust, and is calculated to convey a still more false impression of the actual state of prophetic exegesis. The most objectionable passage is the following:—

"In our country each successive defence of the prophecies, in proportion as its author was able, detracted something from the extent of literal prognostication, and either laid stress on the moral element, or urged a second, as the spiritual sense. Even Butler foresaw the possibility that every prophecy in the Old Testament might have its elucidation in contemporaneous history; but literature was not his strong point, and he turned aside, endeavouring to limit it [what?] from an unwelcome idea. Bishop Chandler is said to have thought twelve passages in the Old Testament directly Messianic; others restricted this character to five. Paley ventures to quote only one."—(p. 65.)

The impression which this language is calculated to leave on the mind can only be the following, viz., that as prophecy has become more studied and better understood amongst us, the learned have gradually cast aside their belief in the Messianic nature of the prophecies of the Old Testament, till at last there are scarcely any which are considered to be strictly prophecies of Christ. Nay, the author seems to give us a descending scale by which we may measure the gradual diminution of faith in prophecy during the last century. "Bishop Chandler *is said* to have thought,"—surely this phrase is strange in regard to a book so well known as Chandler's "Answers to Collins!"* Why should not Dr. Williams

* I refer to the following books:—Bishop Chandler's "Defence of Christianity, from the Prophecies of the Old Testament," &c., against the "Grounds and Reasons of the Christian Religion" of Collins, and his "Vindication of the Defence of Christianity," &c., against "The Scheme of Literal Prophecy considered" of the same author.

have taken the trouble to ascertain what Bishop Chandler does say, before he made so loose a statement?

We shall simply place Bishop Chandler's own words in apposition with Dr. Williams's report of them:—

Dr. Williams.	Bishop Chandler.
"Bishop Chandler is said to have thought twelve passages in the Old Testament directly Messianic."	"But not to rest in generals, let the disquisition of particular texts determine the truth of this author's assertion. *To name them all* would carry me into too great length. *I shall therefore select some of the principal prophecies*, which being proved to regard the Messias immediately and solely, in the obvious and literal sense according to scholastick rules, *may serve as a specimen* of what the Scriptures have predicted of a Messias that was to come."

It seems very clear that Dr. Williams knows even less of Bishop Chandler than he appears to know of Bishop Butler. But before we pass on to Bishop Butler, let me ask those who read this Essay, what faith they can put in any statement it contains after reading these words. The allusion to Paley is even worse. Paley was not writing a book on prophecy, but in treating of the evidences of Christianity he contents himself with quoting only one prophecy, and assigns his reason for limiting his quotation to that one, viz., "as well because I think it the clearest and strongest of all, as because most of the rest, in order that their value might be represented with any tolerable degree of fidelity, require a discussion unsuitable to the limits and nature of this work." He then refers with approbation to Bishop Chandler's dissertations, and asks the infidel to try the experiment whether he could find any other eminent person to the history of whose life so many circumstances can be made to apply. It is not that he "ventures to quote" only this as if he were afraid to meet the question, but he actually refers to the book where these questions which lie out of his own path are specially treated. And now, what becomes of the list of prophecies, "fine by degrees and beautifully less" as years roll on, which Dr. Williams would persuade his readers have been given up till a grave divine "ventured to quote" only one! The subject is really too sacred, too solemn to be treated in a manner like this. On any subject, such misrepresentation would be very discreditable, but in treating of the evidence for the truth of Holy Scripture, it becomes positively criminal.

But if Paley and Bishop Chandler are thus misrepresented, what shall we say to the insinuation about Bishop Butler?* Instead of Bishop Butler having turned aside from a future prospect of probable interpretations, he distinctly grapples with those that have been made on this principle, and denies that they have any weight. So that in the representation of Bishop Chandler, Dr. Paley, and Bishop Butler, the author of this Essay may be said to have misrepresented every one of them, and to have interwoven his misrepresentations together into a statement which it would be difficult to parallel for its contempt of truth. I have no wish to charge the author with *wilful* misrepresentation, and I trust he may not have thought of the impression his words would inevitable leave on the mind of any reader

* The assertion that "literature was not his strong point" is really beneath criticism; though coming in the midst of a sentence which it is an act of courtesy to designate as English, it may excite something like wonder. It rather resembles another attack upon an eminent prelate of our Church—I mean Bishop Pearson. Dr. Williams accuses him of making the prose of the Jewish rabbinical writers more prosaic. I never understood that they professed to write poetry, and therefore, if Bishop Pearson has made them intelligible, he will be excused for not rendering them into poetry. But to say the truth, most persons who read what Dr. Williams has printed in the form of stanzas at the conclusion of this Essay, will feel that the author's notions of poetry are rather peculiar. These sneers at great and eminent men are so unworthy of a man of learning, that we will pass them by, only hoping that Dr. Williams may one day be entitled to a tithe of the reverence due to those whom he has thus depreciated.

of his book, but I appeal with confidence to every reader of plain common sense, whether that is not the only impression they are calculated to make? Bishop Butler's is not a work on prophecy, but in enumerating the sources of evidence for Christianity he cannot well overlook prophecy. He is not attempting to expound prophecy, but shewing how it bears upon the evidence of Christianity, and answering some objections which are commonly made against its testimony. He adduces and answers three lines of objection: 1. The obscurity of parts of the prophecies; 2. The objection that, considering each prophecy distinctly by itself, it does not appear to be intended of the events to which Christians apply it: to this he answers, that "a series of prophecy being applicable to such and such events, is in itself proof that it was intended of them," &c.; 3. "That the shewing, even to a high degree of probability, if that could be, that the prophets thought of some other event, in such and such predictions, and not those at all which Christians allege to be completions of such predictions,—or that such and such prophecies are capable of being applied to other events than those to which Christians apply them,—that this would not destroy the force of the argument from prophecy, even with regard to those very instances." And after he has given his reason for this decision, he says, "Hence may be seen to how little purpose those persons busy themselves who endeavour to prove that the prophetic history is applicable to events of the age in which it was written, or of ages before it." And he then argues the case in regard to Porphyry, and concludes his remarks. What colour does this course of argument give for insinuating that Bishop Butler foresaw the possibility that every prophecy in the Old Testament might have its elucidation in contemporaneous history, and "turned aside" from the thought? It was an objection which *had been* often made, it formed a strong point of attack, and Butler quietly points out that it has no force. To those who have a knowledge of the writings of Chandler, Butler, and Paley, or to those who have the patience to examine each assertion of this author, and place it at its true worth, these observations would be wholly unnecessary. I do not address myself to them, but I address myself to those who might be expected to look to a man of the reputation and position of Dr. Williams for guidance in such matters, and would receive his statements with trust. Such persons, whatever Dr. Williams may have meant, would be entirely deceived. They would suppose that belief in prophecy in England was well-nigh exploded among the learned, and left only to platform orators; while the insinuation that upon the Continent only about two or three doubtful passages are now believed to testify of the Messiah, and one of the destruction of Jerusalem, seems completely to banish all faith in prophecy from the world. And this is effected by a series of misrepresentations, which it would not be easy to parallel. Let those therefore who read these pages endeavour to learn from the examination of such assertions as these, what dependence they may place on other portions of this Essay where they have less means of testing the justice of the statements.

As Dr. Williams has the reputation of an experienced controversialist, it may be desirable to point out one subterfuge, to which he has no right to have recourse: I mean by a quibble on the words "*directly* Messianic." If he professes to mean no more than that the prophecies were in the first place applicable to some other subject, but were intended by the Holy Spirit to testify of the Messiah, he concedes the whole question. His whole Essay is constructed on the principle that there are no real "predictions" in the Bible, with two or three insignificant exceptions. This Essay would take away all belief in such predictions, and utterly banish inspired prophecies as a source of evidence. If he admits that they are inspired predictions, it matters not whether they are so in a primary or a secondary sense. And it is well to suggest to his readers, that although Dr. Williams appears to think it sufficient to deny each prophecy individually to apply to Christ, no attentive reader of the Bible can fail to see that the image of the Messiah is foreshadowed and pourtrayed in its integrity by the combination of these individual features, each of which may be contained in a single prophecy. They are full of wonder when considered individually, but united, their strength is, or ought to be, irresistible.

Before we leave the general notion of prophecy as having a real element of prediction, we would ask those persons who have been led astray by the assertions—I cannot call them arguments—of this author to read attentively the prophecies in which the fall of the great powers of the world is predicted, and to compare the predictions with the present state of those powers, e.g. of Egypt, of Tyre, and of Babylon.* These are among the most striking of the secular predictions, if we may so call them, of the Bible. Let the candid enquirer well consider these side by side with the assertions of this Essay, and he will then be enabled to form some judgment of the prejudice and one-sidedness against which the believer in the Bible has to contend.

There is another subject also to which we may here allude in a few transient remarks: it is the manner in which the Essayist has argued against the inspiration of the apostles by a manifest misconception of a very plain passage.

In a note at p. 67 Mr. Mansel is reproved, because in his Bampton Lectures "recognised mistranslations and misreadings are alleged as arguments." Mr. Mansel is so abundantly able to make answer for himself, that it would be superfluous for any friend to answer for him. But these words are quoted to shew how very prone we are to commit the very fault which we attribute to others. Dr. Williams, both in his Essay, and in his "Rational Godliness," p. 309, uses as an argument against the inspiration of the apostles, the words

* Babylon—Isa. xiii., xiv., &c. Tyre—Isa. xxiii.; Ezek. xxvi.—xxviii. Egypt—Ezek. xxix. These are not the only prophecies, but sufficient as a basis for the enquiry. Bp. Newton in his "Dissertations on the Prophecies" will supply more, as well as the prophecies relating to Nineveh and other great powers.

of St. Paul when he assured the Lycaonians that he and Barnabas were "men of like passions" with themselves. Is there a mistranslation more recognised than this, or can there be an argument more entirely alien from the subject into connection with which it is dragged, than this quotation of Dr. Williams? What argument can it afford against *any* theory of inspiration, that the apostles acknowledged to those who were about to worship them as gods, that they were mortals like themselves, subject to suffering, sickness, death? Had the author taken counsel on the subject with a well-educated fifth-form boy he would, I am willing to believe, have cancelled this argument.

But Dr. Williams is not content to throw contempt on the great men of modern days, on Bishops Pearson and Butler, and on men of reputation in our own day, like Mr. Mansel,—he wings his shafts against the great men of ancient days also, and has especially selected Jerome for his mark. It does not appear very probable, after some fourteen centuries in which the name of Jerome has been held in high reverence, even by those who would demur to some of his opinions, that this eminent Father would sink into contempt even though assailed by one who was thoroughly conversant with his weakest points. But when the attack is so made as to shew the weak points of the assailant himself, the effect becomes rather ludicrous than serious. It seems a pity for the reputation of the Essayist that when he selects a few crowning absurdities, as he imagines, from the whole works of this Father, he should flounder at every step in a manner which almost excites our compassion. One feels something like compassion for a man, who with the pages of an eminent expositor of Scripture before him, indulges in the littleness of picking out a single specimen of what appear to him to be absurdities, and then produces it in a manner which evidently shews either that his acquaintance with the author is very slight, or that he is unwilling his readers should know anything more than the bare assertion which, quoted by itself, sounds strange to our ears.

Dr. Williams, after telling us that to estimate rightly Bunsen's services in exhibiting the Hebrew prophets as witnesses to the divine government would require from most Englishmen years of study, proceeds thus :—

"Accustomed to be told [i. e. the English] that modern history is expressed by the Prophets in a riddle, which requires only a key to it, they are disappointed to hear of moral lessons, however important. Such notions are the inheritance of days when Justin could argue, in good faith, that by the riches of Damascus and the spoil of Samaria were intended the Magi and their gifts, and that the King of Assyria signified King Herod; (!) or when Jerome could say, 'No one doubts that by Chaldæans are meant Demons,' and the Shunamite Abishag* could be no other than heavenly wisdom, for the honour of David's old age; not to mention such things as Lot's daughters symbolizing the Jewish and Gentile Churches."—(pp. 63, 64.)

For this attack upon Jerome we have the authority quoted in a note. The authority is thus stated, p. 64 :—

"On Isaiah xliii. 14, 15, and again on ch. xlviii. 12—16. He also shews on xlviii. 22 that the Jews of that day had not lost the historical sense of their prophecies, though mystical renderings had already shewn themselves."

In another note, p. 65, we have the following remark :—

"When Jerome Origenises he is worse than Origen, because he does not, like that great genius, distinguish the historical from the mystical sense."

These are very hard words; but the Fathers have had the vials of wrath showered down upon them so often that an ounce or two, more or less, of the virtuous indignation of the nineteenth century at their shortcomings, can make but little difference. But when the nineteenth century begins to depreciate the fourth and fifth centuries in theology, it would be well that the matter should be stated quite fairly. It will be of no avail for Dr. Williams to state, as he did in reply to an

*** This is not worth answering. It occurs in a private letter to Nepotianus, and is simply a case of etymological trifling.**

anonymous critic, that he speaks "in a style abundantly clear, though with rapid condensation," &c., for in the present instance he selects his own point of attack, and if he quotes any statement of an author, he is bound to quote it with sufficient detail to place his reader in possession of the whole case. I have no means of testing the familiarity of Dr. Williams with the works of Jerome; and as he bears the reputation of a learned and candid man, I should wish to believe that he is not quoting from a random plunge or two into the depths of that Father's Commentary, although I can scarcely imagine that any candid man would endeavour from such a passage to create so unfavourable an impression of this eminent commentator, if he really knew much about him! Throughout these valuable remains of ancient exegesis, Jerome compares the Hebrew text and that of the LXX, and points out the difference of the interpretations to which they naturally lead. He occasionally gives his opinion on other interpretations, and gives his reasons for rejecting or accepting them. Often two different interpretations are found in the commentary on the same passage, and the sagacity of the reader must be exercised in judging between them. While he gives one of these interpretations, he uses the language which fits that interpretation, whether it expresses his own sentiments or not. What are we therefore to think of the fairness of a person who picks out and isolates a single sentence from the middle of a mystical interpretation, and then presents it to his readers as a specimen of the exegesis of Jerome? If he only meant that the simple fact that such a statement could ever enter into any mystical interpretation at all, is a proof that exegesis was at a very low ebb, and that Jerome was not much above his contemporaries, then his proof would be worth nothing, and he would only exhibit *pro tanto* his own incompetence to measure the intellectual power of the age. If he meant to exhibit this as an average specimen of Jerome's powers, then such a proceeding needs only the simple detail which I have given to shew its unfairness. It would be unfair to take it as a *speci-*

men if it were shewn to be Jerome's own opinion and enounced generally. But when it is shewn to be a part of a great interpretation, which is immediately followed by the words, "But the sense according to the LXX is entirely different," what shall we say of such a quotation? And that too on the supposition that Dr. Williams has given a true interpretation of the words he has quoted? Any competent Hebrew and Latin scholar, on reading these words, "De Chaldæis nullus ambigit quin Dæmones sonent," would be directed by the words *Chaldæi* and *sonent* to a *paronomasia* or play on words between the Hebrew name for the Chaldæans and the word for Demons.* If he looked for Jerome's own interpretation of the word among his Hebrew words, there he would find that the Hebrew word for Chaldees is rendered by Jerome, "Chasdim, quasi Dæmonia, vel quasi ubera, vel feroces." So that after all this contempt of Jerome, it appears that he is only enouncing, in connection with a particular interpretation of a certain passage, an etymological fact, not an exegetical principle. The unlearned would understand from the account in the Essay that Jerome meant to lay down as a rule of interpretation, that wherever Chaldeans are mentioned, Demons are intended, whereas all that Jerome does say is this, viz., that the Hebrew text lends itself to a mystical interpretation, by which Babylon is represented as the world, and there is no doubt that the word Chasdim may be interpreted 'Dæmones,' etymologically speaking. He immediately adds that the sense is entirely different according to the LXX. I invite all those who have the requisite acquirements to study this portion of Jerome, and to test the account which I have given of his meaning with the utmost severity. I now ask, if this account be true, can any reader trust the author of this Essay for a faithful portrait of one of the Fathers? † But this is by no means

* כשדים, *Chasdim*, or *Chashdim*. Now this is, otherwise pointed, equivalent to "like Demons," the word שדים occurring for Demons in the Pentateuch.

† I must not be misunderstood, however. I quite acknowledge that

all the retribution due from the author of the Essay to the memory of this eminent Father. So far from being anxious to interpret Scripture thus mystically, and to make out the Chaldeans to be Demons, Jerome actually reproves Origen for this very fault on more occasions than one.

Any person who desires to judge more fairly of Jerome, after this paltry attack of Dr. Williams, may consult, among other passages, his commentary on Isaiah xiii., with its preface.* He will there see how carefully he rejects the spiritual interpretation of Eusebius, who was not a person commonly run away with by his imagination, and cleaves to the simple historical view of the passage, and how he repudiates the allegorizing spirit of Origen. Or, again, let him turn to Jer. xxv., where he will find the judgment of Jerome on the allegorical interpretation of Origen: "The allegorical interpreter" (i.e. Origen) "here talks nonsense, and puts force upon the historical interpretation." Indeed, he seems to think the mere statement of such an opinion here a sufficient refutation. Let him turn again to Jeremiah xxvii., where he finds these words: "The allegorical interpreter" (i.e. Origen) "interprets this passage about the heavenly Jerusalem, because the inhabitants of that city are to descend into Babylon, that is, the confusion of this world, which is in the wicked one, and to serve the king of Babylon, that is without doubt the devil." This is his account of Origen's interpretation, and the reader will remark that he makes here the king of Babylon the devil; but he immediately adds, "But *we* follow the simple and true history, that we may not be involved in clouds and delusions."

Surely no reader will require further proof that, if he desires to estimate the character of Jerome fairly, he

this etymology is farfetched, and that this is an unsound mode of interpretation. But to charge Jerome with flagrant absurdity for a single expression like this, is simply ridiculous and unworthy.

* There can be no doubt that Jerome's translation is faulty here. כדיבים cannot be in the nominative, but is in the genitive after "the doors," "the doors of the princes," but this makes no difference as to the general sobriety of his interpretation of this passage.

must go to some other source than Dr. Williams. If Dr. Williams really knows much about Jerome,—a question I do not presume to answer, although I may have formed an opinion upon it,—it is quite clear that he does not intend his readers to benefit by his knowledge. He *may* be capable of giving them a just notion of this Father, but he is quite determined to thrust upon them an unjust view, and depreciate Jerome in order to libel modern writers who differ from the rationalists.

The specimen already adduced of the method of this author in dealing with general questions, such as the interpretation of prophecy and the character of great patristic authorities, are sufficient to shew that no confidence whatever can be placed in his statements. But perhaps it may be thought that he is more happy in his exegesis or explanation of particular passages of Scripture. Dr. Williams has ventured, fortunately for us, and as we deem unfortunately for himself, to give us his opinion on certain difficult passages of Holy Writ. If he had not ventured on this experiment he might have maintained the reputation of being a very competent Hebrew scholar; but if in the opinions he delivers he shews a thorough want of appreciation of the nature of the passages he brings forward, he must be content to sink down into the common herd of authors, who write on what they do not take pains enough to understand.

Whether this is the case with Dr. Williams will appear from the following statement.

All Hebrew scholars are well aware that some diversity of opinion has existed, especially in Germany, as to the interpretation of that portion of the prophecy of Jacob in Gen. xlix. which relates to Judah and Shiloh. The English reader who is not acquainted with Hebrew and German is, of course, unable to refute any misrepresentation of the state of the question, and if Dr. Williams writes for them, he is bound to state it fairly. If he writes for the learned I need scarcely say that they will only smile at the presumption of a scholar who, in regard to a passage on which there has been a division of opinion, considers himself qualified to overturn the decision of the best authorities and the tradition of more than two thousand years, and to declare that except for doctrinal perversions this view would never be maintained. Let us now examine the passage and the authorities for the two divergent views.

The words as translated in our version are, "The sceptre shall not depart from Judah, nor a lawgiver from between his feet, until Shiloh come." And such has been the translation from the earliest days till within a comparatively modern period, when the last clause has been translated by some Hebrew scholars, "until he come to Shiloh."

If we enquire into the support on which these two translations respectively rest, we shall find that there was till within the last two centuries an almost* unanimous concurrence in the translation given by our version, as far as the subject of the verb "to come" is concerned. It was almost universally translated "until Shiloh come," although some understood by Shiloh "He to whom it belongs," and others understood "rest" or "peace" as a name of the Messiah. It is one of those prophecies which might seem to press hardly upon the Jews after the utter dispersion of their nation; but all their writers, as quoted in the *Pugio Fidei*, maintain the old interpretation which their Targums put upon the passage," "until Messias comes." A few modern commentators, as well as Gesenius and other rationalists, have however translated the passage "until he comes to Shiloh," and this translation Baron Bunsen has accepted. And of this his reviewer remarks:—

"The famous Shiloh (Gen. xlix. 10) is taken in its local sense, as the sanctuary where the young Samuel was trained;

* I find a statement in Reinke's *Die Weissagung Jacobs, &c.*, p. 124, which leads me to suppose that Rabbi Lipmann supported this view, but I am unable to ascertain that he understood the town Shiloh under this word. His view is given in his poem as published in Wagenseil's' *Tela Ignea Satanæ*, pp. 113, 114, and answered pp. 264–328. In the *Nizzachon Vetus*, in the same volume, there is another attack on the Christian interpretation, p. 27.

which, if doctrinal perversions did not interfere, hardly any one would doubt to be the true sense."—(p. 62.)

The Jews, against whom our interpretation presses very severely, have had every motive for adopting the new view, yet we see they adhere to the old. Let us then look at the teacher of Gesenius, I. S. Vater, a man entirely free from any bigoted prepossessions in favour of theological tenets. After enumerating the different views, and giving that in which Shiloh is taken for the sanctuary a very complete examination, he adds,—

"All this would be very suitable under the supposition that this song was sung at a time in which Shiloh was the centre of the theocracy. The possibility of such a supposition cannot be denied. Nor can the possibility also that it was sung under the influence of a deep feeling of the pre-eminence of the tribe of Judah in David and his race of kings," &c.—(*Commentary*, vol. i. p. 321.)

Such is the language of a very calm rationalist commentator, and yet Dr. Williams quietly tells us that nobody would maintain our translation except from "doctrinal perversions." But in fact, the new translation, though patronized by Dr. Williams, really entails a series of difficulties, which nothing but very strong "perversions," whether doctrinal or not, could enable a competent scholar to overlook. What era did the fixing of the tabernacle at Shiloh commence? What historical importance, except in the religious history of the people, does it possess? And could the tribe of Judah be said then to exercise any pre-eminence when the leader of the people of Israel was Joshua of the tribe of Ephraim?* If this song, as Vater disrespectfully calls it, was forged in the time of Samuel, what a very clumsy forger its author must have been! The man who swallows this camel may well strain out the few gnats which he finds in the Authorized Version. If Dr. Williams desires to maintain his reputation as a Biblical scholar, he will avoid assertions by which

* It has been well observed, that in the time of the Judges, Othniel alone was certainly of the tribe of Judah. Ebzon is doubtful.

nothing can be proved, except that he has a very arrogant mode of attributing bad motives to those who differ from him, even when it is almost demonstrable that he is in the wrong. All that can be said is, that in a passage of some difficulty, Dr. Williams has taken the side which has not only an overwhelming weight of authority against it, but has very little in its favour, and, not content with this, he denounces all who differ from him, very much in the style of a person who is wholly ignorant of the strength of the case of his opponents.*

Such is the impression which this first essay of Dr. Williams in Hebrew criticism in the present Review is calculated to make on those who have any competent knowledge of the original passage.

But we have several other passages despatched in almost as summary a manner, and with about as much regard to the real circumstances of the case. Take for example his view of the second Psalm, or rather one expression of it. Dr. Williams in describing the opinions of Bunsen on various prophetic announcements of Scripture, seems to take the position of one leading a poor English neophyte through these dangerous mazes in order to familiarize his mind with the notion that all Messianic interpretations have been given up and are untenable. He speaks thus of Bunsen's views of Psalm ii.:—

> "If he would follow our version in rendering the second Psalm, 'Kiss the Son,' he knows that Hebrew idiom convinced even Jerome the true meaning was 'worship purely.'"

In a note he quotes as much of Jerome as suits his purpose, thus:—"Cavillatur . . . quod posuerim, ... *Adorate pure* . . . . ne violentus viderer interpres, et Jud. locum darem." Now so far from Jerome's being convinced by the Hebrew idiom that this is the real meaning of the passage, he states clearly that one word

* Those who read German will find a good account of the different opinions on this passage in *Die Weissagung Jacobs, &c.*, by Dr. L. Reinke, (Munster, 1849,) pp. 58–129. The English reader will also find much information in Hengstenberg's "Christology," vol. i.

is ambiguous, and although, to avoid *calumnies* from the Jews in regard to such an ambiguous word, he translates in the text *Adorate pure*, he appears in his notes clearly to prefer the other translation, 'Kiss the Son.' Now could any unlearned reader dream that this was the state of Jerome's mind as to this passage from the bold assertion of the text of Dr. Williams and the very cautious dotted extract which he gives in his note?

I here subjoin an exact translation of the whole passage:—

"He is also said to blame me, because in interpreting the second Psalm, instead of that which is read in the Latin, *Apprehendite disciplinam*, 'Learn instruction,' and which is written in the Hebrew, נשקו בר, *nascu bar*, I have said *Adorate filium*, 'Worship the Son,' and then, again, in turning the whole Psalter into the Roman tongue, as if I had forgotten the former interpretation, I have put *Adorate pure*, which it would seem is a contradiction evident to all. And, indeed, we may pardon him for not being accurately acquainted with Hebrew, when he sometimes is in difficulty in Latin. נשקו, *nascu*,—if we are to translate word for word—is equivalent to κατφιλήσατε = *deosculamini*, 'Kiss ye,' and being unwilling to translate it baldly, I followed the sense rather [than the words] so as to translate it *adorate*, 'Worship ye,' because they who worship are wont to kiss the hand and bow the head, which blessed Job declares that he had not done to the elements and to idols, saying, 'If I have seen the sun when it shone, and the moon walking in brightness, and my heart in secret rejoiced, and I kissed my hand, which is a great sin, and a denial of the most high God;' and the Hebrews, according to the idiom of their language, put *deosculatio*, 'kissing,' for *veneratio*, 'worship.' I have translated that which they, to whose language the word belongs, understand. But בר, *bar*, with them has different meanings, for it means 'son,' as in Barjona, 'son of a dove;' Barptolomæus, 'son of Ptolomæus;' Barthimæus, &c. It means also 'wheat,' and a 'bundle of ears of wheat,' and 'elect' and 'pure.' What fault have I committed if I have translated an ambiguous word in different ways? In my Commentary, where there is an opportunity of discussing the matter, I had said *Adorate filium*, 'Worship the Son,' [but] in the text itself, not to seem a violent interpreter and not to give occasion to

Jewish *calumny*, I said *Adorate pure sive electe*, 'Worship purely or in a choice manner;' as Aquila and Symmachus had translated it."—*Hieron. adv. Ruffinum*, lib. i.

The reader will observe how entirely Dr. Williams omits all reference to Jerome's views, as expressed in his *notes*, and how cunningly he cuts out the word *calumny*, as applied to the Jewish objectors. Can the unlearned English reader trust such a guide as this? I must also add that, although Ewald and Hupfeld, as one might expect, reject the Messianic view, Delitzsch, the last learned commentator on the Psalms, maintains it very strongly.

There is an amount of misrepresentation in these statements which entirely precludes any confidence in an account given by Dr. Williams, either of the views of any writer on a given passage or of the real state of the case in regard to that passage. In one of these instances he has not only pronounced *ex cathedrâ*, as it were, an opinion on the meaning of a prophecy against the weight of authority and the general bearing of the passage, but he has coupled the expression of his opinion with the attribution of bad motives to those who do not agree with him. In the other, he has told half the truth as to Jerome's opinion, but only half the truth, and he has shaped his quotation from that Father in such a manner as to conceal the fact that the rest of it altogether makes against him.

The same spirit of rash assertion marks his treatment of the Messianic passage in the 22nd Psalm, where it is very difficult to ascertain the genuine reading; but Dr. Williams would persuade the unlearned reader that the cause has been entirely settled, and that the evidence is all in his favour. So far is this from being the case, that it is one of those passages where learned men find it difficult to make up their mind what the true reading and interpretation are. My own belief is, that upon the whole the evidence preponderates for our rendering; but it is a point on which, from the evidence of the Old Testament MSS. alone, there are some difficulties, though the certainty, from the quotations in the New Testament, that other portions of this Psalm are Messianic, is a great argument in favour of the Messianic nature of this verse.*

These are specimens of the manner in which the evidence for the Messianic interpretation of particular passages of Scripture is dealt with; it will hardly be expected that an answer should be given to every one, for this would need a volume. A single sentence conveys an objection the answer to which must, if complete, extend to several pages.

But we will now enter upon a larger field of interpretation. The Essayist has given us one interpretation of a prophetic chapter. It is a chapter in the interpretation of which all our deeper feelings of Christianity are so intimately interwoven that a religious man might be expected to approach it with reverence, and if the force of evidence compelled him to give up the old and Christian interpretation of that chapter, he would announce his change of view, if not with sadness, at least with gravity and sobriety. The last thing which a religious man would be expected to do with the 53rd chapter of Isaiah would be to play with its interpretation—as if it were a matter of utter indifference whether a vital prophecy were entirely irrelevant or not to the mission of the Redeemer of the world. We are not to be led by our preconceived notions, but at all events a religious heart might be expected to part with some of the most striking evidences of our faith with some regret. And truly, when the question concerns a prophecy which has almost invariably been held to be one of the most striking in the Bible, to which the New Testament sometimes in sublime silence gives

* To examine this passage properly would require several pages: it is a question both of reading and interpretation. Bp. Pearson considered this one of the passages confessedly altered by the Jews: but later researches have rather altered the conditions of the question. I shall now only refer to De Rossi's "Collations," vol. iv. pp. 14–20; Pfeiffer, *Dubia Vexata*, pp. 305–309; Delitzsch and Hupfeld on the passage; Davidson's "Hebrew Text Revised," and Reinke's *Messianische Psalmen*, vol. i. p. 266, &c. Of these, all but Hupfeld and Davidson either adopt the sense of "piercing," or consider the evidence nearly balanced. Reinke, as usual, is very full and valuable.

a wonderful testimony,* the last thing we should expect would be very high praise of an ingenious interpretation, nay an elaborate exposition of it, where the author after all acknowledges that it does not persuade him. Why then so elaborately display it? and why add, that if any individual can be thought to fulfil the prophecy that individual would be judged to be Jeremiah, unless by a kind of insane crusade against the ordinary view of the passage the author wishes to deprive the humble Christian of any possibility of using this passage as a prophecy of the Messiah? Now if either of these interpretations,—that which makes collective Israel the subject of the prophecy, as Dr. Williams appears to believe, or that which makes Jeremiah, as Bunsen maintains,—were proved to fulfil the prophecy in some sense, it would be no proof that it was not intended in a fuller and higher sense to describe the Messiah. But the truth is that if the prophecy be taken as a whole, there are insuperable objections to both these interpretations, which it suits Dr. Williams to ignore, that he may throw a little dust in the eyes of those who are unfortunate enough to lean on him as an interpreter of Scripture. Great humiliation, and that voluntary, and undergone by an innocent man for the benefit of others, and the most lofty exaltation, these are the characteristics of the subject of that prophecy. It is quite true that once Jeremiah was taken from a dungeon, and so (if this were not a "recognised mistranslation") "he was taken from prison,"† but where was his lofty exaltation? The interpretation fails in a cardinal point, and the Jews themselves have given it up. The German periodical before referred to, says they gave up the Messianic interpretation "on paper," that is, in controversy with the Christians; but if Dr.

* When our Lord was silent before Pilate, "insomuch that the governor marvelled," no specific reference is made to the passage, but the prophecy flashes on our minds at once.

† This translation is generally discarded now, so that even this trifling coincidence is nullified. See Gesenius, M'Caul, Drechsler, and Henderson. There is a difference of opinion still as to the exact *meaning* of the passage; but none of these interpreters dream of "prison."

Williams will read their liturgies he will see that they still retain it in reality. Any person well acquainted with Rabbinical writings knows that frequently they used in their commentaries to say "This passage applies to the Messiah, but to answer the Christians we must apply it to some other person;" but when their books began to be published, in many instances they withdrew these words as being discreditable to them.

The language of Dr. Williams is somewhat unguarded. After sketching out Bunsen's reasons for applying the prophecy to Jeremiah, he adds:—

> "This is an imperfect sketch, but may lead readers to consider the arguments for applying Isaiah lii. and liii. to Jeremiah. Their weight (in the master's hand) is so great, that if any single person should be selected, *they prove Jeremiah should be the one.*"

They may prove it to the Essayist, though what the cogency of a *proof* may be which fails to produce conviction, I must leave him to explain; but I doubt whether he will find many to agree with him. Let us examine one or two of his quotations. It is true that Jeremiah appears to have wished to intercede for the Jews, and the Essayist refers to Jer. xviii. 20, xiv. 11, xv. 1, in proof of this; from which passages (xiv. 11 and xv. 1) we learn that God forbade Jeremiah to intercede for them as he had done, for the judgments must come upon them; and in xviii. 20 he says, "Remember that I stood before Thee to speak good for them, and to turn away Thy wrath from them." It is a pity that the Essayist omitted to give the sequel of this intercession found in xviii. 21, the very next verse, which runs thus:—"Therefore deliver up their children to the famine, and pour out their blood by the force of the sword; and let their wives be bereaved of their children, and be widows; and let their men be put to death; let their young men be slain with the sword in battle. Let a cry be heard from their houses, when Thou shalt bring a troop suddenly upon them: for they have digged a pit to take me, and hid snares for my feet. Yet, Lord,

Thou knowest all their counsel against me to slay me: *forgive not their iniquity, neither blot out their sin from Thy sight*, but let them be overthrown before Thee; deal thus with them in the time of Thine anger*."

It may suit the Essayist to ignore this sequel to the declaration of Jeremiah that he had formerly interceded for the people, in whose prosperity, should it come, he himself would have shared, and he may consider this a striking fulfilment of the prophecy; but who will follow him in this perversion? I speak not for the Christian sentiment only, but I simply ask what shall we

* And yet in the very face of these denunciations of his persecutors, Baron Bunsen ventures to use the following language, which I translate literally from the German original:—"Jeremiah says, in speaking of the cruel persecutions of the citizens of his native town, xi. 18, &c., 'The Lord has given me knowledge of it, and I know it: then Thou shewedst me their doings. But I was like a lamb or an ox that is brought to the slaughter.' And afterwards kings and nobles wrought all in their power to realize this anticipation of the prophet. And if Jeremiah, when Pashur cast him into the dungeon, broke out into loud lamentations on his misfortune, and prayed God to ennoble his reputation by the punishment of these men who denied his truth; yet we find in the last most bitter trial to which he was subjected in Judæa, no word of impatience escape him, still less a word of desire that God should revenge him on his enemies. *But on the contrary*, there runs through his whole life the very inmost (*die innigste*) *intercession for the transgressors!* to which allusion is made in the end of the celebrated chapter of Isaiah."—*Gott in der Geschichte*, vol. i. pp. 205, 206.

It is true that one-half of a verse of Isaiah appears to be fulfilled by the declaration of Jeremiah, that he is "led as a lamb or an ox to the slaughter," but the slightest amount of attention, one would think, would have sufficed to show that such a fulfilment utterly contradicted the rest of the verse! The sheep of Isaiah is dumb, and opens not his mouth, but Jeremiah utters loud complaints not unmixed with denunciations! We are now entitled to ask where the prejudiced view lies? With Baron Bunsen, who *is determined that the prophecy shall be no prophecy*, or with us who believe the prophecy, and find its fulfilment where the Church of Christ has found it for 1800 years? But above all, how can Bunsen dare to say, that *throughout the life of Jeremiah* he was constantly interceding for the transgressors?

And again, though not a word is said of Jeremiah's death, Baron Bunsen *assumes* that he perished by "a cruel murder," because the great prophet of truth could "scarcely" be expected to escape martyrdom. And this fact, (!) for which he appeals to his own conjecture, rather than the tradition preserved in Jerome, and these contradictions to the prophet's own words, form the basis of Bunsen's application of this prophecy to Jeremiah. And this absurd speculation, which scarcely deserves a refutation, gains for the author from Dr. Williams the high praise of being from the hand of a master!

think of an exegesis which can refer to passages like Jer. xviii. 20, followed as it is by these denunciations, as a fulfilment of the prophecy of "interceding for transgressors;" and dare to prefer it to that most thrilling, most awful prayer of mercy, which rose from the lips of One in the very agony of a painful death, when He who even then spake as never man spake, made that sublime intercession for His persecutors, "Father, forgive them, for they know not what they do."

It cannot be needful to go through the weary task of examining each quotation in detail, here; I would only recommend those who have any desire to investigate the question, to do as I have done—examine them carefully; and I believe that the conclusion of such persons will be the same as mine, that no more unfounded assertion was ever made than that, if any single person should be selected, *they prove Jeremiah to be the one!* The English and the argument of this sentence are nearly on a par, but it is useless to cavil about trifles when such momentous questions are at issue. The discrepancies between the history of Jeremiah and the words of the prophecy are so manifest, that Saadias Gaon has found few followers till Bunsen revived this palpable controversial device. Even Abarbanel himself, one of the most bitter opponents of Christianity among the Jews, says, "In truth I do not see even one verse that can prove the truth of its application to him." And yet Bunsen is spoken of as a "master" in exegesis here, not for proving the truth, but for his ingenious defence of a theory which the Essayist himself rejects. His notions of a masterly exposition and a "proof" are so manifestly peculiar, that we must conceive these words to belong to a private vocabulary of the English language in use at Lampeter, but not current elsewhere.

Abarbanel proposed both Josiah and the Jewish nation. Josiah is scarcely worth considering. But what particular interpretation Dr. Williams does adopt, it would be difficult to say. His words are these:—

"Still the general analogy of the Old Testament which

makes *collective Israel, or the prophetic remnant*,* especially the servant of Jehovah, and the comparison of chaps. xlii. xlix. may permit us to think *the oldest* interpretation the truest; with only this admission, that the figure of Jeremiah stood forth among the Prophets, and tinged the delineation of the *true* Israel, that is, *the faithful remnant* who had been disbelieved—just as the figure of Laud or Hammond might represent the Caroline Church in the eyes of her poet.

"If this seems but a compromise, it may be justified by Ewald's phrase, 'Die wenigen Treuen im Exile, Jeremjah und Andre,' (the few faithful in the captivity, Jeremiah and others,) though he makes the servant idealized Israel."

It would be convenient in considering this author's views, to be able to ascertain exactly what they are, but as he does not seem to be quite fixed in any one view, it is a hopeless task. *Collective Israel*, or *the faithful remnant*, or *the prophetic remnant*,—though I suppose by "the faithful remnant" he means the faithful prophetic remnant,—appear to prefer almost equal claims to acceptance; and the author seems to oscillate between them with a beautiful impartiality, throwing in only a word in favour of Jeremiah, which leaves us as much in the dark as we were before. Can Dr. Williams believe that these interpretations are synonymous, or that an amalgamation of all of them can possibly stand? If he does, his character for critical acumen will scarcely survive such palpable incongruities! And this, it is to be observed, is the criticism of a man who thinks he is not interpreting a *prophecy* but an *historical narrative*, where a writer would describe events without ambiguity.

But these vacillations are trifles compared with the assertion that the interpretation now in favour with the Jews is the "*oldest* interpretation." Our own interpretation is at least coeval with the New Testament, (see 1 Pet. ii. 24, &c.) a clear proof that it rests upon an older basis still. And though Origen informs us

* The italics are mine, not the author's. The reader will observe that Dr. Williams leaves it open *which* of these interpretations we are to choose, as if either would do.

that in a dispute with learned Jews one of them attempted to evade the force of this prophecy by such an interpretation, this is a very slender evidence that they generally accepted it, even then. And, if we enquire of the Jewish authorities themselves, we find them acknowledging that the ancient Jews interpreted this prophecy of the Messiah. The Targum distinctly recognises it, the most ancient Jewish interpreters acknowledge it: even in the present day, liturgies of the Jews testify their adherence to the ancient view in a manner which is far more convincing than a controversial statement would be.

Before however I pass on to another subject, it will be right to mark the treatment Bishop Pearson receives at the hands of Dr. Williams. His vast attainments and his great power have obtained for him an homage, which has scarcely ever been refused by those who are competent to test his learning. But, as the late Archdeacon Hare used to say, "Many an empty head is shaken at Plato and Aristotle;" and in a similar manner we find occasionally a perverse disposition which seems to rejoice in throwing a stone at departed greatness. Thus the Essayist remarks, "*It is idle with Pearson* to quote Jonathan as a witness to the Christian interpretation, unless his conception of the Messiah were ours." The transparent absurdity of this remark strikes the mind so forcibly, that it would be a matter of surprise that the author did not reject it himself, if we did not find many other illogical remarks throughout the Essay. So then, it is really the opinion of Dr. Williams that we do nothing, even if we shew that all the ancient Jews considered this prophecy as clearly relating to the Messiah, unless they will acknowledge that Jesus is the Messiah! I fear that even the first class at Lampeter will hardly be contented with husks like these; and men of plain sense will consider it of rather more importance that the whole of the ancient Jewish Church accepted this view, than that Bunsen applies it to Jeremiah, and Dr. Williams to the collective Israel! Bishop Pearson was probably almost as good a judge of the cogency of arguments—if we may presume to compare any one to Dr. Williams—as the Essayist himself. And I do not very much fear that the reputation of Bishop Pearson will suffer much damage from so puerile an attack.

But before I leave this part of the subject, it is only justice to Dr. Williams to remark that he only denies that these great declarations of Scripture are *predictions;* he professes to acknowledge that their moral teaching has its highest fulfilment in Christ. His words are: "A little reflection will shew how the historical representation in Isaiah liii. is of some suffering prophet or remnant," (which?) "yet the truth and patience, the grief and triumph, have their highest fulfilment in Him who said 'Father, not My will but Thine.' But we must not distort the prophets to prove the Divine Word incarnate, and then from the incarnation reason back to the sense of prophecy." *

I was not aware of the intention with which the remark in the latter part of this paragraph was made, till I happened to find an allusion in Mr. Mansel's Bampton Lectures to the views of Dr. Williams on the 53d of Isaiah, as developed in his "Rational Godliness."

Mr. Mansel (p. 418) argues that if we believe one such miracle as the incarnation of our Lord, we have no reason to disbelieve another, such as the prediction of future events under the inspiration of God. And this Dr. Williams calls reasoning back from the incarnation *to the sense* of prophecy. It seems strange that a man of any acuteness could fail to see that Mr. Mansel did not reason back *to the sense* of the prophecy; the sense of the prophecy must be determined

* A little more of the same sort follows. Israel would be acknowledged as in some sense a Messiah, &c., but the Saviour, who fulfilled in His own person the highest aspirations of Hebrew seers and of mankind, thereby lifting the words, so to speak, into a new and higher power, would be recognised as having eminently the unction of a prophet whose words die not, of a priest in a temple not made with hands, and of a king in the realm of thought, delivering His people from a bondage of moral evil, worse than Egypt or Babylon, &c.

by just principles of interpretation; but Mr. Mansel argues that if it must be interpreted of Christ, we have no reason to reject it from *à priori* and general objections to miracles. The only possible effect this can have on the interpretation of this special prophecy or any other is this, that it leaves us at liberty to take the *predictive* sense, if other considerations lead us to it.* As we do not therefore reason back from the incarnation "to the sense of prophecy," I feel no inclination to enter on the defence of a course which we do not adopt.

We shall simply remark that Christ and His apostles tell us that the Hebrew Scriptures testify of Him, and they expressly ascribe a *predictive* sense to the prophecies. We have therefore, on the one hand, Christ and His apostles, who assure us that the prophecies are predictions; on the other, we have Dr. Williams and the critical school, who assure us that they are not. The question is therefore simply this,—Will you believe Christ and His apostles, or will you believe the critical school? The pretence of a moral fulfilment is only a device to cover the barefaced impudence of denying the very words of the Saviour and His apostles, but is too flimsy to deceive even the most ignorant. I will not accuse Dr. Williams of placing it there intentionally to deceive the ignorant: I suppose that he himself considers this moral fulfilment as more than equivalent to the real fulfilment of a *bonâ fide* prediction. But as this is a peculiar view, and as those who think with me believe that it cannot be maintained without falsifying the words of our Saviour and contradicting His own account of the Scriptures, Dr. Williams must excuse his opponents if they speak very plainly as to the worthlessness of his admissions.

* Mr. Mansel says indeed, "Once concede the possibility of the supernatural at all, and the Messianic interpretation is the only one reconcilable with the facts of history and the plain meaning of words." He finds out the plain meaning of the words from a true exegesis; and he only argues from the Incarnation that you have no right to reject this sense because it implies a miracle.

The observations which have been made may serve to shew with how little justice the Essayist has attempted to exhibit this wonderful prophecy as a piece of historical writing of a date posterior to the time of Isaiah. This is all which I am here concerned to shew, but if a commentary on this most astounding prophecy be required, I may state that great assistance may be derived towards its exegesis from the Essay of Hengstenberg, either in its early form as translated in Clark's "Biblical Cabinet," or in its more developed condition as found in the "Christology of the Old Testament," (published also by Messrs. Clark,) and from the pamphlet of Dr. McCaul, or Dr. Henderson's "Translation of Isaiah." From all these sources together, the mere English reader will obtain a very sufficient refutation of the non-Messianic interpretations, and he will be able also to elicit from a comparison of the various views of each verse, an interpretation of the whole which will give him much satisfaction. The works of Bishops Chandler and Lowth, as well as that of Prebendary Lowth, may be consulted with advantage.

In the indiscriminate onslaught upon prophets and prophecy, it could not be expected that Daniel, whose predictions are the most definite of all included in the sacred volume, should escape proscription. We have however, in Bunsen and Dr. Williams, very little which is new. It seems sometimes to be imagined that the attacks upon Daniel are due to some new discoveries, and that the Germans have brought a host of new arguments against the genuineness of this portion of Scripture; but if we look at the selection of topics made by Dr. Williams to overwhelm this prophet, we shall find that even down to the very words selected as proving that the language is later than his time, they are all the old *crambe repetita*. The simple fact is, that the Germans and Dr. Williams follow Porphyry and Collins, while others consider that their arguments are insufficient to warrant their conclusions. It is true that Bunsen and Ewald have added each his own particular theory to the general medley of speculation upon this prophet, but they have met with little favour, even in Germany. The extraordinary facility with which a prophet or two is extemporized in Germany, would surprise those who are not aware of the strength of the theorizing faculty in the German mind. 'If one Isaiah or one Daniel will not solve the question satisfactorily, take two,' appears to be the rule, and accordingly an earlier Daniel is supposed by Baron Bunsen to have lived, not at Babylon, but at the Assyrian court, about twenty-two years before Sargina (the Sargon of Scripture and the father of Sennacherib) overturned the ancient dynasty of Assyria. The history of Daniel is partly derived, according to this view, from traditional tales about the older Daniel, and some of the prophecies are a traditional reconstruction of these, with sundry confusions between Assyria and Babylon It is hardly worth while to spend our time in considering so gratuitous an hypothesis, for even the German rationalists assure us that Baron Bunsen has done for Daniel very little except to add to the perplexity in which his history is involved. Bleek, who also supposes another Daniel of a more ancient date than ours, entirely repudiates the suppositions of Ewald and Bunsen, and closes his remarks upon them with these words: "By such assumptions the explanation of the existence of our Book of Daniel in its present condition is by no means rendered more easy, but on the contrary, more difficult."

It must be clear to every man of plain common sense, that if the license *quidlibet audendi* which was conceded to poets and painters is assumed by German critics, the theological world cannot be expected to disprove each hypothesis separately. The question must be argued in a different manner. If the objectors to the genuineness of Daniel are content to rake up again and endorse all the miserable mistakes and perversions of Porphyry and Collins, we are surely entitled to assert that they have entirely failed to make out their case, without writing a volume to confute a sentence.

I shall merely remark with regard to the arguments, that they chiefly rest on two assertions:—

1. That the prophecies of Daniel are so clear as to Antiochus Epiphanes, and so manifestly end with him, that it is to be inferred that they were written shortly after his time.

2. That the language is not that of the time of Daniel, and that Greek words occur in Daniel, especially in the names of the musical instruments,* which proves that its author lived long after the time in which Daniel is placed according to the Bible.

These are the two main grounds, and neither of them is capable of any satisfactory proof. The first proposition is also manifestly false in one of its assertions, for the prophecies extend to far later times than those of Antiochus. Indeed, the supposition that Antiochus Epiphanes is intended in some parts of those prophecies of Daniel which are so confidently applied to him, is attended with insuperable difficulties, as any one who is disposed to enquire into this matter may learn from Bishop Chandler, especially pp. 140—157, and Bishop Newton on the prophecies. In chapter vii. (see Chandler, pp. 206—282,) the little horn cannot be Antiochus Epiphanes, although in another chapter (the eighth) some things may be attributed to him which belong to the little horn. But if the fourth kingdom be the Roman, (and what other will answer its description?) then the fifth kingdom can be no other than the kingdom of Christ. We may not be able to explain every part of these prophecies, but we know enough to shew that Antiochus Epiphanes could really fulfil only a very small part of them, and that those who attempt to apply the rest to him, involve themselves in inextricable contradictions. It is manifestly impossible to

* With regard to the names of the musical instruments, the objectors fail in two primary points. They entirely fail in proving that they are derived from the Greek; and, if they did, they cannot prove that this would necessarily bring down the date to a later period than 536 B.C. They might almost as well deduce the *Akkadimi* mentioned in Rawlinson's Memoir on Nineveh from *Academus*. See also Dr. Mill's "Historical Character of St. Luke's First Chapter Vindicated," pp. 65—69.

answer a general statement like that of Dr. Williams, because we do not know how many of the prophecies he applies to Antiochus Epiphanes, nor how he explains them.

Again, with regard to the suspicious words, if the enquirer will consult either Hävernick's "Daniel," or Hengstenberg's *Die Authentie des Daniel und die Integrität des Sacharijah*, he will see with how little reason this argument has been alleged. Modern philology, upon the whole, has rather tended to remove this objection than to confirm it.*

The same remark must apply to the statements regarding Zechariah. I have now before me two volumes in German, in one of which the author appends a defence of the integrity of Zechariah to that of the genuineness of Daniel, viz., the volume of Hengstenberg to which I have just referred; the other is a Commentary on Zechariah, by W. Neumann, published at Stuttgart in the course of last year, which does not seem to think the hypothesis of the authorship of the book being divided between Zechariah and Uriah worth mentioning. These hypotheses being endless, it is of course impossible to refute them. If objections are raised against one, another is ready to take its place. And with regard to Daniel, it must be observed that while these hypotheses are as plentiful as blackberries, no one seems to advert to the utter improbability that a spurious book should be inserted into the canon of the Jewish Scriptures between the time of Antiochus Epiphanes and our Saviour, and that no suspicion of this ill dealing should ever arise till Porphyry denied the prophecies because they were clear, and declared that they must be historical narrative and not prediction. The camel is swallowed, and the gnat very carefully strained out. The German rationalists find no difficulty

* I may direct those who do not read German, and cannot therefore make use of Hävernick and Hengstenberg, to an Essay in the "Journal of Sacred Literature" for January last, on the Chaldee of Daniel and Ezra, for a great deal of information on this subject.

in believing in the genuineness of Ossian, while they repudiate that of the Pentateuch.*

We have now examined a very considerable portion of the statements, if they deserve the name, of Dr. Williams, and we have not found one which has the common merit of fairly representing the truth. An examination such as this must necessarily be imperfect, but if it is shewn that the representations of the author are such that no person who is unable to investigate thoroughly the questions of which he treats, can gain any just notion of the state of those questions, but, on the contrary, is certain to imbibe a most prejudiced and untrue view of them, the mischief which his statements can do will be diminished. To those who are competent to discuss these questions, I do not think that a single word of reply would be needed. There is not an objection brought forward with which they are not familiar, and the only thing which they can deem novel is the positive and arrogant tone in which our acceptance is challenged for what most of them will believe to be by far the least probable interpretation of the passages to which allusion is made.

It may perhaps be expected that a few words should be said about the remarks on the Trinity and the doctrines of St. Paul, but they appear so harmless from

* We must not altogether omit all notice of Bunsen's views on Jonah, because they have been made in the pages of this Essay the occasion of a sneer at the English. Baron Bunsen, in his *Gott in der Geschichte*, defends the genuineness of Jonah's prayer, but treats the history of Jonah, though warranted by our Saviour's own words, as a mere myth. On this, Dr. Williams, with his usual courtesy towards English believers, remarks, "One can imagine the cheers which the opening of such an essay might evoke in some of our own circles, changing into indignation as the distinguished foreigner developed his views." My belief is that no well-informed Englishman would feel any exultation at finding that Bunsen accepted his views, because, if he knew much of Bunsen, he would feel his judgment to be so fallible and weak, that his opinion on a point of genuineness would be of little value. And in the very chapter in *Gott in der Geschichte* which treats of Jonah, he would find a remarkable confirmation of his distrust of Bunsen's judgment on a question of genuineness, for the author there declares his belief that a very trumpery poem found in Ælian, which professes to be the song of Arion, is really the production of this individual. To account for the inferiority of the style, he tells us that we must remember that Arion was not a poet, but a ballet-master.

the superficial and sketchy manner in which they are delivered, and from their extreme weakness, that it would be unwise to give them importance by raising up serious objections to them. If any person believes that the language of Scripture can be explained in regard to the relation of Father, Son, and Spirit, by considering these terms as equivalent to will, wisdom, and love; as light, radiance, and warmth; as fountain, stream, and united flow, &c., he is beyond the reach of argument. Let a person take any one of these triads, and read the first chapter of St. John, substituting the middle term of this triad for the Word, and the first for God, and he will soon perceive the vanity of this mode of explanation; or let him attempt to explain the epistles of St. Paul on the principles enounced in p. 81 of this Essay, and he will very soon leave the guidance of Bunsen, if he desires either to understand or explain St. Paul. There is nothing in this portion of the Essay to overthrow the truth of Scripture facts, and the view of the doctrines is not profound enough for the learned nor attractive enough for the simple reader. It may, therefore, safely be left to its native weakness. No attempt will be made to expose its imbecile weakness unless it is supported by fresh developments and new arguments. It will be left to take its place with other ambiguous endeavours to explain the Epistles of St. Paul in a non-natural sense, such as that of Taylor on the Epistle to the Romans. If there is any truth in the statements which have here been made against Dr. Williams, they are sufficient to ruin the credit of his Essay, and to shew that it is full, even to overflowing, of misrepresentations, which are highly discreditable even if they proceed from ignorance and carelessness, but if they are made with a consciousness of their nature, deserve a still deeper reprobation.

A large portion of this Essay having now been subjected to examination, it may be desirable, before we conclude our remarks, to recapitulate the results to which we have attained. We believe that it has been shewn,—

1. That the author in his account of the present state of theological literature in Germany has entirely misrepresented its condition; that he has greatly exaggerated the achievements of the critical school, and appears utterly to ignore its miserable failures, blunders, and extravagances; and that either from his ignorance of the fact, or from a wilful suppression of the truth, he gives the impression that there is an almost unanimous acceptance of these views among the learned in Germany, while the real truth is that the rationalist cause is daily losing ground in that country.

2. That in describing the course of prophetical interpretation in England, the author has entirely misrepresented the whole case. That he has specified three persons in particular as giving indirect testimony to his views, viz., Bishop Chandler, Bishop Butler, and Dr. Paley, and that in every case he has utterly misrepresented their testimony. Of Bishop Chandler's views he appears wholly ignorant; Bishop Butler's argument he has entirely misunderstood; and with regard to Dr. Paley, he has misrepresented his selection of one case only as a virtual abandonment of the rest, while the author himself expressly obviates in the strongest possible terms any such inference from this selection.

3. That in the exegesis of particular passages* the author has shewn by the arrogance with which he treats those who differ from him, even in the most difficult passages, that he is either wholly ignorant of the weight of argument and authority against him, or unable to appreciate it; and that in order to favour his views he has in one case misrepresented the views of Jerome, and garbled his text so as to favour his misrepresentation; that he has attributed to Jerome exegetical absurdities on a very partial examination of his words, to which a further acquaintance with Jerome would give a very different colouring; and that no person desiring to know the truth on any of these ques-

* The assertions and interpretations which are not examined here are not one whit more trustworthy, but those which have been selected offer the most *definite* tests of their inaccuracies.

tions would derive any assistance from the remarks of the Essayist, but, on the contrary, would necessarily derive a very false impression from them.

4. That in regard to the interpretation of Isaiah lii., liii., the Essayist has given the highest praise to Bunsen for an interpretation which has very little to recommend it, and what he has exhibited in some particulars is flatly contradicted by the very passages adduced to prove it; that notwithstanding his high praise of this interpretation, he rejects it himself, and yet most strangely endeavours to amalgamate it with two, if not three, other interpretations with which it is wholly incompatible; and that he has thus given to the world a specimen of utter incompetence in the interpretation of Scripture, which must take away all confidence in his opinions, until he shews that he has better grounds for them than any which he has hitherto put forth.

5. That in regard to Daniel, the Essayist has done nothing except to assert a few of the oldest and the most commonplace objections to the genuineness of this part of Scripture; that he takes no notice of the fact that they have frequently been refuted, but brings them forward as if they were irresistible, only because he yields assent to them himself.

If these charges against the Essayist are founded in truth, the least which can be claimed for them is this, that the Essayist is entirely disqualified as a guide of those who are unable to pursue such enquiries for themselves. They prove, if they are established, that no person who desires to have a true view of the evidence for Scripture or for the interpretation of prophecy, can possibly attain it from the statements of this writer, and consequently that his Essay, instead of assisting the well-informed and able enquirer in his search after truth, is only calculated to mislead the ignorant, and to induce him to embrace falsehood rather than truth.

These are heavy charges, but the author can have no reason to complain, because the reason for each assertion is given. They are not simple assertions, as his are, without proof. Each charge is supported by evidence, and if the evidence is insufficient, the author has an opportunity of answering it. The assertions of the rationalists are dangerous only when they are made without the arguments on which they are founded, because it is usually impossible really to refute an assertion unless the grounds on which it is made are alleged, except in regard to matters of positive fact or of mathematical or scientific truth. If a person asserted that the three angles of a triangle are greater than two right angles, the falsehood of such an assertion might be demonstrated, but if we are told that the contents of Daniel prove that it is later than the period to which it is assigned, we cannot answer the statement until the specific manner in which the anachronism occurs is indicated.

In answering Dr. Williams, we are obliged to confine ourselves to a destructive process, without attempting a constructive argument. It is necessary to shew those whom he misleads that they cannot trust him. Had this Essay been addressed to men capable of discussing the questions to which they relate, no answer would have been required, but as it is calculated to mislead the uninformed, the truth demands a defence. I know not with what feelings these authors may regard the circumstance, that infidel societies have assisted in promoting the reading of these Essays in cities and large towns, by buying copies to cut them up and lend them out at a penny per Essay! and clubs were formed that those who could not afford to purchase this expensive luxury might at least have the satisfaction of learning that the Church of which all the Essayists, except one, are ministers, is teaching them doctrines founded on a book full of the grossest untruths and the most extravagant myths, and based upon miracles which are unworthy of any belief. But this is the fact.

Such is the practical result of this "free handling" of sacred subjects. If the conclusions to which the Essayists would lead us were true, it would be our duty to accept them, with all their awful consequences, with all the confusion they would bring into our knowledge, all the uncertainty they throw on the prospects of a life beyond the grave. But as these views, instead of being an advance on our present knowledge, are really a miserable return towards ignorance and heathenism, every Christian man, who can examine and expose them, is bound to the utmost of his power to oppose them. Neither the knowledge nor the judgment shewn in any of the Essays appear to me to warrant the tone in which the volume is written, for the knowledge of the subject shewn in the Essay of Dr. Williams appears to be of the most superficial kind, and the judgment for the most part seems to lead the author almost invariably to embrace the weakest side, and where I have given any time to the examination of the rest, I have found that they have no superiority in these respects. For instance, in the Essay on the "Religious Tendencies of England from 1688—1750," the whole weight of the argument, such as it is, is produced by ignoring the literature of that period which was not devoted to evidences, and a great deal of its infidel literature. No notice is taken of the "Oracles of Reason," a book constantly referred to in the earlier part of the last century, and very little is said of the various works of Collins. The author attributes to the age a sort of *monomania* for manufacturing evidences, and of course with such a theory it is very convenient to ignore almost all the infidel literature which called forth these replies. Indeed, I cannot think that any person can be very much misled by a writer who makes Humphrey Prideaux, who died in 1724, a voucher for the state of public opinion in 1748, and who, in talking very confidently about the controversies as to the origin of the Gospels, blunders irretrievably between Marsh's *Michaelis* and his Lectures at Cambridge! These may be slips of the pen, but there is too much besides in the Essay which indicates a very hasty and superficial view, to permit the author to escape censure under this plea. When we behold defects like these, and can discover nothing that contributes in any degree to advance our knowledge of sacred things, the arrogant tone and the assumption of superiority which characterize this volume would provoke a smile, if they did not stir up deeper feelings in the heart,—feelings of sorrow for the ignorant who have been misled, and the certain infidelity and immorality which must result from principles like these being disseminated among the half-educated and the ignorant. For, after all, it is to these classes that the mischief is done. So far from deprecating the fullest discussion of Scripture difficulties among the learned, I am rejoiced when any question is thoroughly discussed, because I am sure the truth will prevail; and I firmly believe that the truth is with those who believe in Scripture as the inspired word of God, and bow before its authority. For myself, I am happy to have been obliged to examine very carefully some portions of the evidences for the truth and the inspiration of Scripture, because I bring from that examination the most profound contempt for arrogant assertions, and the most convincing proofs to my own mind that they alone who build on Scripture as the only solid foundation of religious truth, are like the wise man who laid the foundations of his house in the solid rock. Every attempt of Dr. Williams to disparage Scripture as an inspired book which I have been obliged to examine, has only impressed on my mind more deeply the wonderful nature of that revelation which God has been pleased to make to man, and the unassailable strength of the evidence by which He has recommended it to our acceptance. The endeavour to reduce it to a mere moral phenomenon, and to reject, as Bunsen professes to do, all external revelation as a fable, appears to me to rest on nothing but the determination to resist all evidence, and to discard all the rules of sound criticism in interpreting a volume which is still in some unaccountable way supposed to represent the will of God. We have no right to attribute the opinions of Bunsen to Dr. Williams, for he carefully abstains from making himself directly answerable for them, however strongly he may indirectly recommend them to the unwary. But we have a full right to bring him face to face with the consequences of that system which he thus indirectly and by inference supports, and to those whom he is misleading we are bound to present the contradictions and absurdities in which they involve themselves by following such principles. And in concluding this review I will endeavour to bring the matter to a fair conclusion. Whenever Dr. Williams officiates in the devotional services of the Church, he repeats an old—perhaps he may think an obsolete—form of words, I mean the Apostles' Creed. Now this Creed asserts that our Saviour was crucified, dead, and buried, and that after three days He rose again from the dead and afterwards ascended into heaven. I give Dr. Williams credit for a belief in that which his lips thus utter, and I ask him whether he believes that He who thus died and rose again, and who claimed to be Son of God, is to be supposed less acquainted with the truth and the meaning of the Scriptures of the Old Testament than Baron Bunsen and the critical school of Germany, with the additional authority of Dr. Williams himself. He declared that the Scriptures did testify of Him, and that they did *predict* His sufferings and His death; Baron Bunsen and the critical school tell us that they did not. He instructed His apostles also in the meaning of those Scriptures, and they declare that holy men of old prophesied as they were inspired by the Holy Spirit of God, and that they did *predict* the great facts of the Gospel, and that God intended by this means to give testimony to the truth of that Gospel; Baron Bunsen tells us, and apparently with the approbation of Dr. Williams, though he will not make himself answerable for it, that they did not. The personal faith of Baron Bunsen, of Dr. Williams, and the critical school of Germany is of very small importance to the world at large; but for every living man who feels that he has an everlasting soul, "What shall I believe that I may be saved?" is a vital question, and where the broad *facts* of revelation are admitted, I believe that there will not be many who will be content to take their doctrines from the critical school of the present day in preference to Christ and His apostles. If the *facts* of revelation, the central facts brought together in the Apostles' Creed, are denied, then we have to deal with simple, open infidelity, and our arguments must be addressed to that condition of the mind. But let us not have an insidious foe, let us have no ambiguity in so vital a question. Let us steadfastly refuse to hear men who acknowledge Christ as the Son of God in words, but deny Him in reality. They acknowledge that He was the Son of God, and that He is ascended into heaven, and sits at the right hand of God, and yet they believe that they know more of the Word of God than He did! He declared that the prophets predicted His coming, and they declare that they did not! This brings the question to the true issue. We must make our choice between these two authorities, and I trust when this issue is fairly tried that there will be very few, who know and understand the state of the question, who will not exclaim with a holy man of old, "Let God be true and every man a liar!" who will not prefer to believe that man's criticism may be erroneous, to accepting the monstrous dogma that the Son of God could either deceive or be deceived in the interpretation of the Word of God!

NOTE ON THE "EDINBURGH REVIEW,"

No. 230.

SINCE the publication of the "Essays and Reviews," a defence of them has been attempted in the "Edinburgh Review," No. 230. It would be unnecessary to offer a single remark on so feeble a performance, if it were not desirable to correct one or two misrepresentations which occur in it.

The first passage on which we shall offer a few remarks is the following:—

"The relative importance of the moral and predictive elements in prophecy, and again of the historical circumstances to which, in the first instance, the predictions were applied, have been discussed by Davison and Arnold in a style hardly less repugnant to the literal views of Dr. M'Caul or Dr. Keith, than anything in Professor Jowett or Dr. Williams. One of the passages deemed most fatal to the orthodoxy of the Essayist just named, [Dr. Williams,] ('only two texts in the Prophets directly Messianic,) was anticipated almost verbally even by Bishop Pearson: 'Wherever He is spoken of as the Anointed One (or the Messiah) it may well be first understood of some other person, except it be in one place in Daniel.' (Pearson on the Creed, Art. 2.) 'The typical ideas of patience and glory in the Old Testament,' says Dr. Williams, 'find their culminating fulfilment in the New.' This is the positive side of his view of prophecy, and it is, in fact, coincident with all that the best interpreters of Scripture have said since the Reformation."

It would seem from this passage that the study of "Essays and Reviews" has so familiarized the mind of the Reviewer with dishonest misrepresentations, that he has lost the faculty of distinguishing truth from falsehood. Bishop Pearson acknowledges that prophecies *which are real predictions of the Messiah* may be applicable, in the first instance, to some other person, although intended to testify of the Messiah and to predict the manner of His coming. Dr. Williams maintains that, except in two cases, there is no such thing as a prediction of the Messiah at all in the Old Testament; and the Reviewer holds these views to be equivalent. He also seems to consider an assertion that the moral excellence and beauty of the New Testament are the fulfilment of the prophetical ideas of the Old, to be equivalent to a belief that these prophecies were inspired predictions which were literally fulfilled in the facts of the New Testament. Until he asserts this, he leaves a world-wide difference between the learned, the reverent, the holy Bishop Pearson, and the Essayist; and if he does assert it, we must decline to characterize his assertion. The complaint against Dr. Williams is, not that he maintains that the prophecies may *primarily* be applied to some other person, but that he denies that they are intended in any way to be *predictions* of Christ. Until the Reviewer can see the difference between these two propositions, he will do well to abstain from theological discussions, for which he is evidently unfitted. But if Dr. Williams is compelled to acknowledge that, although spoken in the first instance of other persons, these prophecies were still intended as *predictions* of the Messiah, we shall have gained something by the controversy. Such a statement would be a contradiction, if not to the words, to the spirit of his whole Essay, and we should understand for the future how to estimate his assertions.

Having considered the case of Bishop Pearson, we come to those of Arnold and Davison. Of Dr. Arnold little need be said, as he was comparatively little known in theological literature. His biographer publishes his opinions on Daniel, but unhappily without the arguments on which they were founded. Thus the *prestige* of his name—and he was highly popular and much beloved—is brought to bear on a question which depends entirely on argument and historical fact. This is the only mischief we have to fear. Where reasons are given and arguments adduced, they can be answered, and we have no fear of the result, for in nearly two thousand years the faith of Christ has never yet been trampled in the dust, nor the heel of the foeman planted on the neck of the Christian warrior. Arguments can be answered, but no answer can be given to the mere influence of a name.

With Mr. Davison the case is very different. There may be positions in his excellent book on "Prophecy" on which theologians might differ, but to identify his clear decisive testimony to the *predictive* element in Scripture prophecies with the denial of Dr. Williams that they contain any such element at all, is to confound truth and falsehood. The writer who can do this is scarcely worthy of an answer. Mr. Davison sees in the Psalms "the most considerable attributes of the reign and the religion of the Messiah foreshewn. There is a king set on the holy hill of Sion," &c. He sees there "His unchangeable priesthood; His divine Sonship; His exalted nature and early resurrection outrunning the corruption of the grave," &c. Again, he admits the twofold sense of prophecy by which the establishment of the kingdom of David is a type of that of Christ, and many "memorable events and objects of the first, the older dispensation," foreshadowing "the corresponding events and objects in the New." He expressly states in a note on this passage that it is highly probable that "the profanation of the temple by Antiochus, and the corresponding profanation of the Christian Church by the great Apostacy, the tyrannic corruption of Antichrist, are rightly joined together as correlative terms of a joint prophecy." (p. 206.) Mr. Davison declares that in "the abyss of the Babylonian bondage Daniel *weighed* and *numbered* the kingdoms of the earth. There also he measured the years to the death of the Messiah," &c. Indeed, his whole volume teems with declarations such as these. We will add only one extract on the prophecies of Daniel, which may serve as an antidote to part of the mischief of the Essay. Bunsen makes the fourth empire of Daniel "the sway of Alexander," to which the Essayist adds the remark, "as is not uncommonly held." Any moderately well-informed reader knows that the Roman empire is *commonly* held to be the fourth; but that would imply more prescience in Daniel than the followers of Bunsen are willing to concede, and accordingly they deny it. But we hasten to give Davison's own words. After repudiating the notion that the prophecies of Daniel could possibly have been written in the age of Antiochus Epiphanes, and stating what he thinks "may amount to a refutation of this hypothesis," (p. 497,) Mr. Davison explains in part the prophecy of the four empires. In the course of the lecture the following passage occurs:—

"Once more the *termination* of the Fourth Empire by its subdivision into a multitude of separate kingdoms is a further ingredient in the information of the prophecy, and a new test of its prescience. Those separate kingdoms are indicated to be ten. The *definite* number may or may not be a strict postulate of the prophecy; a multifarious division unquestionably is denoted. That multifarious division took place in the cluster of petty contemporary kingdoms which replaced the Roman empire upon its dissolution. In that cluster of kingdoms the ten horns of the fourth beast, diverse from all the rest, find their interpretations, and their corresponding realities.

"So long, therefore, as the civil history of the ancient world shall last, under the scheme of its four successive empires; so long as the introduction of Christianity, in the place and order previously assigned to it, shall remain upon record, and its visible reign exist; so long as the conclusion of the Iron Empire of Rome shall be known in the promiscuous partition made of it by the host of Northern and Eastern invaders; so long there will be a just and rational proof of the inspiration of these illustrious prophecies of Daniel. If we try to refer such discoveries to any ingenuity of human reason, they have too much extent and system for the substituted solution. In that attempt of solution we are cramped by improbabilities on every side. One adequate origin of them there is, and that alone can render them intelligible in their manifest character, if we consent to read them as oracles of God, communicated by Him to His prophets, and by them to others, for the manifestation of His foreknowledge and over-ruling providence in the kingdom of the earth; and next for the confirmation of the whole truth of revealed religion. In that light they fall into order. In that same light, too, their origin and their use explain each the other."

These passages sufficiently indicate the views of Davison on prophecy. He believed that while these prophecies sometimes shadowed out the events of the first dispensation, it was chiefly when those events were the counterpart of the Gospel history that these prophecies were strictly intended by the Holy Spirit of God to predict what actually took place in the life of our Saviour and the events of the Gospel, and that they were *literally* fulfilled. He believed the prophecies of Daniel to be genuine, scouted the absurd notion that they were written in the time of Antiochus Epiphanes, and in the partition of the Roman empire he acknowledges the fulfilment of the prophecy of the ten horns. The fourth empire, in his opinion, was undoubtedly the Roman.

There is only one point more in this article that deserves remark here. It is the statement about truth and falsehood. It is contained in the following passage of the review:—

"The truth or falsehood of the views maintained is treated as a matter of indifference. The lay contributor, however offensive his statements, is dismissed as 'comparatively blameless.' But the Christian minister it is said 'has parted with his natural liberty.' It is almost openly avowed (and we are sorry to see this tendency as much among free-thinking laymen as among fanatical clergymen) that truth was made for the laity, and falsehood for the clergy; that truth is tolerable everywhere except in the mouths of ministers of the God of truth; that falsehood driven from every other quarter of the educated world, may find an honored refuge behind the consecrated bulwarks of the sanctuary."

It is needless to spend much time in answering so manifest a mistake in the apprehensions of the Reviewer. He really requires a course of logic before he ventures to write on theology. The simple question before us is this, Whether it is reputable for men to profess one set of principles and teach another? Does the Reviewer think that it is for the interest of truth that men who have ceased to believe in the resurrection of our Saviour, or any other great fact of the Creed, should remain ministers of a Church which requires them publicly to profess their belief in that fact? What difference can the abstract truth or falsehood of the fact or dogma make to the character of the man who professes to believe it with his lips, when he secretly believes it to be false?

I have instanced the resurrection of our Saviour because allusion is made to that great central fact of our religion in another passage in the review, but the argument is equally applicable to any other doctrine or fact.

It surely cannot be needful to add another word in reference to this argument of the Reviewer. The plain good sense of the English mind is incapable of admitting such a view for a moment, and the Reviewer must seek some other ground, if he desires to vindicate his friends.*

I will only, in concluding these remarks, express my hope that the discussion which has been caused by these "Essays and Reviews," may not only result in the firmer establishment of the great doctrines of our faith, but may induce the writers themselves to reconsider the questions they have treated so inadequately, and bring them to a frame of mind in which they may seek the glory of God, not by denying His miracles or explaining away His word, but in the earnest belief and the practical enforcement of those great truths which the Church of Christ has received for nearly two thousand years, and which have been the stay and the hope of countless millions from the first formation of that Church.

* It must be acknowledged that the Reviewer is candid enough to say, that considering the ability with which the Essays are written, it is strange that they should have added little or nothing to our knowledge of the subjects on which they treat.

MIRACLES.

"*On the Study of the Evidences of Christianity. By BADEN POWELL, M. A., F. R. S., Savilian Professor of Geometry in the University of Oxford.*"

"PROFESSOR POWELL," says the author of an apology for the "Essays and Reviews," "has passed beyond the reach not only of literary criticism, but of ecclesiastical censure.*" He has indeed passed beyond the reach of ecclesiastical censure; but unhappily his work survives him: and while it does so, it cannot claim exemption from criticism.

Its subject, as set forth in its title, is "The Study of the Evidences of Christianity." It would have been designated more accurately had its title been narrowed into more exact keeping with its real object, which is to shew that Miracles have no place among those evidences.

The Essay may be considered as divided into two parts: After an Introduction (pp. 94—100), in which the author deprecates the want of candour and impartiality with which, as he affirms, the subject of miracles is often approached, and intreats a fair hearing, he endeavours to shew (pp. 100—115) that the antecedent incredibility of miracles is such that no amount of evidence is sufficient to establish the proof of one: this is the *first* part. The *second* (pp. 115—129) is occupied

* Edinburgh Review, April, 1861, p. 475.

with the consideration of the evidential force of miracles —a labour, by the way, which he might have spared himself, as needless, if he had proved his point in the preceding part. The remainder of the Essay (pp. 129—144) is of a more discursive character, and is occupied chiefly in gathering up fragments, which might seem to have been dropped from parts I. and II., and which the author was either unable to arrange in their proper places, or which he thought would serve his purpose more effectually if reserved for the end.

It is a hard matter at the outset to know how to deal with a writer who occupied the position of Professor Powell. As a Christian, and a clergyman of the English Church, we should naturally expect that on the subject of which he treats we should have much common ground with him,—that, in fact, almost the only question between us would be, not whether the Christian miracles are to be acknowledged as miracles, or whether they are to be appealed to at all among the evidences of Christianity, but to what extent they are evidential. But on examination we find the case to be widely different.

The reality of the New Testament miracles is denied, or, if granted in any wise, is granted,—to use Professor Powell's own words in another work, of certain writers whom he censures,—merely as "a nominal homage to the prejudices of a religious party, a profession in name, covering a denial in substance, as transparent as that of the Jesuit commentators on Newton, in their professions of unlimited deference to the Ecclesiastical dogmas,—'Cæterum latis a summis pontificibus contra telluris motum decretis nos obsequi profitemur,'—while they deliberately contravened them in promulgating, illustrating, and demonstrating the prohibited doctrines." *

* B. Powell, "Order of Nature," p. 222. See "Essays and Reviews," pp. 140, 142, 143; and compare Bp. Van Mildert's account of some of the promoters of infidelity in the sixteenth and seventeenth centuries:—"Some, with strange inconsistency, called themselves Christians, and even contended for the necessity of faith in the doctrines of the Gospel, while they acknowledged that faith to be altogether at variance with the philo-

Further,—the Scriptural account of the Creation is ignored, and Mr. Darwin's "masterly volume," which established "the grand principle of the self-evolving powers of nature," is accepted as an authority which summarily overrides the Mosaic record.* And thus, such is the credulity of unbelief, this writer, who cannot bring himself to believe a miracle except under a protest, is ready, without hesitation, to acquiesce in a theory which would deduce the descent of all the animals that live or have ever lived on this earth, man included, from one or at most four or five common progenitors.† There are others, it seems, than the "ignorant," of whom it may be said with truth, that they are "as obstinate in their contemptuous incredulity, as they are unreasonably credulous." ‡

The existence of a God is indeed acknowledged, but it is of a God very different from the God whom the Bible sets before us; of a God subjected to the laws which govern the material universe; laws possibly of His own framing, but which, once framed, like the laws of the Medes and Persians, may not be altered even by Himself. The world, it would seem, is a piece of clock-work, which having been wound up in the beginning,—if indeed it ever had a beginning,—was

sophical opinions which they espoused."—*Boyle Lectures*, Serm. IX., vol. i. p. 322.

* Essays and Reviews, p. 139. See also, in the same page, the nonchalance with which the author sets aside the Scriptural record of the origin of mankind:—"Never, in all that enormous length of time which modern discovery has now *indisputably assigned* to the existence of the human race!" Again, p. 129:—"More recently the antiquity of the human race, and the development of species, and the rejection of the idea of 'Creation,' have caused new advances in the same direction," (towards the "dissociation of the spiritual from the physical.") Of a piece with this is the following from another work by our author:—"I can only add an expression of surprise, that so leading and liberal a journal as the 'Edinburgh Review' should have so far lost sight of all sound philosophy, and shewn itself so far behind the advance of enlightenment, as to introduce in a recent article a new attempt to revive the credit of Bible geology. *The whole argument proceeds on the assumption—as if uncontroverted—of the authority of the Judaical Scriptures in the matter.*"—*Order of Nature*, p. 219.

† Darwin on the "Origin of Species," p. 518.

‡ Mill's "Logic," vol. ii. p. 165.

then set a-going, and left to go, in a perpetual motion, without further interference on the part of its Maker. Strange that it should be thought more agreeable to sound reason to believe of Him who has given to the creatures which He has made both the will and the power to control the operations of the laws of matter to an almost indefinite extent, that He has divested Himself of the same, than that He has both retained them, and exercises them according to the dictates of His infinite wisdom!

What the author's view of revelation is, it is not easy to understand. He seems expressly to acknowledge a revelation of some sort;* but it is a revelation, which, however it may differ in degree, does not appear to be different in kind from that accorded to "poets, legislators, philosophers, and others gifted with high genius;"† and yet it is a revelation of truths, some of which at least transcend the utmost reach of reason; nay, according to the author's principles, require a sacrifice of reason upon the altar of faith.‡ Moreover it is, as this account of it might lead one to expect, an internal revelation, not an external one. But by what means its claims, in those points which transcend the reach of human reason, and which form, as miracles are said to do, "the main difficulties and hindrances to its acceptance,"§ are to be enforced on those to whom it has not been *directly* communicated, does not appear. One would be strongly tempted to suppose that none but those to whom it has been *directly* communicated are under an obligation to receive it. This, at least, was Lord Herbert of Cher-

* Essay, pp. 142—144.

† P. 140. "If the use of fire, the cultivation of the soil, and the like, were divine revelations, the most obvious inference would be that so likewise are printing and steam. If the boomerang was divinely communicated to savages ignorant of its principle, then surely the disclosure of that principle in our time by the gyroscope was equally so. *But no one denies revelation in this sense; the philosophy of the age does not discredit the inspiration of prophets and apostles, though it may sometimes believe it in poets, legislators, philosophers, and others gifted with high genius.*"

‡ Essay, pp. 140—142. § P. 140.

bury's conclusion (and a just one), from premises very similar to those of Professor Powell.*

These will serve as specimens of the author's teaching. But I have no intention of following him into every particular in which his questionable opinions come out to view. My object is simply to deal with the subject of Miracles, which is *the* subject of his Essay. If I touch upon other subjects, it will only be as they stand related to this.

Before proceeding to the main question, Professor Powell "premises a brief reflection upon the spirit and temper in which it should be discussed." † He would have it approached with the candour and impartiality which befit a judge, not with the bias of an advocate. And though those who deal with it may have no doubts or difficulties of their own, he would have them appreciate those of others, and make allowance for them.

This is all very just. Especially it behoves that there should be no want of sympathy with minds perplexed with difficulties, which they are honestly seeking to have resolved. Harshness is not the treatment proper for such cases,—not to mention that he who exhibits it is, by that token, wanting himself in a very important qualification necessary for the attainment of truth, and may well doubt whether that which he holds, and would enforce so imperiously, is truth; or if it is, at the least whether he holds it practically and to any salutary purpose. But sympathy with those who are perplexed and troubled with difficulties, and are conscientiously seeking their way out of them, must not be suffered to run on into a countenancing of those who have turned aside from the way of truth themselves, and are availing themselves of their position, and of the influence which their position gives them, to turn others aside from it.

That we should approach the question with candour,

* See Van Mildert's Boyle Lectures, Serm. IX., vol. i. pp. 326, 327.

† Essay, p. 95.

and with an honest desire to arrive at the truth, is a caution very necessary to be borne in mind in other matters as well as in the one before us. But it is to be remembered that there may be an undue bias *against* as well as *for*. Dr. Whewell, in his Bridgewater Treatise, has assigned reasons for believing that what he calls deductive habits as opposed to inductive, —habits formed by following out the discoveries of others, as opposed to those formed by prosecuting the work of discovery ourselves,—"may sometimes exercise an unfavourable effect on the mind of the student, and may make him less fitted and ready to apprehend and accept truths different from those with which his reasonings are concerned."* And a critic, certainly not hostile to our author, said of him in a review of a previous work, some time before the appearance of the present, as though finding in him an exemplification of the truth of Dr. Whewell's remark, "It would not be a harsh criticism to say that Professor Powell shews a marked fondness for what is new and arduous in philosophy; and takes pleasure in stigmatizing as hindrances to truth in physical science all

* Chap. vi., "On Deductive Habits; or, On the Impression produced on Men's Minds by tracing the Consequences of Ascertained Laws." Bridgewater Treat., p. 329. See also p. 334:—"We have no reason whatever to expect any help from the speculations (of the mechanical philosophers and mathematicians of recent times), when we attempt to ascend to the First Cause and Supreme Ruler of the universe. But we might perhaps go further, and assert that they are less likely than men employed in other pursuits to make any clear advance towards such a subject of speculation. Persons whose thoughts are thus entirely occupied in deduction, are apt to forget that this is, after all, only one employment of the reason among more; only one mode of arriving at truth, needing to have its deficiencies completed by another. Deductive reasoners, those who cultivate science, of whatever kind, by means of mathematical and logical processes alone, may acquire an exaggerated feeling of the amount and value of their labours. Such employments, from the clearness of the notions involved in them, the irresistible concatenation of truths which they unfold, the subtlety which they require, and their entire success in that which they attempt, possess a peculiar fascination for the intellect. Those who pursue such studies have generally a contempt and impatience for the pretensions of all those other portions of our knowledge, where, from the nature of the case or the small progress hitherto made in their cultivation, a more vague and loose kind of reasoning seems to be adopted." See Burgon on "Inspiration and Interpretation," p. 241.

such opinions as are fostered by ancient and popular belief, including those which assume Scriptural authority for their foundation." And presently afterwards, referring to certain views, which are reproduced here, relating to the "transmutation of species," and the asserted "creation of animalcule life" in the experiments of Messrs. Crosse and Weekes, he adds,* "*We have the constant feeling that the leaning is too much to one and the same side in these questions*,—we might fairly call it the paradoxical side; while admitting at the same time, that paradoxes are often raised into the class of recognised truths." †

So much for candour and dispassionateness in the conduct of discussions of this kind. At the same time, it is to be confessed, that they who believe our Lord to have been what He claimed to be, and acknowledge the New Testament to contain an authentic record of His teaching and that of His apostles, cannot approach the subject but with a foregone conclusion in favour of the reality of the Christian miracles. With them the question is already settled, upon authority which admits of no dispute. For it is impossible to deny that the reality of those miracles is perpetually implied throughout the New Testament. Not the shadow of a doubt is ever cast upon it. If the Christian miracles were not real miracles, what becomes of our Lord's truthfulness? Whatever may be thought of His apostles, He at least, on such a supposition, must stand before us in the character of a deceiver. It is not too much to say, therefore, that the question is vital as regards Christianity. And it cannot be matter of surprise, that they who have embraced the Gospel, on whatever grounds, and have staked their dearest hopes upon its promises, should look upon the denial of the

* See Essays and Reviews, pp. 138, 139.

† Edinb. Review, July, 1858. Campbell makes a like observation respecting Hume:—"No man was ever fonder of paradox, and, in theoretical subjects, of every notion that is remote from sentiments universally received. This love of paradoxes, he owns himself, that both his enemies and his friends reproach him with."—*On Miracles*, Part I. § 4.

reality of the Christian miracles as a sacrilege of the worst description.

All this Professor Powell seems to have felt; and therefore, while asserting in the most positive manner, that "in nature and from nature, by science and by reason, we neither have nor can possibly have any evidence of a Deity working miracles," he adds, as though providing a loophole by which he might escape from the necessity which seemed to lie upon him of denying miracles altogether, "for that, we must go out of nature and beyond science;" * and he adds presently,—

> "In the popular acceptation, it is clear the Gospel miracles are always *objects*, not *evidences* of faith;" (*objects* of faith they must certainly be to Christians, as we have seen—*evidences* they are also, as I shall hope to shew;) "and when they are connected especially with doctrines, as in several of the higher mysteries of the Christian faith, the sanctity which invests the point of faith itself, is extended to the external narrative in which it is embodied; the reverence due to the mystery renders the external events sacred from examination, and shields them also within the pale of the sanctuary; the *miracles* are merged in the *doctrines* with which they are connected, and associated with the declaration of spiritual things which are, as such, exempt from those criticisms to which physical statements would be necessarily amenable."†

What have we here but the hateful principle by means of which, in so many instances, infidelity has eaten out the heart of religion, while it has left the outward form of it untouched,—that opinions may be philosophically true yet theologically false, or, conversely, philosophically false yet theologically true? ‡ Woe be to the individual by whom such a principle is

* Essay, p. 142. † P. 143.

‡ "To such lengths did some of these Schoolmen proceed, that, when accused of advancing tenets repugnant to the Scriptures, instead of repelling the accusation, they had recourse to the dangerous position, that opinions might be *philosophically true yet theologically false;* a position obviously mischievous in its principle, and opening a door for the admission of infidelity into the very bosom of the Church."—*Van Mildert, Boyle Lect.*, vol. i. p. 250.

accepted! woe be to the Church in which it gains currency!

The miracles to which Professor Powell's concession refers are obviously those which circle more immediately around our Lord's Person,—His Incarnation, Resurrection, Ascension.* But, it is clear, from what has been already urged, that the concession, if made at all, must be extended to the Gospel miracles generally, seeing that the truth of our Lord's word is bound up with them. And at the same time, it is to be considered that if the reality of but one single miracle be granted, of whatsoever kind,—say, for example, the Resurrection,—the objection on which the whole stress of our author's argument rests is done away. What has been in one instance may have been in another, in ten others, in a thousand others. The principle is conceded. There is no longer any antecedent incredibility to be overcome.†

But, in truth, Professor Powell's concession, as will be seen in the sequel, is but verbal after all. And I take this opportunity of remarking, that repeatedly, in the course of his Essay, one has the conviction forced upon one, either that he had a difficulty in expressing

* See "Order of Nature," p. 69.

† "In one respect, this semi-rationalism, which admits the authority of revelation up to a certain point and no farther, rests on a far less reasonable basis than the firm belief which accepts the whole, or the complete unbelief which accepts nothing. For whatever may be the antecedent improbability which attaches to a miraculous narrative, as compared with one of ordinary events, it can affect only the narrative taken as a whole, and the entire series of miracles from the greatest to the least. *If a single miracle is admitted* as supported by competent evidence, *the entire history is at once removed from the ordinary calculations of more or less probability.* One miracle is sufficient to shew that the series of events with which it is connected is one which the Almighty has seen fit to mark by exceptions to the ordinary course of His providence: and this being once granted, we have no *à priori* grounds to warrant us in asserting that the number of such exceptions ought to be larger or smaller. If any one miracle recorded in the Gospels,—the Resurrection of Christ, for example,—be once admitted as true, the remainder cease to have any antecedent improbability at all, and require no greater evidence to prove them than is needed for the most ordinary events of any other history. For the improbability, such as it is, reaches no further than to shew that it is unlikely that God should work miracles at all; not that it is unlikely that He should work more than a certain number."—*Mansel's Bampton Lectures*, p. 252.

himself clearly, or else that, on occasion, he designedly involved his meaning in a mist of words because he feared that, if seen in clear sunshine, it would be too much for the prejudices of his readers.

I.

At all events, as to the point in question, it is plain that the whole drift and tendency of the Essay is to deny the reality of miracles altogether. The argument lies within the smallest possible compass,—The antecedent incredibility of a miracle is such as absolutely to preclude all *à posteriori* reasoning on the subject.

And that antecedent incredibility rests on "the grand truth of the universal order and constancy of natural causes, as a primary law of belief," a belief "so strongly entertained in the mind of every truly inductive inquirer, that he cannot even conceive the possibility of its failure*." Wherever we turn our eyes we see the operation of fixed laws. The world, in all its parts, is ordered and governed upon an established plan. As science extends her domain and pushes her discoveries into new regions, cases which once seemed exceptional are found to conform to the general rule. If in any instance the conformity cannot be traced, yet the instances in which it can are so innumerable, that there can be no reasonable doubt that in this also the rule holds.

"The very essence of the whole argument," as the author expresses himself in another work of a similar tendency with the one under consideration, "is the invariable preservation of the principle of order: not necessarily such as we can directly recognise, but the universal conviction of the unfailing subordination of everything to some grand principles of law, however imperfectly apprehended or realized in our partial conceptions, and the successive subordination of such laws to others of still higher generality to an extent transcending our conceptions, and constituting the true chain of universal causation which culminates in the sublime conception of the *Cosmos*."†

* Essay, p. 109. † Order of Nature, p. 228.

Professor Powell's view, it will be observed, differs from Spinoza's and from Hume's, to both of which at first sight it bears some resemblance.

Spinoza held that a miracle is absolutely impossible, because it would be derogatory to the Deity to depart from the established laws of the universe,* an argument which appears to be identical with that of Wegscheider referred to by Professor Powell, "that the belief in miracles is inconsistent with the idea of an eternal God consistent with himself."†

Hume did not absolutely deny the possibility of a miracle, but he denied its capability of being proved from testimony. With him the matter is simply a balancing of probabilities, and in his judgment it is always more probable that the testimony to a miracle is false, than that the ordinary course of nature has been deviated from.‡

Professor Powell does not, with Spinoza, presume to determine what it *behoved* God to do; nor, with Hume, does he trouble himself nicely to adjust the balance of probabilities. His reasoning is built upon analogy. He concludes peremptorily from the analogy of God's dealings in the material world in every instance in which His operations can be traced, from the *cosmos*, the order which pervades the universe, that a miracle which, according to his notion, is "a violation of the laws of matter, or an interruption of the course of physical causes,"§ is simply incredible.

But it is this very notion of a miracle, unguardedly countenanced, it is true, in some instances, by writers of eminence, which makes his whole argument wide of

* "Hinc clarissime sequitur, leges naturæ universales mera esse decreta Dei, quæ ex necessitate et perfectione naturæ divinæ sequuntur. Si quid igitur in natura contingeret, quod ejus universalibus legibus repugnaret, id decreto et intellectui et naturæ divinæ necessario etiam repugnaret; aut si quis statueret Deum aliquid contra leges naturæ agere, is simul etiam cogeretur statuere, Deum contra suam naturam agere, quo nihil absurdius."—*Spinoza*, *Tract. Theol. Polit.*, c. 6.

† Essay, p. 114. ‡ Hume's Essay, "Of Miracles."

§ Essay, p. 132.

its mark, as it does also that of Spinoza, which in this respect agrees with it.*

A miracle, in the Scriptural notion of the word, is a *violation* neither of the laws of matter, nor of any other of the laws of nature. It is simply the intervention of a Being possessing, or endued with, *superhuman* power,—an intervention, which, though it temporarily modifies, or suspends the operation of, the laws ordinarily in operation in the world, is yet itself exercised in strict accordance with the law of that Being's nature, or *superindued* nature, by whom it is exercised.

It is true that Professor Powell distinctly acknowledges that lower laws are continually held in restraint by higher, and quotes Dean Trench with approval as affirming such to be the case.† But there is one clause in his quotation, the meaning of which, he confesses, is not clear to him, that, namely, in which "moral laws" are spoken of as "controlling physical."

And this is precisely the point to which Professor Powell's philosophy seems to have been incapable of reaching. His mind appears to have been so engrossed with the study of what is called natural science, his eye so exclusively fixed upon the material world around him, that he overlooked the fact, that the world contains other elements besides material, that it has other forces besides physical, and that as matter is perpetually acted upon in all imaginable ways by those other forces, so the laws of matter are perpetually, not "violated," but interfered with, moulded, controlled, kept in check, as to their operation, by those forces.

The human will is the element, the action of whose disturbing force upon the material system around us comes most frequently or most strikingly under our notice. Man, in the exercise of his ordinary faculties, is perpetually interfering with, or moulding, or controlling the operation of those ordinary laws of matter which are in exercise around him. He does so if he does but disturb one pebble in its state of rest, or stay

* See Dean Trench, "Notes on the Miracles," p. 15.

† Essay, p. 134.

the fall of another before it reaches the ground. He does so to a vastly greater extent when, by means of the appliances with which art, instructed by science, has furnished him, he projects a ball to the distance of four or five miles, or constrains steam, or light, or electricity, or chloroform to do his bidding. Still his doings are not miracles, because they do not extend beyond the range of his unassisted powers. But are we sure that God may not, on special occasions and for special ends, have endued some men with *superhuman* powers, by which the laws of the material world may be controlled to an extent beyond what could have been done by *unassisted* nature? or that He may not have directed or permitted beings superior in might to man to exercise such powers?* That He has done so, in sundry instances, Scripture affirms. What is there in the reason of things to make the affirmation incredible or even improbable? To say that it is contrary to experience is to beg the whole question at issue.

The fact is, once admit that there is a God, and even beings who have to do with this earth, inferior to God but superior in might to man, or admit that man himself may, for special reasons, be endued with superhuman power, and you grant that there are *agents* who have it in their power to interfere with or control the laws ordinarily in operation in the material world, so as to work miracles.

Admit, further, that there may be an *occasion* calling for superhuman interference,—and such surely is the authentication of a revelation containing truths which

* "What degrees of power God may reasonably be supposed to have communicated to created beings, to subordinate intelligences, to good or evil angels, is by no means easy for us to determine. Some things absolutely impossible for men to effect, it is evident may easily be within the natural powers of angels; and some things beyond the power of inferior angels, may as easily be supposed to be within the natural power of others that are superior to them, and so on. So that excepting the original power of creating, which we cannot indeed conceive communicated to things which were themselves created, we can hardly affirm with any certainty that any particular effect, how great or miraculous soever it may seem to us, is beyond the power of all created beings in the universe to have produced."—*S. Clarke*, *Evidences*, p. 298.

it was of the utmost consequence for man to know, but of which, except by revelation, he could know nothing, —and the possibility is advanced to probability. We have, if we may without irreverence use the heathen poet's words in such connection, both a *vindex*, and a *nodus dignus vindice.*

Such a revelation Christianity professes to be. It professes to direct man towards the attainment of the true end of his being, to instruct him in the knowledge of God, and to teach him how to serve God acceptably, and it assures him (an assurance which he could not otherwise have had) of the continuance of his existence in a future state of happiness or misery after death, that happiness or misery depending upon his conduct here. Underlying the information thus described are such truths as the incarnation, the death and passion, the resurrection, the ascension of the Son of God, and the descent of the Holy Spirit, together with an account of the respective offices of both of these divine Persons in the economy of man's salvation. These are subjects to the knowledge of which unassisted human reason could by no possibility have attained, and yet that knowledge, seeing that sundry most important duties grow out of the relationships involved,* cannot but be of the utmost consequence to us.

If then it was not to have been expected antecedently (as who could have ventured to predict beforehand how God would deal thus in such a case?) that Christianity, if true, would be attested by miracles, yet now that it does claim to have been so attested, there is sufficient reason apparent why it should have been so. Indeed, it seems inconceivable, how, without miracles,—including prophecy in the notion of a miracle,—it could sufficiently have commended itself to men's belief? Who would believe, or would be justified in believing, the great facts which constitute its substance, on the *ipse dixit* of an unaccredited teacher? And how, except by miracles, could the first teacher be accredited? Paley, then, was fully warranted in the assertion which

* See Butler's "Analogy," Pt. II. ch. i. p. 216, Oxford, 1820.

our author censures, that "we cannot conceive a revelation"—such a revelation of course as Christianity professes to be, a revelation of truths which transcend man's ability to discover,—"to be substantiated without miracles." * Other credentials, it is true, might be exhibited *in addition* to miracles,—and such it would be natural to look for,—but it seems impossible that miracles could be dispensed with.

And in this respect Christianity is entirely consistent with itself. Had it made no appeal to miracles, its teaching, considering what the substance of its teaching is, could scarcely have gained credit. Had its teaching been such as men might have attained to by their unassisted powers, suspicion might fairly have rested on its appeal to miracles.

Assuming, then, that it has pleased God to make a revelation, such as Christianity claims to be, to man, what have we in the ordinary course of the world's affairs analogous to it, on which to raise the conclusion that miracles are incredible, or even improbable? The case is one entirely *sui generis*, except in so far as it has associated with it other revelations, intimately connected with it, belonging to a former dispensation. As Bp. Butler remarks,—"Before we can have ground for raising what can with propriety be called *an argument* from analogy, for or against revelation, *considered as somewhat miraculous*,"—or, as it might be added with equal truth, for or against *miracles*, as authenticating a revelation,—"We must be acquainted with a similar or parallel case. But the history of some other world seemingly in like circumstances with our own is no more than a parallel case, and therefore nothing short of this can be so."† It follows, then, that the analogy of the ordinary course of nature affords no sufficient ground for doubting the reality of miracles said to have been wrought in attestation of a revelation which has nothing analogous to it in nature. The generalization which would conclude from thence that there can be no

* Essay, p. 119. † Analogy, Pt. II. ch. ii. p. 237.

such thing as a miracle is an over-hasty one, large as is the induction on which it rests.

If it be urged that the reasoning which has been employed hitherto does but remove the question of probability or improbability, of credibility or incredibility, a step farther back,—viz. from the case of miracles to that of revelation in general,—this is granted; but at the same time, he who thus compels us to go back with him one step, must be content to go with us one step more. For before we can venture to affirm the improbability or incredibility of revelation generally, we ought to be sure that there are no truths essential to man to know, of which yet man cannot attain the knowledge without supernatural instruction.*

Professor Powell, indeed, is not indisposed to acknowledge a revelation, provided it be not an external one.† And no doubt a revelation by internal illumination is perfectly conceivable. Indeed Scripture recognises such a revelation repeatedly. But it is to be observed that if that revelation be a revelation of truths of which man could not by the exercise of his natural faculties have attained the knowledge, we have at once something which transcends nature, that is, in other words, a miracle,—not indeed a physical miracle, but a moral one.

Let thus much suffice for the question of antecedent

* That a revelation is not antecedently improbable, would appear from the circumstance that Socrates is represented by Plato as intimating not only his belief in a future life, but *his belief that some Divine communication would one day be made concerning it.—Dean Lyall*, *Propædia Prophetica*, p. 155.

† Compare "Order of Nature," p. 282:—"Those who have felt the greatest difficulty in admitting *physical* miracles, have no hesitation in accepting the assertion of any amount of *purely moral and spiritual* influence, even to the extent of those exalted conditions of soul in which the favoured and gifted disciple was enlightened by immediate disclosures of Divine truth, or endowed with internal energies and spiritual powers, beyond the attainment or conception of the ordinary human faculties: and theistic reasoners have held it more consonant with the Divine perfections to influence mind than to disarrange matter."—*But man's moral and spiritual nature, by all analogy, must have its laws as well as his physical nature. And a departure from the former is as truly a miracle,—as truly indicates supernatural interference,—as a departure from the latter.*

credibility or probability. But indeed, we are but feeling about in the dark while we are discussing such questions in a matter where we are, after all, so little competent to determine antecedently what is credible or probable, or are following out analogies where we are so little competent to determine to what extent the analogies hold, or whether indeed they hold at all. The really important question is, *as to the facts reputed to be miraculous.* And it is surely inconsistent in those who lay so much stress, and justly so, on the necessity of weighing every fact which bears upon their theories in matters of science, summarily to override facts, when they do not accord with their theories in matters of religion.

That the *facts* of the Christian history which are reputed miraculous really did take place, rests, as has been often urged, upon such testimony as would be accepted as sufficient, and much more than sufficient, in all ordinary matters.

We are told, indeed, that testimony "is, after all, but a second-hand assurance, a blind guide; that it can avail nothing against reason;" nay, that even our own senses may deceive us.* And it is very true that both testimony *may* mislead, and our senses *may* deceive. But these results depend upon the character of the testimony, and upon the condition in which our senses are, or the opportunities which they have for taking cognizance of that which comes under their notice. Testimony *may be* sufficiently established; our senses *may have* sufficient certainty in their observations: and it is as much a law of our moral nature that we should place reliance upon testimony when sufficiently established, and upon our senses, when they are not disordered and at the same time have sufficient opportunities of observing, as it is a law of our physical nature that we should feel pain if wounded, or that we should fall if not supported.

But then it is to be observed to what extent the report of testimony and the observation of our senses are

* Essay, pp. 141, 142.

claimed. There are two elements to be considered in an alleged miracle—the *fact*, and the *author* of the fact; all that is claimed for testimony, all that is claimed for the senses is, that they are competent to establish the *fact;* as to the *author*, this point is to be arrived at on other considerations.

The reality, then, of the Christian miracles, so far as the fact is concerned, rests, as has been said, on the most ample testimony. They were wrought openly; in many instances before enemies. They were asserted in the most public manner by those who professed to have been eye-witnesses of them, and that in the country in which they were said to have been wrought, and while there were numbers still living who could have contradicted the assertion if false; numbers, too, who had every disposition to contradict it, if they could have done so with success: yet no contradiction, that we know of was ever made. The enemies of Christianity,—though they refused to acknowledge the finger of God in them, and so denied them to be miracles, or rather *divine miracles*,—never denied the facts. They endeavoured, indeed, to *account* for them; but the very circumstance of their doing so afforded the strongest testimony which they had it in their power to yield to their reality, *as facts*.

It is true the prevalent belief in magic, and in the power of evil spirits and their sensible interference in the world, made men more ready to believe reports of supernatural or superhuman occurrences than they might have been otherwise. Still, when every allowance has been made on this account, it is inconceivable that facts, such as the Christian miracles were affirmed to be, could have been accepted, *as facts*, by enemies, who had every opportunity of testing them, and actually did test them in some instances most rigorously, unless they had really taken place.

And it is much to be observed that many of them were of a kind respecting which, as far as the fact is concerned, it is incredible that deception could have been practised, or mistake or delusion have occurred.

The walking upon the water, the instantaneous hushing of a storm, the healing of a paralytic, the cleansing of a leper, the giving of sight to the blind, the making whole of the maimed, the feeding of great multitudes with a few loaves and fishes, the restoration of the dead to life in the presence of many witnesses, in one instance four days after death was said to have occurred, and when the grave had to be opened in which the body lay; these are facts, which, however it may be pretended to account for them, could not have gained credit unless they had actually taken place.

And what is also especially worthy of note, they, together with the other Christian miracles, are *not a few*, and those *isolated* facts; but *a multitude* which cohere together, and, like the several stones of an arch, mutually support and strengthen one another.

Of these facts the central one,—the key-stone, so to speak, of the arch,—is our Lord's Resurrection. This rests *independently* on the strongest evidence, our Lord having been seen alive after His death many times and by many different persons,—in one instance "by above five hundred brethren at once," of whom, says St. Paul, referring to the circumstance, "the greater part remain unto this present, but some are fallen asleep." But besides the independent evidence on which it rests, it is sustained on the one side, by the manifold signs and wonders, such as those above referred to, which our Lord did antecedently to His death; on the other, by His ascension, and by the descent of the Holy Spirit,—the former witnessed and attested by the eleven apostles, the latter manifested, not only by the marvellous works wrought by the apostles, and the gifts of power bestowed largely through the laying on of their hands upon the first disciples, but also—which is very much to be observed—by the moral change effected both in their own characters, and in the lives and conversations of those who received their testimony; for this, though not a miracle physically, was at least a fact, and as such, a witness to the reality of that gift of the Holy Spirit, which is represented as consequent upon our

Lord's ascension, and by which miracles are said to have been wrought.

And to all these must be added another great and most important fact,—that Christianity made its way in a world whose interests and prejudices were arrayed against it, avowedly from the very beginning appealing to the miracles of its Founder, and to the miraculous powers possessed and exercised by its first preachers, as well as by others to whom they imparted the gift. For however men may now, while professing to accept Christianity as of divine origin, attempt to eliminate the miraculous element from its system, nothing could be farther from the thoughts of its first preachers. Mistakenly or not, they both believed and taught that miracles, especially that chief miracle, the Resurrection of its Founder, were part and parcel of Christianity. And as they believed and taught, so their converts believed and confessed. And both preachers and converts, in repeated instances, laid down their lives in proof of the sincerity of their convictions.

It is of no avail to refer to the countless pretences to miraculous powers which have since been made, whether by heathens or Christians, as though these, as a matter of course, invalidated the Gospel miracles. Both the Gospel miracles and other alleged miracles are to be tried severally upon their own merits; and if the facts alleged are established upon sufficient evidence, they are to be received *as facts:* whether as miraculous facts or as divinely miraculous facts, is a subject for further consideration. At the same time, if there should be ground for believing, as doubtless there is, that many of the later miracles are spurious, this is no more than was to have been expected in the reason of things; no more than our Lord and His apostles had prepared the Church to expect. And indeed, to a certain extent, such spurious miracles are even witnesses to the reality of some miracles. For, as one has remarked who will not be suspected of an undue bias in this direction, "The innumerable forgeries of this sort which have been imposed upon mankind in all ages are so far from weakening the credibility of the Jewish and Christian miracles, that they strengthen it. For how could we account for a practice so universal of forging miracles for the support of false religions, if on some occasions they had not actually been wrought for the confirmation of a true one? Or how is it possible that so many spurious copies should pass upon the world, without some genuine original from whence they were drawn, whose known existence and tried success might give an appearance of probability to the counterfeit?" *

There can be no reasonable pretext, therefore, for denying the facts supposed to be miraculous in the Gospel history. Nor, truly, does Professor Powell absolutely and in every instance deny the facts. It is only when no reasonable prospect of a solution upon his own principles offers itself that he denies them. And even then his denial is couched in such ambiguous terms, that, if we had not a more explicit statement of his views elsewhere to guide us, it might be somewhat difficult to ascertain his precise meaning.

But let us hear his own account of the way in which he would deal with the Christian miracles. He is speaking, indeed, of alleged miracles in general, but of course with his eye specially directed to those of the Gospel:—

"An alleged miracle can only be regarded in one of two ways;—either (1) abstractedly as a physical event, and therefore to be investigated by reason and physical evidence, and referred to physical causes, possibly to *known* causes, but at all events to some higher cause or law, if at present unknown; it then ceases to be supernatural, yet still might be appealed to in support of religious truths, especially as referring to the state of knowledge and apprehensions of the parties addressed in past ages; or (2) as connected with religious doctrine, regarded in a sacred light, asserted on the authority of inspiration. In this case it ceases to be capable of investigation by reason, or to own its dominion; it is accepted on religious grounds, and can appeal only to the principle and influence of faith. Thus miraculous narratives become invested with the character of articles of faith, if they be accepted in a less positive and cer-

* Middleton, quoted by Bp. Douglas, "Criterion," pp. 245, 246.

tain light, as requiring some suspension of judgment as to their nature and circumstances, or perhaps as involving more or less of the parabolic or mythic character; or at any rate as received in connexion with, and for the sake of the doctrine inculcated."*

It appears then, that in the first place the fact of the alleged miracle is to be subjected to a rigid scrutiny, and if there be no apparent ground for rejecting it, we are then to consider whether it is not capable of being referred to some *known physical* cause.

If there is no such cause to which it can be referred, still,—as no one can pretend to set bounds to nature,—it may reasonably be supposed that, if our knowledge were sufficiently enlarged, we should be able to assign a cause, in accordance with the laws of nature,—a natural cause as distinguished from a supernatural one; and we may rest in that supposition.

If, however, the character of the miracle, or possibly the constitution of our own minds, be such, that we cannot bring ourselves to acquiescence in such a supposition,—then, as a last resource,—we must accept the narrative which contains the account of it,—supposing it to be one of the Scriptural narratives,—"as an article of faith," "on the authority of inspiration."

In doing this, however, we must be content to regard the narrative "in a less positive and certain light, as requiring some suspension of judgment as to its nature and circumstances:" in other words, we must presume that we have been mistaken in looking upon it as literally and historically true. And we must either leave it to "await its solution," without venturing to offer a solution of our own, receiving it "in connexion with, and for the sake of the doctrine inculcated," or we must have recourse to "ideology," and suppose that the narrative has "more or less of the parabolic or mythic character," or, as our author expresses himself elsewhere, is "of a designedly fictitious or poetical nature." †

* Essay, p. 142.

† Compare "Order of Nature," pp. 274, 275:—"We have adverted

Professor Powell is ingenious in the method which he has devised for maintaining his theory. Other opponents of miracles have been content to rest their opposition each on a single principle; Professor Powell has a second and a third in reserve, if the one which he had first put forward fails. It is a matter of no little difficulty in dealing with him to know, in the case of any particular miracle, the precise ground on which he is entrenching himself. At the same time, however, it is to be observed, that, as regards the Christian miracles, it is a matter of necessity that he who calls them in question must choose the principle on which he proposes to deny them, and adhere to it throughout. If, for instance, it be granted in any case that the narrative is a narrative of fact, though possibly of a fact which happened according to the ordinary course of nature, it is impossible to believe that others of the

to the kind of examination we should make of a marvellous event occurring before our eyes. The same critical scrutiny could not be applied to a marvellous event recorded in history. But in general, if such an event be narrated, especially as occurring in remote times, it would still become a fair object of the critical historian to endeavour to obtain, if possible, some rational clue to the interpretation of the alleged wonderful narrative. And in this point of view, it is sometimes possible, that, under the supernatural language of a rude age, we may find some real natural phenomenon truly described according to the existing state of knowledge.

"But marvels and prodigies, as such, are beyond the province of critical history and scientific knowledge; they can only be brought within it when, either certainly or probably, brought within the domain of nature. It is almost needless to add, in reference to any such historical narrative, that it is of course presumed, as preliminary to all philosophical speculation, that we have carefully scrutinized the whole question of testimony and documentary authenticity, on purely archæological and critical grounds.

"But in other cases, where such marvels may seem still more to militate against all historical probability, and where attempts at explanation seem irrational, we may be led to prefer the supposition *that the narrative itself was of a designedly fictitious or poetical nature.* And this alternative opens a wide and material field of inquiry, which can only be adequately entered upon by those who unite in an eminent degree the spirit of philosophic investigation with accurate critical, philological, and literary attainments; and which embraces the entire question of the origin and propagation of those various forms of popular *fiction* which are, and have been in all ages, so largely the expression of religious ideas, and often convey, under a poetical or dramatized form, the exposition of an important moral or religious doctrine, and exemplify the remark, that parable and myth often include more truth than history."

narratives are "of a designedly fictitious or poetical" character; and *vice versa*, if it be granted that any of them are designedly fictitious or poetical, it is impossible to understand others as narratives of facts. They are all so obviously of one and the same character that they must stand or fall together.

1. With regard to the theory which would attribute the Christian miracles to natural causes:

It is not denied that some few of them, *stripped of the circumstances connected with them*, might admit of being explained without the supposition of special divine interference. But *take those circumstances into account*, and the natural at once "lifts itself up into the miraculous." * That a piece of money, for example, should be found in a fish's mouth, is an occurrence which might possibly happen in a natural way: but add the coincidence that our Lord directed Peter to go to the sea and cast in a hook and take the fish that should first come up, and told him that he should find in its mouth the very sum of money which he was in want of for the particular occasion, and it seems impossible to deny that "the finger of God" was in the whole transaction. In like manner, that a sudden storm upon the sea of Galilee should speedily be allayed, is perhaps not extraordinary; but that when it was at its height, and the sailors were alarmed at the prospect of instant destruction, our Lord should rise up, and speak the words "Peace, be still," and it should forthwith die down and be succeeded by a great calm,—here was a coincidence which cannot be believed to be fortuitous. Those who witnessed it, at least, were deeply impressed with the conviction that there was an exercise of other than human agency: "What manner of man," they exclaimed, "is this, that even the winds and the sea obey Him?" †

But though some few of the miracles, apart from the circumstances connected with them, might possibly be accounted for in a natural way, the great major-

* Trench, "Notes on the Miracles," p. 13.

† Matt. viii. 27.

ity refuse to be so dealt with. It is true that a *naturalistic* construction has been devised systematically for the whole of them;* but that I may here use Professor Powell's own words,†—"the immense multitude of coincidences and combinations of circumstances and extraordinary occurrences, which it thus becomes necessary to suppose concentrated in one short period, presents too complex a mass of hypotheses to furnish a real and satisfactory theory of the *whole series* of evangelical miracles."

If the theory will not answer for the whole series, it can be of little service in the case of the very few to which it might seem to admit of application, nor, when the abatement necessary to be made for the concomitant circumstances is taken into consideration, can it be of any service even for them.

Professor Powell, while implying that some of the facts of the Gospel narrative commonly described as miracles are in reality to be ascribed to natural causes, goes on to say that such "might still be appealed to in support of religious truth, especially as referring to the state of knowledge and apprehension of the parties addressed in past ages:" in other words, they might be dealt with on Schleiermacher's principle, as *relative* miracles.

But the boon thus offered is one which, even if the solution suggested were acquiesced in, the whole tone ot the Gospel narrative would forbid us to accept. Our Lord constantly appealed to His miracles *as real miracles*, as superhuman works, as testimonies borne to Him by His Father. Whatever therefore might have been the effect of such marvels upon those who deemed them to be of heaven, when indeed they were but of the earth, on us, to whom a deeper insight into nature had revealed their true character, it would only be to excite indignation and disgust.

If it be urged, that the deeper insight into nature possessed by our Lord and communicated by Him to His apostles by which He and they wrought marvellous

* By Paulus. † Order of Nature, p. 333.

works, might fitly be "appealed to in support of religious truth," without impeachment of His or their sincerity, inasmuch as the very possession of it, in the age in which it was exercised, implied superhuman knowledge, this truly is to grant the principle which we contend for. Here is a miracle in the strictest sense of the word: not indeed a *physical* miracle, though it produced physical effects, but something which was *above humanity and above nature.*

But indeed we do but trifle while we speculate on such matters. With all the insight into nature to which modern science has introduced us, we are as far removed at this day as were the contemporaries of our Lord and His apostles from comprehending the means by which such works as those recorded in the New Testament are to be wrought. We can travel with such speed as almost to outstrip an arrow in its flight, we can send a message over hundreds of miles in a few seconds, we can transfer an instantaneous likeness of ourselves or of the scene around us to paper with an exactness which no pencil could equal, we can cheat pain of its victims, we can weigh the earth, we can foretell the eclipses of the sun and moon, and even of the satellites of other planets,—but we are as incapable of communicating instantaneous sight to the blind, hearing to the deaf, speech to the dumb, health to the sick, life to the dead, or of doing any other of the mighty works ascribed to our Lord or His apostles, as was the simplest and most unlearned of those who witnessed them.

2. The second theory which Professor Powell calls in to his aid is one, which, like the preceding, he is far from adopting universally. It is only when other methods fail, or when this has some special advantage to recommend it, that he has recourse to it. And even so he appears to do so with some hesitation. The narrative, it is suggested, may "perhaps involve more or less of the parabolic or mythic character." It doubtless contains important instruction as symbolizing certain truths, but it is not literally and historically true.

We must read it as we read the parable of Dives and Lazarus, or that of the unjust steward. We must apply it as St. Paul has taught us to apply the history of Sarah and Hagar, only, it should be added, with this difference, that whereas St. Paul's application was built upon the literal truth of the history, the theory under consideration rejects the literal truth and substitutes the mythic in its stead.

To unfold on system the mythic or allegorical application of which the Scripture narratives may be thought capable, may serve as an exercise for ingenuity; and this, in his coarse, ribald style, was the method pursued by Woolston in his assault upon the miracles. But that such application should be accepted, in suchwise as to exclude the literal and historical sense, by any sincere lover of truth, I do not say in all, but even in one of the narratives, is impossible. Those narratives bear every appearance of reality on their surface, and no skill or ingenuity can discover anything of a different character underneath the surface. The actors are real, the actions are real, the conversations, the discussions, which accompany or arise out of the actions, and the proceedings which result from them are real. Let any one read over, for instance, the account of the raising of Lazarus and of the measures taken by the Jews in consequence of it, or of the giving of sight to the man who had been born blind and of the investigation instituted by our Lord's enemies into the reality of the miracle,* and he will rise from the perusal with the conviction that it is an insult to his understanding to ask him to allow a so-called ideological application to supplant the natural and obvious meaning. And if this would be his feeling on reading one or two of the Gospel narratives, it would be so in a much greater and more intense degree on reading the whole of the historical books of the New Testament with the subject specially kept in view.

Woolston made large and confident appeals to the Fathers in support of his system: and it cannot be denied either that allegorizing was in much use in the

* John ix.

early Church, or that it was carried to excess in some instances by individual Fathers. But of that excess, reaching so far as occasionally to exclude the literal sense and to substitute an allegorical in its stead, we have no instance till towards the middle of the third century. Origen set the example; * and he was followed occasionally by men whose names carry greater weight than his.† Yet even Origen, in his work against Celsus, uniformly argues, as does Celsus also, on the principle that the narratives of the Christian miracles are to be understood literally, however they may admit or solicit an allegorical sense besides. He repeatedly appeals to the miracles as real, not only in a general way, but with the specification of particular instances; such as the feeding of the multitudes with a few loaves and fishes, the three several cases of the dead raised to life, the healing of the sick, the giving of sight to the blind, and the enabling of the lame to walk.‡

* "Strong as the appetite of the Fathers certainly was on all these accounts for figures, I do not think any instance can be produced from those before Origen of the literal meaning of a passage of Scripture being evaporated in the figurative. . . . He is the first of the Fathers of whom it can be said, that he refines the fact away in the allegory: and even of him it can only be said under great restriction. Origen's general notions upon this question seem to be most fairly represented in his work against Celsus,—the soberest of his works,—viz. that we are to consider the narrative of Scripture as having an obvious sense, but that we are not to rest in the obvious; nor, in interpreting the law, are we to begin and end with the letter: and in like manner, in contemplating the incidents related of Jesus, we shall not arrive at the spectacle of the truth in full, unless we are guided by the same rule."—*Professor Blunt*, "*On the right use of the Early Fathers*," pp. 213—215.

† "Sed etiam Hieronymum video tantum insaniisse, ut scriberet ad Nepotianum, in Epistola de Vita Clericorum, Historiam Davidis et Abisæ Sunamitis figmentum esse de mimo vel Atellanarum ludicro, si sequeris literam. Apage vero has allegoristarum nugas, quibus, propter nonnulla vere typica in Sacra Scriptura, et alia quædam vel tropice prolata, vel ambiguæ interpretationis, magni alioqui viri, dum aliis prodesse volebant, suam ipsorum famam læserunt."—*Routh*, *Reliquiæ Sacræ*, tom. iii. p. 434.

‡ Thus, e. g. (lib. i. p. 5, ed. Spenc.) he appeals to prophecy and miracles as evidences of Christianity, in accordance with the Apostle's words, 1 Cor. ii. 4, *ἐν ἀποδείξει πνεύματος καὶ δυνάμεως*, as he explains them:—*Πνεύματος μὲν, διὰ τὰς προφητείας, ἱκανὰς πιστοποιῆσαι τὸν ἐντυγχάνοντα, μάλιστα εἰς τὰ περὶ τοῦ Χριστοῦ· δυνάμεως δὲ, διὰ τάς τεραστίους δυνάμεις ἃς κατασκευαστέον γεγονέναι καὶ ἐκ πολλῶν μὲν ἄλλων, καὶ ἐκ τοῦ ἴχνη δὲ αὐτῶν ἔτι σώζεσθαι παρὰ τοῖς κατὰ τὸ βούλημα τοῦ λόγου βιοῦσι.* See also pp. 30, 34, 53, and lib. 2 pp. 70, 87, 88.

And in so doing he is but acting in conformity with the principles of the earlier Fathers as well as of the sounder part of the later. To whatever extent they might employ allegory,—and no doubt they did in many instances to a great extent,—their rule was to make the literal and historical truth the basis of the allegory which they built upon it.*

3. One other principle of solution is put forward by Professor Powell. He is willing, in certain cases, to accept the miracle "on religious grounds," "in connection with and for the sake of the doctrine inculcated," —as "an article of faith," not as a matter respecting which our senses can have any cognizance.

If by this he meant that there are certain miraculous *facts*, which transcend our reason, but which nevertheless we believe *as facts*, on the authority of revelation,—such, for instance, as the incarnation of our Blessed Lord,—the principle is most sound, and every Christian will acquiesce in it cordially. Only it follows immediately, as has been already intimated, that if it be conceded but in a single instance that a miracle has been wrought, the ground on which Professor Powell's grand objection to miracles rests is cut away from under him. What has been in one instance may have been in others. There is no longer, even on his own principles,

* "Tunc namque allegoriæ fructus suaviter carpitur, cum prius per historiam in veritatis radice solidatur."—*Gregory the Great*, *Hom.* 40 *in Evang.*, quoted by Dean Trench, "Notes on the Miracles," p. 82. See also St. Augustine, *De Civ. Dei*, lib. xiii. c. 21, where, animadverting upon those who would put an allegorical interpretation on Gen. ii. to the exclusion of the literal sense, he says:—"Tanquam visibilia et corporalia illa non fuerint, sed intelligibilium significandorum causa eo modo dicta vel scripta sint. Quasi propterea non potuerit esse paradisus corporalis, quia potest etiam spiritualis intelligi: tanquam ideo non fuerint duæ mulieres, Agar et Sara, et ex illis duo filii Abrahæ, unus de ancilla, unus de libera, quia duo Testamenta in eis figurata dicit apostolus; aut ideo de nulla petra Moyse percutiente aqua defluxerit, quia potest illic figurata significatione etiam Christus intelligi, eodem apostolo dicente, 'Petra autem erat Christus.'" Then, after giving two different allegorical expositions of the description of Paradise, he adds:—"Hæc, et si qua alia commodius dici possunt de intelligendo spiritualiter Paradiso, nemine prohibente dicantur, dum tamen et illius historiæ veritas fidelissima rerum gestarum narratione commendata credatur."—See also *De Genesi ad Literam*, lib. viii. c. 1.

any shadow of reason for maintaining that a miracle is antecedently and absolutely incredible.

Whether the sense above referred to is that which Professor Powell really intends, is not easily to be collected from the work before us. He speaks more plainly however in his book "On the Order of Nature." And there it appears that while he professes to accept such miracles as the incarnation, the resurrection and the ascension, in what he calls a "spiritualized sense," "in connection with and for the sake of the doctrine inculcated," he has the utmost repugnance to receive them as physical facts. The truth is, he has already become convinced, on antecedent considerations, that there can be no such thing as a miracle; and not even the authority of the inspiration which he professes to accept is of avail to shake his conviction. Even while acknowledging the *name*, he is at pains to deny the *thing*.

But let us hear his own words:—

"If we turn to the New Testament, and acknowledge in its later writings, especially those of St. Paul, the fullest development of apostolic Christianity, we there find, in a very remarkable manner, that no reference is made to any of the Gospel miracles, except only those specially connected with the personal office and nature of Christ; *and even these are never insisted on in their physical details, but solely in their spiritual and doctrinal application.*

"Thus the Resurrection of Christ is emphatically dwelt upon, *not in its physical letter*, but in its doctrinal spirit; *not as a physiological phenomenon*, but as the corner-stone of Christian faith and hope,—the type of spiritual life here, and the assurance of eternal life hereafter. . . .

"So in like manner the transcendent mysteries of the incarnation and ascension *are never alluded to at all by the apostles in a historical or material sense*, but only as they are involved in points of spiritual doctrine, and as objects of faith. . . .

"And *in this spiritualized sense* has the Christian Church in all ages acknowledged these divine mysteries and miracles, '*not of sight but of faith;*' not expounded by science, but delivered in traditional formularies, celebrated in festivals and solemnities by sacred rites and symbols, embodied in the creations of art, and proclaimed by choral harmonies; through all which the spirit of faith adores the great mystery of godliness, —manifested in the flesh, justified in the spirit, seen of angels, preached unto the Gentiles, believed on in the world, received up into glory."—*Order of Nature*, pp. 458—460.

The whole drift of these remarks obviously is to deny, if not in express words yet by implication, the reality of our Lord's incarnation, resurrection, and ascension in any physical sense.*

The other miracles of the Gospel, it seems, are not even referred to in the later writings of the New Testament. Had then the apostles, in "the fuller development of Christianity" to which they had attained, learnt to regard their earlier belief on this point as a delusion?

Even if it were true, however, that there is no reference in the Apostolic Epistles to the miracles of the Gospel, this would be no matter of surprise, unless (which requires to be shewn) the subject in any particular instance required, or at all events suggested, the reference. The fact is, however, that there are occasional, though not frequent, references by the writers to their own miracles, and these distinctly as literal facts.† And if they spoke of their own miracles as such, we may be sure they would have had no hesitation, had the occasion required, in speaking of their Lord's miracles as such.

* In confirmation of the construction which I have put upon Professor Powell's words, I may refer to an article on the "Essays and Reviews," in the "Edinburgh Review" for April, 1861, in which the apologist, (for this is really the character which the writer sustains,) after asserting that, though many parts of the Bible are confessedly figurative and parabolic, there still remain events, such as, above all others, our Lord's Resurrection, where the historic reality must be admitted, proceeds,—"But our own assurance of this and of like occurrences far less important ought not to blind us to the fact, that the very events and wonders, which to us are helps, to others are stumbling-blocks. And though we shrink from abandoning any thing which to us seems necessary or true, yet we are bound to treat those who prefer to lean on other, and, as they think, more secure foundations, with the tenderness with which we cannot doubt they would have been treated by Him, to whom the craving for signs and wonders was a mark, not of love and faith, but of perverseness and unbelief."

† See Gal. iii. 5; Rom. xv. 18, 19; 2 Cor. xii. 12; Heb. ii. 3, 4. The transfiguration and the voice from heaven are expressly appealed to, and that as strictly literal and historical facts, 2 Pet. i. 16, 17.

The miracles, however, which are connected with our Lord's Person and office are "never," we are told, "insisted on in their physical details, but solely in their spiritual and doctrinal application." The resurrection, for instance, is "emphatically dwelt upon, not in its physical letter, but in its doctrinal spirit."

One is at a loss to conceive how any one could make such an assertion as this, unless he thought by its bold confidence to impose upon himself and overbear the reclamations of others. Most persons would rise from the perusal of the 15th Chapter of the First Epistle to the Corinthians with the thorough conviction that how much use soever the Apostle may make of our Lord's resurrection doctrinally, he does most emphatically dwell upon it in its *physical letter.* Its *literal truth* as a "*physiological phenomenon*" is the very basis and substratum of all that is said on the subject. It is implied throughout the whole of the Apostle's argument: "I delivered unto you first of all," says the Apostle, reminding the Corinthians of the doctrine which he had taught at Corinth, "that which I also received, how that Christ died for our sins according to the Scriptures; and that He was buried, and that He rose again the third day, according to the Scriptures: and that He was *seen* of Cephas, then of the twelve. After that, He was *seen* of above five hundred brethren at once. . . . After that, He was *seen* of James; then of all the Apostles; and last of all, He was *seen* of me also. . . . Now if Christ be preached that He rose from the dead, how say some among you that there is no resurrection of the dead? But if there be no resurrection of the dead, then is Christ not risen: *and if Christ be not risen, then is our preaching vain, and your faith is also vain. Yea, and we are found false witnesses of God; because we have testified of God that He raised up Christ: whom He raised not up, if so be that the dead rise not.* For if the dead rise not, then is not Christ raised: *and if Christ be not raised, your faith is vain; ye are yet in your sins.* Then they also which are fallen asleep in Christ are perished. . . . . *But now is Christ risen from the dead, and become the first-fruits of them that slept.*"

Will any one venture, after such a passage as this, to talk of a merely "spiritualized sense," as though the resurrection of the "fullest development of apostolic Christianity" were of a different kind from that which was recognised on the very day on which the history relates that it occurred, when our Lord shewed the assembled disciples His hands and His feet, and bade them handle Him and see that His body was a real body, and by consequence His resurrection a real resurrection, literally and physically true?

It would be a waste of time to adduce further proofs, whether as regards the resurrection, or the incarnation, or the ascension, that whatever doctrinal instructions the apostles might *graft upon* these great and cardinal truths, they neither held nor taught any other faith respecting them than that which pervades the whole volume of the New Testament. They regarded them *as facts*,—"*physiological phenomena*," to use Professor Powell's phrase,—and they denounced those who denied their literal truth,—whether by explaining them, as Hymenæus and Philetus did the resurrection, in a "spiritualized sense," or as the *Docetæ*, by attributing to our Lord a phantom body and denying that He was really "come in the flesh,"—as heretics and antichrists.*

So much, then, for the several solutions which Professor Powell offers in explanation of the Christian miracles. I have endeavoured to shew of each in turn that it is wholly unsatisfactory. But, indeed, there is no need of a laboured refutation. The simplest and the most convincing exposure of their unsatisfactoriness is that which each one may derive for himself from an attentive persual of the New Testament narratives. Let any candid person read the accounts there given, and, as he reads, ask himself from time to time, whether it is possible that there could be room for *illusion*, and that in so many and such various instances, so that

* 2 Tim. ii. 17; 1 John iv. 3.

what he has been accustomed to regard as facts were not facts; or whether it is conceivable that what was done or happened can be accounted for, all the concomitant circumstances being considered, *by a reference to natural causes;* or whether it can be believed that the writers of the Christian books could have intended their narratives to be understood, not as literally and historically true, but *only ideologically*, or in a "*spiritualized sense;*"—if any one, on reading these accounts, should affirm that one or the other of these suppositions is credible, is conceivable, is possible, he must be beyond the reach of argument; I know of no further consideration which would be likely to have weight with him. The difficulty, however, is to prevail upon those who have already determined with themselves on antecedent grounds to reject the Christian miracles, to read the narratives of those miracles with any measure of candour. Hume owned that he had never read the New Testament with attention;* and there is reason to fear that not a few of those who have arrived at conclusions similar to those of Hume, strengthen themselves in the same by a like disregard of that sacred Book and the witness which it bears.

To gather up, then, what has been said thus far:—We have seen, 1st, that they who, on the ground of antecedent incredibility, are for rejecting miracles summarily and without even entering into the question of evidence, have no warrant for such a course; 2dly, that the real question at issue is, What are the *facts* of the case? and that, as regards the Christian miracles, there is the strongest reason for believing the facts,—while at the same time the solutions offered by our author, when he would dispose of their claim to be recognised *as miracles*, are wholly unsatisfactory. Being facts, it is idle to speak of an allegorical or a "spiritualized" sense, such as shall exclude the literal. And they are facts which it is impossible to account for by a reference to causes ordinarily in operation. No such solution is conceivable. They must be acknowledged

* Boswell's Life of Johnson, vol. ii. p. 19, ed. 1823.

to be beyond the power of man, and above nature: they must be accepted *as Miracles.*

II.

But it may still be a question, How far are miracles to be accepted as evidence for a divine revelation,—or, to confine the matter within narrower bounds, as evidence for Christianity? This is Professor Powell's second consideration, though one, as has been already observed, which he might well have spared himself the labour of discussing, supposing that he had proved his point in the preceding part of his Essay. For to what purpose is it to discuss the value of the evidence afforded by miracles, if we are already persuaded that no such thing as a miracle was ever wrought? As it is, indeed, he does not so much discuss the question, as though it were one which admitted of debate, as ring a variety of changes upon the principle, which he conceives he has already made good, of "the universal order and constancy of natural causes." This being the case, whatever might be the evidential force of miracles, with those whose preconceived notions disposed them to acquiesce in them as miracles, to others, whom modern science has enlightened, it can be of no account.

But that principle, as we have seen, has not been established. And we may therefore proceed to discuss the question of the evidential force of miracles upon its own merits.

And this question involves a previous one, By what tokens may miracles, acknowledged such, be proved to be from God?

By many, indeed, such an inquiry would be thought superfluous, inasmuch as a miracle having once been granted to be real, there would seem no room for further question. The appeal to miracles, however, is one which has been repeatedly made by rival sects in support of their respective claims: and though probably enough without any foundation of truth to rest upon in the vast majority of cases, yet Scripture, as it distinctly recognises the existence of superhuman beings, evil as well as good, so it not less distinctly warns us that miracles, even real miracles it should seem, may be wrought by the agency of such beings, God so permitting, where the workers are evil, whether for the trial of His servants, or, judicially, for the punishment of those who wilfully blind themselves against the truth.*

Let us see to what extent the same Scripture affords us a test whereby we may try the miracles whether they are of God.

"If there arise among you a prophet or a dreamer of dreams, and giveth thee a sign or a wonder, and the sign or the wonder come to pass, whereof he spake unto thee, saying, *Let us go after other gods, which thou hast not known, and let us serve them;* thou shalt not hearken unto the words of that prophet, or that dreamer of dreams: for the Lord your God proveth you, to know whether ye love the Lord your God with all your heart and with all your soul . . . And that prophet, or that dreamer of dreams, shall be put to death; because he hath spoken to turn you away from the Lord your God." †

This, then, was the rule under the Old Testament: a miracle wrought, or pretended to be wrought,—and it mattered not which,—*in support of a system opposed to the revelation already given*, was not to be hearkened to for an instant.

And it is much to be observed that a tacit reference to this rule pervades our Lord's intercourse with those who opposed his claims. That He did many miracles they could not and they did not attempt to deny. But they endeavoured to put him down summarily on the ground that His teaching was at variance with their law. While He, on the contrary, continually appealed to that law, bidding them search the Scriptures, for they testified of Him, and affirming, that had they be-

* 2 Thess. ii. 9, &c. See Cudworth's "Intellectual System," p. 706; and Clarke's "Evidences of Natural and Revealed Religion," p. 306.

† Deut. xiii. 1—5.

lieved Moses they would have believed Him, for he wrote of Him.

Precisely similar, it may be added, to the rule under the Old Testament, is the rule under the New:—"Beloved, believe not every spirit, but try the spirits whether they are of God: because many false prophets are gone out into the world. Hereby know ye the Spirit of God: Every spirit that confesseth that Jesus Christ is come in the flesh is of God: and *every spirit that confesseth not that Jesus Christ is come in the flesh is not of God.*" * "Though we or an angel from heaven *preach any other Gospel unto you than that which we have preached unto you*, let him be accursed." † Here is the same test; and though miracles are not specified in connection with it, yet it is obviously designed to apply to *whatsoever credentials* might be adduced, miracles in the number. No one is to be hearkened to, no, not for a moment, let him come with what pretensions he may, *whose teaching contravenes a revelation already given.*

In what has been said thus far, it will be seen that the subject has been regarded from the point of view of those only who are already in possession of a divine revelation. If it be asked, How the case stands with those who have had no previous revelation to guide them?—It must be confessed that such persons are, so far, comparatively at a disadvantage. Still there are certain great principles of moral and religious truth written on men's consciences, though in many cases well-nigh obliterated, which, *as far as they go*, must serve to them instead of a precedent revelation. No miracle ought to be accepted by a heathen as divine, the object of which is to confirm a system of teaching plainly repugnant to those principles. On the other hand, there being no antecedent presumption on such grounds against the teaching, the appeal to miracles would be entitled to a candid and patient consideration.

If the case, instead of being that of a heathen, were

* 1 John iv. 1—3. † Gal. i. 8.

that of an unbeliever living in a Christian country, the only difference would be, that such a one would have the advantage of a truer and higher moral standard to judge by,—the standard, namely, which had been furnished by that very revelation on which he was sitting in judgment, and of which he was unconsciously reaping the benefit.

And now we may see the extent to which the doctrine is a test of the miracle. And it is highly important that we should have a right understanding on this point, seeing that certain dicta, such as that "the miracles prove the doctrines, and the doctrines approve the miracles," have got into current use, which, though they are perfectly true if taken rightly, often have an unsound sense put upon them.

The doctrine, then, taught by him who appeals to miracles as a proof that he has a commission from God, must itself be tried *by the revelation already given.* Under the Old Testament dispensation, that doctrine would have been self-condemned, and the miracles to which it appealed together with it, which taught men to forsake the worship of the one living and true God. Under the New Testament, the case is the same where the doctrine denies that Jesus is the Christ, or contravenes any other of the fundamental truths of the Gospel. Where neither the Old Testament nor the New can be appealed to, then, and then only, must men be content with that standard of truth and morality, an imperfect one at best, to which, by whatsoever means, those who know nothing or believe nothing of a precedent revelation have attained. To appeal to any such standard, when the benefit of a precedent revelation is enjoyed, would be as superfluous as to light a candle in full sunshine.

Professor Powell, after referring to such passages as those which have been above cited, and inferring most justly, "that the unworthiness of the doctrine will discredit even the most distinctly alleged apparent miracles," adds, that the worthiness or unworthiness of the doctrine "appeals solely to our moral judgment." * It does so, no doubt; but then it is to our moral judgment, if we are already in possession of a revelation, *enlightened by that revelation.* Scripture distinctly recognises the standard of natural conscience, *where men have no safer and truer guide.* † But where they have, its language is, "*To the law and to the testimony: if they speak not according to this word, it is because there is no light in them.*" ‡

It will be observed that the test referred to makes proof, not whether the facts in question are miracles or not, *of any sort;*—it is no test of that:—but whether they are *divine* miracles; whether they are to be referred to God as their author, or to "the working of Satan," and are to be classed with those "signs and lying wonders" (τέρατα ψεύδους),—not necessarily counterfeit miracles, but, in some cases possibly enough, real miracles, wrought for the upholding of a lie,—wherewith the Evil One is permitted to deceive those "who receive not the love of the truth that they may be saved." §

It must be borne in mind, too, that the test referred to is, after all, but a *negative* test. It *disproves* in certain cases; *it does not prove* in any. If the doctrine taught contradicts a revelation already given, or, where there is no precedent revelation, those great principles of truth and morality which are written on men's consciences, no works of wonder wrought in support of it are even to be admitted to a hearing: they are to be rejected summarily. But if the doctrine be in accordance with a revelation already given, or with those principles, it does not necessarily follow that the alleged miracles are divine or even real miracles; these points are to be determined upon other considerations: but at least there is no reason, which there would have been otherwise, why they should not be admitted to be tried.

To pass, however, from *negative* criteria to those of a *positive* description.

* Essay, p. 121. † Rom. ii. 14, 15. ‡ Isa. viii. 20.
§ See Cudworth, p. 708.

It may be granted, at the outset, that there is no test which, *taken singly, by itself*, is absolutely sufficient to stamp an alleged miracle with the seal of God. But yet, notwithstanding, there may be presumptions afforded by various considerations, and there may be concurrent circumstances of such weight, that *the joint result* may be to place the matter beyond question. And it is important to remember that it is *by such joint result*, rather than by any single test, that divine miracles are to be ascertained. Though even so, Scripture warns us that there is need of an honest and truth-loving heart, otherwise the proofs afforded, be they what they may, will be fruitless.

Of the presumptions referred to, one is supplied by *the alleged miracle itself.* Its character may be such, that, as it is inconceivable that it should have been wrought but by power more than human, so it is inconceivable but that that power must have been divine. This was Nicodemus's conclusion drawn from the character of our Lord's miracles: "We know that thou art a Teacher come from God, because no man can do these miracles that Thou doest, except God be with him."

Another presumption is afforded by *the character of the Person* by whom the alleged miracle is wrought; for though it is possible enough for Satan to transform himself into an angel of light, and the world has had too many proofs that the teachers of false doctrine may be men of blameless lives,—(and truly it is this very circumstance which, more than any other, has contributed to the first establishment of heresies)—yet, doubtless, if a man of sound judgment, whose word has never been falsified, whose life is eminently holy, claims to work miracles in attestation that he has a commission from God, and if there is nothing in the character of his teaching to invalidate his claim, his integrity and truthfulness do afford a presumption that his claim is well founded.

And the same may be said of *the doctrine taught.* It is true, as I have observed above, that the test afforded by the doctrine, so far as that test is absolute and decisive, is negative, not positive;—doctrine which is contrary to a revelation already given being at once and summarily conclusive against the claims of any miracles, or alleged miracles, to be regarded as divine; but doctrine which is not contrary to such revelation being not necessarily conclusive in their favour. Still a proof is one thing, a presumption is another. And if the doctrine, in attestation of whose divine origin miracles are alleged to have been wrought, be so eminently holy, and inculcate truth and righteousness to such a degree, and carry on the face of it such an air of goodness that it is impossible to conceive that it should have proceeded from the Evil One, here also, however there may be an absence of absolute proof, there is surely *presumptive* evidence that the appeal which is made is founded in truth.

One other presumption is afforded by *the object*, for which the miracle is said to have been wrought. If that object be trifling and apparently unworthy of the divine interference, or if the end could have been gained by natural means, then there is at once a presumption against the idea of a divine miracle. But if, on the other hand, the object be of grave importance, and especially if there be no way apparent by which otherwise it could so well have been attained, there is here also a presumption that the miracle is from God.

Now each and all of these presumptions are found in the case of our Lord's miracles. Those miracles carried what might well be thought a divine stamp upon their forefront; and that stamp was recognised by those, who, as Nicodemus, brought with them candid and truth-loving hearts. They were commended, further, by the life and conversation of Him who wrought them, and by His doctrine so entirely in accordance with that life and conversation; and the object for which, as it is alleged, they were wrought was one, if any, eminently worthy of divine interference.

Still, these are but presumptions,—only, be it observed, presumptions which mutually strengthen and confirm one another. For, let it be considered for a moment how the case would have stood, supposing that one or more of them had been wanting. If, for example, our Lord's miracles had been such as we find attributed to Him in some of the Apocryphal Gospels, trifling, or malevolent, or vindictive, or in any other way unworthy of Him who professed to have come forth from God; or, the character of the miracles affording no ground for remark, if the life and conversation of Him who wrought them, or the tendency of His teaching, had been exceptionable; or, these also being free from blame, if the object, for which it was professed that the miracles were wrought, had been apparently unworthy of the divine interference,—in any of these cases it is obvious how greatly the force of that presumptive evidence which they yield, now that they are combined, would have been impaired, if not indeed destroyed altogether.

But, besides these presumptions, there is another circumstance to be taken into the account, of a much more substantive and determinate character.

Prophecy, in foretelling the advent of the Messiah, had described the circumstances of His coming and the characteristics by which He should be known. Among these characteristics it had intimated that He should shew signs and wonders,* and it had even particularized some of these. It had foretold that "the eyes of the blind should be opened, and the ears of the deaf should be unstopped, that the lame man should leap as a hart, and the tongue of the dumb should sing." † And such works "were held by the Jews to constitute the distinctive marks of the Messiah, according to the prophecies of their Scriptures." ‡ There were intimations also, more or less distinct, of those still greater marvels which should circle round His person,—the Incarnation, the Resurrection, the Ascension,—and of the outpouring of the Holy Spirit upon his followers.

Now the works of Jesus and the other marvellous circumstances connected with Him accurately corre-

* See Deut. xviii. 15—22. † Isa. xxxv. 5, 6.
‡ Professor Powell, "Essay," p. 116.

sponded to these predictions and these intimations. And even where, as in some instances might be the case, the prophecies were obscure or of doubtful application, the works threw light back upon the prophecies, while at the same time the prophecies stamped the works as divine.

It was with an evident though tacit reference to these prophecies,* that our Lord bade John's disciples, who had been sent to Him with the question, "Art Thou He that should come, or look we for another?" return and tell their master what things they had seen and heard, (He had in their presence, as of set purpose, "cured many of their infirmities and plagues, and of evil spirits; and unto many that were blind He had given sight,") "How that the blind see, the lame walk, the lepers are cleansed, the deaf hear, the dead are raised, to the poor the Gospel is preached. And blessed is He, whosoever shall not be offended in me." † And in like manner His Resurrection was constantly appealed to, both by Himself prospectively, and by His apostles after the event, not only as a sign,—(it was, in fact, the great and crowning sign,)—whereby He might be known as the true Messiah, but as a sign which the Scriptures had foretold. And the Church,

* St. Jerome, commenting upon Isa. xxxv. 5, 6, says, "Quod, quanquam signorum magnitudine completum sit, cum Dominus loquebatur discipulis Joannis qui ad eum missi fuerant, Euntes renuntiate Joanni quæ audistis et vidistis, &c., tamen quotidie expletur in gentibus, quando qui prius cæci erant et in ligna et lapides impingebant, veritatis lumen aspiciunt," &c.; which is a distinct acknowledgment that, though the passage will bear a spiritual sense, yet primarily it is to be understood literally. And Origen deals with the prophecy in a similar manner, interpreting it first literally of bodily cures, and then building upon the literal interpretation, though with something of an apology, a spiritual one:—Ἐγὼ δ' εἴποιμ' ἂν, ὅτι, κατὰ τὴν Ἰησοῦ ἐπαγγελίαν, οἱ μαθηταὶ καὶ μείζονα πεποιήκασιν ὧν Ἰησοῦς αἰσθητῶν πεποίηκεν· ἀεὶ γὰρ ἀνοίγονται ὀφθαλμοὶ τυφλῶν τὴν ψυχὴν, κ. τ. λ.—*Contr. Cels.*, lib. ii. p. 88. To the same purpose Tertullian, *De Resurrect. Carnis*, c. 20. Justin Martyr, in the passage quoted below, *Trypho*, § 69, interprets the prophecy literally.

† Luke vii. 21—23. So St. Matthew represents Isa. liii. 4 as fulfilled in our Lord's miracles of healing, Matt. viii. 16, 17. And St. Peter refers to Joel ii. 28, 29 as fulfilled in the outpouring of the Holy Spirit on the apostles and those who were associated with them, Acts ii. 16, &c.

taking up the very words of St. Paul,* and incorporating them into her Creed, echoes on the same teaching to this hour, declaring her belief, not only that "Christ rose again the third day," but that He so rose "*according to the Scriptures.*"

This correspondence between the Gospel miracles and the prophecies which foretold them was a criterion on which the early Christian writers laid especial stress, as proving those miracles to be divine. It has been truly remarked that the prevalent belief in magic, as it afforded a subterfuge to the enemies of Christianity, by which they sought to escape when they were pressed with the argument from the Gospel miracles, so it made those who maintained the Christian cause more slow than they would have been otherwise to avail themselves of that argument. Still they did avail themselves of it without hesitation; and, when they did so, they were careful for the most part to couple their appeal to the miracles with an appeal to prophecy; not merely to prophecy which described beforehand our Lord's person, and character, and office, and the establishment of His religion and its growth and increase, but also specifically to prophecy which foretold that He should work miracles, and described the miracles which He should work.† Such a concurrence, it was justly

* 1 Cor. xv. 4.

† Thus Justin Martyr:—Ὅπως δὲ μή τις ἀντιτιθεὶς ἡμῖν, Τί κωλύει καὶ τὸν παρ' ἡμῖν λεγόμενον Χριστὸν, ἄνθρωπον ἐξ ἀνθρώπων ὄντα, μαγικῇ τέχνῃ ἃς λέγομην δυνάμεις πεποιηκέναι, καὶ δόξαι διὰ τοῦτο υἱὸν Θεοῦ εἶναι; τὴν ἀπόδειξιν ἤδη ποιησόμεθα, οὐ τοῖς λέγουσι πιστεύοντες, ἀλλὰ τοῖς προφητεύουσι πρὶν ἢ γένεσθαι κατ' ἀνάγκην πειθόμενοι, διὰ τὸ καὶ ὄψει ὡς προεφητεύθη ὁρᾷν γενόμενα καὶ γινόμενα· ἥπερ μεγίστη καὶ ἀληθεστάτη ἀπόδειξις καὶ ὑμῖν, ὡς νομίζομεν, φανήσεται. . . . Ἐν δὴ ταῖς τῶν προφητῶν βίβλοις εὕρομεν προκησυσσόμενον, Παραγινόμενον, γεννώμενον διὰ παρθένου, καὶ ἀνδρούμενον, καὶ θεραπεύοντα πᾶσαν νόσον καὶ πᾶσαν μαλακίαν, καὶ νεκροὺς ἀνεγείροντα, καὶ φθονούμενον, καὶ ἀγνοούμενον, καὶ σταυρούμενον Ἰησοῦν τὸν ἡμέτερον Χριστὸν, καὶ ἀποθνήσκοντα, καὶ ἀνεγειρόμενον, καὶ εἰς οὐρανοὺς ἀνερχόμενον, κ. τ. λ.—*Apol.* i. § 30, 31.

In his Dialogue with Trypho, § 69, he cites Isa. xxxv. 1—7 in proof that our Lord's miracles had been foretold, and then proceeds to shew the fulfilment of the prophecy in Him:—Ὃς καὶ ἐν τῷ γένει ὑμῶν πέφανται, καὶ τοὺς ἐκ γενετῆς καὶ κατὰ τὴν σάρκα πηροὺς, καὶ κωφοὺς, καὶ χωλοὺς ἰάσατο, τὸν μὲν ἅλλεσθαι, τὸν δὲ καὶ ἀκούειν, τὸν δὲ καὶ ὁρᾷν, τῷ λόγῳ

urged, placed those miracles beyond the reach of cavil, and afforded a conclusive proof that He whose mission was thus attested must have come from God.

Our Lord's miracles, then,—and the same holds of the miracles of the apostles,—were, by all the tokens which have been mentioned, plainly proved to have proceeded from God as their author. Negatively, there was nothing in the teaching of those who wrought them

αὐτοῦ ποιήσας· καὶ νεκροὺς δὲ ἀναστήσας καὶ ζῆν ποιήσας, καὶ διὰ τῶν ἔργων ἐδυσώπει τοὺς τότε ὄντας ἀνθρώπους ἐπιγνῶναι αὐτόν.

And yet the author of the article above referred to on the "Essays and Reviews," in the "Edinburgh Review," says, "In the early ages of the Church, Justin Martyr in his 'Apology' rarely, *if ever*, appeals to the miracles of the Gospel in proof of its divinity." It is not obvious which of Justin's "Apologies" is meant, nor why one of his works should be singled out, when, besides the two "Apologies," there is another equally apologetic in its character, nor why he alone of the writers of "the early ages of the Church" should be appealed to. It must be confessed that Justin's appeals to the miracles are not frequent; but the passages which have been cited shew that he did not hesitate to appeal to them when the occasion required, and that when he did, he did so in no faltering tone. Other passages to the like effect will be found in "Trypho," cc. 11, 35, and 39. Bp. Kaye, in his analysis of the contents of the first "Apology," regards Justin's appeal to miracles and prophecy as of sufficient prominence to have a separate head allotted to it,—"III. Direct arguments in proof of the truth of Christianity *drawn from miracles and prophecy.*"—*Kaye's Justin Martyr*, p. 13.

To the same purpose as Justin, St. Irenæus writes, lib. II. c. xxxii. § 3, 4:—Εἰ δὲ καὶ τὸν Κύριον φαντασιωδῶς τὰ τοιαῦτα πεποιηκέναι φήσουσιν, ἐπὶ τὰ προφητικὰ ἀνάγοντες αὐτοὺς, ἐξ αὐτῶν ἐπιδείξομεν, πάντα οὕτως περὶ αὐτοῦ καὶ προειρῆσθαι, καὶ γεγονέναι βεβαίως, καὶ αὐτὸν μόνον εἶναι τὸν Υἱὸν τοῦ Θεοῦ.

Origen, *Contr. Cels.*, lib. ii. p. 87, ed. Spenc., expressly refers to Isa. xxxv. as fulfilled in our Lord's miraculous works:—Ὅτι μὲν οὖν χωλοὺς καὶ τυφλοὺς ἐθεράπευσε, (as Celsus had acknowledged, though he had spoken with a ὡς ὑμεῖς φατε of the miracles of raising the dead,) διόπερ Χριστὸν αὐτὸν καὶ Υἱὸν Θεοῦ νομίζομεν, δῆλον ἡμῖν ἐστιν ἐκ τοῦ καὶ ἐν προφητείαις γεγράφθαι, Τότε ἀνοιχθήσονται ὀφθαλμοὶ τυφλῶν, κ. τ. λ. See also Com. in Matth., tom. xii. 2.

Lactantius, in like manner, appeals to the correspondence between our Lord's miracles and the prophecies which were fulfilled in them, as a criterion by which they might be known to be divine:—"Fecit mirabilia; magum putassemus, ut et vos nuncupatis, et Judæi tunc putaverunt, si non illa ipsa facturum Christum prophetæ omnes uno spiritu prædicassent." Again, "Exinde maximas virtutes cœpit operari, non præstigiis magicis, quæ nihil veri ac solidi ostentant, sed vi ac potestate cœlesti, quæ jampridem prophetis nuntiantibus canebantur."—Lib. v. c. 3, and lib. iv. c. 15. In connexion with the latter passage he cites Isa. xxxv. See Dr. Ogilvie's Bampton Lectures, Serm. II., and Appendix, pp. 248—255.

which was contrary either to the great principles of moral and religious truth written on men's consciences, or to the revelation which God had previously given. Positively, there was every presumption in their favour, whether from the nature of the miracles themselves, or from the character of those who wrought them, or from the tendency of their teaching, or from the object for which they were professedly wrought; and, what was beyond these presumptions, there was a marked correspondence between them and the prophecies which had foretold the signs by which the Christ should be known. There could be no doubt but that such works were to be ascribed to God.

And as they were to be ascribed to God, so they bore witness to those by whose instrumentality they were wrought, that they had a commission from God. And as such they were repeatedly appealed to by them; sometimes, as we have already seen, in conjunction with the prophecies which foretold them, at other times simply and absolutely, and without any such reference;—"If I do not the works of My Father," said our Lord to the Jews, "believe Me not. But if I do, though ye believe not Me, believe the works: that ye may know and believe that the Father is in Me and I in Him." * And the apostles held the same language:—"Jesus of Nazareth, a man approved of God among you, by miracles and wonders and signs, which God did by Him in the midst of you, as ye yourselves also know." † And the miracles of the apostles are appealed to in similar terms, as proving that they also had a like commission:—"How shall we escape, if we neglect so great salvation; which at the first began to be spoken by the Lord, and was confirmed unto us by them that heard Him; God also bearing them witness, both with signs and wonders, and with divers miracles, and gifts of the Holy Ghost, according to His will?" ‡

* John x. 37, 38. So Matt. xi. 20—24, xii. 38—40; John ii. 18—22, v. 33—36, xiv. 11, xv. 24.

† Acts ii. 22. So St. John xx. 30, 31; Acts v. 30, 32; x. 37—39.

‡ Heb. ii. 3, 4; so St. Mark xvi. 20; Acts iv. 29—31, xiv. 3; Rom. xv. 18, 19; 2 Cor. xii. 12; Gal. iii. 5.

And on this appeal to miracles, both our Lord's and those of the apostles, the Church of Christ was built up in the beginning. True, miracles were not the only foundation on which the superstructure was raised; but they were *one* of the foundations, and a very important one,—so important, that, when we look back upon the Church's earliest history, it is impossible to conceive, how, without some foundation of the same or of like description, it could have been raised at all.

For what are the facts which that history sets before us?—A few Jewish peasants go forth into the world, and declare everywhere that they have a commission from God to teach a religion diametrically opposed to the prejudices, the associations, the habits, the worldly interests of those to whom they address themselves. It is true, that this religion inculcates a morality so pure and exalted, that it cannot but commend itself to the minds and consciences of such as are really in earnest in seeking to know and do what is right, though even so not without the admixture of some precepts which must seem foolishness in their eyes: but together with this, and inseparable from it, it contains assertions of the most improbable kind, and such as one would imagine the most credulous must revolt from. It affirms that the Son of God had become man; that He had been born into the world, not as a mighty prince, surrounded with earthly pomp and splendour, but as an obscure Jewish peasant. It affirms, further, that he had been regarded by those of His countrymen whose learning and authority entitled them to the utmost deference, as an impostor; that as such He had been delivered over by them to the Roman Procurator and put to an ignominious death; that He had come to life again, however, and after shewing Himself sundry times to those who had been His followers, had ascended up to heaven in their presence; that thence He will come again at some future day to judge the world, and that then all who ever lived will be summoned before Him, the dead raised from their graves, the living called from their occupations; and that He will award to every one his final and irreversible destiny according to his works. This was the strange story which the first preachers of the Gospel carried forth with them wherever they went. This was the very heart's core of the religion which they taught, and for which they required men to abandon the beliefs of their forefathers, without the faintest prospect of worldly advantage, but, on the contrary, with every reason to expect derision and ridicule, the loss of goods, the estrangement of friends, even imprisonment and death. And the expectation was realized. Those who embraced it "ligabantur, includebantur, cædebantur, torquebantur, urebantur, laniabantur, trucidabantur, et—multiplicabantur." * The religion in a brief space spread itself over the whole civilized world. Is it conceivable that it should have done so unless it had appealed, and had been able to make good the appeal, to superhuman attestations in proof of its divine origin? As St. Augustine forcibly urges, "You have two alternatives to choose between: either you must believe the miracles; or you must believe, what is itself a miracle, that the world was converted without miracles:" "Si miraculis non credatis, saltem huic miraculo credendum est, mundum sine miraculis fuisse conversum." †

Yet we are told that this goodly fabric of the Christian Church, whose existence at this day is none of the least of the proofs of the divine mission of its founder, was built up upon an unsound and insecure foundation:

* S. August., De Civ. Dei, xxii. 6. 1.

† De Civ. Dei, xxii. 8. 1. Origen had urged the same argument:—*Οὐκ ἄν χωρὶς δυνάμεων καὶ παραδόξων ἐκίνουν τοὺς καινῶν λόγων καὶ καινῶν μαθημάτων ἀκούοντας πρὸς τὸ καταλιπεῖν μὲν τὰ πάτρια, παραδέξασθαι δὲ μετὰ κινδύνων τῶν μεχρὶ θανάτου τὰ τούτων μαθήματα.*—*Contr. Cels.*, lib. i. p. 34. St. Augustine, on another occasion, has the following striking passage referring to the miracle of our Lord's Resurrection:—"Jam ergo tria sunt incredibilia, quæ tamen facta sunt. Incredibile est Christum resurrexisse in carne, et in cœlum ascendisse cum carne; incredibile est mundum rem tam incredibile credidisse; incredibile est homines, ignobiles, infimos, paucissimos, imperitos, rem tam incredibilem tam efficaciter mundo, et in illo etiam doctis, persuadere potuisse. Horum trium incredibilium primum nolunt isti, cum quibus agimus, credere; secundum coguntur et cernere; quod non inveniunt unde sit factum si non credunt tertium."—*De Civ. Dei*, xxii. 5.

—"Miracles which would be incredible *now*, were not so in the age and under the circumstances in which they are stated to have occurred." And the appeal to them, however cogent with those to whom it was addressed in the first century, has lost its force in the nineteenth: nay, "it might not only have no effect, but even an injurious tendency if urged in the present age, and referring to what is at variance with existing scientific conceptions."*

It has been my endeavour to shew, in the preceding part of this Essay, how utterly groundless is the insinuation which is here cast upon the Christian miracles; that as their reality as facts, and facts not only superhuman but divine, rests upon the most convincing proofs, so they are as surely to be believed now, with the full light of modern science streaming upon them, as they were believed in the age of comparative darkness in which they were wrought. But apart from this,—What, on the supposition referred to, becomes of the truthfulness of Him, who, as we have seen, rested His claim to be heard on the appeal to those miracles? For it is undeniable that when our Lord *did* appeal to them, it was on the ground that they *were miracles*, superhuman works, works wrought by the power of God, and indicating the finger of God, that the appeal was made.

No,—if the appeal to miracles is not valid now, it was not valid when it was made by our Lord. And if it was not valid then, there was an insincerity in it, as made by Him, which communicates a taint to the whole of His teaching. It is of little consequence by what other arguments the cause of Christianity is sought to be sustained. We may admire much that we see in it; but we can no longer regard it as a religion on which the seal of God is set. The great articles of its Creed must henceforth take their place among the myths and legends of men's invention.

We cannot then, as reasonable men, we dare not as Christian men, make light of the argument from miracles, or even give it a subordinate place among the

* Essay, p. 117.

Christian evidences. It may have been dwelt upon too exclusively, and have been pushed into undue prominence in some instances; but that is only a reason why we should be especially on our guard, lest, by a change of fortune naturally enough to be expected, it should be thrown into the background and unduly depressed in others.*

Most true it is indeed, that miracles, though forming an important part of the evidence for Christianity, form but a part. But it is a part intimately connected with the other parts, and, together with prophecy,—both prophecy which received its fulfilment in our Lord's life and ministry, and prophecy, in some instances uttered by our Lord and His apostles, which has been fulfilled subsequently, and is still being fulfilled,—so essentially underlying those other parts, that without it they have no sufficient foundation to rest upon.

There is one portion indeed of the Christian evidence, and a most important one, which might seem, at first sight, to have little connexion with external proofs, —the assurance, namely, which the Christian derives from his inner consciousness of the purifying, sanctifying, and ennobling influence of the Gospel upon his

* I am not acquainted with Coleridge's works: but, judging from the use which Professor Powell and others have made of them, I cannot but think that he has in this respect, through dread of one extreme, contributed "to thrust the pendulum back with too violent a swing" towards the opposite. And yet, in the context immediately connected with one of the passages quoted by Professor Powell, (Essay, p. 120,) I find him adding what shews that in reality nothing was farther from his own thoughts than the disparagement of the external evidences:—"But most readily do I admit, and most fervently do I contend, that the miracles worked by Christ, *both as miracles and as fulfilments of prophecy*, both as signs and as wonders, *made plain discovery, and gave unquestionable proof of His Divine character and authority;* that they were to the whole Jewish nation *true and appropriate evidences* that He was indeed come who had promised and declared to their forefathers, 'Behold, your God will come with vengeance, even God with a recompense; He will come and save you.' *I receive them as proofs, therefore, of the truth of every word which He taught who was Himself the Word*, and as sure evidences of the final victory over death, and of the life to come, in that they were manifestations of Him who said, 'I am the Resurrection and the Life.'"—*Aids to Reflection, Aphorisms on Spiritual Religion, note prefatory to Aphorism xxiii.*

own heart and life. And the conviction produced by this assurance, where the soul is thoroughly penetrated by the influence of Christ's religion, is such, as no arguments drawn exclusively from external considerations could have effected. The Christian's answer, to those who might interrogate him respecting his belief, would be like that of the man who had been born blind, to whom our Lord had given the gift of sight, when questioned about his Benefactor,—"Whether He be a sinner or no, I know not: one thing I know, that, whereas, I was blind, now I see." *

But it is to be observed that this assurance comes under the head of confirmation rather than of proof. It does not precede, but follow, the reception of Christianity. No one is susceptible of its force but he who is already a believer. It rests therefore eventually on the same basis as that on which Christianity itself rests. And thus, though not directly, yet indirectly, it also is inseparably connected with the evidence afforded by miracles, however unconscious the person who is under its influence may be of the extent to which he is indebted to that evidence.

There are those whose happy lot it is to have been nurtured in the knowledge and love of Christ from their infancy, and never to have known a doubt. And there

* John ix. 25. They are words deserving to be well weighed and pondered, which were written, on the review of a long life, by one who had had large experience in dealing with other men's consciences, and had been a close observer of his own:—"I am now more apprehensive than heretofore of the necessity of well grounding men in their religion, and especially of the witness of the indwelling Spirit. For I more sensibly perceive that the Spirit is the great witness for Christ and Christianity to the world. And though the folly of fanatics long tempted me to overlook the strength of this testimony while they placed it in certain internal affections or enthusiastic inspiration, yet now I see that the Holy Ghost is in another manner the witness of Christ and His agent in the world. The Spirit in the prophets was His first witness; and the Spirit by miracles was the second; and the Spirit by renovation, sanctification, and illumination, and consolation, assimilating the soul to Christ and heaven, is the continued witness to all true believers. . . . And therefore ungodly persons have a great disadvantage in their resisting temptations to unbelief; and it is no wonder if Christ be a stumbling-block to the Jews, and to the Gentiles foolishness."—*Richard Baxter*, *Narrative of his Life and Times, in Wordsworth's Eccl. Biog.*, 1st ed., vol. v. p. 568.

are those who once did doubt, but have been convinced by the force of the Christian evidences, and doubt no longer. These, as far as their personal belief is concerned, have no need to resort to the argument from miracles. But then it is because they have advanced to a higher stage, and they have no occasion for the steps by which that stage is to be reached.

It was to such persons that the Apostolic Epistles were addressed; and the appeal, consequently, was no longer, as doubtless it had been before their conversion, "to outward testimony or logical argument, but to spiritual assurances." * It was of such persons that St. Chrysostom spoke when he said, in words which Professor Powell quotes, "If you are a believer as you ought to be, and love Christ as you ought to love Him, you have no need of miracles." †

But there are others, who stand on different ground. They, it may be, have never yet believed, or they may have had doubts and difficulties suggested to them, whether from within or from without, which affect the very foundations of the faith; while, at the same time, they are not sufficiently advanced in religion to be conscious of the force of those internal evidences which have been referred to. To such persons the evidence afforded by miracles is of pressing urgency; and he who would disparage it and teach them to regard it as of little or no account, is so far a hinderer of their faith and of their salvation. They are like men struggling for life amid the waves, and he is snatching from their grasp that plank on which they might have buoyed themselves up and have escaped, bidding them meanwhile, as though in cruel mockery, lay hold on another, which, however serviceable it might prove to them hereafter, is at present beyond their reach.

* Essay, p. 124.

† St. Chrysostom, Hom. 23 (al. 24) in S. Joan., quoted by Professor Powell, p. 128.

THE IDEA OF THE NATIONAL CHURCH:

(CONSIDERED IN REPLY TO MR. WILSON.)

SECTION 1. Theories of "National Religion" in England.
" 2. Outline of the Essay on 'Broad Christianity.'
" 3. Religious Idea of 'Broad Christianity.'
" 4. 'Broad Christianity' and the Apostolic Age.
" 5. "Exclusiveness" of Primitive Christianity considered.
" 6. Ethical Basis of 'Broad Christianity.'
" 7. Appeal to History, as to 'Broad Christianity.'
" 8. Adjustment demanded.

Preliminary Note.

[*Numerous writers have criticized the "Essay on the National Church," praising the style or blaming the tone, marking inaccuracies or deprecating tendencies, without examining its subject. It can matter little, however, to the world at large, whether the writer of that Essay be as eloquent, or rash, or obscure, or heterodox, as his various critics have shewn. But with his subject-matter we must all be concerned; to that therefore the ensuing papers will be given.*

*It is not here proposed to offer what has been termed a "counter-essay," which might be regarded as a merely literary prolusion; but to attempt a real discussion of a practical matter.**]

§ 1. *Theories of National Religion in England.*

"Omnis Ecclesia Anglicana."—Spelman, A. D. 668, Abp. Theodore.

THE CHURCH OF ENGLAND still bears the name which she has borne for a thousand years, "the National Church." The Acts of Uniformity now assert for her in the Statute-book,

* For many minor details, and for the examination of most of Mr. Wilson's incidental statements, the reader may be referred to a work entitled "The Reviewers Reviewed and the Essayists Criticized," published by J. H. and Jas. Parker, Oxford and London.

as really as they did in 1662, or 1559,—as really as synods had done it ten centuries before,—a National position; and even in the popular mind the belief of that "Nationality" yet lingers, though with growing indistinctness. It is not now the idea of the Caroline or of the Elizabethan times, still less of the pre-Reformation period; it is not the idea of even fifty years ago. The name remains, while the reality has greatly changed, more than once. We are even now in a period of transition.

The name of the "National Church."

Time was when the decisions of our "National Church" in synod, confirmed at Rome, bound every subject of the realm. The theory on which our ancestors then proceeded was Ecclesiastical; the unity compulsory, and therefore co-extensive with the nation.—Disputes as to Investiture, the Constitutions of Clarendon, the Great Charter, the Statutes of Provisors, and Præmunire, are the practical witnesses against it from age to age: but, while it lasted, doubtless it had conscientiousness, if not of the highest type.—Again, time was when the king, as head of the State, commanded the Religion of the whole people. The theory was Political: to dispute the spiritual Supremacy of the Crown was "high treason," and the penalty was sternly inflicted, whether the offender had the grace of a Fisher or the dignity of a More. But the theory came to an end; and that very soon; for it revolted the conscience of the majority in England, of more than a majority in Scotland, and of the whole of Ireland. Gradually within a hundred years, the resolute Royal assumption, that the whole nation must follow the conscience of the sovereign, perished, and the clay, the stone, and the iron, of the great image of Tudor Supremacy that had been set up, could no more cohere.

Pre-Reformation forms of "Nationalism." William II. and Anselm. Henry II. and Becket. John & Langton. Richard II.

Tudor form.

35 Hen. VIII. c. 3.

1 Mary, c. 1. s. 5.

Henceforth Religious Unity seemed hopelessly broken. Between the days of Edward VI. and Charles II. a fundamental change had taken place in the sentiments and feelings of those who formed the

Transition form.

lower stratum of the British people. They had been Roman, and they had become Puritan. A change scarcely less vital had come over the higher classes of the nation. At the Reformation, the rich (and they who sought to be rich) were progressive and protestant; at the Restoration they were conservative, and hierarchical. The sympathies of both classes had been reversed in one century: but an effort was still to be made to gather together once more, if not to unite, the dissolved elements of society. When the time for this effort arrived, let us mark how it was attempted.

Its Occasion;

To do this we must revert to those theories of the past on which, in some form, the Restoration had to fall back. Of course the old pre-Reformation views were not to be thought of. The bare dread of a possible return to Romanism, a few years later, overthrew the dynasty which had been restored. Some modification of the old Tudorism seemed to be all that remained practicable. Among her sons, the Church (notwithstanding her great names) had "none to guide," no great ecclesiastic. Sancroft and his brethren had been taught in the school of Andrewes and Laud, who had strained the Regale to the utmost; the former against Rome, the latter against both Rome and Geneva. The great divines of the Restoration, as if hopeless of ascertaining the limits of lawful State-interference with Religion, indistinctly acquiesced in political intervention, thankful that it happened on the whole to be orthodox. The Tudor theory, in all its transitions, had preserved a vague adherence to the distinction inherently existing between the "spiritualty" and "temporalty" of the nation, and recognised alike by the Constitution and by the popular instincts. To this, Churchmen and Statesmen alike recurred; and though the practical compromise to be attempted might involve some theological surrenders, it seemed actually inevitable.

Its later Revival;

And character.

No doubt indeed the original Tudor spirit urged Royal Authority as the ground of the Nation's faith.

A. D. 1530. The "Act of Submission" of King Henry's Convocation, (under an unjust præmunire,) while really Henry VIII. and Wareham. giving up all to the king, had still feebly intended to assert a principle when the words "quantum per CHRISTI legem licet" were added by the Lower House. But the conscience of the people retained, far more faithfully, the high principle so implied; and, as we know, vindicated it severely at last. Elizabethan form. —Elizabeth saw the fatal defect of her father's spiritual claim, declined the title of "Head The "Reformatio Legum" given up. of the Church" worn by her three predecessors, (of which it had been treason to "deprive" her,) and hesitated to proceed as her father had done, by "Royal Commission," to reform the A. D. 1571. Ecclesiastical Constitution. She sought, and yet feared, to supply by Convocation a Spiritual sanction to her religious government; and there she A. D. 1604. paused.—So, too, King James I. had his synod and his canons; and Charles I. had his; but the theory of "the spiritualty" remained still uncertain.— A. D. 1640. And such was the modification of "Supremacy" taken up and revived in 1662, to last in its vigour little more than twenty years.

It was not (as has been intimated) that the Church- Restoration form. men or the politicians of the Restoration proceeded on a defined theory. Necessities of state seem often to oblige measures of which men consider not at first the intellectual or moral ground. But it was resolved at all events that the Religion of the country should be "National;" and, in forgetfulness of the changed conditions of the whole case, men fell back as far as they could on the ideas of the previous Protestant reigns. To the Royal Supremacy and the sanction of Convocation, they added, more stringently, A. D. 1662. the authority of Parliament; and the "Act of Uniformity" was the result. But "canons" never followed.

The short-lived hope that the Nation might henceforth be "of one language and of one speech" in Religion, finally perished in 1688. The "Act of Toleration" formally registered the fact, that henceforth, whatever the "National Church" might mean, it did not imply Religious Unity. The condition of Scotland and Ireland only confirmed the same general conclusion. On what terms the Government and the Church should go on together, remained once more to be seen.

1 William and Mary, c. 1. s. 18.

The Sixth section of the "Toleration Act" preserved the temporalities of the Church from all invasion; and a Tudor subterfuge was thus again introduced, that ecclesiastical property and ecclesiastical duties need not be co-extensive.—In 1717 the action of "the Spiritualty," the Convocation, was suppressed. It was naturally the next step.—Every act of legislation for the ensuing hundred years, which touched on ecclesiastical affairs at all, attenuated the connexion between the Church and the State; till in 1828 it was not deemed necessary even for members of the Church to submit to the "test" of being Communicants. Then came the admission of the Roman Catholics to Parliament; and the legislation of the next thirty years formally abolished all that remained of the coercive Discipline of Courts Ecclesiastical,—(which on Ash-Wednesday is still deplored!) The "National," or quasi-national, position being gradually restricted, the law still sought to dictate in some instances the Doctrine to be believed within the "Establishment;" and in some, actually impinged on the most sacred convictions of all who had accepted the teaching of the Prayer-book as not simply "authorized by statute," but actually *true*.

Revolution form. Uniformity arrested.

The "Spiritualty" as represented in "Convocation," suspended.

9 Geo. IV. c. 17.

Further restriction of the quasi "Nationality."

(The Divorce law.)

Can it be thought surprising, that the design is now at length distinctly avowed, by a considerable party in the State, to bring to a conclusion what seems to it a struggle for no intelligible principle on the side of the Church?—and which is thought to involve the progress of liberty for the people?

Proposal to abrogate "Nationalism."

It is easy, perhaps, to see, as we look back, that when nonconformity was tolerated by the Act of William and Mary, it was the Church's duty, believing in her old position, to have consolidated in every parish some Discipline for her body, as a Spiritual Community. The temptation was great, no doubt, to accept all Englishmen as Churchmen still, unless formally joined to some external congregation. It swelled the Church's numbers for the time, and seemed to give, that which had been her snare before, political strength; but it hopelessly broke down the conscience of her laity to the worldliest level, and conduced to all the secularism which followed; led to the too frequent profanation of the most sacred offices of the Church without enquiry, and at length even without reluctance; and almost to the loss of the idea (in our times) among the multitude, that the "National Church" ever had a CREED higher than human laws could give.

Retrospect.

It is impossible to regret that, at such a crisis as this to which we have now come, attention should be earnestly called to the question, What shall be the future relation between the State and the Church, between Politics and Religion,—must we not say, between Civilization and Christianity? Men who are termed "practical" are in the habit of thinking that they can go on without a theory. Half thinkers perhaps generally do so. They are forgetful, or unaware, that a course of action always implies a principle, avowed or unavowed. The many will sometimes bear with action, while unprepared to admit its real basis. But conscience and act refuse to be for ever separate. Men speak out at length, and say that which their conduct has all along been meaning. What is seen to be an hypocrisy, perishes at last. It is this which the present generation is witnessing, not only in our own country, but in all Europe.

Present crisis.

Some theory inevitable.

And now we seem to be met by two classes of thinkers—those who would abolish, and those who would fundamentally remodel,

"Abolitionism" and Secular Nationalism.

the National profession of Religion. Hitherto it has been roughly assumed by all parties among us, that Religion has chiefly to deal with the future world, and policy with the present, and that their mutual action and relation arise from those mixed questions, both ethical and social, which affect in different ways both the "life which now is and that which is to come." This is no longer a common assumption. There are those who would entirely separate the spiritual and the secular; and others who would identify them, on the pagan principle, that religion, like morals, is, as M. Comte would say, "a phase of humanity."

Abolitionism has no philosophy.

The "Abolitionists" have scarcely at present any philosophy; but they would be content, apparently, that the State should stumble on, with no hypothesis, practically assuming the non-existence of all questions of a future life. They must know, indeed, that these questions will still be smouldering, and often dangerously, in the individual breasts of millions; but they would risk a total ignoring of them by the politicians. They point to the American Republic as a State successfully constituted without a recognised Religion; which is not only a premature boast, but in other respects ill serves their argument. The most recent act, for example, of the American President, Mr. Lincoln, by which he appoints a day of "National Humiliation, Prayer, and Fasting," is a clear invasion of the principles which demand entire separation of religion and politics; and it will be regarded by perhaps a majority of Americans as insulting to their convictions and inconsistent with their political professions.—But, indeed, before we can listen to the Abolitionists at all, as teachers of a Civilization of the future, we have a right to call on them to give some account of the past. Are all the efforts of fifteen centuries to adapt Christianity to the nations of Europe, for instance, to be supposed to tend to nothing? Is there no philosophy of all this history? Does it belong to no law of human progress?—If they maintain this, very few at present will follow them.

Our primary concern is, at all events, with those who would make Religion a branch of Politics, and leave indeterminate all questions of a possible future.

The latter an English form of "Positivism."

The followers of M. Comte in France and America conceive that they have worked out what they term a "Positive Religion," from which they have "eliminated Catholicism;" and they claim adherents in our own country among all those who would in like manner withdraw the Creeds from the religion of Christendom, and criticize the Bible on the same level as all other literature. They speak with confidence of the growth of their principles among the educated classes of our country; in them they discern (can it be said untruly?) a daily increasing disinclination to every dogma, and a reduction of every doctrine once thought sacred to the level of an opinion. Religion (as Christians have thus far received it anywhere) *is* more and more remitted to the region of speculation; and it is regarded as the extreme of uncharitableness to suspect the future safety of any man, on account of his creed. It is obvious, too, to observe that some theories which have sprung up independently among ourselves of late,—such as "Christian Socialism," and what has been termed "Essayism,"—so far harmonize with the "Positivism" of M. Comte as to aim, on principle, to divert attention from the distinctive hope of "salvation" hereafter, and direct it to the primary consideration of the affairs and duties of this world.*

"Christian Socialism" and "Essayism," phases of Positivism.

Abolitionism not the most immediate danger.

It is to this class of theories we have now to address ourselves. Few Churchmen, and indeed few thoughtful politicians, can be supposed as yet to have sympathy with the plans of those who would abolish all National profession of Christianity. Our immediate attention belongs to others, who would still retain a "National Church" in name, but in truth deliberately set aside all its supernatural claims, and gradually abate every portion of our Bible

* Essay, p. 196.

and Prayer-book, according as the level of popular feeling sinks lower and lower.

The proposition is formally laid down and defended among us,—That a "National Church" is as simply, "as properly, an organ of the National life, as a magistracy or a legislative estate!" * Leaving "speculative doctrine" to philosophers, a "National Church" has for its one object, it is said, to "concern itself with the ethical development of its members."† To do any justice to this view, to understand how it arises or takes shape in the mind of one who still retains any hold on the Prayer-book and the Scriptures, it will be necessary to take in at a glance the whole outline of the Essay in which it is developed: we shall then be in a position to compare the "National Religion," so suggested, both with the history and the fundamental ethics of Christianity.

Secularism, or the New Nationalism,—proposed in "the Essays."

For in truth the questions raised are "fundamental," not only as involving the objective certainty of the Christian facts, but the individual recognition of all moral and spiritual truth. If "National Religion" be nothing but the expression of the general life and public opinion of a people, it is very little more than an abstract idea; and the question then arises, whether the rightful freedom of each individual conscience (for which the "free-thinkers" declaim at other times so strongly) be not unjustly interfered with, by the proposed authoritative promulgation of the so-called "religious truth?" From this point of view, those who would abolish all national professions of faith, would seem to be the more consistent reasoners. For the Essayist, it will be seen, encourages freedom of individual thinking, up to a certain point, and then stops. He would have men free to reason themselves into a *denial* of their "traditional Christianity," and then acquiesce in the authoritative promulgation of a "generalized system" reflecting the views of the day.

Fundamental nature of the questions here raised.

Latent irrationality and intolerance of this Secularism.

The term by which these—as they may be called—

* P. 190. † P. 195.

semi-free-thinkers describe the theory they defend is "Multitudinism," a term of foreign origin, about equivalent to "Nationalism." The opposite view (which they reject) is that Religion makes its appeal to each separate conscience; (because men's future condition will not be determined in masses, but in accordance with individual character;) this they call "Individualism." The two views recently came into collision, in a discussion which arose in Switzerland; and the Essay, an outline of which here follows, formally arises out of that discussion.—Persuaded, as every honest mind must be, that to misstate any position when about to oppose it, is an offence against the truth itself, the ensuing Outline will, it is hoped, be such as the Essayist himself will acknowledge to be a true representation of his entire drift and meaning.

This Secularism called also "Nationalism," and abroad known as "Multitudinism."

§ 2. *Outline of the "Essay on Nationalism," or 'Broad Christianity.'*

'In the city of Geneva, a controversy lately arose, —Whether Religion is to be regarded as a National or an Individual concern?—M. Bungener defended the former, or Multitudinist, idea. His position admits of better defence in England perhaps; as our "Nationality" is so strong. The signs of the times, too, among us, warn us that a broader basis of Religion is demanded. Grave doubts have arisen, whether our future Civilization is bound to Christianity at all; and these are the doubts of earnest, sincere, and educated minds, whom our existing religion has shocked. The masses, *de facto*, are recoiling from us and our narrow traditions. This scepticism is the result of thought and knowledge, not pride of reason or culpable hostility. We shall find it impossible to maintain much longer the *necessity* of faith in Christ. If Scripture seems to teach it, either Scripture is wrong, or we interpret it wrongly. Our Revelation has never reached a fourth part of the world we now are acquainted with. We must not any longer say that Christ came just in the fitness and "fulness of time." Was not Budhism a Gospel for India 600 years before Christ?—The solution must be, that men will be judged according to the law and light they have. If we hold this of the heathenism of past ages, so also of that of the future.'—(*Essay*, pp. 145—158.)

'In advocating, then, a broader basis for Christianity, we are encouraged by the fact that its triumphs thus far have been on the "Multitudinist" principle. Primitive Christianity was doctrinally and ethically *broad*. It appears not as a theory of personal salvation, but as a moral and social system; (except in the fourth Gospel.) And the relative value of doctrine and morals in the Apostolic age may be judged by the compatibility even of a denial of the Resurrection with membership of the Christian body. Nor can we suppose that even immorality shut men out from the Christian brotherhood.—The first Churches being thus "Multitudinist," tended too, from their local character, to Nationality. True, dogma came to be more insisted on in the days of Constantine; yet a Multitudinist Church is not *necessarily* either dogmatic or hierarchical; but the reverse.—The ethical view, that the "world lieth in wickedness," is St. John's rather than Christ's.'—(pp. 159—168.)

'Nationalism (or Multitudinism) is, in fact, a necessity of human society. In Heathenism, in Judaism, and Christianity, it is alike found; though the Nationalism of Judea is miscalled a "Theocracy." Christ offered His religion to the Jews nationally; when they rejected it, it appealed (by a kind of temporary necessity) to individuals, and so it "filtered" into society by "conversions." Conversion of nations, *en masse*, was however the natural tendency, though checked by the disruption of the empire and other causes; and by old fetters, such as the assumption of an objective "faith once delivered" to us.'—(pp. 169—174.)

"The actual basis of our own Nationalism may be termed—Scripture, *without defined Inspiration*. In our sixth Article, the Protestant feeling of our nation just satisfies itself, in a blind way, with an anti-Roman view. But extreme Scripturalism cannot be charged on Art. VI., for it leaves us free to interpret most things as we will. An Englishman agreeably fancies that one portable book makes him independent of his priest; but the result is disappointing. The circulation of Scripture, excellent and divine as it is, (though with a human element,) has issued in a puzzle. A National Church, true to Multitudinism, will leave us more and more free to judge the Bible.'—(pp. 175—180.)

'At present the *ex animo* subscription to the Thirty-nine Articles seems a restraint on the clergy; but it is very vague. What the legal restraint amounts to, when all the canons are considered, is hard to imagine. We acknowledge the Articles to be "agreeable to the Word of God;" but not of equal authority with it. There may be certain erroneous statements in the Articles; and if so, we fall back on Scripture. True indeed an old Statute (13 Eliz., cap. 12) requires "assent" to the Articles; but that could not be enforced now. The Articles are flexible, and there is latitude of interpretation,—with many open questions. Not that this state of things ought to last, in a Multitudinist Church. Obsolete tests should be repealed; and it may easily be done by withdrawing the old statute, and the subscription which hampers us. Subscription being abolished, the Articles themselves might remain, (to gratify anti-Roman feeling.) At present it enervates us, to oblige us to prove the Articles "agreeable to Scripture or to antiquity;" or become Dissenters.'—(pp. 181—190.)

'Then as to the Endowment of the "National Church;" it is National Property; and so, in one sense, is *all* property. But a ministry supported by endowments may perfectly reflect the National mind; and be quite suitable to a Multitudinist Church. And the National interest lies in preserving such endowment, as it tends to unite all classes in the community. Each one of us when born into a Nation is born into a Spiritual Society. The Nation has one spiritual life; and its Church is the expression of its social and ethical development. The Gospel would be narrow and one-sided, if it did not quicken Nationality, but only provided isolated "salvation,"—a notion which unfits men for this life. At least there should be no needless obstacles to National Unity, even if it cannot be perfectly secured. Without aiming unreasonably at "comprehension," all barriers should, if possible, be thrown down. Intellectual differences should be allowed for; they are inevitable. All may verbally accept Scripture, in some sense. Ideal methods of interpretation may go far at last to unite all.—The accounts, e. g. of our Descent from Adam, or of the Flood, or the destruction of Sodom, and other catastrophes and marvels, may be "ideologically" viewed. Our Lord's Transfiguration or His "miracles" may be put in a light to satisfy various minds. The "ideologian" is not disturbed by difficulties, or defects in evidence, or by gross notions of Apostolic descent of the ministry, or by the Millennium: Christianity (to his view) is not a theology of the intellect, nor an historical faith; but may be received *generally*. This ideology may be but the philosophy of the few; but it denounces none,—believing that *all will at last be received to the bosom of God*.'—(pp. 191—206.)

All verbiage apart, we have here, at one view, the entire course of the thought of the Essayist, simply disengaged from the incidental and ornamental additions. What the speculation means as a whole, is here faithfully exhibited; and it may be confessed, that there lies before us a real theory corresponding with the facts of our Religious life as a Nation, to a serious extent. If that theory were accepted by us, and further acted out, it must involve (as will be seen) the rejection of the entire Christianity of the Bible, or the Church, ancient or modern. This is the point to be made clear, and not, of course, barely asserted, by those who differ from "the Essayist."

The tone here adopted towards Christianity by the advocate of this "new Nationalism," is certainly not a

The general Challenge given to Christianity.

flattering one. For 1,800 years our Religion has been in the position of an intellectual and moral superior, and could generally make terms, as such, with a decaying or uncouth civilization wherever it came. But the nineteenth century, it is said now, professes to be intellectually and morally in advance of us,—an alienation between the Church of the past, and the times we live in, is even boasted of. True, indeed, society cannot go on without Religion, but the world is at present on most unsatisfactory terms with Christianity everywhere; nor does there appear to be much probability of an early concordat between the "spirit of the age" and the spirit of the Christian Revelation: but the professors of the present forms of Christianity, Roman, Anglican, and Puritan, are all now warned that a broader system than theirs is demanded, to which the *name* of "Christianity" shall yet be given. We are bidden to "set our house in order." Intellectually, of course, we may "hold our own" if we can; politically, we may content ourselves awhile with any position that may be offered by the accidents of the hour. But the *supernatural character* hitherto attributed to the Religion of Christ is not only denied, but declared to be a subsequent development, and no necessary part of the teaching of our Divine Master.

§ 3. *Religious idea of a Broad National Christianity.*

The scheme of Generalized Christianity challenged by us,—

as the Ideal of Multitudinism.

It is supposed, then,—for the question must be put in some tangible form,—That Christianity may be received in a *generalized way*, without men's being bound to acknowledge all the details of any existing part of the Christian body, or all the various books of the Old and New Testament, as true. This, of course, opens every religious question among us, *de novo*; and we are bound to ascertain what this Generalized Christianity,—which is the "idea" of Multitudinism, its ἀρχὴ and τέλος,—really means. For to say, you will accept the Bible, and hold yourself at liberty afterwards to reject it piece-meal, seems simply, to-most persons, unintelligible, if not absurd. We cannot permit the assertors of the rights of *reason* to stultify their subject and their argument, without challenge. We are not asking too much if, in the name of reason, we do our best to ascertain what educated men *mean*, when, with an air of superiority, they profess to believe in Christ, not only apart from the history and tradition of His followers, but apart from the record of His life and teaching in the four Gospels. To this we must first of all address ourselves. Let us have the theory clearly expressed and logically worked out, to some extent, of a GENERALIZED CHRISTIANITY, independent of historical creeds, historical Scriptures, and historical continuity. It is hard to ask us to commit ourselves to such a scheme, without knowing something about it.

Christianity to be reduced to a merely "Documentary Revelation."

The course taken by our eclectic opponents seems to be this. Accepting in a literary way the existing volume of Scripture, as usually admitted, and separating it as a purely *Documentary Revelation*, from "all the work of the Spirit of God, from the day of Pentecost till now," they proceed to examine it part by part, as they would "any other book." * How far, or in what sense, they think any part of Scripture sacred, or even true, they abstain at first from saying. They receive, and even praise it, as a whole.

Popular aspect of this:—the "one meaning of the one Book."

Thus they may secure the hasty suffrages of the ignorant and the toleration of the pious, who fancy that all is simplified if they have *only* to ascertain the one "plain meaning" of one well-known Volume; forgetting that all are not critics. The Protestantism of the age is pleased, too, by such appeal to a purely Documentary Revelation, is soothed by the deference to "private judgment, and hoodwinked by the rejection of "antiquity." The new theorists have been thriving on the delusion. Yet is there not something thoroughly unworthy of men engaged in a great intellectual and moral work, in *ad captandum* appeals *as if* to the

* Essay, p. 377.

"Bible only,"* addressed to the reverent sentiment of the untheological masses, whose whole faith they are about to sweep away?

For the very next step to this *general* reception of the Bible, is to separate the Old Testament from the New; and in the latter, to distinguish the Gospels from the Epistles. Then, the Gospels are reduced to the lowest point by separating the supernatural from the "natural" portions of the narrative; and the words of Christ Himself from the incidents recorded by the Evangelists; and again, His ethics from His doctrine! Not that the process of "criticism" stops here, though by this time the unlearned allies of the critics must take alarm; and before long the whole cause of Scripture investigation even by scholars is discredited.

Insidious progress of this attempt.

This way of proceeding is to be indignantly deprecated by honest thinkers.—The direction of the spiritual course of our time (if the truth is to be owned) has not, with all men's pretensions, been intellectual. The progress of education and taste a few years ago led to the partial revival of old theological learning and ritualism; and it was not a further progress of education that checked it. It was arrested by political and social causes, and, more than all, by panic; instead of being met by any counteracting efforts of a thoughtful kind. There followed indeed a temporary religious re-action of a Puritan spirit,—but with no intellectual life. And now, "Essayism" (if the term be allowable) has not been unwilling to pretend to espouse the Chillingworth doctrine, which ever pleases the crowd; and unworthily has thought to blind the unthinking many with the offer of a "*freely*-handled Bible."

The panic of the allies of Rationalism at the "free-handling" of the Bible.

The alarm which has followed, however, now that the insidious nature of the proposal has been understood, has occasioned a recoil, which was not unnatural. The generality, so painfully appealed to, doubtless lean on Scripture, (for they feel that they must have something:) they

* Essays, p. 426, &c.

cannot themselves examine much of it, and they see not what is to become of them, if they are to be given over to the authority of "critics;" for that seems as great an invasion of the "rights of Englishmen" as the "voice of the Church" had ever been. They thought the Bible had been criticized enough before their time; and that "private judgment" now had only to "interpret" it. To submit to scholars,—might it not at once lead to a narrower and more stringent tyranny than that of ecclesiastics?—and equally interfere with the absolute right and assumed competency of every man of average powers to interpret the vernacular Scriptures as he pleased, for himself?—They did not see, at first, that to reduce Revelation to the rank of mere literature, was to hand it over to the *literati*.

The concessions of the alarmed semi-critics.

Among those who now shrink the most from the critical destruction of Scripture as the substance of our Religion, there are some who are ready to concede its partial mutilation. There is an attempt here and there, of a crude and hasty kind, to make "concessions" to the enemy. Like mariners in a storm, certain religionists have been looking about to see what they can part with, to make their vessel "more safe;" or like besieged men who have to consider how much they had better abandon, before they retire to make desperate resistance, perhaps at the citadel.—The philosophers are not unpleased at the commotion; and the irreligious are beginning to suspect that they may soon get rid of many a terror, which thus far has held their conscience in bondage.

For those who share none of these fears, the course to be pursued with the defenders of this "Generalized Christianity," is (as we shall repeat) to insist on their *producing* it for the examination of all men. Let them tell us, in no misty or evasive sentences, what their "Christianity" *is;* and where they will get it, after they shall have reduced the Religion of Christendom to a "Document," and ascertained the uncertainty, if not the doubtfulness, of every part of it?

To have any anxiety as to the ultimate results of the

The position of Churchmen.

most searching investigation of Scripture would betray, in any case, a feebleness of faith, which the well-taught Christian would but pity. They who know that their "house cannot fall," for it is "founded upon a rock," * must not be supposed to be fearful for themselves because they are willing to help others who are tossing on the waves. All that the most patient and penetrating learning, or the most advanced science, shall ever teach, the truth-loving Christian will welcome. They, on the other hand, who have surrendered the ancient Creeds, (and with them so much of the living grace of the Gospel,) must make the best defence they can of all that remains to them of the "deposit of faith."—It is *their* concern, pre-eminently, to deal with this portentous scheme of a "Generalized Christianity," the residuum that is to remain to them after the latest critical sifting of the text of the Christian Scriptures. The Churchman refuses the postulate, (without which the generalizers cannot proceed one step in their argument;) he denies that the Sacred Record was designed to be cut off, as a mere "document," from the *de facto* Christianity of all ages. The Churchman's defence will not avail the merely literary believer.

Definition of "Generalized Christianity"—the ideal of Multitudinism.

But, accepting for a moment the assumption with which the generalizers of our religion would begin, it is not difficult to see how, step by step, the whole order of the "new creation in Christ Jesus" may be undone, and chaos arrived at. Let us follow for a moment one of the lines of thought which the writer of the "Essay on the National Church" suggests to us, and see what it comes to:—

Example of the Process of Generalizing.

'The Descent of mankind from Adam and Eve,—the destruction of the world by the Flood,—the overthrow of Sodom and Gomorrah,—are all thought objectionable by a growing class of "critics." † But they are only parts (it must be urged) of the *Hebrew* Scrip-

* St. Matt. vii. 25.

† Essay, p. 200, &c.

tures; and on examining them, many great scholars have rejected them as of doubtful credibility! As Christians, are we *bound* to accept as true the entire Scriptures of Judaism? The three points objected to are not *essential* then to Christianity! We find ourselves in the difficulty, no doubt, that Christ and His apostles accepted all these "errors" as truths; or at least the New Testament represents them as so doing. Christ says, that "from the beginning God made them male and female;" * and He refers, in proof, to this "erroneous" Jewish record as Divine. He equally mentions the catastrophe of "the days of Noah," † the destruction of the world by the Deluge, and the overthrow of the cities of the plain; ‡ and this not once, but several times. But may we not conclude that Christ thus deferred to the national prejudices of His countrymen? or perhaps, that His biographers have reported untruly His words on all these subjects?—This obliges us, indeed, at once to give up as much as several important passages of the Evangelists; and to doubt the *authority* of those writers on other points. For if they have not truly reported CHRIST'S words, how can we trust them as to His deeds?—say e. g. the "Transfiguration," mentioned by St. Luke. Is it possible to accept the words of that Evangelist, who tells us § that Moses and Elias came from the invisible world to hold a supernatural conversation with Christ on the Mount, ‖—when we have been compelled to reject, or suspect, what he says about Sodom and Gomorrah?

(Baden Powell's "Christianity without Judaism.")

'It becomes imperative, then, to advance a step further; and ascertain rather *the spirit* of the teaching of Christ, to be learned from the Evangelist; without binding ourselves to any *facts* which seem to a "just criticism" to be improbable. The difficulty, however, of accepting the spirit of a book which we have been obliged to think untrustworthy as to its facts; or of *ascertaining* the spirit of Christ's teaching when we

* St. Matt. xix. 4—8. † Ibid. xix. 38. ‡ St. Luke xvii. 29.
§ St. Luke ix. 30. ‖ Essay, p. 202.

can no longer be certain of one of His words,—is enhanced at every step. The inherent beauty of any passages of the so-called "Discourses of Christ" might well save them from being consigned to neglect; but the Miracles can hardly be admitted now, without better evidence than that of such "biographers." The "supernatural element," too, of His birth, (as well as His Resurrection,) would need other vouchers!'

But enough of this.—A similar course of thought might arise from any of the miserable suspicions thrown out by these "critics," till nothing of the Gospel remained but this:—That a person, or persons, of the name of Jesus, appeared in Judæa 1800 years ago, who greatly influenced many minds at the time; and whose alleged history was recorded some thirty or forty years after the events!—All beyond this being a "human accretion" on the divine teaching which 'produced so remarkable an effect at the time!'

Conclusion against Generalized Christianity, the Ideal of Multitudinism.

Such, then, is GENERALIZED CHRISTIANITY. And let it not be said that the specimen is extravagant, or beyond what any one has dreamed. It is strictly deduced from the principles of "Essayism." Much more might be said without overstepping logical propriety. A Christianity *without certainty of a single fact of the Gospel*, from the Incarnation to the Resurrection of Christ,—that is the shadow of religion to which these eclectics and critics would lead our nation. Or, if all this be denied, and they mislike this plain language, once more, in the name of all reason and fairness, we repeat our challenge, and call on our new teachers to tell us openly, in their own word, what their "Generalized Christianity" is to be? and where we are to find it?

Reserving all charity.

It is not said, or implied for a moment, that the scheme of vague religion here delineated has taken definite form in the minds of all those now living among us, who are teaching its first principles. What we must rather say is, that these writers accost us, not as hard, bold, English reasoners, but as half-German, half-fanatical, credulous, imaginative, illogical; quite capable of going on holding premises and denying conclusions.

Let these halting and feeble-minded thinkers be made to take *any* part of the New Testament, in which there is any reference to the Old, and reason from it.—Suppose the advocate of "Generalized Christianity" to decide on receiving as "genuine" the reported words of Christ in any *one* of the Gospels; he will see our Lord there referring to "all the prophets,"*—Isaiah, Jonah, Daniel, and the rest; and making quotations from the Psalms, or the Pentateuch, mystically, typically, spiritually, hardly ever "literally," or in the way any secular book would be understood. And he will then stand in this dilemma :—Either he must reject those words of Christ which fix His *imprimatur* on the old prophets, and on a special way of interpreting them; or he must accept them, with all their consequences. If the latter, then he is committed to the Old Testament as divine Scripture, "which cannot be broken;"† if the former, he is bound to shew *what rule he has* to determine, Which of Christ's words are to be accepted? And which not? In the one case his Christianity will be no abstraction, it will be special doctrine; in the other, doubtless his view will be a very generalized one; but he must say how he will prevent it from fading down to the thinnest indisputable truisms, which may be gleaned from the fewest sentences, of the least mystical discourse, reported in the briefest Gospel.

Further Examples.

§ 4. *Broad Christianity compared with the Apostolic Age.*

But the generalizers of our religion are not consistent. They cannot, or do not, *reason*. For, after using the language of utter

Another enquiry.

* St. Matt. xv. 7; St. Luke iv. 17; St. John xii. 38; St. Matt. xii. 40, xxiv. 15, iv. 4, 7, 10; St. Luke xxiv. 27, 44.

† St. John x. 35, v. 38, 39.

scepticism, we find them, perhaps in the next page, referring (without hint of "criticism") to the documents of the New Testament as in some sense trustworthy evidence still, for some of the facts of Primitive Christianity, which are incomprehensibly declared to accord with "Multitudinism!" It is urged (as will be seen by the Outline) that their broad and general idea of Christianity may be vindicated, as, after all, more "apostolical" than the exclusive views, prevalent since the first age, as to definite faith in Christ, or as to the idea of "salvation" in a future state. Let this then be examined in the next place,—Whether, from the first, it was the intention of Christianity (as affirmed) to provide a "generalized religion" for the multitude, of an *inclusive* kind? And whether this can be fairly learned from the Christian Scriptures, which are here happily, though inconsistently, called to give evidence, by those who regard them as so very uncertain, if not also frequently false?

Whether, in fact, Primitive Christianity was broad?—or exclusive?

It will not avail to say, in reply to what will be alleged, that the authority of the texts quoted is disallowed; that is not the question. It has been distinctly assumed, that the Christian Scriptures may be appealed to in support of this "Multitudinism," or "New Nationalism," which is recommended to us. We deny this; and it therefore becomes a question of *fact.* For whether the inclusiveness, argued for by these writers,—or the exclusive claims, urged by us for our Religion,—be to be *preferred*, is not the enquiry; but which is in fact borne out by the New Testament? —and there must be no mystification as to this precise issue.

Of course a Christian cannot consent, that the theory of his Religion should be lowered to the level of the facts; but the one will undoubtedly serve at all times to throw light on the other, though the attempt must be made to distinguish them; since it would be unreasonable to suppose, either that the high spiritual aim of Chrisianity was always attained, or that the practical derelictions

The theory, and the facts, of Christianity to be distinguished.

of moral agency should be chargeable on the Gospel as its design.

Its acknowledged aspect towards "the life that now is, and that which is to come." (1 Tim. vi. 6.)

Religion, we affirm, has two aspects,—one towards this world, and one towards the future. It raises and ennobles the present, and that all the more because it points to immortality. None will deny that its action on the present is frequently generic: the many are affected by it, and affected in masses. Hence we speak of Christianity as "influencing civilization" in all its great developments. There is not so much dispute as to this; but rather, as to which is the *primary* object of religion, this world, or the next? for, upon the determination of this, the merits of Multitudinism and Individualism will easily be ascertained by any one. If Roman Christianity—itself often a corrupt form of Multitudinism—have helped to confuse men's thoughts, in some degree, as to this distinction, let it not be thought tedious if it be somewhat enlarged on, since so much depends on it.

Idea of the Christian life, as primarily a "life of Faith."

Hitherto, so universal has been the belief among religous people of all kinds, with the rarest exceptions, that earthly duties, however sacred, are but preliminary to an eternal "life to come," that some (as the Pelagians) even conceive the present to be the means of *meriting* the future reward; and though this is heretical, it is but a dogmatic exaggeration of what Scripture says, and all persons feel, that we shall hereafter be "judged according to our works." * While faith sees, and lives for, "the Invisible," (as witnessed by all the men of faith since the world began,) the "fruits of faith," being good works, have been acknowledged by all to have their temporary use and salutary action in this world. But Christianity distinctively proposes a "life of Faith;" while Multitudinism *declines* the consideration of the future.† Whether, indeed, even for this life, "individualism" be not more ethically true, shall also be considered; but at present the question of fact is to be looked to,

* Heb. xi. 27.

† Essay, pp. 159–161.

—whether primitive Christianity, as learned from its only records, was "multitudinistic," and broad, and directed to the present? or whether it was "exclusive," and sought access to the individual conscience of the few, (indirectly approaching the many,) and chiefly contemplated the eternal world?

Alleged Scripture grounds of Multitudinism.

The Ten following grounds have been suggested for the position, that "Multitudinism" has the support of the New Testament.

1st Ground. Essay, p. 159.

1st. That "though the consequences of what the Gospel does will be carried out into other worlds, its work is to be done here."

The reply to this it is needless to repeat, as it is contained in what has been just said as to the primary and secondary objects of Religion.

2d Ground. Essay, p. 160.

2d Ground. That "neither in doctrine nor in morals did the primitive Christian communities (if judged by the Apostolic Epistles) approach the idea formed of them;" but are much more like communities of general professors of Christianity, than societies requiring individual strictness.

The reply is a plain one. The same Epistles which inform us of the moral failures of the primitive Churches warn and rebuke *individuals;* and in no case complain of their moral state as a result of organic defect, or of corporate false action. Special duties of Christians, man by man, woman by woman, child by child, form the subject-matter of apostolic exhortation. A generic remedy, singularly enough, is not perhaps *glanced* at as much as once by St. Paul (as it might have been) in his thirteen Epistles. He had "not so learned Christ;" but his preaching, he says, was "warning *every man* and teaching *every man* . . . . that we may present *every man* perfect in Christ." *

3d Ground. Essay, p. 160.

3d Ground. "That the doctrinal features of the early Church are more undetermined (and inclusive of many opinions) than would be thought by those who read them only through ecclesiastical Creeds."

* Coloss. i. 28.

But here the reply naturally is, that the Multitudinist is bound to shew, if he would establish his conclusion, that there were *no* essential "doctrinal features" at all.—Perhaps indeed the earliest profession of faith may have been little more than "*believe* on the Lord Jesus Christ and thou shalt be *saved*;" but such a profession, in the simplest imaginable form, still required *individual* reception, and supposed the need of "salvation;" and the very form of Baptism (taking every person singly) was *individualistic;* nor could sacramental administration well be otherwise. Baptism, the foundation of every Church, early or late, carries with it the doctrine of "the Father, the Son, and the Holy Ghost," from the beginning. Men, e. g., who "had not heard whether there were any Holy Ghost," * and had been baptized only by John the Baptist; and one who was already an "eloquent" expounder of Scripture, had to receive, somewhat later, more perfect baptism, or (as the case might be) more exact instruction in the Christian dogma.†

4th Ground. "That the doctrine taught by the Lutherans of justification by *subjective faith* was never the doctrine of any considerable portion of the Church till the time of the Reformation. It is not met with in . . . . . the apostolic writings, *except those of St. Paul.*"

4th Ground. Essay, pp. 159, 160.

Reply:—Whether the "Lutheran" expression of the doctrine of "justification by faith" be Scriptural, is not our concern; but Whether faith as a subjective grace in the soul,—whether faith as *dwelling in a man*, (and not simply as the general opinion of a "multitude,")—be truly exhibited to us in Scripture? For, as to making the writings of St. Paul "exceptions," when examining what the New Testament evidence is, it appears most unreasonable and tortuous; unless it be at once avowed that St. Paul's Epistles (constituting nearly half the New Testament) are 'untrustworthy.' It is forgotten, (when this doubt is thrown in about St. Paul's inspiration,) that the point under examination is,

* Acts xix. 2. † Acts xviii. 26.

whether his record of a "fact" is to be admitted? For undoubtedly, *he says*, that faith was an indwelling and individual gift, in the opinion of Christians then. In proof, the examples of Timothy, his mother, and his grandmother, may be taken: the Apostle thanking God "for the unfeigned faith that was in him, which *dwelt first* in his grandmother Lois, and his mother Eunice." * —But we are not obliged to refer to the Epistles of St. Paul only. Our Lord Himself, in the Gospels, (if we are to credit *them*,) assigns mercy to individuals "according to the faith that was in them;" † and His apostles, in the Acts, imitating their Master, blessed the cripple at Lystra, "perceiving that *he had faith* to be healed." ‡ And the expressions, "*purifying the heart* by faith," "*sanctified* by faith," § and others which we meet with, describe an effective work of individual elevation and conversion. St. Peter and St. James speak of the "trial of faith" in the soul; the former as "precious and praiseworthy in the day of the Lord," ‖ the latter as "working patience." ¶ And St. James in almost all instances refers to faith as *indwelling in the individual*, even when warning Christians against attributing to it a false value. St. Peter classes "faith with *hope*," ** as indwelling graces directed towards *God* as their outward object, as subjectively as St. Paul had done; and he, too, speaks of "salvation of souls" as the end of that inward "believing." And, finally, St. John in the Apocalypse makes no difference between "faith," "charity," and "patience," †† so far as their indwelling character is concerned. The word "faith" is used sixteen times by St. James, and five times by St. John; but in only one instance does St. James, and only twice St. John, use "faith" to describe the Religion of Christ as a system; and in every other to exhibit its internal character as a Grace in the believer's soul.

* 2 Tim. i. 5.
† St. Matt. ix. 22, xv. 28; St. Mark x. 52; St. Luke xvii. 19.
‡ Acts xiv. 9. § Acts iii. 16, vi. 5–7, xi. 24, xv. 9, xxvi. 18.
‖ 1 St. Pet. i. 7. ¶ St. James i. 3. ** 1 St. Pet. i. 9, 21.
†† Rev. ii. 19; xiii. 10.

5th Ground. 'That the doctrine of the Nicene and Athanasian Creed is less definitely, or in other words more broadly, stated in Scripture than in the symbols of the later Church.'

5th Ground. Essay, p. 160.

This has been answered, by anticipation, in what has been said in reply to the "Third Ground."

6th Ground. 'That the Gospels of St. Matthew, St. Mark, and St. Luke, afford evidence to Christ's own words; and these words, taken in conneyion with the Epistle of St. James and the 1st of St. Peter, leave no doubt that the general character of Christianity was chiefly *moral*.'

6th Ground. Essay, pp. 161-2.

Reply:—Supposing this were admitted, it would not lead to the conclusion desired by the advocate of "Multitudinism." For morality is only sound when it has its hold on *individual* conviction. A general conformity to the public opinion, in matters of duty, may often lead to good average results; but we could not praise the morality of any man who had no conscience as to the *rectitude* of the rules to which he socially conformed. And indeed the whole of the attempted reasoning connected with this subject in the place referred to,* is rather *opposed* to "Multitudinism;" inasmuch as it represents Christ's moral design to be, to "penetrate to the root of Conscience,"—which of course, is to address the individual, rather than the corporate life of man.

7th Ground. Three facts are referred to as implying Multitudinism. First, our Lord's lament over Jerusalem for their national rejection of Him, which proved "that He had offered it to them nationally, in a broad and general way." Secondly, the conversion of 3,000 on the day of Pentecost; for, "that they cannot be supposed to have been individual converts; but only a mass of persons brought in as a body;" and, thirdly, the alleged existence "among the Christian converts in the early

7th Ground. Essay, pp. 146, 153, 171.

* Essay, p. 162.

Church of those, for example, who had no belief in a corporeal "resurrection;'* and therefore, 'that even a denial of doctrine, such as the Resurrection of the body, ought to be permitted in a Broad National Church intended for all.'

Reply:—The first alleged fact is contrary to all that we read in the Gospels. For it does not appear that our Lord, on any one occasion, laid His claims before the authorities, for an official investigation; but in every instance called out individuals, and appealed to consciences.—The second supposition is even more distinctly contrary to the record, in which the "pricking of the heart," "repentance," and "baptism" are attributed to *every one;* and it is added, that "fear came upon EVERY *soul.*"† The whole narrative is as strongly *individualistic*, as if written for our argument.—The third supposition‡ is founded on St. Paul's remonstrance in the Epistle to the Corinthians, "How say *some* among you that there is no resurrection of the dead?" Why (it is asked) did not St. Paul§ excommunicate such Sadducees if he thought their opinion ought to exclude them? Now let the same argument be urged a verse or two further on, in the same chapter, and it might plausibly enlarge the boundaries of this "broad Christianity" to include even those who had *no true* "*knowledge of God*" at all; for, among these Corinthians it is said, that there were even "some who had not the knowledge of God,"‖ and the Apostle adds, "I speak this to your shame." Let our "Multitudinist," who uses this surely preposterous argument, decide whether open idolaters, sceptics, or atheists, are to be admissible, with "Sadducees," to his comprehensive Church? Of the one class as much as of the other the Apostle said there were τινὲς, "some," among the Corinthians. To those who are not Multitudinists it will seem plain enough that there would, in that unformed and unfixed condition of things at Corinth, be many half-persuaded, many ignorant, many only preparing

* Essay, pp. 146, 163. † Acts ii. 37, 38, 43. ‡ Essay, p. 164. § 1 Cor. xv. 12. ‖ Ibid., ver. 34.

for baptism; and there is no reason whatever to think that these rebuked Sadducees, and unbelievers in God, had been yet baptized. So far indeed from a denial of God or of the Resurrection being compatible with membership of the primitive Church, the Apostle shews how "Jesus and the Resurrection" *must* stand together, when he declares that the whole structure of Christianity must fall if the Resurrection be denied;* and that for "some to be without the knowledge of God"† was utterly "shameful" to a Christian community.‡

8th Ground. 'That the relative value of doctrine and morals in the primitive Church may be judged by the preference given in the Apostolic Epistles to the latter beyond the former; and that latitude as to doctrine may be fairly inferred from this.'

8th Ground.
Essay, p. 162.

Reply:—We are not left to mere inference in estimating the vital importance of sound doctrine as well as morals. St. Paul says, "A man that is an heretic after the first and second admonition *reject.*" § He left Timothy in Ephesus, to "charge some to teach no other *doctrine;*" and to urge "charity, out of a pure heart, a good conscience, and *faith unfeigned:*" ‖ he warns him to "take heed to himself and *to the doctrine,*"¶ *διδασκαλία,* and that "the time would come when men would not endure *sound doctrine.*" St. John uses our Lord's own word, *διδαχή,* and describes apostasy as a not "abiding in the *doctrine* of Christ," ** and forbids Christians to receive those who do not "come with this *doctrine;*"—(and the special doctrine there alluded to is the Divine Sonship of our Lord.) In fact, two-thirds at least, if not four-fifths, of the Apostolic Epistles are Doctrinal; and if their evidence is to be taken, it seems scarcely possible to have a point more conclusively settled against the Comprehensionists and Anti-doctrinists.

* 1 Cor. xv. 17, 18.
† 1 Cor. xv. 34.
‡ Acts xvii. 18, 32.
§ Titus iii. 10.
‖ 1 Tim. i. 3, 5: *μὴ ἑτεροδιδασκαλεῖν.*
¶ 1 Tim. iv. 16.
** St. John ii. 9, 10.

But the preference given to morals above dogma in this argument proves to be but short-lived; and it is soon seen that, in arguing his case, it was not that the Multitudinist loved Morals more, but Doctrine less. Observe the

9th Ground. Essay, p. 165.

9th Ground. "That if any called a brother were a notoriously immoral person, the rest were to be enjoined, 'no, not to eat with him,' but he was not to be refused the name of a brother or Christian."

Reply:—The injunction "not to eat" with a gross ill-liver applies also to *religious* eating, at "Communion:" the participation in a common meal cannot be supposed to be the whole of the Apostle's meaning, since he forbids all "keeping company" with such an immoral person. And if this be so, excommunication (in the Scripture sense *) is implied in this very passage. Even if, indeed, it were granted that the Christian Church was at first unable to exclude profligate members, that would not shew the desirableness of now reverting to such a state of things, and deliberately, as a theory, adopting its "comprehensiveness." But the very instance referred to evidences beyond a doubt the individualistic aim of the Church, and indeed the personal inspection of every member.

10th Ground. Essay, p. 165.

10th Ground. "That the Apostolic Churches took collective names from the *localities* where they were situate," and so 'tended from the first to be Multitudinistic.' And thus 'Nationalism' is to be regarded, not merely as a providential fact in the history of our religion, and so dealt with; but as the theory of Christianity from the first.

Reply:—It is difficult to conceive of anything more natural, or inevitable, than the designation of any institute from the name of the place where it is fixed. Until it can be gravely shewn that to call any other institution by the name of the place where it stands is a proof that it comprehends the whole neighbourhood in its plan,

* 1 Cor. v. 11, &c.; 2 Thess. iii. 14, compared with Acts x. 28, [συναναμίγνυμι and κολλάω;] 1 Cor. vi. 16, 17.

we shall not be able to see any argument in this *hypothesis*—(for it is nothing more)—as to the tendency of the Apostolic Churches to Multitudinism, shewn by their names. To argue a theory of our Religion from this, is somewhat weak.

The entire "Scripture evidence" alleged in behalf of the supposition, that this new "Nationalism" was the original intention or tendency of Christianity, has now been reviewed; and it is difficult to repress astonishment at the state of mind which could explore the New Testament, and then produce these "proofs" that it meant to teach a Religion with no exclusive Doctrines or exclusive Morals!

We proceed to a different thesis.

§ 5. *The Exclusiveness of Primitive Christianity Examined.*

The Scripture evidence for Individualism next to be heard.

If we produce the unambiguous testimony of our Divine Master, Christ Himself, and of His chosen Apostles, as to the *fact*, that in Christianity we are appealed to, singly, conscience by conscience, let those who are not ashamed to be "Christians" take heed how they turn from it. If the New Testament witness to "Individualism" (as it is termed) make it appear indeed what men call "narrow and exclusive," be it remembered that we are not now examining the philosophy of our religion, nor its ethical vindication. That may be done elsewhere. Neither will the criticism of a few phrases help the objector. It is to the matter of fact we are pointing, (whether it be pleasing or not,)—the broad fact which is patent to every eye, that Christianity, according to the Scriptures, *has a Doctrine*,—has a strict *Moral* system,—asks to *include none* who will not rise towards its standard of truth and purity, anticipates frequently *narrow results*, aims always at the *individual* conscience, and points, primarily, to an "*eternal life*" beyond the grave.

I. Our Saviour Christ's own warnings.

And first let us hear the words of Him who is "the Truth."

"What is a man profited, if he shall gain the whole world, and lose his own soul? or what shall a man give in exchange for his soul?" *

"It is profitable for thee that one of thy members perish, and not that thy whole body be cast into hell." And "Fear Him who is able to cast both body and soul into hell." †

"Labour not for the meat which perisheth, but for that meat which endureth unto everlasting life." ‡

"Lay up for yourselves treasures in heaven, where neither moth nor rust doth corrupt, and where thieves do not break through nor steal: for where your treasure is, there will your heart be also." §

"Provide yourselves bags which wax not old, a treasure in the heavens that faileth not." ‖

"When the fruit is brought forth, He putteth in the sickle, because the harvest is come." ¶

"The harvest is the end of the world; and the reapers are the angels." **

"Strait is the gate, and narrow is the way, which leadeth unto life, and few there be that find it." ††

"If ye believe not that I am He, ye shall die in your sins: . . . . and whither I go ye cannot come." ‡‡

No ingenuity can possibly extract from such words a theory of "Multitudinism;" a Religion *for this world in preference to the next;* a broad and "comprehensive" scheme lowered to the feelings of the crowd, the "*many*, whose love shall wax cold" §§ in the latter days.—It is not to the point to say here, "if Scripture teaches exclusiveness, Scripture is wrong." ‖‖ We are only examining the question of *fact*, What does Scripture teach? Is it a "little flock," ¶¶ or a great flock, to whom "the kingdom will be given?"

* St. Matt. xvi. 26; St. Mark viii. 36.
† St. Matt. v. 29, 30, and St. Luke xii. 5.
‡ St John vi. 27. § St. Matt. vi. 20, 21. ‖ St. Luke xii. 33.
¶ St. Mark iv. 29. ** St. Matt. xiii. 39. †† Ibid., vii. 14.
‡‡ St. John viii. 24 and 21. §§ St. Matt. xxiv. 12.
‖‖ Essay, p. 154. ¶¶ St. Luke xii. 32.

One more sentence from Christ Himself shall conclude His warning witness to us all. The question was formally raised for His decision :—

"Lord, are there few that be saved? And He said unto them, Strive to enter in at the strait gate: for many, I say unto you, will seek to enter in, and shall not be able. When once the master of the house hath risen up, and hath shut to the door." *

II. The witness of Apostles, and others.

If we pass on to the witness of those who came afterwards and enquire how they understood the Lord's apparently unworldly and exclusive teaching, we now cannot be surprised to read thus :—

St. Peter. "Lord, to whom shall we go? *Thou* hast the words of eternal life. And we believe and are sure that Thou art that Christ, the Son of the living God." †

St. John and St. Peter. "Neither is there salvation in any other: for there is *none other* Name under heaven given among men, whereby we must be saved." ‡

St. Paul. "I am not ashamed of the Gospel of Christ: for it is the power of God unto *salvation to every one* that believeth." §

The Apostle to the Hebrews. "Without holiness *no man* shall see the Lord." ‖

St. Jude. "Contend earnestly for the *faith once delivered* to the saints." ¶

St. Philip the Deacon. "If thou believest *with all thy heart*, thou mayest be baptized. And he said, I believe that Jesus Christ is the Son of God." **

The Angel at Joppa. "Call for Simon, who shall tell thee words whereby thou and all thy house shall *be saved.*" ††

If the idea of 'exclusive salvation for those who believe and obey the Gospel' be not here placed before

* St. Luke xiii. 23, &c. † St. John vi. 68, 69. ‡ Acts iv. 12.
§ Rom. i. 16. ‖ Heb. xii. 14. ¶ St. Jude, 3, 4, &c., 17, &c.
** Acts viii. 37. †† Acts xi. 14.

the individual conscience, it seems impossible to say in what form it could have been naturally expressed at all.

Nor is it any "abstract Christianity" which is thus put forward. The greatest of the writers of the New Testament leaves on record this authoritative sentence, twice uttered, and conclusive against all other versions of our Religion than the original message:—"Though we, or an angel from heaven, preach *any other* Gospel unto you than that which we have preached unto you, let him be accursed! As we said before, so say I now again, If any man preach any other Gospel unto you than that ye have received, *let him be accursed!*" *

It is not as though "eliminating" two or three obstinate texts would relieve the case. The facts which lie on the surface, or those most deeply imbedded in the structure of the whole record of our Religion, equally attest the sense which primitive believers had of the everlasting importance of a right faith in "Him whom not having seen they loved," † and for whom they would "suffer the loss of all things," and "count them as dross," if they might but "win Christ, and be found in Him" ‡ at last.

III. The testimony of Apostolic Deeds.

And see how urgent they became, therefore, "hearkening to God's voice." §—In "adding to the Church" ‖ the newly baptized, it was for "*salvation.*" Whether to the alarmed jailor of Philippi, or to the quiet Church settled at Rome, or to the scattered Jews who had believed, the message was the same, "Believe on the Lord Jesus, and thou shalt be *saved.*" "We shall be *saved from wrath through* Him." ¶ "We are not of them who draw back unto perdition: but of them that believe to the *saving of the soul.*" **—Let men risk their puny view that all this was bigotry if they will; but was it not a characteristic of original Christianity, such as no impartial reader (believer or not) can dispute?—If not,

* Gal. i. 8, 9. † 1 St. Pet. i. 8. ‡ Philipp. iii. 8.
§ Acts iv. 19. 20. ‖ Ibid., ii. 47. ¶ Acts xvi. 30, 31; Rom. v. 9.
** Heb. x. 39.

then the heathen who complained of the heat and zeal of Paul and Barnabas* were right. Unless Christianity were essential to each soul to whom it came, why should the sincere adherents of old religions have been so roughly and needlessly disturbed? Why should even Jews be told, that in rejecting Christ they were "counting themselves unworthy of everlasting life?" † Why should "father be set against son and son against father, mother against daughter and daughter against mother, mother-in-law against daughter-in-law and daughter-in-law against mother-in-law?"‡—Why see we that life-long eagerness to "spend and be spent" § for souls;—to move about among *willing* moral agents, and pass the rest;—to listen to a vision, if it beckoned to Macedonia as a field of success;—or to hasten to bear the "good tidings," when informed of "much people" in a certain city willing to hear it;—or to be reluctantly turned away from another 'unwilling' region as hopeless, being "forbidden of the Holy Ghost?" ‖ —If in foregoing all that the world holds dear, encountering all perils and hardships, and facing a daily martyrdom,¶ those first missionaries were under the belief that the issues of Eternity were at stake, and trusted that by their toil they might "by any means save some," **—bring even "one of a city, or two of a family," †† to "Him whom to know was life eternal," ‡‡—*then* their conduct was reasonable, their self-devotion most noble. But if they only meant that they desired for Him whom they preached one niche in the Pantheon of the nations; if they "turned the world upside down" §§ in order that the Gospel might be accepted *as one Religion among many*, it is impossible not to deplore what must then be considered the cruel and terrifying language of their addresses,—in a word, impossible perhaps to overrate the actual mischievousness of such unmeasured enthusiasm.

* Acts xiv. 5; xix. 28. † Ibid., xiii. 46. ‡ St. Matt. x. 35–37.
§ 2 Cor. xii. 15. ‖ Acts xvi. 9, xviii. 10, xvi. 6.
¶ Acts xv. 26; 2 Cor. vi. 4–10, xi. 23–28.
** Rom. xi. 14; 1 Cor. ix. 22; 1 Tim. iv. 16; Jude, 23.
†† Jer. iii. 14. ‡‡ St. John xvii. 3. §§ Acts xvii. 6.

It may be concluded, then, unless a common-sense view of the whole subject is to be refused, that enough has now been adduced to justify the conviction that Apostolic Christianity, as learned from the New Testament, required Individual Conscientiousness, Individual Faith.

In whatever form this "exclusive Christianity" be objected to hereafter, let us not in the face of all facts be told, that *Scripture* does not teach this "necessity of faith in Christ;" or that the Primitive Churches *designed* to include nominal professors of the Gospel, and did not primarily contemplate the salvation of individual souls.—We now pass on.

IV. The testimony of the Apostolical Canons;

No question appears to have gravely been raised, as to the "exclusiveness" of every form of Christianity in the next age after the apostles. Of some dim Gnostic semi-heathenism it were vain to speak; and it may be supposed that the system of the "Apostolical Canons" (as, for brevity, it may be termed) was too indisputable, to invite criticism of a fact perhaps more indisputable than any other in the Christianity of the second and third centuries,—its rigid demarcation, alike from Judaism and from the world.* The Creeds, the Ritual, the Discipline of the whole Christian body of those ages, may be deprecated by enemies, or repudiated by false friends; but their "growing exclusiveness" is a fact of which even our critics will remind us: and while we accept their testimony, we will add that no one in those days seems to have questioned that such exclusiveness was a true "following of the apostles," up to the days of Constantine;—of which hereafter.

and the First Three Centuries.

Perhaps no greater service could be done at this time to the cause of practical Christianity, than to gather together all the incidental records,† and to exhibit the actual relation of the Church and the world

* St. Justin M., Dial. with Trypho.

† See Gibbon, and his authorities, ch. xv., xvi., xvii.

in detail, in the times between St. John and St. Athanasius. It would need a more minute knowledge of the social and domestic life in the great cities and villages of the Roman world than is often found among scholars, (even such as Albert de Broglie, "Pressensé," or Neander,) to convey the true magnitude of the Church's spiritual and separating influences on her individual members. But it needs to be done: for under God's Providence, and led by His promised Spirit, by no mere accident did it come to pass that the Church had to work out the Divine plan at first, unaided by the powers of the world.—Our generation certainly needs to see, *how* Christ's Church aimed to found the "city of the living God;" * to raise the "building fitly framed together to grow to an holy temple in the Lord;" † and anticipate "the kingdom that cannot be moved." ‡

§ 6. *Ethical Basis of Broad Christianity.*

Ethical view "of Multitudinism."

The assertion now disproved,—That Christianity expressed itself at first in "Multitudinism,"—was intended apparently to lead to the position, that what the Multitude shall in future be pleased to hold, shall be the "Christianity" of the age to come. It appears to have been conceived that the course of the Gospel, and the course of the human mind, had hitherto diverged. Revelation, and the general Conscience of mankind, had thus far moved in distinct orbits; but they had at length arrived at the point where they would coincide, and might (by some happy neutralizing of the original forces) continue to take one and the same direction in future. This dream, it may be hoped, is somewhat dissipated: but let us glance at the theory of this "general Conscience"—(this "public opinion," or opinion of the majority, which was to be the Rule of Religion, the "Gospel" of the future, §)—before we wholly lose sight of it.

We have seen that a "Generalized *Christianity*" is

* Heb. xii. 22. † Ephes. ii. 21. ‡ Heb. xii. 28.
§ Essay, p. 195.

impossible, if we accept the New Testament at all. A Religion without a Doctrine, or "dogma," must be so transcendental as to lie beyond even the region of metaphysics. Dogma, we find, insists on definition; and "vague thinking" is a misnomer, commonly betraying only incapacity. But the idea of a "generalization of *Conscience*" or abstract "ethical development," is still to be considered.

Vague Thinking and vague Feeling contrasted.

No one will question, that in matters of feeling and sentiment there actually is an *average* standard, in any civilized community. It rises and falls, with many circumstances; but it is specially elevated by the elevation of individual hearts and aims; and a single hero will sometimes raise the standard of the age, as a single saint has often thrilled the hearts of millions in the Church. Such an admission, therefore, of "average conscientiousness" will not assist "Multitudinism" inasmuch as it depends for its very existence on the action, inward and outward, of each man for himself.

Even "Heathen Nationalism" must have been somewhat based on "conscience,"

It has been said that Nationalism, based thus upon the general sentiments of an age or country, has existed even in Heathenism;* and this will not be denied; yet even so, in every instance, it has had some individual origin, and lives on by the inward life of individual souls, far more than by any formal enactments or corporate acts. But, without pausing upon this,—(for we have here no concern in constructing a moral defence for the old religions of the world before or apart from Christ,)—it has been recognised among Christians, and we depend on it as one glorious distinction of our Revelation, that we have been taught in a special way the grandeur of Individual Responsibility. The absence of this, the Christian feels, is the fatal defect of every philosophical scheme of polity—from Plato,† down to Hobbes. The value of each immortal soul of man, suspected before, is the open announce-

* Essay, p. 169.

† In the "Republic"—where the Individual is utterly crushed.

ment of the Gospel; * and it will be seen that the theory of a "Multitudinism" crushing all men into one general mould of thought, is prepared to undo, as far as in it lies, that elevating work which the Religion of Christ would accomplish for each of us.

In thus urging, we do not attribute to the "Multitudinist" a conscious denial of Individual Responsibility, but the maintenance of a position which virtually destroys it. He subordinates the sense of right to the existing average of propriety, when he limits the sphere of Conscientiousness, practically, to this world.

The real issue before the enquirer.

At the risk of seeming to elaborate—what many will of course admit at once—the priority of the claims of CONSCIENCE, it will be necessary to explain with care what is so fundamental. Let men see what the "Broad Christianity" to which they are invited implies *morally*. Intellectually, it would aim destruction at *all* Creeds and Doctrines,—reckless of the fact that to deny Christianity as a "theology of the intellect" † is to banish it from the realm of truth. It would also, as we have seen, reject its "Historical character," ‡ and so consign it, after due "criticism," to the region of fable. But there was a step further in disparagement which it seemed possible to take; and the "Broad Religionists" are, we find, prepared for it. They would remove our Christianity from its lofty Moral eminence also. The Soul, and its future, they set aside: and reversing the injunction alike of Moses and St. Paul, bid men "follow the multitude," § and "conform to this world, and *not* be transformed for another." ‖

Irrelevant questions to be here omitted.

It is easy, no doubt, to hamper any investigation of the rights of Individual Conscience, with collateral considerations. It might be urged, and truly, that Society is bound to protect itself against the aberrations of some, and the moral obliquity of others. Again, it may be said,

* St. Matt. vi. 26. † Essay, p. 205. ‡ Ibid.
§ Exod. xxiii. 2. ‖ Rom. xii. 2.

the equity and benevolence of the Divine government may be believed to provide some alleviation of the heavy weight of Individual Responsibility, in the widely varying circumstances of mankind; and that this alleviation may be found in the just influences of a well-ordered Society. This, and much more, may be admitted, beyond question; but must not interfere with what is now before us.

For there still remains, all the more firmly established by these very considerations, what may be termed the substratum of *Will* to be dealt with, in every man. Take away the solemn enquiries, or sublime anxieties, of each Individual, and Morality as well as Religion must cease to have real meaning; there must remain, even confessedly, no more than a *nominal* adherence to that which can only by courtesy be called "Faith,"—an acquiescence so morally base, as to amount to a repudiation of the first conditions of all possible Duty.

Christianity objectively true, and as such demanding individual recognition.

No thoughtful believer could doubt that Christianity really stands in all its parts on a true foundation of philosophy; however imperfectly that may have been ascertained by us. The proof, indeed, that it makes its appeal to our Moral nature is accessible to every man who will but examine his own Moral Responsibility, as man, in any transaction of his life. There is no sentence of praise or blame, social or religious, pronounced by us on the conduct of others, or by them on us, which does not imply such Responsibility as results from Self-government; which is commonly known as "Moral."—The error which lies at the root of "Multitudinism" will be found to be a misconception of the whole character of Moral Responsibility in man, and a confusion of that idea with a very different one, viz. his Political, or his Social, Responsibility, as member of a Community.—Let this be examined.

Of Man as a self-governing being.

Man is so far intended by nature to be a "Self-governing" being, that his highest Moral perfection lies in his most perfect Self-control. If all men usually attained this, the functions of external government would be limited to a guarding of the (still possible) errors of individuals; and the progress of political knowledge is teaching men, more and more, the wisdom of non-intervention with personal liberty of will and action; so that it has become almost a kind of axiom in politics, that that is the best government for men which is able to interfere the least with each individual, and simply restrains the wrongful interference of one man with another. All external governments are no doubt inherently imperfect, (except that of the Divine Being,) when thus considered as *restraints* on Individual will and Power, in the manifestation of which Moral Agency consists. How deep a Moral confusion, then, must enter into the speculation of theorists who transfer the great Moral work of human life, formally, from the Individual to the Government! And this is what these "New Nationalists" would do.

Of man's Political Responsibility,—regulated by mutable law.

Let it not be hastily imagined that any doubt is here to be thrown on men's *real* Responsibility to the State; or to any Community in which their sphere of moral agency lies. But the ideas must be distinguished. Our Responsibility as *men* is prior to our Responsibility as citizens; and it is founded in our very constitution. MAN is not only capable of originating action, but he is so constituted as to know that he *ought* to originate it, in accordance with some anterior and unchangeable principles of truth and righteousness. But his Responsibility as a *citizen* is at present regulated by ever-mutable law.

What distinguishes Moral Responsibility.

It is a distinction of all Law, that it carries consequences to the law-breaker; and that is what may be termed "Political Responsibility." But there is this further distinction of *Moral* law,—that our inward Consciousness more or less accompanies the principle, and its results. We have a knowledge, in the case of other laws, that they are vindicated by such and such sanctions, and will be attended by certain consequences; but in the case of Moral laws, we have a further conviction that thus it *ought* to be.

Illustrations:

A man, for instance, is truly enough said to be "obliged" by the laws of the country or society to which he belongs. He is in such wise "responsible" to the laws, that if he violates them he incurs punishment. This kind of responsibility has nothing certainly Moral in it. The law may be good, or it may be bad; yet this responsibility of the person is real, while the law remains: i. e. if he violates the law, he abides the penalty. This Political Responsibility no doubt ought to be Moral also,—(because States ought to conform their laws to the essential rules of right);—but Responsibility to the State is a distinct idea from Moral Responsibility, even when the one happens to coincide with the other.

1. Political.

Again; Communities within a State, (and more limited in their nature in every respect,) may have customs, habits, and rules, which infer more or less of obligation on the members. The individual perhaps may withdraw, if his Conscience disapprove; but while his membership continues, he has a Social Responsibility; which may be described, however, as a mere "liability to consequences."

2. Social.

What is thus said of Political and Social laws may, in some sense, be also affirmed of the Physical. A "law of Nature" cannot be broken with impunity. If we violate it, we incur the penalty. We are Responsible. Yet in this case also the consequence follows absolutely, whether our inward Consciousness accompanies it or not.

3. Physical.

But the idea of a true *Moral* Responsibility is far more than this; it is no less, indeed, than Chalmers vindicates as a "*Supremacy* of Conscience."[2] It implies, not only that we are, but, *ought to be*,—accountable for our own doings. For, we can well conceive that one who had come under the extremest

4. Moral.

(Chalmers' Bridgewater Treatise.)

censures of some *de facto* political or social law; or had become the victim of some difficult or imperfectly known physical law; might be regarded with the deepest sympathy and compassion. The martyr for liberty wins our approbation, though he perish beneath some legal tyranny. The philanthropist, who unsuccessfully withstands some evil social custom, obtains eventually the applause of the human Conscience. The votary of knowledge, whose struggle for science has involved him in accidental suffering, has the good-will of his fellow-men to attend him in his disaster. But, on the other hand, let us be told of a man who has done a deed of injustice and cruelty, yet (miscarrying in his object) has been overtaken by apparent *Retribution;* there is no sentiment of approbation for him. We do not feel that his disaster ought *not* to be; but just the reverse,—that it *ought.* Our Conscience records its approval.

There may be a thousand theoretical difficulties in connexion with this high truth; but there is a divinity in it that will surmount them all.

But the subject must not further be pursued here, though most important and attractive. A distinction should, however, be pointed out between the idea of the Responsibility, and that of the Probation, of moral agents; and it is by considering moral agency in its *Social* position that we shall best ascertain the distinction between the two.—The formation of the character of the Individual through the action of his own will, amidst the habits and influence of Society, is not an "end,"—not a final object, or τέλος. The man is intended to act on the community of his fellow-men, for their well-being; and, so far, perhaps, as Society is concerned, Moral Responsibility might be conceived to terminate in this. It is a result which satisfies the phenomena of Social Moral agency. But, viewed relatively to the Individual himself, this certainly is not enough. And it is the Individual that we must consider, unless we imagine every man to exist for

Distinction of Responsibility and Probation.

How far the perfecting of the individual may be a τέλος.

the sake of some other man, and no man for his own sake,—(so that the well-being of a thousand men is worth obtaining, but the well-being of one is not to be considered!)—which is absurd. We must conceive, then, that the forming and perfecting of the character of each Moral Agent for his attainment of the Highest Good, is the *end* of present Probation.—Whether, indeed, this perfecting of the individual be not the determining of certain ultimate relations of the creature to the Creator—the finite to the Infinite,—is an enquiry which would now lead us too far.

Relation of the Individual to the Highest Good.

But it may be well to add that, prone as we are to crave for something less changeable than the decision of our own will as Individuals,—(and tempted therefore to rely on the greater seeming stability of the laws and habits of Society,)—we may find our best corrective in the thoughts here suggested. We shall not be in danger of lowering our moral tone to the fascinating level of the Multitude, if we throw ourselves on the noble belief that our Individual Conscience is in direct communication with the Moral Governor of the world, the Supreme Reason, the Highest Good; and that our Individual struggle for good and against evil,—(conducted under His eye, who will not let the Moral World become chaos at last,)—will ultimately be vindicated by Him, whether its present issue appear with us successful or not.

It cannot be necessary to point out to any one who has followed the course of thought here pursued, that a "Broad Nationalism," without definite Truth and without the individual approval of Conscience,—(for such is its intended "breadth,")—has no ground of philosophy; but involves an entire disbelief of all Personal Virtue, as well as Faith. Knowing, as the Christian does, the need which Conscience has of illumination and guidance, still he must insist on its real action. If Mr. Mill * can afford to risk entire freedom for the

* Mill on Liberty.

intellect, we may at least maintain that Conscience may be equally trusted

But there is one further aspect of the subject, and bearing directly on Political Responsibility, which must not in this place be omitted. Many who may have acquiesced in what has been said as to the Supremacy of Conscience and the Individuality of responsible action, may still enquire,—Has the State, *as a* State, no duties towards Religion? And nothing which has been said ought to cast doubt on the solemn fact that the State has such duties. To put the question in more philosophical terms,—it amounts to an enquiry into the Mutual Relations of the Individual Conscience, and the Society of which it is a member.

Relations of Conscience and Society.

It is evident that these relations are subject to change, as civilization advances. In earlier stages, Society, or the State, might have almost paternal duties towards the individual. It must be remembered too, that the human individual is intended at all times to develope in Society,—a fact which of itself implies duties of the whole to the parts, as well as of the parts to the whole. But the laws of the Society and the convictions of the individual having thus, alike, an ethical basis, must be judged ethically. In the best conceivable polity a law would always be moral,—i. e., not only politically, but ethically good. We cannot even conceive of the permanent existence of a system of law condemned by every individual conscience. The *de jure* relation of law and morals is therefore assumed in such passages as St. Paul's,—"the law is not made for the righteous man," and "it is not a terror to the good but to the evil." *

It is the duty then of the State always to aim to express in Law the highest ethical convictions of the Consciences of individuals.

Duty of the State.

A large class of Mixed questions, connected with personal and domestic rights,—such as Education, Marriage, Inheritance, Service,—may long need for their

* 1 Tim. i. 9; Rom. xiii. 3.

settlement the exercise of political patience. In the meantime, if the Church be free to inculcate her divine principles,—which bear on all social subjects directly or indirectly,—the majority of individual consciences will be so elevated to the Christian standard, that the Law and Morality of the State will become necessarily Christian.

§ 7. *Appeal to History in behalf of 'Broad Christianity.'*

The appeal to History.

Having traced the character and pretensions of this projected "Multitudinism" thus far, and shewn that it has no Scriptural and no Ethical vindication, but is afraid of the fair operation of all Conscience; * it might seem superfluous to go further, and shew that the references made to History, in support of this hypothesis of comprehension, are worthless.

But as History has been very confidently invoked,† we have no option. They who make the appeal must take the consequences.

Christianity appeared on earth when the old Mythologies of Greece and Rome had lost their hold on man. The Individual Conscience had parted from them; they had become "Multitudinistic,"—and therefore must perish. The new Religion made the appeal that was needed to Conscience. In Apostolic and post-Apostolic times there was uniformly an effort to create a *Personal Religion* in connexion with a Baptismal Creed, as has been already shewn. The age of Constantine stands next, and has been referred to for a kind of formal "inauguration" ‡ of the principles of 'Broad Christianity.' Up to that time it is allowed, that there was a "gradual hardening and systematizing;" in other words, fixed principle was always desired.

Constantine. A. D. 313.

Constantine, by the Edict of Milan and succeeding acts, restored to Christians their lost property, and gave them (notwithstanding all professions of general toleration) an as-

* Essay, p. 189. † Ibid., p. 37. ‡ Ibid., p. 166.

cendency in the Empire which they did not possess before.* But great as his interference with Christianity, both for good and for ill, no disposition was shewn, either by him or by any party in the Church, to dispense with a definite Creed. This is acknowledged by those who supposed "Multitudinism" to have been set up by him.† The Christianity patronized by the Imperial favor was also hierarchical and sacerdotal, as well as dogmatic. It was therefore vitally different from that which the "Broad-Nationalists" would seek; and no arguments deduced from it can, in any fairness or justice, be available by them. There was one point, however, in which the Imperial encouragement of Christianity may be regarded as "Multitudinistic;" viz., its employment of Secular influences to spread the name of the Christian Religion beyond the limits of its Spiritual system. The attempt to make the whole framework of the Church coincident with that of the Empire was broad enough, no doubt, though not so broad as the "New Nationalists" of our day would ask. It was natural (may we not add, noble?) for a Roman Emperor to desire to use Religion as a bond of Unity for his dominions; but the effect was unhappy. It was "the new cloth and old garment." The whole body of the Church resisted. Bishops in their councils, and missionaries in their remoter spheres, remonstrated, and recalled with affection the memory of the Ante-Nicene freedom. The whole body of the laws, framed by the Church from age to age, for the Spiritual Discipline of all her members, were one protest against it.‡ The spread of an *Imperial* Christianity beyond the Church's real influence was a primary cause of the withdrawal of tens of thousands of stricter Christians

Multitudinism of the West.

Some effects of the Imperial edicts.

Hosius and others.

* See in Fabricius (the Imperial Edicts for and against the Christians)—*Lux Salutaris*, c. xii.

† Essay, pp. 155—167.

‡ See Mr. Bright's "History of the Period from Nicæa to Chalcedon;" also, my Lectures on "Ecclesiastical Jurisdiction;" and Montalembert's *Moines D'Occident*.

to the deserts of Africa and the mountains of Asia; and what then remained?—The Church of the Empire, exhausted of so much of its active spirituality, soon ceased to be the "salt of the earth." The energy of heathenism had died out; the energy of Christianity (which is Sanctity) was driven out; and the half-Christian, half-heathen "Multitudinism," which had spread without the Individual Conscience, utterly enervated the whole Empire; and in a hundred and fifty years Western Rome was an easy prey to the barbarians.

Fall of the Western Empire. A. D. 476.

Nothing would be easier than to trace the progress of the secularization of Christianity, and the ruin of Nations, side by side,—from the fifth century to our own,—alike in the East and the West. But the task is superfluous to those not wholly unacquainted with the history of Europe, and useless to all others. From the time when patriarchs corresponded in rank with "prefects," and when each "diocese" of the Empire had its primate, each province its metropolitan, and each metropolitan of necessity his suffragans, a nominal Christianity sprung up faster than the Church could sanctify it. Being unconscientious, it could but ruin the nations.—The attempts of Theodosius, and afterwards of Justinian, to digest the laws of the Church and the Empire, were resolute efforts of great minds to find some theory to combine the facts existing around them; but they were vain. The fall of the exarchate of Ravenna to the barbarians, in the year 753, is commonly assigned as the era of the extinction of the Roman law in Italy; and of the failure with it of the great imperial schemes for "comprehending" the world in the Church, or rather, for amalgamating the two.

Justinian's Institutes.

A. D. 753.

Each nation of the West, from Charlemagne onwards, in its turn aimed at the same impossible end,—impossible while man is a moral agent,—coercive National Unity in Religion and Policy.

Charlemagne.

The great systems of Feudal Law which prevailed among the tribes which overwhelmed the Roman civilization,—the Salic law, the Ripuarian, the Burgundian, the Lombard, and others,—were all impregnated with the Roman spirit, and equally desired a National Unity, partly secular and partly spiritual. Here, for the first time, we find the Religious element predominating, and not unfrequently preserving the social system from extinction. Imperialism had sought to mould the Church to its great earthly purposes; Feudalism assisted the Church in moulding, for some higher end, the character of nations. But under the influence of Feudalism, all Europe tended to become one great Hierarchy, from the days of Charlemagne to those of Hildebrand.

Feudal Law.

See the Treatises appended to the Justinian collection.

Now it has been said, that Christianity, in fact, made its great triumphs by means of the mediæval Multitudinism.* Nations were "born in a day." The assertion involves a *petitio* of the whole question; for those who believe Religion to be an imposture, apart from individual Conscience, will demur altogether to these alleged "triumphs." If France became Christian in a multitude, Spain became Arian in a multitude, and had an obstinate *State*-Arianism for some hundred years. The leaven of "Multitudinism" is so defiling that it may soon degrade any Church to a mere *establishment*, in half its elements; an Establishment as debased as that of Louis XIV. supported only by *Dragonnades*.—(Anywhere, indeed, where Savonarolas are burnt and Kens are driven out, Establishments instead of "triumphing" preside over a wide Moral Ruin.)—Or, to look in another direction.—The masses who were baptized by St. Vitus in the North returned in masses to heathenism, and adored, in their favourite idol, "Santovitch," † the saint who had once preached to them of Christ. Was that a "triumph?" The crowds,—received as crowds,—by the illustrious Xavier in India, faded away in crowds once more into

* Essay, pp. 146, 159. † See Hoffman.

their original Hinduism. Undisciplined for Christ, the nominal Chistianity came to nought.—"Multitudinism" failed everywhere.

"Multitudinism" of the East.

How was it in the Byzantine Empire? There surely, if anywhere, the principle of "Multitudinism" had a sphere for eleven hundred years, so far as it could have it in connexion with a definite Creed and an authorized Hierarchy. The great work which Trebonius and his nine coadjutors, under Justinian's auspices, so ably achieved; those fifty books which digested with such care the codes of Theodosius, of Gregory, and Hermogenes, and the Constitutions of succeeding Emperors; exhibit the rule of the Eastern civilization, from the rise of Constantinople in the fourth century to its fall to the Mahometans in the fifteenth. Can any one refer with pride to that course of "Multitudinism" in those long ages of growing decrepitude? Is there much in the spectacle to encourage the attempt, political or religious, to *force* into existence an Ecclesiastical and Civil Unity?

Nomo-canon of Photius.

If, from the fourth to the ninth century, the Eastern Church made some struggle to act on the ancient Discipline of Christ, as an independent reality, it is evident that from the time of Photius the struggle was practically over. The Nomo-canon fixes the character of the Byzantine Church and State henceforth. A "discipline," degenerated to a dead formalism, consummated doubtless a "Unity," but it was at the cost of Moral life. It was put to shame by the new-born vigour of Islamism,—a successful, because a confessedly sensual "Multitudinism," defying the Christian name. As the Feudalism of the West ended in Papacy, so the "Photianism" of the East was, at length, what we now term "Erastianism," of the most unreserved type that the civilized world has known. It has received its retribution since 1453, beneath the Ottoman rule! Its whole lesson to us is a *warning*. There is something, indeed, sublime

Mahometanism. A. D. 1453.

in the continued existence of Christianity at all, "amidst the fires, unconsumed" so long!—If, in the future Providence of God, it may be permitted to emerge from the ordeal of lengthened degradation and suffering, may it have unlearned its unhappy traditions of Secular policy, and abandon at last a "Multitudinism" which wrought out the chains of a miserable Captivity, though it paralyzed the tyrant hand that forged them!

Oriental Multitudinism not an example; (as intimated in Prof. Stanley's Lectures, p. 60.)

But our own concern is with the Western, rather than the Eastern civilization; and to this the discussion (as has been intimated*) rightly must return; and the more so, that we may have a summary view of our own position now.

England inherited the Western form of the problem which the present age, or the future, must solve, as to the position of the State and the Church; the relations of Society and the Individual Conscience. Speaking generally, our institutions were, under God's Providence, of Feudal origin; and the feeling of Nationality was strong in us, as in all the Northern races. This was shewn, without question, in the Anglo-Saxon period,—(at least from the time of Theodore, himself an Oriental); but it was modified by many influences *ab extra.* Separated by the sea from the continent of Europe, our National life had a distinctive development. We became Roman, but remained National. We had lost that union with the civilization of Europe which in some degree was ours till the old Romans left us to that National self-government which in the fifth century began to be a reality; but the union of the Heptarchy, and still more the Norman conquest, re-established our relations with Rome, on a footing which Augustine's mission could not attain. Nevertheless, from the Conquest to the Reformation there was a struggle of the "two

England follows the West.

The Heptarchy.

The Conquest.

* Essay, p. 147.

powers," the spiritual and the temporal, conducted without a definite appreciation of the exact issue. The Church would not have deliberately said that prelates, with the pope at their head, ought really to supersede kings, parliaments, and magistrates; the State would not have said that it could give validity to sacraments, and salvation to souls, and could therefore afford to do without bishops and priests. Each party stood in need of the other; and each felt it. Vacillating, irritated, and just conscious that the right settlement of Church and State had not been attained, our Nation remained till the sixteenth century; when the strong will of Henry VIII. interfered.—We in England have certainly tried fairly to fight out the battle between these "two powers;" so have some Roman Catholic nations abroad: the Lutherans smothered the struggle.

The pre-Reformation Unity of England.

But in the pre-Reformation times there was this advantage on the Ecclesiastical side,—it was not subject to the same organic changes as the State. The people, as a whole, might be divided as to the succession of their kings; but not as to the Creeds and Sacraments. Had the temporal been as one, as the ecclesiastical power, the theory of "Multitudinism" would for the time have seemed to have a triumph. The National Oneness was arrested by a divided allegiance in the pre-Reformation days; as truly as by divided opinions in religion in the times which followed.—(And this is the inherent weakness of all "Multitudinism," that it must follow the fortunes of two masters.)—But the Religious unanimity of England in the mediæval age, though great, was not distinctively *local;* and the same causes which broke up the unity of the Church elsewhere, operated here with equal power. Then came the Tudor and Stuart transitions; and the great change of 1688, as delineated at the outset of this enquiry; to which we revert.

Revolution.

The Revolution was a political necessity, which for the time bewildered the consciences of the people. The relations of Church and

State settled themselves very greatly, to human eyes, by hap-hazard. Attempts were made by such writers as Burnet and Wake on the one hand, and Leslie on the other, to adjust the claims of the "Regale and the Pontificate;"—but, after this, all parties among us took up that position which, with some variations, they have since maintained. The Act of Uniformity had, in some sort, closed up enquiry into such fundamental questions; and the suspension of Convocation, and the extradition of the Nonjurors, completed the *de facto* settlement. Conscience, through every historical change, secretly clung to the truth that Religion is a spiritual concern of each Individual. "Practical men" despaired, however, of a solution of the old difficulty of *imperium in imperio*, on paper; and a compromise was the resort of all sides, with some surrender of truthfulness, perhaps with all.

(Burnet's rights of Princes. Wake on Convocation. C. Leslie.)

The old "Church and State" party had triumphed in 1688, by abating their Churchmanship, and henceforth they could only maintain their ground against different classes of opponents by permitting, and using, different "schools of thought," (as we have since expressed it,) and by adopting different, and scarcely consistent, methods of defence. Against Rome the controversy was still carried on, on the principles of Andrewes and Laud; against Rationalism and Nonconformity on those of Warburton. But eventually the Nation grew to doubt the grounds of the actual religious compromise; and wearied of attempts to modernize ecclesiastical machinery, as antiquated as the costume of the middle ages. A Church only too willing to become "Multitudinistic" was gradually losing its life. Its better members "endured,"—as if tacitly reserving to themselves the right to schism, when things might become intolerable. The Conscience of the Nation made some gallant efforts to right itself; but in vain. Outside the Church, the Tolerated Nonconformity,—while denying priesthood, sacraments, and rites,—vindicated the "distinction of spiritual and temporal," and so intrenched itself in the consciences of the uneducated and sincere.—From Owen and Patrick, down to Secker, that distinction had been fought for. Then came an ominous silence of nearly a hundred years;—and, Where are we now?

From Owen to Secker.

§ 8. *Adjustment Demanded.*

It has seemed to some, that we are rapidly drifting towards the entire Separation of the Church, as a Church, from its union with the State, and the adoption of that position, as Christians, which our Religion held, 1,600 years ago.—Are we then to retrace our way through all the wilderness of so many ages, as though Providence had misled us all along?—The question is a grave one; let it be well weighed before our future becomes hopelessly complicated.

Apparent position.

Need of some adjustment.

Doubtless in those first ages of the Church and the Empire, when the old religions were decaying or decayed, there was entire independence on both sides; but there followed not only jealousy, discord, and persecution, but even a disruption of society, rendering some adjustment absolutely necessary; and in that adjustment the Church, and not the sects, naturally took the lead.—The nature of Man has not changed; he needs Government. The nature of Religion is not changed; it needs freedom of conscience. May it not be for our own Nation, leading so prominently the van of civilization, at length to teach the truth in this also,—that, while learning to do the work which is proper to them, all wise States must leave to the Christian Church, in all its parts, the task of doing its own work, more and more unimpeded? Our "Nationalism" in Religion can only be real, when it is conscientious. And Conscientiousness, as we have seen, is *individual.* But why may not the "Toleration" of the nineteenth century, and the Individualism of the first, or second, or third, here at length coincide?—Some sectarian jealousies may yet be hard to deal with; but let the Christianity of the age to come be free among us, and it will have no need to fear the intellectual and moral struggle which lies before us.

The Anglican Church, and its right to consideration.

But at this point the question is naturally raised by some,—How has the Church of England, "the Church of the XXXIX Articles," any more right, in virtue of this demanded "freedom," to assume the Religious direction of the people, than any other Christian community among us? Granting that some form of Christianity must take the lead, in the settlement of those mixed questions where social interests and moral truth are likely to touch; or in the general instruction of the people;—What right has the "Church of the Prayer-book" to claim this position beyond all others?

Hereditary claim.

It will not be expected that, in reply to this enquiry, a discussion as to the truth of the Anglican doctrines should be opened. It would not only be out of place, but interminable. The answer is a practical one. The Anglican Church has not claimed for herself a position, she has inherited it; and there is no sect which could with any probability compete for it with her. She has it by historical continuity and descent. The Church of the Monks of Bangor, the Church of Augustin, the Church of Theodore, of Dunstan, of Stigand, of Becket, of Warham, of Parker, of Andrewes, of Laud, of Pearson, Wilson, Butler, has gone through all the National phases of all our generations, and has preserved, through all, the *same Creeds* of the Ecumenical Councils, the *same Canonical Scriptures*, the *one Baptismal Rite*, the *one Eucharistic Consecration* in the ancient words of the first Liturgies, and an *unbroken Hierarchy*. A multitude of questions may be ingeniously raised as to all these, but they are irrelevant here. There is no disputing the broad fact. No one can pretend that the *de facto* Church of England is, or ever has been, in the position of a sect forcing itself, *ab extra*, on the Nation. It has come down with the Nation, through all its varied fortune, and shared its destiny. Of course this does not prove that she ought to have perpetuity among us; but it accounts for the position actually occupied. The theory of some might be, that if there is to be "an alliance," the State should be free to choose her own Church; but history is stronger than theory; and history, recording the mutual action of Church and State on each other, assigns no such sublime function of religion-choosing in the abstract to either Parliament or Monarch; on the contrary, any assumption which has ever looked like this, for a moment, has always been a failure.

Whether that form of our Church which it received when the XXXIX Articles were imposed shall for ever continue without change, is a question which cannot be answered on principles of the past; the future will deal with it on its own principles. The idea of a "Parliamentary Revision" belongs to the past. It is more than 200 years old. The idea of relaxation of subscription" by the authority of the Crown, is of the past. It is Tudor. The adjustment of the future must be based on higher principles, or it will be rejected as no fit religious settlement for a people which has outgrown the folly which could recognise the Secular as Divine.

The present position of the Anglican Church is this:

Present position.

She is believed by her own sons to have possession of that Divine Revelation, with its vital gifts of Grace, bestowed by Christ on our world 1,800 years ago. She has certain local *peculiarities* also, some of them restraining her use of that Revelation, and among them this,—that she is not free to act as a corporate body, as all other religious bodies around her are. She is hampered by accidents of her historical position from which she ought, as a spiritual body, to be free as the first Christians at the Pentecost. The advance of education, civilization, science, social economy, and law, all warn her that "old things are passing away." She will need all the energy, power, and grace which Christ has bestowed, if she is to fulfil her mission now. The sooner the State learns, that to treat the Church as an *unspiritual* body is to make her worthless as an instrument even of Civilization,—the better it will be for the Nation. The Church pretends to be more; she must *be* what she pretends, or *abandon the pretence*,—and be abandoned by the conscience of the people. The Spiritual Freedom of the Church is her right, and it can neither honestly *nor safely* be withheld. Let her be put to the fair trial of her sacred powers; if she cannot grapple with a free and intellectual age, then let her, in the Name of Him who is True, take the consequences, whatever they be. But let not the unjust and ignominious course be adopted, of employing and overstraining her "spiritual" character* for some purposes, and denying it for others; using and yet half-outlawing her higher intellects. That can only end in the most hopeless National Infidelity. And let her not be bound to the cowardly political traditions of the least spiritual era of our history. Let her be free to reform her Convocation, reform her spiritual laws, and regulate her internal Discipline; and if then she cannot deal with the age in which her lot is cast, her place may be taken by some loftier and better teacher.

Unreasonableness and unfairness of distrust.

The State may fairly be enquired of by us, "Why are you afraid of us? You can trust all the sects to do their own will, within fair legal restrictions for mutual protection; and why not us? You upbraid us warmly for our deficiencies at times; and then refuse to allow us to act on our own highest principles! What means this subtle sort of homage to our spiritual character? If your clergy be, as they are sometimes told, a 'learned clergy,' (at least in comparison of others,) if, considering their numbers, they are (not untruly) thought in some respects exemplary,—on what reasonable ground shall a nation which proclaims itself educated and free, insist on shackling the intellectual and spiritual activity of its teachers?"

The extent, truly preposterous, to which the under-

* As, for instance, in the licences issued to non-conformists by archidiaconal and other courts—which confuse the consciences of those who receive, as well as of those who give them.

miners of our whole Christianity claim for themselves a monopoly of intellect and fearless "pursuit of truth," forces upon us this great subject. Divine Revelation being *true*, must deal with the intellects no less than with the passions and interests of mankind. But this means not the mere action of isolated intellect, apart from all the corporate and social conditions of the mind.* We can take no narrow view of the field of human thought. It is we who are for freedom, and the courageous following up of every ascertained truth, and this will yet be seen; but we shall be certainly put to work at a fearful disadvantage, through the intrusions of many a pedantic half-scholar, half-recluse, (for whom the Church is little answerable,) unless we may be free *as a Body* to do all our great Master's will among men.

Our intellectual freedom.

Too often the term "intellectual freedom" seems as if identified with a departure from all the foundations of the faith; which is as reasonable as if the demand for moral freedom were supposed to imply a surrender of all the grounds of morals, thus far admitted among mankind. But let us be reasonably understood, and we can recognise no danger in claiming for the Church of Christ all the freedom which He bequeathed, and we believe that that alone will secure the harmonious development of all the spiritual nature of man.

* The mutual relation of our corporate duties, and our Individual Moral life, can only be rightly adjusted—perhaps only rightly apprehended—when the greatest freedom of action has been conceded. Professor Goldwin Smith, in his Lectures, (p. 65,) has suggested some difficulties in connexion with the occasional sacrifice of the Individual—as in acts of heroism for the benefit of communities, or of human nature; or as in the toil of the present generation for the future. In addition to what I have already said on this subject (*infra*) in the latter part of the section on "the Ethical View," (pp. 51—54,) it is obvious to mark that the *Virtue* of Action, in each case supposed by the Professor, first pertains to the *Individual*—though certain advantage flows to others. The relation to the individual probation may, and indeed must, be very intricate; because we know so little of the *whole* moral condition of any individual. But this does not throw the least doubt on the *reality* of Personal Responsibility, in any case; any more than all the other incidents of life in which the influence of others so constantly touches us. Indeed, many an act of heroism would cease to be noble, were it not for the Personal responsibility of the hero.

Not that the satisfaction of those who are deemed the intellectual classes is the principal end to be aimed at by a Church which has to care for all. Perhaps the hardest fact to be encountered, and the most humiliating, is that the lowest forms of Puritanism are still popular with the ignorant multitude and therefore with their politicians, and by them even identified with Spirituality. But while the temptation to pander to this must be withstood, it implies also a condition of things to be wisely ministered to.—A fact, however, scarcely less hard and less degrading, is the prevalence of a quasi-scientific spirit, which is afraid to look into its own conclusions, and has a greedy faith in the latest uncouth imagining of some "free-thinker," who never escaped in his life from the trammels of sham-philosophy, but just has a scepticism as to the Bible, and a horror of a close thinker, if he happens to be a theologian. Bishop Berkeley in his day chastised some such.*

Our sphere and its difficulties.

1. Popular.

But in becoming equal to the requirements of the age to come, the Anglican Church will have to conform her Ecclesiastical System to new positions. Only, if she be a Church,—really and spiritually so,—she must be *free* to do it.—It may not unjustly be thought a providential circumstance that so many organic questions, connected with the Church, have thus far been staved off. Not "Church Rates" only, but (and far more) the "comprehensive measure" which has been threatened as to our Ecclesiastical Courts, has been postponed time after time. May it not seem as if designed to give us space for reflection?

2. Ecclesiastical.

At present, if any question be referred to Ecclesiastical Courts, sympathy is evoked for the persons concerned, as if they were victims of antiquated oppression. Yet how loud is the outcry raised if scandals, either religious or moral, are unchecked by authority!—If the

* In "The Analyst" and "Alciphron;" and his replies to the Cambridge Mathematician, &c.

purely spiritual or religious questions which are stirred in the Anglican Church were settled with no more intervention of legal authority than if they were litigations among Baptists, the world would soon learn whether this learned and extensive Anglican Church had a life of its own. Then let purely spiritual be separated from mixed questions, before any measure is adopted as to Courts Ecclsiastical.

How the Church may still, in this free nation, be "National."

The Church, confident in her Faith, and able, without jealousy, without fear, to act on every Conscience, will not fail to be "National:" for she will possess (she knows) the high intellects and best hearts of the time. Since the conflict, to which Christianity is to be called in these days, must be a more vital one than it has yet known, is it too much for the Church to ask to be allowed to meet it with her own weapons, and in her own way? And if then she carries with her, as she will, the individual convictions of the great mass of the thoughtful laity of England, the idea of even ruling "by a majority" for a while, is not so unfamiliar, as to forbid the expectation that even on that ground the Church will yet receive a "National" homage and support.

Uselessness of political hypocrisy.

Of course, if men regard Religion only, or chiefly, as it tells on this world, they must soon arrive at practical conclusions widely different from all those of Churchmen, with whom the engrossing thought is as to the destiny of each soul in the world beyond the grave. With the all-important enquiries arising out of the question,* "What shall I do to be saved?" it is impossible here to deal. The great doctrines of our future happiness or ruin, reward or retribution, belong to the foundations of all Moral responsibility. But even to the mere politicians of the present hour it may not be useless to point out the *impossibility* of their dealing much longer with Christianity on *their* hypothesis. Things *cannot* continue as they are. Some may of course be quite willing to go on, on the tacit assumption that the Christian

* Essay, pp. 153, 161, 196.

Scriptures, and generally the Christian System, may be used as far as convenient, and then dropped; but the advancing education and understanding of mankind will demand intelligible Principles, and put it beyond the power of politicians to deal thus immorally with religion. As to the assumption of the Eclectics, that the Moral argument is against an "exclusive" Christianity; we meet it, at present, by urging, that the alternative now is an Exclusive Christianity, or none.

The people will certainly require statesmen to speak out their real meaning: for the people's conscience is more with us than the statesmen. Once let it be understood that there is nothing supernatural in the "Religion of the nation," and, as Romanists well know, its days are numbered. A sacred book (disobeyed in more than half its rules) will not save it. To take out of the Bible a few "leading principles," and leave the rest, satisfies no honest conscience. If this were lawful, why complain of the "free-handling" critics?—what do they more than this?—Then, again, let men well consider what it means to submit spiritual questions to the arbitration of a Parliament consisting of four or five *different* religions. None can fail to see that it must hopelessly widen the growing distance, between men of thought and cultivation, and all popular Christianity. The whole English people will certainly perceive that it implies a denial of all Objective Religious Truth. They will feel how impossible it must be for a real Church to go on, with its principles and its practices more and more at variance. This must lead to infidelity, social despair, convulsion. Roman Catholics have a system and theory to which some of their people at least conform, and others attempt it, and all abstain from denying it; the same may be said of all classes of Non-conformists; but a great mass of population, nominally left to the Church, are taught to consider themselves Christians, without as much as an *attempt* on their part to follow any distinct Christianity at all,—such, for example, as the system implied in any one of St. Paul's Epistles. To the Bible they do not conform, nor to the Prayer-book; and with a half-traditional modification of Natural Religion, they frequently are more like "Positivists" than Christians; that is, they are vague believers in *one another*, and what is called "public opinion."

Real membership of a Church, whether national or not, what it is.

Well will it be if the present controversy bring back honest minds to the principle impressed on the history of all Christendom from the Pentecost onwards,—that the Communicants of a Church, with their baptized dependents, *are the Church.* "We being many are one Body: *for* we *are all* partakers of that one Bread." * A departure from this point towards any other "comprehension," is a departure in the direction of ultimate infidelity,—which only a lack of the logical faculty fails at once to detect. For the *world's* sake, no less than the Church's, the sacred rites of our religion *must*, before long, be more discriminately used. The Church cannot for *ever* go on lamenting her "lack of Discipline." The State cannot continue nominally to acknowledge our Christianity as Divine, and then brow-beat it—(as capriciously as Indians their idol when deaf to their prayers.) This will never be tolerable, to a people who, whatever they become, will not be Indian in superstition.

Commination Service.

Let men ponder well the theory, whether it be called "Positivism," or "Multitudinism," or this ideal "Nationalism," which "philosophers" have propounded for them, as thinking the world is now ripe for it. "Broad Christianity," as if to put us to shame, has been held up as a glass before the mind of this generation; it is represented as demanded by the character and needs of the age. And yes,—this "Multitudinism" is truly the only idea which will fairly account for the treatment which our Religion has submitted to receive,—a theory of UNPRINCIPLE. The Conscience of the Church has been so frequently crushed, the free expression of her mind so restrained, that bolder

The theory brought to shame us.

Unprinciple.

* 1 Cor. x. 17.

thinkers than our statesmen have not hesitated at last (as has been seen) to put out as a theory for future action that which has, however unconsciously, been almost a theory of the past,—a "Multitudinist" National Church, of which "public opinion" is to be the rule, and from which every creed and article may be withdrawn, and only such portion of the New Testament be admitted as each individual may approve as genuine, and "interpret" to his own mind!

Its impossibility.

(Gladstone's "State in its Relation with the Church.")

Neither for the Nation, nor for the Individual, can it be safe to go on *without Principle.*—Conscious of this, a modern statesman, at the beginning of his political life, gave himself with steady devotion to the careful examination of the theories of law and philosophy and government, by which in past generations the facts of our religious and social life had been interpreted; and he ended by abandoning theorizing. *Solvitur ambulando!* There was everything that was noble in the effort; but may it not have been nobler in its cessation than in its action, (needful as that may certainly have been,)—*if it be clearly seen*, that there are first truths of Political as well as of Moral science, which are anterior to definition and proof? Gamaliel's lesson, to "let these men alone," if their work may be of God,* is no mean result to gain.—To have missed a theory, and to have arrived at a *Principle of action*, is worth all the intellectual toil.

The principle

And this is the Principle, that Christianity aims at *each Conscience*,—and must be left to do its own work. Fearless for the Truth, and patient, it welcomes every honest effort of the human mind. It bears a message from the Eternal, to each undying soul; and "whoso hath ears to hear, let him hear."† Thus it has the courage to win even a minority from the ranks of the world to the "knowledge of the Truth;" and yet claim for them to be the "salt of the whole earth." If for a time "not many wise, not many mighty, not many noble,"‡ be her promised adherents, she still

* Acts v. 38. † St. Matt. xi. 15. ‡ 1 Cor. i. 26.

would refuse to reckon a merely nominal adherence to her faith; for that would be *morally base*, a falsehood, a denial of Duty and Conscience. And if despair of theorizing has taught statesmen this at last, it shall indeed be well! And this great and glorious England of ours, with a Church "National," not in name only, but in Conscience, may have a moral future such as the world has not yet seen.

Illustrated. There have been speculators before now, who have determined that the soul of man is equally diffused throughout his body; there have been others, who have located it personally in the brain, or even in one special gland: but that our Personality is truly *one*, however difficult its definition, none have questioned. And if a Church by its spiritual and moral energy shew itself to be the Soul of any people, there will be no dispute as to the law of its diffusion, or as to its being "National." It will be the free utterance, for the body of that Nation, of its highest aspirations after Truth and Goodness; and it will remain the reverenced Minister of "hopes full of immortality."

Its opposite. Let no one imagine so vain a thing as that a practical people will tolerate a generalized "ideal of Christianity" *as* Divine. As little also will a free people bear any form of compulsory Religion. Yet will "the public" ultimately demand something more spiritual than its own "opinion." It will have an "historical Christianity." A narrow few may have already persuaded themselves to "give up the Church, and fall back on the Bible;" but what will they do with the "critics?"—Certainly they will *need* a learned clergy; and what then shall become of the fanatics? Will they do as they have done before,—avail themselves of the scholarship which shields them, and then go on awhile, until they need a fresh deliverance?

The prospect. But let us hope for better things. A noble spectacle it may be for the world, if this free land, with its illustrious Monarch and free Parliament, should teach observant Europe, that a highly educated Church may be *trusted* to fulfil her spiritual mission.

A statesman really worthy of the name, seeing among our twenty thousand clergy some, and not a few, foremost in science, and all eager for the spread of real knowledge; seeing others (and they too not a few) giving their high gifts and hard lives to difficult enterprise for Christ's cause in the whole habitable globe; seeing, once more, the vast multitude of them engaged in the ten thousand villages of our nation, in life-long work for the Gospel,—such an one might believe that such a Church, freely and generously trusted, might make Christianity Catholic in our land. Our Church's character is marvellously "National" now; it is one with the people, even in its faults no less than its efforts; and it doubts not that its future, in the truest sense, shall be "National." Nor would it be less speedily so, but far more, if the Church were even as free as the judges in their proper sphere,—that sphere being *entirely* Spiritual.

Real "Nationality."

It will not detract from the National character of the Church, if her inner and spiritual affairs be untouched by the State.—Look at the ten thousands of English homes of which, in uncounted examples, it may be said in the touching words of an Apostle, there is a "Church in that house!"* Are they not the glory of the "Nation?" Have they no inner life beyond that which statesmen can regulate? Are they not "National?"

And so, in a far higher measure, and with yet fuller authority and grace, the "Nationality" of our Church of England, if she may do her own work, shall yet abide,—founded on the "hidden life" which Christ has given her, and sanctifying the souls of the people, for Him who "purchased" them for His own.†

* Col. iv. 15. † Acts xx. 28.

THE CREATIVE WEEK.

There is no attaining a satisfactory view of the mutual relations of Science and Scripture till men make up their minds to do violence to neither, and to deal faithfully with both. On the very threshold, therefore, of such discussions as the present, we are encountered by the necessity for a candid, truthful, and impartial exegesis of the sacred text. This can never be honoured by being put to the torture. We ought to harbour no hankering after so-called "reconciliations," or allow these to warp in the very least our rendering of the record. It is our business to decipher, not to prompt; to keep our ears open to what the Scripture says, not exercise our ingenuity on what it can be made to say. We must purge our minds at once of that order of prepossessions which is incident to an over-timid faith, and, not less scrupulously, of those counter-prejudices which beset a jaundiced and captious scepticism. For there may be an eagerness to magnify, and even to invent difficulties, as well as anxiety to muffle them up and smooth them over,—of which last, the least pleasing shape is an affectation of contempt disguising obvious perplexity and trepidation. Those who seek the repose of truth had best banish from the quest of it, in whatever field, the spirit and the methods of sophistry. The geologist, for example, if loyal to his science, will marshal his facts as if there were no book of Genesis. Even so is it the duty of the interpreter of the Mosaic text to fix its sense and investigate its structure as though it were susceptible of neither collation nor collision with any science of geology.

If we cancel the disturbing divisions of chapter and verse, which are certainly one mask on the face of the record, and liberate the parallelism,—the suppression of which, if parallelism there be, must needs constitute another,—the Scripture account of creation, with slight though not gratuitous deviations from the Authorized Version, will stand as follows:—

In the beginning God created the heaven and the earth.

And the earth was desolate and void :
And darkness was upon the face of the deep :
And the spirit of God moved upon the face of the waters.

And God said, Let there be light :
And there was light :
And God saw the light that it was good :
And God divided the light from the darkness :
And God called the light Day :
And the darkness He called Night :
And the evening and the morning were the first day.

2.

And God said, Let there be a canopy in the midst of the waters :
And let it divide the waters from the waters :
And God made the canopy :
And divided the waters which were under the canopy from the waters which were above the canopy :
And it was so.
And God called the canopy Heaven :
And the evening and the morning were the second day.

3.

And God said, Let the waters under the heaven be gathered together unto one place :
And let the dry land appear :
And it was so.
And God called the dry land Earth :
And the gathering together of the waters called He Seas :
And God saw that it was good.
And God said, Let the earth bring forth shoots :
The herb yielding seed, the fruit-tree yielding seed-enclosing fruit, after his kind, upon the earth :

And it was so.
And the earth brought forth shoots:
The herb yielding seed after his kind, and the tree yielding seed-enclosing fruit, after his kind:
And God saw that it was good:
And the evening and the morning were the third day.

4.

And God said, Let there be lights in the canopy of heaven to divide the day from the night:
And let them be for signs and for seasons, and for days and years:
And let them be for lights in the canopy of heaven to give light upon the earth:
And it was so.
And God made two great lights:
The greater light to rule the day:
And the lesser light to rule the night:
He made the stars also.
And God set them in the canopy of heaven to give light upon the earth:
And to rule over the day and night:
And to divide the light from the darkness:
And God saw that it was good:
And the evening and the morning were the fourth day.

5.

And God said, Let the waters bring forth abundantly the moving creature that hath life:
And let fowl fly above the earth in the open canopy of heaven:
And God created great leviathans:
And every moving creature, which the waters brought forth abundantly, after their kind:
And every winged fowl after his kind:
And God saw that it was good:
And God blessed them, saying:
Be fruitful and multiply, and fill the waters in the seas:
And let fowl multiply in the earth:
And the evening and the morning were the fifth day.

6.

And God said, Let the earth bring forth the living creature after his kind:
Cattle, and creeping thing, and beast of the earth after his kind:
And it was so.
And God made the beast of the earth after his kind:
And cattle after their kind:
And everything that creepeth on the earth after his kind:

And God saw that it was good.
And God said, Let us make man in our image, after our likeness:
And let them have dominion over the fish of the sea:
And over the fowl of the air:
And over the cattle:
And over all the earth:
And over every living thing that moveth upon the earth.
So God created man in His own image:
In the image of God created He him:
Male and female created He them:
And God blessed them, and God said unto them:
Be fruitful, and multiply, and replenish the earth, and subdue it:
And have dominion over the fish of the sea:
And over the fowl of the air:
And over every living thing that moveth upon the earth.
And God said, Behold I have given you every herb bearing seed, on the face of all the earth:
And every tree which has seed-enclosing fruit:
To you it shall be for meat:
And to every beast of the earth:
And to every fowl in the air:
And to everything that creepeth on the earth, wherein is life:
I have given every green herb for meat:
And it was so.
And God saw everything He had made, and behold it was very good:
And the evening and the morning were the sixth day.

7.

Thus the heavens and the earth were finished:
And all the host of them:
And on the seventh day God put period to the work which He had made:
And He rested on the seventh day from all His work which he had made.
And God blessed the seventh day, and sanctified it:
Because that in it he rested from all his work which God created and made.

Now every reader looking with a fresh eye on this sublime composition, must be struck, first of all, with its indubitable *unity*. All its parts cohere in the strictest symmetry, and bind up into an integral and indissoluble whole. There is here the same organic unity which marks the Decalogue, or the Lord's Prayer, or the parable of the labourers in the vineyard: or, if we go out of the Bible for comparisons, it combines with lyric breadth of treatment and stateliness of tread, all the compactness of some solemn sonnet freighted with a single thought from beginning to end,—severe and yet exhaustive,—in which abridgment would be mutilation, and addition excrescence. It therefore occasions no surprise to find at Gen. ii. 4 the clearest marks of a break and a transition; * one strain of composition closed, a fresh strain begun. Verse 4 is a bridge, or rather stepping-stone, from the one monograph to the other. How this is to be critically accounted for is no part of the present enquiry. Whether, as has been thought probable from the change of the divine name,† and for other reasons, certain sections of the book of Genesis are to be viewed as recensions of more ancient materials, and, if so, what those sections are, does not here concern us. Adoption, in such case, is equivalent to authorship. Some parts of the Pentateuch, indeed, are certainly more recent, if others are perhaps more ancient, than Moses; just as one at least of the Psalms is held to be of earlier, and many are known to be of later, date than the age of David.‡ Whoever believes that the Spirit of prophecy spoke before the Hebrew lawgiver,§ as It spoke after him, will not deem the freest of free criticism, in this province of research, inimical to the authority of Scripture. Be the explanation what it may,—variety in a pre-existing basis or deliberate change of strain,—the record of the creative week is one record, what follows is another. Sceptical

* "Post enumerationem et expositionem dierum septem interposita est quasi quædam conclusio, et appellatus est Liber creaturæ, &c., Gen. ii. 4." —*St. Augustine*, *De Genesi contra Manich.*, ii. 1.

"Even a cursory perusal will convince us that they consist of two distinct sections."—*Kurtz*, *Bible and Astronomy*, Edinburgh, 1859, ch. i.; also Wiseman, "Connection between Science and Revealed Religion," vol. i. p. 150.

† From Elohim to Jehovah-Elohim. The latter the plural of Majesty, Intensity, or Fulness of Divine Perfection, the consistency of which with pure Monotheism is proved by Deut. vi. 4, "Jehovah our Elohim is one Jehovah." Adam Clarke connects Elohim with the Arabic *Allah* = the Adorable. Most critics interpret it as "the Mighty One." On the plural see Kalisch, "Historical and Critical Commentary on the Old Testament," p. 80.

‡ Deut. xxxiv.; Ps. xc., cxxxvii.

§ Jude, ver. 14.

criticism may deny that the two monographs are harmonious: this must not provoke refusal to recognise them as distinct.

The Mosaic heptameron is thus a whole in itself: it is further manifest that it *shuts in* a whole. Whatever the work-peopled week be, it is meant absolutely to include and enclasp the creation of the All at the will of the One. Ere this week opened, in the conception of the sacred penman, God had not begun to create: ere this week closed, He had done with creating. Of work prior to the first day the sacred writer knows no more than of work posterior to the sixth. With the first day the series of creative fiats begins; by the seventh they have ceased. "For *in*," that is, *within*, "six days the Lord made heaven and earth, the sea, and all that in them is, and rested the seventh day,"—rested from *all* His work. Accordingly, the record articulates into seven strophes or segments. Of which five are contain*ed*, and two are terminal or contain*ing*. The five are defined in the clearest manner by their opening and close:—"God said . . . . . Evening and morning were the second, third, fourth, fifth, sixth, day." The initial and final sections are necessarily modified, the one as supplying an exordium, the other as forming a peroration or climax. Still the only question that can naturally rise is whether the exordium belongs strictly to the first day, or to the six days in common. *Within* those six days, on either view, all is made that has been made. During six days God works. On the seventh day that rest is resumed, which before the first day had not been broken.

Pursuing our analysis, the exordium in abeyance, it is further evident, not only that six days are broadly homogeneous, and the seventh unique,—a sisterhood of work-days in contrast to a solitary rest-day,—but also that the six work-days part spontaneously into *two groups*, each bearing a very remarkable relation to the other:—

God said, Let there be light:	**God said, Let there be lights:**
And there was light.	**And God made two great lights.**

God said, Let there be a canopy in the midst of the waters: And God called the canopy Heaven.	God said, Let the waters bring forth abundantly: And let fowl fly above the earth in the open canopy of heaven.
God said, Let the dry land appear: God said, Let the earth bring forth shoots, &c.	God said, Let the earth bring forth the living creature, &c. God said, Let us make man. Behold I have given you every herb, &c.

It is manifest that we have here a balance and a correlation of parts, an interlocking of the second moiety of creative working with the first, a prelude and a sequence, a preparation and a development. The story of creation is told at twice. Each day has its double and its consort. In the preliminary triad, light is severed from darkness; a firmament divides the waters above from the waters below; the dry land is disengaged from the waters, and clad with vegetation. In the complementary triad, light is collected and concentrated in sun, moon, and stars; water and air are peopled with marine animals and birds; lastly, the dry land is replenished with terrestrial creatures, and with man himself, and preëxisting vegetation is gifted away to them for food. This ground-plan betokens a delicate co-adjustment of group to group—a fulness and finish of parallelism—which corrects the first impression of simple continuity. The first day *pairs* with the fourth, the second with the fifth, and the third with the sixth: each, to borrow a term from comparative anatomy, a *homotype* to each.* Consequently the structure requires a complex symbol:—

a. 1. Light. b. 2. Firmament between the Waters. c. 3. Dry Land (with plants) above the Waters.	The heavens and the earth,
a. 4. Lights: Sun, Moon, and Stars. b. 5. Water-Animals and Birds. c. 6. Land-Animals—Man.	and all the host of them. (Gen. ii. 1.)

* Compare *Quæstiones Mosaicæ*, London, 1842, p. 31; Dr. Forbes, "Symmetrical Structure of Scripture," p. 162; Kalisch, p. 63.

The mighty mansion is first built, next furnished. A triad of "days" is devoted to its architecture, a triad to its occupants. The former describes a series of *extrications*,—light from darkness, the waters from the air and sky, the dry land from the waters. The latter portrays a series of *formations*,—the heavenly bodies in celestial space, the animal population of the waters and the air, lastly, land-animals and man. Thus the first three days are so many *finger-posts* to the second three.* In consonance with which bipartite arrangement, there may be noted a certain expansion and elaboration of details in the third and sixth days respectively. Each has two creative fiats: the earlier days in both groups have but one.

At this point a sudden light, or what seems a light, breaks in; and the question will suggest itself to most minds at all versant in critical studies, to what ORDER of composition the opening section of Genesis belongs. Which, e.g., does it most resemble in the apparent law of its structure, the 27th of Acts, or the 104th Psalm? To what shall we parallel its "days,"—to the notation of literal week-periods in our Lord's earlier ministry † or in the missionary travels of St. Paul, or to the mystic "hours" of labour in the vineyard, or the lofty refrains of Psalms xlii.,—xliii., and cvii.? Poetry may be detached from reality, or opposed to reality; it may also, and that without ceasing to be itself, or foregoing its appropriate framework, be the highest and most vivid *exponent* of reality. It is enough for the present to indicate this enquiry. We have still to look somewhat more closely into the details of the record.

"In the beginning God created the heaven and the

* God said, Let there be light, and there was light:
Next parted water from the vault of air:
Then bade the land above the ocean rise.

God said, Sun, rule the day, Moon, rule the night:
Next bade fish, bird, the sky and water share:
Last gave the earth its various tenantries.

† St. Luke iv. 16, 31, vi. 1, 6. Σαββάτον δευτεροπρώτον is simply the third in this series: compare Acts xiii. 14, 42, 44.

earth." This is the Hebrew periphrasis for the universe of things=κόσμος, *mundus*.* So, in the Creed, "Maker of heaven and earth" is expounded by "all things visible *and invisible*;" this last probably a development of the meaning present to the mind of the sacred writer, since he only concerns himself with such results of creative power as are palpable to the senses. Whether "created" denotes egress into being from absolute nonentity, or only a moulding and manipulating of self-existent matter, cannot be determined from the word itself. "No language, as the addition *out of nothing* shews, has a single term to express the former idea."† But the intention of the sacred penman may be safely gathered from the tenor of Hebrew belief.‡ Whence the opening sentence of Genesis may be held as announcing that everything save God had a beginning, and had its beginning from Him. Before the "beginning," only God was; "in the beginning," He caused all things to be; and He is thus the unbegun beginner of all that is.§

Creation being conceived as proper or improper, immediate or mediate, the word "create," however, may be here understood either contradistinctively of one or comprehensively of both processes. On the former view the meaning will be,—"In the beginning —*in primo puncto temporis*‖—God brought into being the *material* of all things, the heavens and the earth. And the earth, so brought into being, was not created perfect, but desolate and void," &c. On the other sup-

* Pearson on the Creed, Ed. 1840, p. 74; "Creation and the Fall," by the Rev. D. MacDonald, Edinburgh, 1856, p. 81. "Universa creatura significata est quam fecit et condidit Deus."—*St. August. De Gen.*

† Dr. Pusey, note in Buckland's "Bridgewater Treatise," p. 22. So Bishop Pearson, p. 80:—"We must not weakly collect the nature of *creation* from the force of any word, which may be thought by some to express so much, but by the testimony of God," &c.

‡ Ps. xc. 1; 2 Macc. vii. 28; Heb. xi. 3; 2 Pet. iii. 5.

§ "Omnia formata de ista materia facta sunt, hæc ipsa materia tamen de omnino nihilo facta est."—(*St. August. de Gen.* i. 14.)—"*Created*, caused existence where, previously to this moment, there was no being."—Adam Clarke, *in loc.*; Kalisch, p. 53; Barrow on the Creed, Serm. xii.; MacDonald, p. 65.

‖ Piscator, *in loc.* "In pr." sc. *temporis*. Poli Synops.

position we shall read,—"In the beginning—commensurate and conterminous with the creative week—God made all things, immediately or mediately, out of nothing, or out of substances He Himself had made; and He made them in manner following." According to our estimate of the preferability of either paraphrase, we shall consider the verse as the commencement of the first day's work, or as a proleptic epitome of the entire hexameron. Philologically, the latter view has all likelihood on its side.* "Create" and "make"—*bara* and *hasah*—are constantly used as synonyms throughout the monograph itself, and elsewhere in the Old Testament. God's "*creating* heaven and earth *in the beginning*" is precisely equivalent to His "*making in six days* the heavens and the earth." So "the *day* in which the Lord God *made* the earth and heavens"† is not the *first* day, still less any period preceding it, but the entire *six* days embracing "*all* the work which God created and made."‡ The first verse of Genesis is therefore to be taken as of the same compass and generality with "Maker of heaven and earth" in the Apostles' Creed. It is the condensed summary of succeeding details, the nucleus or embryo of which the sequel is the expansion, the *intrada* to the strain of creative harmony.

The work of the first day follows, the way being paved for its distinctive fiat by a picture of that chaos from which the cosmos sprung. "The earth was without form," &c.,—*tohu-va-bohu*,—desolate and void,§ uninhabitable and uninhabited,‖ "and the Spirit of God moved"—or hovered, or brooded¶—"on the face of the waters. And God said, Let there be light. . . And evening was, morning was, one day."** We

* *Quœst. Mos.*, p. 7.
† Gen. ii. 4.
‡ Gen. ii. 3.
§ Jer. iv. 23.
‖ "Invisibilis et incomposita," St. Augustine (after the Septuagint); "Inanis et vacua," Vulgate.
¶ Deut. xxxii. 11; Ps. civ. 30.
** Compare St. Matt. xxviii. 1, *ἐν μιᾷ τῶν σαββάτων;* and note, Kalisch, p. 67:—"It is futile to assign to this use any mysterious or hidden reason, as Josephus and others insinuate, or to understand it as a *peculiar*

have thus (1.) Day antithetic=light-period, (2.) Day comprehensive=light and night period, νυχθήμερον.

To the day of partition of the light from the darkness succeeds that of severance of the firmament from the waters. "God said, Let there be a firmament in the midst of the waters," &c. "Firmament," *rakia*,* is literally expanse or canopy, and the work of the second day is the spreading the zone of air between the zone of cloud and the zone of ocean; and the constitution in general, so to speak, of the circumterrestrial sphere, or space. "And God called the canopy Heaven." The Hebrews distinguished a first, a second, and a third heaven. Of these the third was the invisible abode of God and His angels, in the second the heavenly bodies were set, on the first the clouds rested.† *Rakia*, or expanse, with an elasticity of meaning like that of our own word *sky*, is used for either of the two inferior "heavens," the interior or the remote: thus in the fifth-day work, as in the second, it is the ethereal floor that props the clouds, and beneath which the birds fly; whereas in the fourth-day work it is the spangled vault, from which the sun looks forth, and in which the stars are burning. Translated into modern phrase, therefore, the *rakia* was either the earth's atmosphere or the cosmical space beyond. And "the waters above the firmament" are simply those lodged in the clouds.‡ "He stretcheth out the north over the

day, a day *sui generis*, or a period of indefinite duration. MacDonald's 'Creation and Fall,' p. 99." Kalisch translates, "It was morning, it was evening, one day."

* Septuag. στερέωμα, Vulg. *firmamentum*. That which gives firmness or *fixity* to the "fixed" stars, holding each in its place and binding all into a "shining frame." Compare *stereotype*. See Dr. M'Caul, "Some Notes on the First Chapter of Genesis," p. 38.

† "That second heaven is not so far above the first as beneath the third (2 Cor. xii. 2) into which St. Paul was caught. The brightness of the sun doth not so far surpass the blackness of a wandering cloud, as the glory of that heaven of Presence surmounts the fading beauty of the starry firmament."—*Pearson*, p. 75. "The Jews say there are three heavens; *cœlum nubiferum*, or the firmament; *cœlum astriferum*, the starry heavens; *cœlum angeliferum*, where the angels reside, the third heaven in St. Paul."—*Barrow on the Creed*, Serm. xii.

‡ See the noble chapter in "Modern Painters," vol. iv. pp. 83—89 :—

empty place, and hangeth the earth upon nothing. He bindeth up the waters in His thick clouds, and the cloud is not rent under them."* The conception is manifestly that of concentric spheres; an inner "firmament" on which the clouds are suspended, an outer in which and along with which the orbs of heaven revolve.

Firmament above, a world of watersbelow; so the second day closes. The third brings the fiat for the rescue and elevation of the dry land. "And God call-

"The account given of the stages of creation in the first chapter of Genesis is in every respect clear and intelligible to the simplest reader, except in the statement of the work of the second day. . . . The English word *firmament* itself is obscure and useless, because we never employ it but as a synonym of heaven. . . . But the marginal reading, *expansion*, has definite value, and the statement that 'God said, Let there be an expansion in the midst of the waters, and God called the expansion heaven,' has an apprehensible meaning. . . . Now with respect to this whole chapter we must remember always that it is intended for the instruction of all mankind, not for the learned reader only; and that therefore the most simple and natural interpretation is the likeliest, in general, to be the true one. An unscientific reader knows little about the manner in which the volume of the atmosphere surrounds the earth; but I imagine that he could hardly glance at the sky when rain was falling in the distance, and see the level line of the bases of the clouds from which the shower descended, without being able to attach an instant and easy meaning to the words 'expansion in the midst of the waters.' And if, having once seized this idea, he proceeded to examine it more accurately, he would perceive at once, if he had ever noticed *any*thing of the nature of clouds, that the level line of their bases did indeed most severely and stringently divide 'waters from waters,' that is to say, divide water in its collective and tangible state from water in its divided and aërial state; or the waters which *fall* and *flow* from those which *rise* and *float*. . . . . I understand the making the firmament to signify that, so far as man is concerned, most magnificent ordinance of the clouds;—the ordinance, that as the great plain of waters was formed on the face of the earth, so also a plain of waters should be stretched along the height of air, and the face of the cloud answer the face of the ocean; and that this upper and heavenly plain should be of waters, as it were, glorified in their nature, no longer quenching the fire, but now bearing fire in their own bosoms; no longer murmuring only when the winds raise them or rocks divide, but answering each other with their own voices from pole to pole; no longer restrained by established shores, and guided through unchanging channels, but going forth at their pleasure like the armies of the angels, and choosing their encampments upon the heights of the hills; no longer hurried downwards for ever, moving but to fall, nor lost in the lightless accumulation of the abyss, but covering the east and the west with the waving of their wings, and robing the gloom of the farther infinite with a vesture of divers colours, of which the threads are purple and scarlet, and the embroideries flame."

* Job xxvi. 7, 8.

ed the dry land Earth, and the gathering together of the waters called He Seas." "Earth," like "day," is thus either inclusively the whole terraqueous globe, or, contradistinctively, the part uncovered by the ocean. Nor is the surface so rescued left a desert. By a fresh creative mandate, the earth brings forth "grass" or "shoots,* the herb yielding seed, and the tree yielding fruit enveloping its seed," each "after his kind." This enumeration may remind us of the old classification based on vegetable magnitudes—herbs, shrubs, and trees. But it is much more likely that "shoots" is the *containing* term for the two which follow, that is, for *food-yielding plants*, which may indeed be held as representative of vegetation in general, but with which alone the sacred writer was prospectively concerned.†

A threefold foundation being now laid, a threefold superstructure is built up. On the fourth day light [Heb. *or*] is consigned to light-bearers,‡ [*ma-oroth*]; passes from its state of diffusion into celestial receptacles; is located and concentrated in sun, moon, and stars. The text says that these were "made;" and therefore means that they were made, not made to appear. Had this latter been the thing to be expressed, the sacred writer who had just set down, "Let the dry land *appear*," had every facility for expressing it. But just as God "*made* the firmament,"§ or "*made* the beast of the earth,"‖ or "*made* man,"¶ is it affirmed that He "*made* two great lights,** and also the stars."†† There is an end to all ingenuousness in the interpretation of Scripture if we foist, in one of these examples, a meaning on "made" which it bears in none of the others. No honest doubts can be appeased by recourse to transparent make-shifts. The Hebrew verb indeed, like *facio*, conforms to its accusative; and may mean, if its regimen so necessitate, to prepare, to dress, &c.

* "Sacred Scriptures, Hebrew and English, by De Sola, &c. Baxter, 1844. Kalisch renders "vegetation."

† Gen. i. 29, 30. ‡ φωστῆρες, *luminaria*.

§ Gen. i. 7. ‖ Ibid. 25. ¶ Ibid. 26.

** Observe also that they are first made, and *then* set to give light, &c.

†† Gen. i. 16.

But the subject must be such as to *dictate* these reflex determinations of sense; and it is preposterous to contend that *fecit luminaria* can be naturally rendered, 'He made sun and moon become visible,' or, 'He cleared away the clouds.' Such is not the meaning which the text puts into an unbiassed reader, but that which a biassed reader or an embarrassed controversialist for a purpose of his own puts into the text. The foundations of faith would be indeed precarious if they depended for their solidity on such artifices of mistranslation.

Sun, moon, and stars, ranked in the ratio of their importance to the earth, as alone consisted with the object of the sacred survey of creation,* occupy the fourth day. To this plenishing of the sky succeeds, on the fifth day, the peopling of the air and the waters. "God said, Let the waters teem with shoals of animate creatures, and let birds fly above the earth in the open expanse of heaven,"† that is, beneath the concave of the lower firmament. "And God created the great animals of the sea, and every living creature that moveth, with which the waters teemed, after their kind, and every winged bird after its kind." The central day of the first triad had prepared a twofold home: the corresponding day of the second triad stocks that home with two vast groups of inhabitants. The cold-blooded fish-reptile family take possession of the deep; the warm-blooded bird wings its flight through the air. A slight rectification of the English version, suggested and endorsed by the best Hebrew scholars,‡ restores consistency, as regards the bird-tribe, between Gen. i. 20 and ii. 19. In the other province of life, while the phrase "every living creature that moveth" is doubtless meant to include the humblest forms of vitality, the type-groups denoted by *tanninim* are clearly those represented by the great water-breathing or water-haunting vertebrates, such as the shark and the croco-

* "Nos enim potius respexit quam sidera, ut theologum decebat."—*Calvin, in loc.*

† De Sola.

‡ De Sola and Kalisch, p. 74.

dile.* These dominating the waters, with the winged fowl careering in the open firmament of heaven, compose the fifth-day aspect of creative power.

A sixth day peoples the earth with those creatures, higher, or lower, for whom, in humble companionship and subordination to man, the earth, on the pioneer third day, had been specially prepared. "God said, Let the earth bring forth the living creature after his kind, cattle, and creeping thing [or *reptile*], and beast of the earth," &c. The sixth day thus introduces "behemoth" to the dry land, as the fifth "leviathan" to the waters.† With "cattle and beast of the earth" there can be no difficulty in identifying the mammalia, or milk-givers, herbivorous and carnivorous, to the latter of whom mediately, as to the former directly, since there can be no fauna without a flora, terrestrial vegetation is the basis of subsistency.‡ And while "creeping thing" may be a term of sufficient generality to include worms and insects, it seems specially pointed at the ophidian "reptile,"§ or serpent-tribe, holding place between these and the nobler animals. Thus the dry land also is tenanted. But the master-creature is still wanting. By the supplementary fiat of the third day vegetable life had been added to inorganic matter. By the supernumerary fiat of the sixth day, the eighth and final fiat of all, there is superinduced on all lower forms of life, vegetable or animal, the rational, spiritual, God-resembling life of man.‖ After solemn counsel

* *Tanninim*, Exod. vii. 9; Isa. li. 9; Job vii. 12; literally 'long-extended:' comp. *Dolichosaurus*. "*Tanninim*—quod significat dracones et omnia ingentia animalia. . . . . Nomen cete commune est omnibus magnis et cetaceis piscibus."—*Cornelius à Lapide*, *in loc.* "Non soli ceti significantur, sed omnes animantes stupenda vastitate et anguinea specie monstra quæ inveniuntur in utroque genere."—*Piscator*, *in loc.* See also MacDonald, p. 278. This work does honour to the theological literature of Scotland.

† Ps. civ. 26; Job xl. 14.

‡ Gen. i. 31.

§ De Sola.

‖ "As it is reasonable to imagine that there is more of design, and consequently more of perfection, in the last work, we have God here giving His last stroke and summing up all into man; the whole into a part, the universe into an individual; so that whereas in other creatures we have but the trace of His footsteps, in man we have the draught of His hand. In him were united all the scattered perfections of the creature, all the

with Himself, shadowing the unique dignity and incomparable endowments of the creature to be brought into being,—σύνδεσμος ἁπάντων,—"God created man in His own image, in the image of God created He him; male and female created He them. And God blessed them, and said unto them,"—unto *them* as alone of capacity to listen,*—"Be fruitful and multiply, and replenish the earth, and subdue it; and have dominion over the fish of the sea, and over the fowl of the air, and over every living thing that moveth upon the earth."

And thus the mighty work is crowned and closed, and the twofold evolution of creative activity—the triad of preparation and the triad of plenishment—subsides in a seventh day of Sabbatic calm. "The heavens and the earth were finished, and all the host of them,"—their tenantry (*ornatus, supellex*) animate or inanimate,† star-peopled space, life-peopled earth, "the round world and all that dwell therein." His plan complete, in both its aspects, "on the seventh day, God put period to His work;‡ wherefore"—whether from the creation or at an after time the text is silent—"God blessed the seventh day, and sanctified it, because that in it He rested from all His work which God created and made."

Now, waiving for the present all enquiry into the literal time-limits of the creative week, these lessons, as it seems, emerge unforced from the record. That creation did not create itself. That matter is not God's coeval, but His creature and servant. That God only had no beginning, and that all things else began to be by His will. That the whole universe is one harmoni-

graces and ornaments; all the airs and features of being were abridged into this small yet full system of nature and divinity: as we might well imagine that the great Artificer would be more than ordinarily exact in drawing His own picture."—*South*, vol. i. Serm. ii. See also the long and admirable note in Kalisch, pp. 74—78.

* God speaks eight times by way of mandate to nature or of deliberation with Himself; twice by way of blessing and benefaction to man.

† Ps. xxiv. 1.

‡ Kalisch suggests "*had* ended his work:" MacDonald, p. 310, with better reason, declines the pluperfect, referring to Exod. xxxiv. 33, &c. So Calvin, "Quia novas species *creare destitit.*"

ous system, the work of one God; the projection of His thought, the transcript of His plan. That such plan bore the stamp of a preconceived progress; and evolved itself in orderly successions, stage after stage, towards a foreseen terminus or goal. That all life, vegetable or animal, came into being, not by the blind operation of natural law, but by acts of divine volition, never put forth capriciously, though "a law unto itself." That each form or type of life was made "after its kind," and owes its characteristic endowments to creative ordination, not to fortuitous development. That the lower life, in the main, antedated the higher; the water-vertebrates and birds preceding the mammalia, the brute mammalia preceding man. That man is not only the latest-born of creatures, but a creature *sui generis*, with the advent of whom, so far as this earth is concerned, the work of creation closed, and a new era of divine government began. That man has not developed into what he is from some bestial type, but holds his prerogatives as a gift direct from the Almighty. That we owe no worship to nature, and all worship to God. That "it is He that hath made us, and not we ourselves;" and that "in Him we live, and move, and have our being."—Such are the teachings of the "Mosaic cosmogony." They may or may not harmonize with modern science. But it will be instructive, before turning to that test, to place side by side with them, though in the merest outline, such rival and partially analogous interpretations of the origin and purpose of things as have prevailed in ancient, or been influentially put forth even in recent, times.

II.

Man, the species, lives. Has he lived for ever? If not, how came he to live at all? How also the myriads of humbler creatures around him? And whence that ordered whole, of sun and sky, and earth and sea, so liberally commissioned to minister to his wants, if inexorably dumb to his questionings?

Man, the individual, dies. How to make the most of life while it lasts? How best to propitiate the unseen powers that can prolong or cut it short, that can make it at their pleasure a curse or a blessing? Moreover, is this life the only life? When a man dies, shall he live again? If so, what can he do here and now, to ensure that it shall be well with him in that great hereafter?

Problems these of perennial and imperishable interest. As the mist of primeval history begins to clear away, we see the human mind grappling with them, and speculation surging round them, throughout the family of nations from the Ganges to the Nile. Not with one set of these questions only, but with both. For they are so interknit that they cannot be parted. A law of life for the individual present, a hope for the individual future, must each repose on a doctrine of the collective human past. All creeds must cast anchor on some scheme of beginnings. Cosmogonies may be sober and sound, or they may be frivolous and foolish. But it was always seen, as it is evident still, that to forego a cosmogony is to dispense with a religion.

The Hebrews grew into a nation in Egypt, and their great lawgiver was learned in all the wisdom of the Egyptians. Were these, then, his tutors in cosmogony? The Egyptian chaos, we are told, is denoted in ancient hieroglyphics by a confusion of the limbs and parts of various animals.* The future heavens and earth are a promiscuous pulp. At last the elements begin to separate of their own accord. Fire, being lightest, springs to the upper region; and air is set in motion next. By the heat of the sun, the earth, plastic and prolific, brought forth multitudes of living creatures, even the largest; though afterwards spontaneous generation became enfeebled in its capabilities, and the larger ani-

* *Quæst. Mos.*, p. 8. On the Egyptian and other Oriental cosmogonies, see Diod. Sic., lib. i. 10, &c.; Euseb., *Præpar. Evangel.*, lib. i. 6, 10, ii. 1; Brucker, *Hist. Crit. Philosoph.*, tom. i. lib. ii. *passim;* Egypt's Place in Universal History, vol. i. pp. 377, &c.; Kalisch, pp. 53—60; Lyell's Principles of Geology, book i. ch. ii.; MacDonald, Part i. sect. iv.; Gibbon, vol. i. ch. viii.; *Quæst. Mos.*, *passim.*

mals could only be perpetuated by propagating themselves.* According as the earthy, watery, or fiery principles preponderated in the composition of each animal, it became quadruped, fish, or fowl. The first men were produced in Egypt from the mud of the Nile. Thus, like the lower creatures, man himself seems to have been considered, by at least one of the Egyptian school, as a hap-hazard birth of the subsiding chaos. Kneph with his potter's wheel, and the tradition of a divine power bringing light out of darkness, shew indeed that worthier conceptions were not unknown to the higher minds of ancient Egypt.† Yet these did not rescue their cosmogony from the grossest extravagances of polytheism. The creed bore fruit. Incapable of religion, the inferior animals are also incapable of idolatry. Man, abdicating his place at the head of creation, and stooping to worship a brute, falls lower than the brute he worships. It would strike us with amazement to see a dog or an elephant crouching in awe before a calf or a crocodile. Yet conceptions of the Most High from which the beasts have been shielded are the product of perverted credence in man. The ox did

* With this ancient conception may be compared the following passage from a modern savant:—"L'effervescence qui se manifeste dans cette matière étant en raison de sa masse, plus celle-ci est considérable, plus il en sort de produits et plus ils sont avancés en organisation. . . . . D'après ces considérations, est-il nécessaire de dire pourquoi dans nos expériences toujours faites sur une si petite échelle, on ne voit apparaître que de si infimes Protozoaires? Nos infusions, nos bocaux ne représentent guère qu'un point métaphysique dans l'espace en comparaison de ces masses incalculables de matières organiques qui purent entrer en fermentation après les grands cataclysmes du globe. Cette idée, que les forces productrices doivent être en raison directe de la masse du substance en action, se présente naturellement à l'ésprit. Aussi beaucoup d'hommes d'une intelligence élevée, ainsi que le fait M. Guépin, se sont demandé si, au lieu de se produire dans un étroit bocal, l'acte génésique avait lieu dans un lac échauffé et renfermant d'abondants matériaux organiques, il n'en résulterait pas des êtres infiniment plus élevés."—*Pouchet*, *Hétérogénie*, p. 494.

Dugald Stewart might well observe, ("Dissertation on Progress of Metaphysics,") "In reflecting on the repeated reproduction of ancient paradoxes by modern authors, one is almost tempted to suppose that human invention is limited, like a barrel-organ, to a specific number of tunes."

† Lyell, ch. ii.; MacDonald, p. 50.

not worship the Egyptian; the Egyptian worshipped the ox.

But Moses, though brought up in Egypt, was a son of Abraham. Does his cosmogony, then, shew a family likeness to those of Mesopotamia and Syria? The Chaldæo-Phœnician belief traced all things to darkness and water,—"a wind of black air, and a chaos dark as Erebus and without bounds."* In this moved misshapen monsters, ruled by a woman named Homoroka, or the Ocean. Bel, or the supreme being, cut this woman in two parts, which became heaven and earth. Then Bel beheaded himself; and the gods, mixing the blood with earth, from this made man.—In the Phœnician myths, wind and chaos produce *mot*, or slime, and that all things; or, otherwise, men and all creatures issue from a gigantic egg, in which they are woke to life by a peal of thunder. With the amplest allowance for the allegorical element, what could spring from such grotesque delineations of the human origin save idolatries as grotesque and grovelling as themselves?

When we pass to the cosmogonies of India and Persia, we exchange the Semitic for the Aryan cycle of tradition. Of this the first and purest embodiment is the very ancient hymn from the *Rig-Veda*, certainly not later than 1200 B. C.:—†

"Nor Aught nor Nought existed; yon bright sky
Was not, nor heaven's broad woof outstretched above.
What covered all? what sheltered? what concealed?
Was it the water's fathomless abyss?
There was not death —yet was there nought immortal:
There was no confine betwixt day and night;
The only One breathed breathless by itself,
Other than It there nothing since has been.
Darkness there was, and all at first was veiled
In gloom profound—an ocean without light;
The germ that still lay covered in the husk
Burst forth, one nature, from the fervent heat.
Then first came love upon it, the new spring
Of mind—yea, poets in their hearts discerned,

* *Quæst. Mos.*, p. 8.

† Translated by a friend of Mr. Max Müller for his contribution to Bunsen's "Philosophy of History," vol. ii. p. 136.

Pondering, this bond between created things
And uncreated. Comes this spark from earth,
Piercing and all-pervading, or from heaven?
Then seeds were sown, and mighty powers arose—
Nature below, and power and will above—
Who knows the secret? Who proclaimed it here?
Whence, whence this manifold creation sprang?
The gods themselves came later into being—
Who knows from whence this great creation sprang?
He from whom all this great creation came,
Whether his will created or was mute?
The Most High Seer that is in the highest heaven,
He knows it—or perchance even He knows not."

In a certain lofty simplicity and meditative grandeur this could scarcely be surpassed, were we to ransack all ancient literature, out of the Bible. Nor are flashes of kindred sublimity wanting in later effusions of the Hindoo mind. But these emerge in depraving alliance with the most fantastic and brain-sick reveries. The Superior Unknown thinks within Himself, "I will create worlds." Water is then brought into being. From a germ dropped into this ocean is developed the mundane egg. In this Brahma creates himself; and then, moving upon the waters, becomes ancestral creator of all things besides. The sun springs from his eye, the air from his ear, the fire from his mouth. From his mouth, his arm, his thigh, his foot, proceed the founders of the chief Hindoo castes. Further, Brahmá divides himself into male and female, whence issues the divine Viradj, who, dividing himself in like manner, gives birth to Manu; who in turn creates gods, saints, giants, the celestial bodies, and mankind.* Brahma, having accomplished his task, "changes the time of energy for the hour of repose." He sleeps during 4,320 millions of years, a day of Brahma, at the end of which period the world is destroyed by fire, and has to be created over again. "For there are creations and destructions of worlds innumerable; the Being, supremely exalted, performs all this with as much ease as if in sport, again and again, for the sake of conferring happi-

* Kalisch, p. 58; Lyell, book i. ch. ii.

ness." At the end, however, of a hundred years, each consisting of three hundred and sixty days of Brahma, he himself, and all things with him, will cease to exist.

Hindoo cosmogony, not satiated with these extravagances, developes in monstrosity as it gathers age. Forbearing to trace its lurid contortions, we may turn to the creed of Zoroaster. In the *Zendavesta*, or Persian Scriptures, the famous doctrine of the Two Principles, or a divine dualism, is propounded as the key to the mysteries of the universe. A Supreme Abstraction, Infinite Time, or Necessity, gives birth to Ormuzd and Ahriman, the deities respectively of light and darkness. In six successive periods, consisting of unequal numbers of days, all together amounting to one year, Ormuzd creates the light, the waters, the earth, the trees, the inferior animals, and man. This is palpably borrowed, with certain emendations, from the Mosaic record. But what is strictly original is very significant. All animals spring from a primeval bull. Ormuzd feasts at each creative interval with his heavenly companions. After the good work has been completed, Ahriman's malignity "pierces Ormuzd's egg." From this all evil ensues. Ormuzd and Ahriman are still struggling for the mastery. But Ormuzd will conquer in the end.

The poems of Hesiod may be said to form a link between the Oriental cosmogonies and the kindred speculations of the Greek philosophers. Chaos, in the ancient Hellenic myth, is the first generated of all things. Earth, sprung from Chaos, begets the sky and the ocean; next a superhuman brood of giants and monsters. There are generations of men, moreover, before the introduction of woman; and woman is depicted as the baneful result of the rivalry between Zeus and Prometheus.* In the dawn of the philosophic period, Thales and Anaximenes propound water or air as the principle of all things. Anaxagoras first distinctly disparts the idea of God from matter.† Aristotle is but the spokes-

* Theogony, 116—146; Works and Days, 59—68.

† Brucker, tom. i. p. 504.

man of all the ancient philosophers, Plato not excepted, in affirming, notwithstanding, that matter is eternal; * and he has but a feeble grasp on its Divine Controller. Not so the author of the *Timæus*, which is, beyond doubt, the most elaborate and representative effort of Greek speculation on cosmical beginnings, and on the mutual relations of Nature and God. To find out the Framer and Father of the universe, Plato teaches, is difficult; to reveal Him to all men through the ministry of speech is impossible. The cosmos was framed after an eternal pattern or paradigm in the mind of the Maker; it the goodliest of works, He the best of causes. Willing all for good, He educed order from chaos. The world is a living and divine thing, strictly one, since it is the expression of one thought of its Architect. Air and water are mediatorial elements between fire and earth. The cosmos is a sphere, because this is the most perfect of all figures. Sun, moon, and the other five planets were created as markers of time, and placed in seven orbits. The divine ideal desiderated four natures to people the universe—gods, winged creatures, aquatic and terrestrial animals. Creating the gods Himself, the Supreme Artificer constitutes these deputy-creators of the lower orders of being, and retires into His wonted repose.† Bad men, after death, in the ratio of their unworthiness, become women, birds, beasts, or fishes. Reverence for the great name of Plato, and recognition of the marvellous insight displayed in portions of this dialogue, especially in its doctrine of the Archetype, need not blind us to the fantastic alloy which renders it so conspicuous a monument of the "follies of the wise." And yet it embodies the highest reach of Greek thought, in the intellectual noon of the nation.

The Augustan age of Rome supplies poetical interpreters of other phases of Hellenic speculation. Pantheism and polytheism find their logical goal in the

* Physics, lib. i. cap. iv. and viii.

† Καὶ ὁ μέν δὴ ἅπαντα ταῦτα διάταξας, ἔμενεν ἐν τῷ ἑαυτοῦ κατὰ τρόπον ἤθει. Compare Gen. ii. 2.

blank unshrinking atheism re-edited with fierce earnestness by Lucretius:—

> "Nam certe neque consilio primordia rerum
> Ordine se suo quæque sagaci mente locarunt;
> Nec quos quæque darent motus pepigere profecto," &c.
> (Bk. v. 420—422.)

All is force, nothing forethought. Atoms wandering in infinite space enter into an infinity of combinations in the lapse of infinite time. Chaos yields to order. The particles of matter combine, like allying itself with like. Ether embraces all things *avido complexu.* Sun and moon appear. Vegetation succeeds. Earth, justly styled on this account Mother, brings forth all sorts of animals. Birds issue from eggs in the genial season of spring. Next are generated beasts and men. This ought to startle no one. Even now, in her old age, the earth can produce small animals spontaneously: she could yield them of any size in her youthful prime. These were nursed in wombs attached to the soil by fibres,—

> "Crescebant uteri terræ radicibus apti,"—

and supplied thence with milk as they were born. Some were monstrous abortions, but only the perfect survived. Exhausted with these efforts, like a woman past bearing, the earth, on this scale, produces no more. Out of chaos she has not very long ago come; to chaos she must inevitably repass. Human language differs only in degree from the cries of brutes. And death consigns to a common nothingness a brute and a man.

In a work of widely different purport, a poet of far inferior calibre to Lucretius becomes the mouth-piece of a worthier reading of creation. No familiarity ought to blunt the perception of the exceeding beauty with which the best results of the unaided thought of ancient times are gathered up in the exordium to the *Metamorphoses.** With this we may consider the cycle of cos-

* To the non-classical reader a condensed translation may be not unwelcome:—

mogony in any sense collateral to the Mosaic as closed. True, the proneness to probe beginnings was not exhausted. Cosmogonies are among the latest as among the earliest efforts of the speculative faculty, and coexist with every stage of thought and culture. Even when faith is not in quest of a resting-place for the sole

"Ere sea and land, the vaulted sky before,
The face of things a common aspect wore:
Chaos its name—a rugged mass and rude,
Inert, incongruous, unformed, and crude;
A lump where lay, in wild disorder blent,
Each undistinguishable element.
No sun as yet his fiery beams had flung,
No hornèd moon had in the heaven been hung;
No orbèd world, to need the glorious pair,
Self-poised, was floating in the ambient air
Nor Amphitrite had spread her arms, and pressed
The lands, far-stretching, to her watery breast.
All things were jumbled—sea and soil were mixed;
That was unyielding, this nor firm nor fixed:
Confusion reigned; the air, uncharged with light,
Left all things warring in unbroken night:
Cold, hot, dense, rare, their various powers would prove,
And hard with soft, and dry with humid, strove.
But God and nature bade them cease to jar,
And lulled to peace the elemental war:
O'er the terrene the archèd heaven He spread,
And forced the waters to their ample bed;
Educed the firmament, serene and clear,
From forth the thick and loaded atmosphere;
And, while He bade the parts asunder roll,
In solid concord bound the gorgeous whole.
* * * * * *
Now burst the stars, and bristle o'er the sky;
The world now teems with various tenantry:
The fishes glide throughout their ocean home,
O'er hill and plain the beasts begin to roam;
While new-fledged birds to lighter realms repair,
And try their pinions on the liquid air.
A nobler creature, of capacious breast,
As yet was wanting to control the rest:
See him at last the infant earth adorn,
Man, heaven-allied, creation's lord, is born!
While brutes are fashioned prone, with drooping head,
And forced to gaze upon the earth they tread,
Him gives his Maker port and brow sublime,
Him bids look upward on his native clime;
And lift, unfettered by terrestrial bars,
Aloft his visage to the sparkling stars!"

of her foot, an impulse of a less legitimate kind takes shape in the attempt speculatively to re-create creation. Despite the tutoring of innumerable failures, the human mind is still found guessing and groping in regions where it can only guess, not know, and only grope, not see. Whether the brood of credulity, or the narcotics of scepticism, these efforts are rife in every age. The same decade which witnessed the publication of the *Principia* welcomed the solemn puerilities of Burnet; * and the contemporaries of Cuvier and Owen have lent an ear to the "Physio-philosophy" of Oken and the kindred romance of the "Vestiges." Theological delusion in our own time, indeed, addicts itself by preference to the end, and leaves the origin of things to its rival. Each does its appropriate work,—the depraving of religion into myth, and the debasing of science into materialism.

The spirit of special pleading is as abhorrent as it would be injurious to the cause of revealed truth. Let the question then be asked in all candour and calmness, whether any of these cosmogonies now passed in review can be placed on the same platform with the Mosaic record. To deny or depreciate flashings of the *mens divinior* in the best of them, would be to stamp primeval man as a castaway from the Paternal Providence, unvisited and unblessed by divine whisperings to the soul. Yet how dense the darkness amidst which that light was flickering! The psalmist of the *Veda* doubts whether the universe is not too hard a problem for even God. The Roman poet betrays the absence of religious insight and earnestness, not only by the conscious inter-

* "In this smooth earth were the first scenes of the world, and the first generations of mankind. It had the beauty and youth of blooming nature, fresh and fruitful, and not a wrinkle, scar, or fracture in all its body; no rocks nor mountains, no hollow caves nor gaping channels, but even and uniform all over. And the smoothness of the earth made the heavens so too; the air was calm and serene, none of those tumultuary motions and conflicts of vapours which the mountains and the winds cause in ours: 'twas suited to a golden age, and to the first innocence of nature."—"The Theory of the Earth, containing an account of the original of the earth and of all the general changes which it hath already undergone, or is to undergo, till the consummation of all things." Book I. chap. vi.

mixture of legend, but by asking, as if in playful bewilderment, which god it was that made man. Plato himself postulates a plurality of sub-creators. The Hindoo conception of periodic renovation is not the sagacious forecasting for which it has been mistaken; since it is simply ebb and flow, and unmeaning repetition, with sheer exhaustion and oblivion as the goal, not progress in a creative plan. These are blots on what is best. To compare the Mosaic record with the residuary fable would be to compare the utterances of right reason and profound devoutness with the incoherent mutterings of some distempered dream.

How *reticent* is that record! How free from the grotesque flights of an unchastened imagination! How abstinent from aught that can be stigmatized as a pandering to a childish curiosity or love of the marvellous! * Above all, how uniquely clear in the grand basis of all religion—the truth that creation is not self-created; and that man, its terrestrial climax, is the child and charge, not of an unconscious nature, but of the living God!

* "How does this picture of creation so singularly distinguish itself above all the fables and traditions of Upper Asia? By connection, simplicity, and truth. . . . I thank the philosopher, therefore, for this bold amputation of monstrous ancient fables."—*Herder*, *Phil. of Hist. of Man*, book x. chap. vi.; see also chap. v. *Quæst. Mos.*, p. 32. "Compared with these rude efforts of the most civilized people to solve the problem of the world's existence, the narrative of the creation in the book of Genesis is remarkable for its sublimity and truth."—*Kenrick*, *Ess. on Prim. Hist.*, p. 9. "All other cosmogonies are founded on the non-recognition of the existence and life of God in relation to the existence and life of the creature; hence the idea of emanation, in various modifications, pervades them all, being found in its most spiritual form in the Indian and Persian cosmogonies, and in one more rude and grotesque in the Phœnician, Babylonian, and Egyptian traditions, which suffer hylotheism to appear more plainly. To the idea of a creation out of nothing, no ancient cosmogony has ever risen."—*Havernick*, *Introduct. to Pentateuch*, pp. 93, 94. "Both systems [Homer's and Hesiod's] have the defect of exhibiting mind as subordinate to matter in the order of mundane development. Of creation in the higher sense, or the calling into existence of habitable animated worlds, by the fiat of a Supreme Eternal Spirit, out of chaos or nonentity, as in the Mosaic system, neither Hesiod nor Homer manifests any conception."—*Mure's Crit. Hist. of Lang. and Lit. of An. Greece*, book ii. ch. xx. Comp. Bishop Thirlwall's Hist. of Greece, vol. i. ch. vii.

III.

The author of the Essay on "Mosaic Cosmogony" is at pains to re-impress his readers with the oft-delivered lesson of the comparative insignificance of the earth, and the contrasting magnitude of the universe. Awe-inspiring, and in a sense appalling as the survey is,* no well-regulated Christian mind need shrink from it. Mr. Goodwin challenges us to look the facts in the face. Be it so. The earth is a planet among planets. An inner group of four comparatively small satellites, an outer group of four enormously larger, and a flock of asteroids between, such, with comets unnumbered, and sub-satellites not a few, the known retinue of the sun. The radius vector of the earth nearly 100 millions of miles in length; that of Neptune, the outpost, marking the frontier of the solar system, in space, about 3,000 millions; the earth's diameter to the sun's as 1 to 100—such the dimensions with which the mind must grapple at the first and lowest stage of this survey.

The sun is a star among stars. If the earth's distance from that luminary be taken as unity, a parallax of one second represents over 200,000.† But no star yields a parallax so large. The nearest, Alpha of the Centaur, gives nine-tenths of a second, Sirius one-fourth, the pole-star scarcely one-tenth.‡ Sirius therefore is about a million times farther off than the sun. Light travels to us from the moon in a second, from the sun in eight minutes, from Sirius in fifteen years. Sirius, moreover, is believed to surpass the sun in bulk and brightness as much as Jupiter, seen from an equal distance, would outshine the earth. On the other hand, certain stars which exceed the sun in volume are his inferiors in mass and density.§ All, however, in a general sense, are bodies of the same order; and their vary-

* See Mr. Keble's fine lines in *Lyra Innocentium*, for All Saints.

† Herschel's "Outlines of Astronomy," 4th edition, p. 540.

‡ "Cosmos," Sabine's translation, vol. iii. pp. 186—190.

§ Lardner, "The Stellar Universe," chap. i. § 35; "Plurality of Worlds," chap. viii. § 5.

ing magnitudes, on a sufficient average, are reasonably ascribed to vista. On this principle the dimensions of the Milky Way have been approximately "gauged." The system to which our sun and Sirius belong is conceived to be a stratum or swarm of about eighteen millions of stars; its shape that of a flattened Y, the sun being near the centre or point of bifurcation.* If the distance of Sirius be as 1, that of a star at any outskirt of the stratum will be as from 200 to 300. Light traverses the diameter of Neptune's orbit, or spans the solar system, in eight hours. It passes, by any of the three routes, from the centre to the extremities of the Milky Way, in about 3,000 years.†

If certain writers on astronomy are to be trusted in their diagnosis of celestial space, we must prepare for a third flight into a third order of distances. The Galaxy itself, they tell us, is but a nebula among nebulæ. Of these nearly 4,000 are already catalogued; and it is often asserted that they are parted from our stellar cluster and from each other by chasms only expressible by light-journeys, not of thousands, but of millions of years. Here at last we pause.

And not too soon; for we have by this time exchanged the sure opinions of science for the waxen wings of imagination.‡ It is not only unproved, but it has been unanswerably disproved, that any cluster of stars within the field of the telescope is coördinate in dimensions or in contents with the Milky Way. Among the cosmical clusters, the Galaxy is as the Australian continent to Polynesia—the mainland of the celestial archipelago. The nebulæ are its outliers and suffragans, not

* Herschel, p. 537.

† "Cosmos," Bohn's edition, vol. i. p. 72; Herschel, p. 541; Lardner, chap. iii. § 75. The elder Herschel (quoted by Lardner) computes 20,000, the younger 2,000, for the passage of light from the centre to an extremity of the Galaxy.

‡ A scientific friend favours me with the following:—"The statements current as to the distance of the nebulæ are founded on conjectural estimates, most diffidently advanced, by Sir W. Herschel, rather as *jeux d'esprit* than as even probable results, but which, by dint of repetition, have come to be regarded as almost of equal authority with the numbers relative to the solar system."

its peers and equivalents.* Of many proofs, one. It is a law of optics that the visibility of a luminous object diminishes with the square of increasing distance: the moon three times farther off would yield only a ninth of the light. Place Sirius then, on an outskirt of the Galaxy,—say 300 times his present distance,—and his light is enfeebled ninety thousand-fold; that is, he will be ninety times less visible to the highest power which can be applied to Lord Rosse's telescope than he is to the naked eye. Place him, however, at the hypothetical distance claimed by some writers for a nebula,—say 1,000 times more remote than this,—and he becomes ninety *million* times less visible! How in that case can he be "resolved?"—The universe of God is vast and awful: its greatness needs no loose exaggeration, no pandering to the vulgar appetite for arithmetical hyperbole. But He alone is infinite. Creation, mighty as it is, has limits. It claims no co-infinity with the Creator.

Authentic astronomy, overwhelming us by its measurements of magnitude and distance, supplies kindred conceptions of cosmical time. In the universe nothing is at rest. The fixed stars are now set free. Among them and along with them our sun circulates in a track for one revolution in which Mädler † demands no fewer than eighteen millions of years. How often have he and his attendant worlds described this round? How often may they be destined to describe it again? To such questionings the only answer is, that as the universe, however vast, is not infinite, so the universe, however ancient, is not eternal. It may be technically true that "neither *astronomical* nor *geological* science affects to state anything concerning the first origin of matter;" ‡ yet *chemical* analysis most certainly points to an origin and "effectually destroys the idea of an external self-existent matter, by giving to each of its atoms the essential characters,

* See an admirably reasoned article on the nebular hypothesis in the "Westminster Review," New Series, No. xxvii. Comp. Herschel, pp. 593, 608, 614; also "Plurality of Worlds," chap. vii. § 11.

† Quoted by Kurtz, "Bible and Astron.," ch. ii. § 16.

‡ Essays and Reviews, p. 218.

at once, of a *manufactured article* and a *subordinate agent.*" * Before the great clock was set a-going, there was an annealing of its materials, and an adjustment of its minutest parts. Law had its seat in "the bosom of God," before it had its expression in the constitution of matter and in the mechanism of the heavens. Motion so regulated presupposes *manipulation*, and therefore a "beginning." Apart, moreover, from the conviction so irresistibly generated by the contemplation of recondite numerical symmetry,† astronomical phenomena are utterly inexplicable unless we postulate *evolution* in cycles, however vast and slow; change, however infinitesimal; a *terminus à quo*, however remote, and a *terminus ad quem*, however obscure. If we combine the nebular hypothesis with the doctrine of a resisting medium,‡ the solar system is now wending through a stage of isolated parts, from a past of vaporous unity to a future of consolidated reunion. It was once all nebula; it will yet, if left to physical agencies, collapse into an exhausted and extinguished sun. That is, all we know of the earth is *an interval* between ejection from and re-absorption into the parent mass. Now the doctrine of the primitive continuity of matter, with high physical probability on its side, is perfectly consistent

* Sir John Herschel's "Discourse on the Study of Natural Philosophy," § 28.

† "Illustrations of the law of multiple proportions abound. Let the reader take for example the compounds of nitrogen and oxygen, five in number, containing the proportions of the two elements so described that the quantity of one of them shall remain constant:—

	Nitrogen.	Oxygen.
Protoxide	14·06	8
Deutoxide	14·06	16
Hyponitrous acid	14·06	24
Nitrous acid	14·06	32
Nitric acid	14·06	40

It will be seen at a glance, that while the nitrogen remains the same, the quantities of oxygen increase by multiples of 8," &c., &c.—*Fownes*, *Elementary Chemistry*, p. 147.

‡ Whewell, "Bridgewater Treatise," bk. ii. chap. viii.; Herschel, pp. 357, 374; Comte, "Positive Philosophy," vol. i. p. 206. Comte feels the above difficulties. With the characteristic credulity of unbelief, he predicts that when all the planets are ensepulchred in the sun, the sun will re-expand into a nebula.

with the enlightened advocacy of final causes. Without a Divine Pilot, how could a mass of nebulosity have *steered itself* into a solar system or a habitable earth? * And yet He, instead of creating, not only each planet, but each wandering fragment of the system, by a distinct fiat of Omnipotence, may have effected the necessary adaptations in concert with the ministry of His own laws. But the nebular hypothesis means "beginning." Subtract a day, or a thousand billions of years, it signifies not; eternity is left as eternal as ever. If matter is eternal, why then is its appointed race not run ere now? With eternity to ripen in, why is the earth so newly ripe? With a resisting medium, why is planetary and even cometary motion still unconquered? With an evolution eternally necessary, why is it still in progress? There is no refuge from the gripe of these questions save that which unites science to the first sentence of the Bible. The cosmos originated, not in physical necessity, but in Divine Will. "In the beginning God created the heaven and the earth."

Supposing, however, thus much conceded,—and the critic of "Mosaic Cosmogony" might perhaps readily concede it,—it will still be urged that science and Scripture dictate very different estimates of the *importance* of the earth,—astronomically, "but one of the lesser pendants of a body which is itself only an inconsiderable unit in the vast creation." † And this would be true were physical magnitude the sole criterion of importance. There are two bars to this surmise. One such consists in the manifest liability to deceptive extension of the principle of final causes. It is not astronomical science, but a vivacious imagination—not a Newton, but a Fontenelle—that builds earth-resembling worlds in the air. Than unnumbered masses of dead matter, be it brilliant or opaque, life is intrinsically nobler. Intelligence is intrinsically nobler, in a single example of it, than a universe of brute life. All the

* Whewell, "Bridgewater Treatise," bk. ii. chap. vii., and Sedgwick, "Discourse on the Studies of the University of Cambridge," Appendix D.

† Essays and Reviews, p. 213.

stars that surrender to the telescope are in themselves less wonderful than the solitary looker through.* Now no analogy can be more precarious than that which postulates the co-extension of matter and life. All the laws of vital development that obtain on this planet must be, not modified, but reversed, if there be any life in the sun. The moon can be inspected as if she were 200 miles off; and is plainly a naked mass of volcanic rock, without water, atmosphere, or trace of vegetation. Comets, compared by Kepler to "fishes in the sea" for multitude, may be peopled by the temerity of the human imagination, but not otherwise. The planets, indeed, are in a different case; there is a very high presumption that some of these at least are prepared homes for living beings. But there is an enormous and perilous stride from life to intelligence. If winged creatures cleave our co-planetary atmospheres, and fish replenish co-planetary deeps, does it follow that observatories crown the heights of Jupiter, or that navies sweep the seas of Mars? And yet, in the absence of reason and its creations elsewhere,—and we have not the shadow of a right to assume that there are libraries in Mercury any more than that there is a printing-press in the moon,—this earth must needs be the prerogative planet of the system. In this there may be physical congruity. The distribution of animal life athwart the globe appears to yield a law, *which there is no reason for supposing peculiar to itself*, of gradual deterioration and ultimate extinction as we recede from a medium temperature towards assignable extremes of either heat or cold. To God nothing is impossible. He *might* sustain life amidst the fires of Etna, or around the chillest pinnacle of the Alps. Life, in like manner, *may* be unfolded in other regions of the solar system, under physical conditions which are always obnoxious or fatal to it on the surface of the earth. But analogy, rightly construed, does not favour the surmise. And he who ponders the incompatibility of all terrestrial life with

* Compare Pascal,—"L'homme n'est qu'un roseau . . . mais c'est un roseau *pensant*," &c.—*Pensées*, Art. XVIII. x.

certain terrestrial locations, will pause before, in idolatry of mere material vastitude, he imposes on the Deity a speculative task, or disparages the noblest of His works that is known to us—the understanding and the soul of man.*

The plurality of worlds is a subject on which it is not prudent to dogmatize either way. That the universe is a lifeless desert, would be a doctrine loaded with improbabilities of which no ingenuity could get rid. But it would be quite as extravagant to insist that all space is swarming with duplicates of the globe we inhabit. We have no right to ask, Why, then, were they made? To what purpose is this waste? is an objection which will only appear of force to those who overlook the disproportion between life potential and life actual, and forget that Prospective Adjustment, though one law of divine workmanship, has Symmetrical Repetition for its colleague.† Who shall assure us that all suns, even double suns, have planets? Or that all planets are habitable, while it is certain that the only celestial body which can be closely scrutinized is "desolate and void?" Still more, who shall predicate from the probable or possible diffusion of life, across inaccessible areas of the universe, the necessary co-presence of reason and mind?

For reason, be it remembered, is but of yesterday on the earth; and it may be with millions of bodies in space, even supposing them inhabited, as it was with the earth for millions of years in time. Civilization

* The argument of this paragraph coincides with that of the "Plurality of Worlds." *Coincides*—for these sentences and that which is here subjoined were written years ago, before the writer had the slightest inkling that the same considerations had seemed of weight to a master of thought. "Our planet has been given by our Maker, so far as we can read His laws, and supposing the laws of life to be uniform, the same advantage *in space* and in relation to other bodies, which an inhabitant of the temperate zone has in reference to the regions," &c. In the same unpublished MS. geological time was insisted on as a counterpoise to astronomical space. Compare "Plurality of Worlds," p. 196. Similar considerations, I find, suggested themselves to Hugh Miller and to the Rev. Dr. King: "First Impressions of England," chap. xvii.; "Geology and Religion," p. 49.

† *e. g.* the female breast was *meant* for suckling, but of what *use* the paps in the male?

has no monument five thousand years old, the age of some still living trees. For the tertiary strata alone, Mr. Darwin demands three hundred millions, which implies his belief that ten times the period is far too narrow a reckoning for the entire sedimentary series. But even the least fanciful geologist will concede that not fewer than one million centuries parts the age of granite from the age of man.* So long, at the least, was the earth a-ripening; who shall say, a-being *wasted?* So long, ere she was freighted with a thinker or a worshipper, or had become the domicile of man and his marvels, our planet performed her rounds as punctually and perfectly as she does to-day. In presence of this fact, how precarious the taunt, and how inconsiderate the sneer, which parades physical bulk as the infallible index whether of created dignity or of creative regards! † As if the earth, when she first received a rational inhabitant, did not thereby become *a value* in the universe which would neither have been impaired nor augmented had she shrunk that instant to the dimensions of Mercury, or expanded that instant to the girth of Sirius.

Were all that has been so eloquently imagined proved; were it to be admitted, not only with due reserve, but with the largest license claimed by the most fervent and fertile fancy, that the luminaries of midnight were not, even to that reckoning, "created in vain," or "called into existence for no other purpose than to throw a tide of useless splendour over the solitudes of immensity," ‡—we might with bold front and sure footing remind the sceptic that if the universe was not too great for God to make, no part of it can be too little for God to care for; and track his faithlessness to its source in a tacit transference of his own short-sightedness to the All-Seeing, and his own weakness to the Almighty. It might be added that any revelation to

* Phillips, "Life on the Earth," p. 126.

† "Shall we measure grace by cubic miles, and God's love by the size of the fixed stars?"—*Kurtz*, p. 83.

‡ Dr. Chalmers, "Astronomical Discourses."

be of use to mankind, must treat the system of things as it is in our perspective, putting in the foreground what is of concernment to us, and leaving the outer universe among the secrets of Omniscience; fulfilling its aim if it tell us with sublime brevity that there are not two, or ten, or ten thousand creators, but that He who made *our* great lights of sun and moon enkindled *all* lights in the spangled space, and "made the stars also." And such vindication would be sound, such reassurance sufficient. Yet it is not all. We owe allegiance to science, but none to romance masquerading in scientific costume. Now if astronomy supplies a survey of space, geology yields an inquest of time. And this latter, by opposing the twin immensity of past duration to the vastness of the starry universe, contributes a salutary and invincible check to gratuitous guess-work in the garb of philosophy. Who shall tell us that wherever matter is life must be, with the moon a naked desert? Who shall tell us that where life is there must also be reason and moral responsibility, with the certainty confronting him that this earth has been ten thousand years the abode exclusively of brutes, for one that it has been the home of man?

Geology, like astronomy, though with still more peremptory grasp, leads us back to a beginning. Its bulging equator and flattened poles, its pavement of congealed lava, which we name granite, nay, the oldest water-woven *carpeting* of that pavement composed of the detritus of the igneous rocks, all attest the emergence of our planet from a primitive temperature and a crisis of forces in which no life could subsist. At a low estimate, as we have seen, a million centuries in-intervene between that period and the present. Which interval, whatever its length, forms a chronicle of the genesis of life, the procession of the types of life, and the advent of man. Now what, in brief epitome, on these absorbing subjects, has the record of the rocks to tell?

Resting on the primitive crust of the globe, and stretching upwards through a thickness of tens of thousands of feet to the old red sandstone, are sedimentary strata,—Silurian, Cambrian, Laurentian,—which it may be convenient to group as the *sub-Devonian* series. In the upper segments of this vast cumulation life abounds; in the lower it fades away to zero. To reach, save approximately, the absolute life-limit, science can scarcely hope: enough that a region has been reached where life is *findable* but not *found*.* So soon as it appears at all,† life presents itself in three of the four familiar types; to which, ere the Silurian system closes, the vertibrate is added. Under the lower garb of fish, this takes possession of the waters throughout the old red, carboniferous, and permian systems, on to the end of the palæozoic period: throughout the entire mesozoic period, it is dominant under the higher though continuous garb of gigantic reptiles—as also of birds—both on land and sea. Faintly and feebly represented during these "middle ages," the mammalia start into strength and supremacy with the dawn of tertiary or cænozoic time. The emergence of all new species has ceased ere man, in the latest portion of this latest period, himself appears.

Thus the crust of the earth is a chronicle in five zones. The history is that of creative ascent from dead matter to life; from invertebrate life to that of the back-bone; from the life of the back-bone, in the fish-reptile series, to that of the breast; and lastly, from the life of the breast to that of the plenarily-endowed brain. Between the exterior zones, azoic and anthropozoic, lie three intermediate brute zones, the sub-vertebrate, vertebrate, and mammiferous. That a *tincture* of vertebrate life is detected in Siluria, or a subdued *prophecy* of mammalian life in the mesozoic rocks, signifies not. The *facies* of each period is unmistakeable. In Siluria, a vertebrate fossil is a straggler and a stranger: the Silurian fish is the mere vanguard of that innumerable host which crowds the ocean for ever after from pole to pole. Just so the few and feeble pioneer

* See Sir Roderick Murchison's great work on "Siluria," p. 20; "Life on the Earth," pp. 68, 214; "Footprints of the Creator," pp. 216—220; and Ansted, "The Ancient World," *passim*.

† "Life on the Earth," p. 71.

mammalia do not give character to the secondary formations; only in the tertiaries do they appear in strength. Geology must be, not extended, but revolutionized, before this generalization can be upset. For it checks the less secure though consistent indications of land-life by the cogent and copious criteria of the life of the sea.*

Can dead matter, of its own accord, become alive? Can an invertebrate animal improve itself into a fish? Can a bird, or a reptile, never suckled itself, improvise an apparatus for suckling its offspring? Finally, can the mere brute burst the bonds of instinct; struggle into the capacity of abstract thought, and its rational expression, language; fall down on its knees and *pray*; and pass either *per saltum* or by slow degrees the gulf that parts the simian from the human brain? If these questions, one and all, must be met by a peremptory negative, the strata of the earth are the register of divine acts strictly creative and supernatural; each marking a step in an ordered progress culminating at last in man. Of him all lower creation prophesies; to him all lower creation tends. The vertebrate structure is the endowment of life with power: the mammalian function superadds love. But the plenary development of neither is possible till wisdom is bestowed through the human brain.† Thus the evolution of ancient nature, through phases that are perplexing only because they are preliminary and partial, steadily converges towards its sublime purpose—the manifesting of God, All-Wise, All-Loving, Almighty. Each act of the long drama contributes to the result, though the enigma is not unravelled till the whole is seen. The dynasty of the lower vertebrate, and the dynasty of the mammal, await their explanation in the master-creature who succeeds to both. The rocks, therefore, which are the monument of a "high and ancient order," are also the receptacle of a natural revelation. Palæontology, like

* Owen, "Palæontology," pp. 408—410.

† "The Three Barriers," (Oxford, J. H. and J. Parker, 1861,) pp. 88—94.

the Mosaic cosmogony, leads up to its "image of God." It lays its finger on a starting-point of which it perceives man to be the goal.* Till man is made, there are many creatures to make; the vegetable and animal life that is summoned into being in the latest tertiary ages has evidently a special relation to his wants: but when he is made, God creates no more.

Nature is a scheme, or it is an accident. It is an evolution foreseen, controlled, and piloted throughout by Divine thought and will, or it is hap-hazard development of unconscious force. To the latter doctrine the rocky archives are in changeless antagonism. Life had its beginning. How? All life that we know of *presupposes* life: † even were its microscopic forms producible from a "corps putrescible," whence that "corps?" ‡ Again, life has its gradations. A lower animal cannot create itself into a higher animal. Throughout the geologic æons, there is indeed most clearly an "ascent in the main;" § a passing from simpler to more specialized embodiments of the creative archetype. But this is a process effected *for* the creature, not *by* it. Transmutation of species, unknown to human experience, is equally unknown to geology. Type after type appears and disappears; but none melts into a something not itself. Each creature, throughout the long succession, comes in as it goes out,

* See the profound and splendid concluding pages of Owen, "On the Nature of Limbs."

† The words of Cuvier are very weighty:—"La vie en general suppose donc l'organisation en general, et la vie propre de chaque être suppose l'organisation propre de cet être, comme la marche d'une horloge suppose l'horloge; aussi ne voyons-nous la vie que dans des êtres tout organisés et faits pour en jouir; et tous les efforts des physiciens n'ont pu encore nous montre la matière s'organisant, soit d'elle-même, soit pour une cause extérieure quelconque. En effet, la vie exerçant sur les élémens qui font a chaque instant partie du corps vivant, et sur ceux qu'elle y attire, une action contraire à ce que produiraient sans elle les affinités chimiques ordinaires, *il repugne qu'elle puisse être elle-même produite par ces affinités*, et cependant l'on ne connaît dans la nature aucune autre force capable de réunir des molécules auparavant séparées."—*Cuvier*, *Le Règne Animal; Introduction*, p. 17.

‡ "The Three Barriers," p. 160.

§ Owen, "Palæontology," p. 411.

and goes out as it came in. When we concentrate attention on the cardinal transitions, the proof becomes overwhelming. If, by the operation of natural law, a sub-vertebrate could produce a vertebrate, or a reptile a mammal, in the old periods of the earth, why not now? Law cannot be supposed conscious of the superfluity of its own action, or cognizant of the critical moment when to stop. For the acts of geology there is therefore but one solution,—the periodical exertion of supernatural power.

To such intervention is it specially necessary to refer the origin of the human race. Between man and all lower existence there stretches a chasm defined by what may be called the language-generating brain. On a centigrade scale of cerebral development, all values of the human organ shade into each other from one hundred downwards to seventy-five; while all values of the brute brain, from the fish to the ape, range upwards in close sequence from zero to about thirty. At both ends of the scale, therefore, the two orders of endowment pass through the assigned range by every, or almost every, shade of transition. *But there is no bridging brain between.* Bounded by cerebral tropics lies a huge zone vacant, nearly equal to *both* the outlying ranges above and below. Even the most abnormally low individual human brain and the most abnormally high individual brute brain leave two-thirds of its normal compass unspanned. Whence this prodigious chasm? Connecting it, as we must needs do, with the perfect hand and the erect attitude, there could be no more signal monument of the interposal of the Creator.*

* "But admitting the foregoing evidence, freely recognising the greatness of its cumulative force, and proceeding to the conclusion to which it leads, we still find ourselves on the shore of *a vast and seemingly impassable gulf* separating the highest of the quadrumana from the lowest forms of man. . . . The wide chasm in cerebral development still remains; and, considered in conjunction with the fact that, so far as we know, man alone possesses the gift of speech, *compels us to confess that the genesis of mankind is a mystery which, for the present at least, science is powerless to penetrate.*"—*Westminster Review*, No. xxxiv. Art. vi.

"The holy gift of speech,"* as it has been aptly called, is to all men common, to man strictly peculiar. Like the parent prerogative of which it is the sign and the satellite, this endowment secludes mankind as of one blood and one brotherhood, between which and the very highest of the manco-cerebral mammalia "a great gulf is fixed."† Moreover, it constitutes an instrument of discovery, and bestows a power of association, ancillary to the dominion divinely delegated to the master-tenant of the world.

Cursory as this review has necessarily been, it may in some degree assist the reader in the task of collating with the teachings of modern science the group of ancient cosmogonies, in the first instance, and the Mosaic record in the second. From that fiery ordeal, how much, say of the *Timæus*, escapes unscathed? And what harm has happened to the Scripture? One point reserved, though not forgotten or evaded, which lesson, of all those our exegesis yielded, have we got to un-

* Wiseman, "Connection between Science and Revealed Religion."

† "Language is our Rubicon. . . . No process of natural selection will ever distil significant words out of the notes of birds or the cries of beasts. In Greek, language is *logos;* but *logos* means also reason, and *alogon* was chosen as the name, and the most proper name, for brute. No animal thinks, and no animal speaks, except man. . . . To think is to speak low; to speak is to think aloud. . . . That faculty [articulate expression of rational conceptions] *was not of his own making*. . . . The science of language thus leads us up to that highest summit from whence we see into the dawn of man's life on earth; and where the words which we have heard so often from the days of our childhood,—'And the whole earth was of one language and of one speech,'—assume a meaning more natural, more intelligible, and more convincing, than they ever had before."—*Max Müller*, *Lect. on Science of Language*, pp. 340—377.

Compare the fine passage of St. Ambrose:—"Erigit bucula ad cœlum oculos, sed quid spectet, ignorat. Erigunt feræ, erigunt aves: omnibus est liber aspectus, *sed soli inest homini eorum quæ aspicit affectus interpres*. . . . Audiunt quoque animantes cæteræ, sed quis præter hominem audiendo cognoscit? . . . Hoc est preciosissimum, quod homo divinæ vocis sit organum," &c.—*Hexaëmeron*, lib. vi. cap. ix. Among patristic expositors of the Hexameron, St. Basil must rank far below the great Latin Fathers. Of recent works on the early chapters of Genesis, one of the most valuable is "Discourses on the Fall and its Results," by Dr. Hannah, Warden of Trinity College, Glenalmond, Perthshire. See especially as corrective of "Essays and Reviews," p. 221, the discourse on the "Image of God in Man."

learn? Astronomy indeed teaches us that the universe is inconçeivably vast, and geology that the earth is immensely old. But does the majesty of the Scripture *collapse* under the new burden of significance it has to bear? True, modern science expands and educates our apprehension of Almighty power. But does it displace or disturb the conception already imbibed from that ancient and reverend record? Does *it* limit the power which spake all things into being? Does *it* teach us of any time when God was not, or give us a lower idea of His duration than this, that He "inhabits eternity?" When the elder Herschel shut up his telescope after sounding the Galaxy through and through into the starless space beyond, did he find nobler language for the celestial revelation than "God said, Let there be light! And there was light. . . . He made the stars also?" When the inquisitors of the earth's strata return from their perusal of those chambers of imagery where the animal dead of uncounted ages lie sealed in stone, have they acquired any knowledge of the creative archetype, and fore-ordained succession of forms, which does not readily fall into the *mould* provided in the written Word?* "Inspiration," indeed, "is not omniscience." Moses did not know the universe as its Maker knew it. But the thing hypothetically required is not the miraculous anticipation of scientific range of research, or the revealing of such knowledge before its time, but such an influence of the Divine Spirit on the mind of the writer as should ensure that, *when the knowledge came*, the general dignity, congruity, and religious impressiveness of the lesson should suffer no harm from the advent of such knowledge. This is all which, on any sober or reasonable theory of inspiration, we have a right to expect. And this we have. True insight into the meaning and method of the extant creation is not falsified, though it is extended, by the unveiling of

* "Ejiciant aquæ *reptilia*, et volatilia *volantia*," (Gen. i. 20.) By comparing "Palæontology," p. 198, on the "artificiality of the supposed class-distinction between fishes and reptiles," with "Essays and Reviews," p. 239, it will be seen that Professor Owen coincides with Moses, though he differs from Mr. Goodwin.

the past. Insight into the geological past it is unnecessary to suppose that the inspired penman either needed or had given him. Enough if the Bible opens with a divinely illuminated survey of creation such as readily *assimilates* the results of that research it was never meant to supersede or forestall; perfect, in scientific as in earlier ages, to all spiritual intents and purposes; so imbued with religious grandeur that it can never be supplanted in its own proper sphere; so far before its time in this respect that it is of *all* time, and leads us upward from the limitations of even a prophet's thought to the presiding and over-ruling influence of that Wisdom "known to Whom are all His works from the beginning of the world." In the estimate of the most *encyclopædic* scientific mind of this century, one psalm, the 104th, "represents the image of the whole cosmos." * Yet what is the first of Genesis but the mother-psalm of which the 104th, section by section, is the daughter, the antiphone, and the echo?

IV.

Of the old Vedic Hymn (p. 304) Mr. Max Müller remarks, "Prose was at that time unknown, as well as the distinction between prose and poetry." † By what epithet shall we designate the Mosaic heptameron? Sceptics call it a myth; or else, more mildly, the speculation of an ancient sage. Most Christians speak of it as a history or narrative. Hitherto, declining either of these terms, we have been styling it somewhat vaguely a "record." The author of an able and learned reply to Mr. Goodwin, written in a most reverential spirit, has come to the conclusion that it is a

* Humboldt adds, "We are astonished to find in a lyrical poem of such limited compass the whole universe—the heavens and the earth—sketched with a few bold touches. The contrast of the labour of man with the animal life of nature, and the image of Omnipresent Invisible Power, renewing the earth at will or sweeping it of inhabitants, is a grand and solemn poetical creation."—*Cosmos*, vol. ii. part i.

† Bunsen, "Philos. of Univ. Hist.," vol. ii. p. 136. Compare that most interesting concluding chapter of Mr. Müller's "Hist. of Ancient Sanskrit Literature."

"parable."* Others suggest that it is a "vision."† One gentleman considers it an account of "plan" as distinguished from fulfilment.‡ We venture to think none of these descriptions satisfactory. The Book of Genesis opens with the inspired PSALM of Creation.

On so transparent a gloss as the "vision"-scheme, words would only be wasted. Nor will many believe that creation *as an idea* is the thing intended, so long as the plainest of plain language assures them that the thing intended is creation *as a fact*. "Parable" has a certain propriety when applied to a single accessory of the record; but it cannot for one moment be accepted as a feasible designation for the 1st of Genesis as a whole. On the hypothesis that we have to do with an ordinary prose narrative, chronicle, or diary, there immediately emerges the great difficulty of the "days." With this it is not too much to say that no ingenuity has as yet grappled successfully. The choice lies between the Chalmerian interpolation of the geological ages before the first day begins, and the Cuvierian expansion of the six days into geological ages. For these solutions respectively, Dr. Buckland and Hugh Miller have each done their best; and more skilful and accomplished advocacy could not be found.§ But the

* Mr. Huxtable, "The Sacred Record of Creation Vindicated and Explained."

† Kurtz, "Bible and Astron.," ch. i., iii.; Hugh Miller, "Testimony of the Rocks;" also "Mosaic Record in Harmony with the Geological."

‡ Professor Challis, "Creation in Plan and in Progress."

§ Among the followers of Buckland, with certain modifications, are Dr. Pye Smith, "Relation between Scripture and Geological Science;" Hitchcock, "Religion of Geology;" Crofton, "Genesis and Geology;" and, so far as they commit themselves, Archdeacon Pratt, "Scripture and Science not at Variance;" Gloag, "Primeval World." Miller's ablest ally is MacDonald, "Creation and the Fall;" and on the same side are Silliman, "Wonders of the Earth and Truths of the Bible;" Gaussen, "The World's Birthday;" Sime, "Mosaic Record in Harmony with the Geological;" McCausland, "Sermons in Stones;" and McCaul, "Notes on Genesis." The Burnet Prize Essay of forty-five years ago, "Records of Creation," by the present Archbishop of Canterbury, although one of the four works which compose collectively the most valuable contribution to the theistic argument since Paley, (Dr. Whewell's "Bridgewater Treatise," Hugh Miller's "Footprints of the Creator," and Principal Tulloch's "Theism," arguments which compelled Hugh Miller to abandon the older method have not been answered. Nor is his own scheme free from the gravest difficulties. Who can bring himself to believe, for example, that when the sacred writer speaks of trees laden for human use with seed-enclosing fruit, he could have had in his mind, or could have so described, the gymnogenous flora of the coal-measures?

Certain writers evade embarrassment by declining to elect among the competing "reconciliations." It is enough, they suggest, that some of them *may* be sound, although it is inconvenient to become responsible for any of them; or they allege that the record was not intended to do what it expressly undertakes and professes to do; or, otherwise, that the time is not come for a comparison between Scripture and geology, since there are points on which geologists are not agreed among themselves.* All this is but a manifestation of anxiety to snatch a cherished dogma from a dreaded foe.† Were the panic well-founded, the belief indebted to such expedients would be only screened, not saved. The combat would indeed be averted, but the enemy would remain master of the field.

Mr. Goodwin cannot be blamed for chastising palpable subterfuges. "Without a sun," it has been observed, "morning and evening are inconceivable to all, save commentators, and *they* have made the matter

being the others,) was written long before the data for a decision had been reached.

* This multiform fallacy of evasion, brushed away by Hugh Miller both in "First Impressions of England" and in "Testimony of the Rocks," is exemplified in Buckland, pp. 12, 33; Archdeacon Pratt, p. 34; King, "Geology and Religion," p. 44; Gloag, p. 110; and Buchanan, "Essays and Reviews Examined," pp. 128, 131. Dr. Chalmers himself, in his private correspondence, betrays a similar hesitance, by speaking of "yet another way of *saving the credit* of the record." It no doubt escaped this great and good man, that his own "way" brought him into direct collision with the "Shorter Catechism," which asserts that God's work of creation consists in His "making all things out of nothing, *in the space of six days*,"—not millions of years before the *first* day dawned.

† "The doubt and perplexity which they affect do not exist: both the principles of the natural sciences and of Biblical exegesis are certain beyond dispute."—*Kalisch*, p. 52.

very clear to us."* If well-meaning harmonizers will lay themselves open to sarcasm, they must take the consequences. Satire will not spare writers who trench, however unwittingly, on the ludicrous, when, under the abused ægis of the "Plurality of Worlds," they identify the planet Jupiter with "the waters that are above the firmament;" or figure Moses as surprised into the ejaculation, "The great Tanninim!" as he describes in cosmoramic trance the saurian monsters of the Oolite.† The worst *dis*-service to the cause of divine truth is that contributed by contorted science and sophistic exegesis.‡ Mr. Goodwin exemplifies, however, the opposite pole of prejudice. Why make difficulties where there are none? Why gratuitously degrade "Spirit" into "wind," converting the image of divine love and energy into an agitation of the air?§ Or why try to tear from *rakia* its true equivalent of *expanse?*‖ Or why refuse to allow for the essentially figurative character of all words descriptive of celestial space and its aspects, in order to fasten an incredible puerility of conception on the "Hebrew Descartes or Newton?" Mr. Goodwin ought to caution the readers of Shelley, in case "build up the blue dome of air" should suggest delusive reminiscences of the dome of St. Paul's. *Uni-verse* ought to be banished from his vocabulary, as implying the diurnal revolution of the

* *Quæst. Mos.*, p. 14.

† The curious reader may collate "Harmony of Mosaic with Geological Record," (Constable, 1854,) p. 98, with the lively and ingenious pictorial restorations in Mr. Page's "Life of the Globe," (Blackwood, 1861,) p. 137, if he wishes to appreciate the "vision."

‡ For example:—"Before sin entered, there could be no violent deaths, if any death at all. But by the particular structure of the teeth of animals, God prepared them for that kind of aliment which they were to subsist on *after the fall*"!—*Adam Clarke on Gen.* i.

§ "Quod nonnulli *ventum* intelligunt, adeo frigidum est *ut refutatione nullâ indigeat.*"—*Calvin, in loc.* "Spiritus *incubabat:* instar avis, quæ incubando ovis, illa fovet," &c.—*Piscator, in loc.* Compare Vedic Hymn, p. 301.

‖ Long before the days of "reconciliations" Calvin wrote,—"Nescio cur Græcis placuerit vertere στερέωμα, quod in firmamenti nomine imitati sunt Latini: *ad verbum enim est expansio.*" So Tremellius and Junius, followed by Piscator, render *expansum.* Compare "spreadest out the heavens *like a curtain,*" Ps. civ. 2; and see previous note, pp. 252, 253.

fixed stars in a frame or "firmament." And it might obviate disappointment were he to drop a warning that we need not look for milk in the Galaxy.

Enough, whether of quibbles or of makeshifts. When we consider the pervading parallelism; the rhythmic refrain*—"the evening and the morning;" the periodic fiat—"Let there be light, a water-parting firmament, land, plants: lights in the firmament, life in the waters, life on the land, Man;" the punctual fulfilment—"It was so;" the retrospect—"God saw that it was good;"—the chief wonder is how it ever was possible to exact from the oldest and sublimest poem in the world the attributes of narrative prose. Yet our surprise abates, not only when we reflect that the error entailed, till these later times, rather a literary than a religious loss, but also when we call to mind how long a similar mask disguised the architecture of entire books of the Old Testament, and obscured the plenary significance of large sections even of the New. Bishop

* Compare the refrain in the fine Vedic hymns (circa B.C. 1000) translated by Mr. Max Müller, "Hist. of Ancient Sanskrit Literature," pp. 540, 569. "Varuna" is *οὐρανός*:—

"Let me not yet, O Varuna, enter into the house of clay:
Have mercy, Almighty, have mercy!
If I go along trembling, like a cloud driven by the wind:
Have mercy, Almighty, have mercy!

* * * * * *

Whenever, O Varuna, we commit an offence:
Whenever we break thy law through thoughtlessness:
Have mercy, Almighty, have mercy!

"In the beginning there arose the Source of golden light:
He was the only born lord of all that is:
He established the earth and this sky:
Who is the God to whom we shall offer our sacrifice?
He who gives life, He who gives strength:
Whose blessing all the bright gods desire:
Whose shadow is immortality, whose shadow is death;
Who is the God to whom we shall offer our sacrifice?

* * * * * *

May He not destroy us—He the Creator of the earth:
He, the righteous, who created the heavens:
He who also created the bright and mighty waters:
Who is the God to whom we shall offer our sacrifice?"

Jebb belongs to this century, Bishop Lowth to the last; yet how much, in this field of hermeneutic, is due to these two names! If a veil was lifted so recently from the face of David or Isaiah, are we to marvel if a veil has lain on the face of Moses? Even some eighty years ago, however, a striking indication of the true affinities of the composition was furnished in a book well known in Scotland as the "Assembly's Paraphrases." The idea was to provide metrical versions of portions of Scripture most closely akin to the Psalms. Of the thirty-two Old Testament selections, one, "O God of Bethel," is a hymn; thirty-one are, in the strict sense, paraphrases. Of these, thirty are based on the poetical books,—Job, Proverbs, Ecclesiastes, and the Prophets. The solitary outsider, linking like with like, *has for pedestal the* 1*st of Genesis.*

None will dispute the presence of parallelism in the Lord's Prayer,—such parallelism as is proper to prayer, or psalm, or parable, or prophecy, or impassioned discourse, but is *not* proper to historical narrative. Yet how closely homologous in structure is the Mosaic heptameron:—

Our Father, which art in heaven:	In the beginning God created *the heaven and the earth:*
Thy Name be hallowed:	Let there be *light:*
Thy kingdom come:	Let there be a *firmament*, &c
Thy will be done, &c.	Let the *dry land* appear, &c.
Give *us* our bread:	Let there be *lights:*
Forgive *us* our trespasses:	Let the *waters*... and fowl, &c.
Lead *us* not into temptation, &c.	Let the *earth* bring forth, &c.
For *Thine* is the kingdom, &c.	Thus *the heavens and the earth* were finished, &c.

If one of these divine compositions is not ordinary prose, neither is the other. The triads of days are as distinctly defined as the triplets of petitions. Only the paralellism, from the correlative interlacement of the groups, is more intricate and complex in the Heptameron than in the Prayer.

He who perceives this has the true key to the concord which he will search for elsewhere and otherwise in vain.

Respect the parallelism, cease to ignore the structure, allow for the mystic significance of the number seven,* and all perplexities vanish. The two groups of days are each perfectly regular, when group, *in its integrity*, is collated with group: neither triad, if it is to exhaust *its own aspect* of creation, can afford to part with, or dislocate, any of its members; and the second triad, as a whole, is rightly and of necessity second, as the first is rightly and of necessity first. And yet it is self-evident that if, for any reason, we trisect or break up the groups, the true *continuation* of day 1 is not day 2 but day 4, of day 2 not day 3 but day 5, of day 3 not day 4 but day 6. And thus the "days" themselves are transfigured from registers of time into definitives of strophes or stanzas,—lamps and land-marks of a creative sequence,—a mystic drapery, a parabolic setting,—shadowing by the sacred cycle of seven the truths of an ordered progress, a foreknown finality, an achieved perfection, and a divine repose.†

* "If Cain be avenged sevenfold" = completely. "To flee seven ways" = a total rout. "Silver purified seven times" = perfectly, &c., &c. "*Per senarium numerum* [1 + 2 + 3 = 6] *est operum significata perfectio. . . . De septenarii porro numeri perfectione* dici quidem plura possunt," &c.—*St. Augustine, De Civitat. Dei*, lib. xi. cc. xxx. and xxxi. On the number seven see also Moses Stuart, "Apocalypse," vol. ii. pp. 425—432, and Forbes, "Symmet. Struct. of Scripture," pp. 159—162.

† Herder was a rationalist, but too candid and clear-sighted to pervert a *symbol*, of which the meaning was evident to him, into a literal register of time. The following passages are very important, as coming from so acute and unbiassed a witness:—

"To remove the false notion of days, let me observe what is obvious to every one on a bare inspection, that the whole system of this representation rests on a comparison by means of which the separations do not take place physically but symbolically. As our eye is incapable of comprehending at one view the whole creation, it was necessary to *form classes*, and it was most natural to distinguish in the first place the heavens from the earth. . . . Thus this ancient document is the first simple *table of a natural order*, in which the term 'days,' while it is subservient to another purpose of the author, is employed only as a *nominal scale* for the division. . . . . Before we approach this crown [man], let us consider a few more master-strokes which animate the picture of this ancient sage. . . . . The sun and stars enter into this picture of nature *as soon as they can*. . . . . With equal truth and acuteness this natural philosopher places the creatures of air and water in one class. . . . . With joy and wonder I approach the rich

Which symbolism, engrafted by permission of the divine wisdom on a division of time astronomically obvious, and embodied in the Psalm of the Almighty's handiwork by

> "That Shepherd who first taught the chosen seed
> In the beginning how the heavens and earth
> Rose out of chaos,"

becomes, in turn, to the Jewish nation at the Exodus, the platform of the law of the Sabbath. God's week is mystical, man's week is literal. But the spiritual *homology* assumed is not disturbed by the inevitable disparity of scale. God did His own perfect work in His own perfect way, and His very rest was but a passing onward to still higher manifestations of His boundless bounty and love. In this, says the Fourth Commandment, *quoting*, though without reference, the familiar religious lesson, "Be ye followers of God. Fill *your* six days as He does *His*, in the Psalm of His creative working, with work that shall, like His, be 'good.' Rest on *your* seventh day, as you have heard *He* rested, not in the torpor of an animal sloth, but in the liberated activities of a devout soul."

description. . . . . Behold the most ancient philosophy of the history of man."—Bk. x. ch. v.

"Our philosopher has unravelled this chaos. . . . . Everything incomprehensible to man his account excludes, and confines itself to what we can see with our eyes and comprehend with our minds. . . . . Men have deemed the Asiatic nations, with their infinite computations of time, infinitely wise; and the traditions of which we are speaking infinitely childish, because, contrary to all reason they say, nay contrary to the testimony of the structure of the globe, it hurries over the creation. . . . . In my opinion *this is palpable injustice.* Had Moses been nothing more than the collector of these traditions, he, a learned Egyptian, could not have been ignorant of those æons, &c. Why, therefore, did he not interweave them into his account? Why, as if in contempt and despite of them, did he *symbolically compress* the origin of the world into the smallest portion of time? Evidently because he was desirous of obliterating them as fables. . . . . Moses leaves every one at liberty to frame epochs as he pleases. . . . . To obviate these follies, he represents his picture *in the readiest cycle of a terrestrial revolution.*"—Bk. x. ch. vi.

So Dr. Henry More, *Conjectura Cabbalistica*, p. 22, makes Moses explain, "It was for pious purposes that I *cast the creation into that order of six days.*" Again, "The hebdomad or septenary is a fit symbol of God."—p. 86.

V.

For more than half a century the Mosaic record of creation has been invested with a peculiar interest. Like the regiment in a great war which goes first into action, or like the outlying rock in a long ridge which has to sustain the full shock of the yet unbroken billow, this portal of the Scriptures, from its being the portal, and from the presumed facilities of successful attack supplied by the young science of geology, has been pre-eminently exposed to the polemic of modern scepticism. One phase, however, of the "conflict of ages" "only dates from the publication of "Essays and Reviews." The Bible used to be assailed by candid and consistent adversaries: it is now, for the first time in the history of religious controversy, impeached by professed friends.

Now we are surely entitled to ask any critic of "Mosaic Cosmogony" *in what character* he proposes to approach it; in plain English, to shew his colours and to take his side. A man may be a Christian or he may be an unbeliever, but he cannot be anything between. There are certain problems which cannot be dealt with piecemeal. Divine revelation must be accepted as a whole, or rejected as a whole; no third course is conceivable. Of the Hebrew lawgiver, in special, has not the Lord of Christians said, "If ye believe not his writings, how shall ye believe My words?" *

We are not indeed bound to imperil the Christian faith on the credibility of every rash and rhetorical exaggeration of a doctrine the over-statement of which might be natural in the ninth, and excusable even in the seventeenth century; although in the present age to transgress in like fashion is simply to play into the hands of adversaries. The sacred writers were pen-*men* and not *pens;* the Divine influence under which they wrote was not analogous to the infusion of such an instinct as makes the bee or the ant an "animated tool," but

* St. John v. 47.

rather to the power of a great human mind over narrower, and lower, and feebler minds. The afflatus was not *mesmeric*, but moral and spiritual: it was rather comparable to thermal currents than to the rigid circumscription of mathematically defined zones. But it is one thing to make frank and full allowance for the human element in the Scriptures, and quite another to forget or explain away the co-presence of the divine. Does a man *accept the supernatural*, yes or no? Does he believe, or not believe, in the resurrection of our Lord from the dead? These are the plain questions to which from any censor of the Scriptures, we are entitled, *in limine*, to exact plain and straightforward answers. If the reply be, "I do *not* accept the supernatural: I do *not* believe that Christ is risen,"—we know what and whom we have to contend with. But if the response be the other way,—"I *do* accept the supernatural: I *do* believe in the Saviour's rising from the dead,"—it is surely, in such case, pertinent to remind him that he must in all consistency accept and believe *much more*. A divine reality in the religion bespeaks and implies a divine element in its records. They stand or fall together. He who professes to hold that the revelation is supernatural, yet argues as if the Bible were merely human, confutes himself. Every mind disciplined in the valuation of evidence must see that the choice is, Neither or Both.

"If Christ be not risen, your faith is in vain." This is one point of apostolic teaching out of which no trick of words can ever juggle us. We cannot pillow our hopes on cloudland; and all is cloudland if we cannot discern in the past the divine Personality of Him who, "when He had overcome the sharpness of death, opened the kingdom of heaven to all believers." Weary human nature lays its head on *this* Bosom, or it has nowhere to lay its head. Tremblers on the verge of the dark and terrible valley which parts the land of the living from the untried hereafter take *this* Hand of human tenderness yet godlike strength, or they totter into the gloom without prop or stay. They who look their last on the beloved dead listen to *this* Voice of soothing and peace, else death is no uplifting of everlasting doors and no enfolding in Everlasting Arms, but an enemy as appalling to the reason as to the senses, the usher to a charnel-house where highest faculties and noblest feelings lie crushed with the animal wreck; an infinite tragedy, maddening, soul-sickening; "blackness of darkness for ever." Christ *not* risen means that there is absolutely nothing, less than nothing, worse than nothing, in the Bible and in Christianity. Christ risen means that His religion is no human device, but a revelation from above; and therefore that those Scriptures to which He set His seal are "given by inspiration of God."

No such *via media*, then, as seems to have floated before the minds of certain "Essayists" can possibly be struck out or maintained. The revelation refuses to be sundered from its records. Between naturalism and supernaturalism we must perforce elect; accepting in full, if we be clear-sighted and consistent, the logical consequences of either decision. In the human past as in palæontology, there are only two ways of it, the creed of Lucretius or the creed of St. Paul,—the "self-evolving powers" of a blind, improvident, unpitying nature, or the unfolding plan of an All-foreseeing Deity. Suppose, then, as regards the geological ages, we adopt the latter solution with Owen and Whewell, rather than the former *no*-solution with Powell and Darwin; in such case the question will immediately press, whether supernatural power and purpose, indispensable postulates in the survey of brute being, can be rationally eliminated from the history of man.

It is God's use, if we may speak it reverently, to repeat Himself; to reproduce His creative ideas with appropriate "variations." Now it has been argued elsewhere* that the ground-plan of ancient nature consists in an ascent, by trenchant transitions, from subvertebrate life to the backbone, as the basis of *power;*

* The Three Barriers, pp. 87—103.

from the backbone to the breast, as the sign and channel of *love;* and from the breast to the human or language-generating brain, as the organ of *wisdom* or rational thought. What, we ask with entire confidence, if this same programme, suitably modified, be reiterated in the upbuilding of each normal human life? What, we ask with due diffidence, assuming human history to be the projection of a divine thought, if an analogous evolution be the key to history?

Childhood, youth, manhood, are familiar divisors of human life; yet far more accurate, it may be, than a fanciful trio of "law, example, and spirit." For the former, if we go in quest of an *equation* for them, are simply the vertebrate, mammalian, and cerebral developments of the perfect man or woman "nobly planned." The rationale of the first period is the building up of physical strength; the affections and the reflective faculties being *kept back*, as it were, and kept low, till that work is done. Animal strength attained, the affections shoot up into supremacy; and these, as life advances, are not deposed, but crowned by ripe reason and judgment. The later gift does not destroy or displace, though it transfigures and elevates what goes before. Each, nevertheless, in its own order.* The keen affections of twenty are dormant at two, the mature judgment of fifty is unattainable at fifteen. How different the capacity of grief, which measures that of love, in an ordinary child of five, from what it is in his brother or sister three or four times the age! Strength pioneer to love, love culminating in wisdom—such therefore the sequence alike in the animal series and in the individual human life.

What if this also be the key to the "biography" of the "colossal man?" Is not the history of our race a chronicle admitting no natural primary division save that into three chapters,—those of childhood and youth, which are closed; that of manhood, which is a-writing still? The *cerebral* period, if we may venture so to des-

* Compare the procession of types in the fœtal brain.

ignate that commencing approximately A. D. 1500,* is sundered from all that preceded it by characters which he who runs may read. Its achievement has been the apocalypse of the universe. What was said of him who, take him all in all, is the representative man of the era,† is true of the era itself:—

> "Nature and nature's laws lay wrapped in night:
> God said, Let Newton be! and all was light."

For the central, or youth-period, we have the first fifteen centuries of Christianity. All that while had God been leavening the heart of man with the lesson of that love which remains His supreme gift to the end of time; passing *into* the world's manhood, not passing away from it.‡ The pre-Christian period, again, was the childhood of our race. It was the merely *vertebrate* age; differing from those that came after as Nimrod from St. Augustine or from Isaac Newton. Its attribute was ferocious force; its law despotic will. Neither the power of divine love nor that of disciplined reason, despite the *prophecy* of each in Greece and Palestine, had as yet entered prevailingly into the temper and doings of mankind. For the last three and a half centuries, history takes its hue from science; the fifteen centuries before are chiefly memorable for their saints; till the Advent, history is monopolized by war. These earliest times were very fierce times; the quality of mercy, the "milk of human kindness," was not infused into them; they were ages not of gold but of blood. The "new commandment" was as yet unuttered; the evangel of "Peace on earth, goodwill towards men," as yet unproclaimed. Force unleavened by love is the

* We may connect with this *cradle-date*, invention of printing, revival of learning, the Reformation; discovery of America; Copernicus, Galileo, Kepler, Newton; modern physiology, zoology, botany, chemistry, geology; steam, the electric telegraph; historical criticism, and the science of language.

† Herschel, "Disc. on Nat. Philos.," § 301.

‡ "That which distinguishes Christ, that which distinguishes Christ's apostles, that which distinguishes Christ's religion—the love of man."—*Milman, Hist. Lat. Christ.*, bk. xiv. ch. iii. Compare Frederick Robertson's Sermon on "The New Commandment."

complexion of history, till the Son of God appears to change it.—May we venture to interpret all this as a *third* edition of the thought legible in the rocky archives, and re-emergent in the individual human life? If so, it is plain that Christian religion, in the historical evolution of humanity, is the analogue and equivalent of the mammalian bond in nature. Those accepting the analogy, and weighing what it imports, will perhaps cease to doubt whence comes this baptism, from heaven or of men.

Thus much at least is certain, that man is the ripe result, and flower, of an immensely ancient terrestrial time. To the impression so often generated by the survey of sidereal space must be opposed the corrective ministered by the quasi-infinitude of past duration. He who built the heavens on such a scale as seemed to preclude the expenditure, even by the Almighty, of minute solicitude on the earth, has garnished it throughout the ages with such profusion of living forms as seemed to leave no time, even to the Eternal, for the plenishing and embellishing of the heavens. And yet all these were but God's *works;* we only are His *offspring.* If one branch of modern science teach, and teach justly, that man's relation to the universe *may be* such as should check his pride, another contemplates the lesson by shewing that his relation *is* such as yields no fuel to despondency. The buried strata have their burden of meaning as well as the rolling worlds. What is there in a million centuries of animal warfare, were all the universe its stage, to take rank in the regards of God with the struggles of its intellectual offspring towards light, towards goodness, towards Himself? Is there no high authentic instinct which whispers to the heart that He with whom we have to do turns willingly away from the shining of His suns and the singing of His morning stars for joy, to listen with a far diviner interest to the prayer of the humble and the cry of the contrite? However wide His universe, and its varied being, He who made us flesh, be we well assured, is in no danger of forgetting that He made us spirit. "Can a woman forget her sucking child, that she should not have compassion on the son of her womb? Yea, she may forget: yet will I not forget thee."

No weapon that is formed against this trust shall prosper. Modern scepticism indeed advances, minatory and menacing, poising in one hand what seems the spear of Ithuriel, and brandishing in the other the hammer of Thor. But the proof of the encounter tells how egregiously she has over-vaunted alike her detective faculty and her destructive strength. In the brunt of collision the weapons exchange attributes; the spear has but the pointlessness of the hammer the hammer but the levity of the spear.

RATIONALISM.

" *Tendencies of Religious Thought in England*, 1688—1750. *By* MARK PATTISON, B. D., *Rector of Lincoln College Ox^ford.*"

IT was the remark some years ago of one of the Essayists themselves, that in whatever direction religious thought in this nineteenth century was tending, no distinctive and characteristic fact had yet occurred, small in itself but pregnant in the inferences to which it should lead, to reveal and to stamp that tendency. So far as England and the middle of the century are concerned, Mr. Wilson and his colleagues have themselves unintentionally supplied the want. Friends and foes, though with different motives, have alike contrasted the fragmentary and cursory character of their volume with the immensity and unexpectedness of the outcry it has occasioned. But the contrast is surely a superficial one. The straw that is cast up by the stream may well be nothing, yet not so the current of religious feeling which it indicates. The book itself, it is true, deals thoroughly with no one subject, puts forward little that is new or original, was written with no idea of producing a panic or a revolution, simply stirs up with an assumption of intellectual and moral superiority almost every possible topic of current scepticism, while dealing seriously with no one in the list. It was merely a bye-work of able men, published with no particular purpose beyond that of accommodating a bookseller with a sequel to an unfinished series. But the crisis of religious thought to which it belongs is of far graver import. And the publication of it will head a notable chapter in any future history of the Tendencies of Religious Thought in England. It were unwise indeed to exaggerate. And little hills close to us, no doubt, may easily be made to look like mountains if viewed through the requisite kind of atmosphere. And one has great faith in the mere *inertia* of religious belief: and still more in the present revived earnestness and life, spiritual and intellectual both, in the Church: and above all, faith in Him who has preserved us hitherto through worse perils. Yet the evil, which the Essayists themselves profess (no doubt honestly) to remedy while they really increase it, is no imaginary one. Infidelity is assailing us afresh, and with a power and under circumstances sufficiently new to invest its assault with a character of special danger. It is no longer the coarse and shallow and unsatisfying infidelity of last century. It appeals, on the contrary, to the deepest and highest faculties in human nature, and it is equipped for the conflict with an array of profound and extensive historical and philological criticism. It claims, more than ever, to speak in the interests of knowledge, morality, and truth, against a theology irreconcilable with them. As the revival of literature in the sixteenth century produced the Reformation, so the growth of the critical spirit, and the change that has come over mental science, and the mere increase of knowledge of all kinds, threaten now a revolution less external but not less profound. And though the Church, in this land at least, is in a position that is strength itself compared with that which it then occupied, yet there are circumstances even now which lend to the threatened assault an undue power. Then it was the Church such as it had grown to be without the Bible. Now it is too much the Bible such as men have made of it for themselves without the Church. Then an external and authoritative dogmatism had sought to crush all minds into unquestioning submission. Now we have the opposite excess of a system of subjective intuitions, and of an individualizing and sentimental faith. And now, as then, morality and divinity are divorced from one another in many men's minds: although then, it was divinity that was in fault through its load of perversions and superstitions, while now out of an undue rationalism men are seeking to pervert the Creeds themselves into a futile conformity to their own supposed moral instincts. And it may well be, then, the crisis of Protestantism among us, as continental spectators of a sceptical turn appear sarcastically to consider it; the sifting, at any rate, of the extreme anti-Church system which abroad usurps the name. It may be the test of the vitality of the Church of England herself, and of the work that has been done to revive her true strength during the last thirty years; which is the light in which it seems to have struck the mind of the greatest of those who have unhappily quitted the English Church because they thought she had lost her vitality. It is, at any rate, a time when religious questions are being sifted with an apparatus of knowledge, and with faculties and a temper of mind, seldom, if ever, before brought to bear upon them. The entire creation of new departments of knowledge, such as philology; the discovery, as of things before absolutely unknown, of the physical history of the globe; the rising from the grave, as it were, of whole periods of history contemporary with the Bible, through newly found or newly interpreted monuments; the science of manuscripts, and of settling texts,—all these, and many more that might be named, embrace in themselves a whole universe of knowledge bearing upon religion, and specially upon the Bible, to which our fathers were utter strangers. And beyond all these is the change in the very spirit of thought itself, equally great and equally appropriate to the conditions of the present conflict; the transformation of history by the critical weighing of evidence, by the separation from it of the subjective and the mythical, by the treatment of it in a living and real way; the advance in Biblical criticism which has undoubtedly arisen from the more thorough application to the Bible of the laws of human criticism, (the honey out of the lion's carcase;) the temper of mind in dealing with the supernatural, which habits of experimental science and enlarged physical knowledge have engendered; and above all, the entire change in the point of view from which men regard all subjects, from the outward to the inward, from the historical to the metaphysical, from the sensuous to the transcendental, from the common sense of last century to the theories of the Absolute and the Infinite which occupy the attention of the present.

Be the crisis however great or small, and whatever share in any recasting of the religious thought of the age, for good or for evil, the "Essays and Reviews" as a whole may be destined to take, the particular Essay, at any rate, to which the present paper relates must in fairness be exonerated from any intentional participation in the furtherance of scepticism. It is a sequel to other valuable papers by the same pen on kindred subjects. And had it occurred alone, the literary world would have welcomed in it a proof that its writer had not deserted those studies which once promised at his hands a really great and enduring work,—a work of which it may be boldly said that it should have taken rank on its special subject with the larger labours of a Hallam. It is an Essay open, no doubt, to literary criticism; searching in its analysis, apt in its quotations, sound in its general view of the age which is its subject, but on the other hand, unfair to some of the writers criticized, fragmentary, and undeveloped; but it is one which would not in itself have stirred the waters of theological polemics. And its writer must have woke up with something of a sense of both surprise and injustice, to the indiscriminate censure which has attached to him the common notoriety of the volume. Without pretending to do otherwise than regret the temper in which it is written, or to underrate the mischievous effect it may probably have, being where it is, upon young and clever students, or to disguise the unsettling impression which it leaves upon the reader, or to deny that its writer has himself to thank for the rashness which originally joined (and let it be added, for the generosity which will not now desert) his colleagues; it must be obvious, nevertheless,—1, that the Essay was not written with any theological object, good or bad, but mainly with a literary one; and, 2, that it is a libel to accuse it of containing either wanton or formal unbelief. It is written in a dissatisfied tone of isolation. It knocks down without building up. It ignores or depreciates objective standards of truth, and speaks of the conflict between faith and infidelity without sufficiently recognising the possibility of any clear grasp of a truth above opinion. It drops here and there harsh-sounding *dicta*, unexplained and undeveloped, which will be read by the light of more pronounced passages in the other Essays, and which therefore in the result, in spite of honest disclaimers of "conspiracy," affix a subsequent responsibility to the writer for all parallel passages in the volume—a responsibility which it would surely be both reasonable and desirable to disclaim. But these things apart—and I have no intention to make light of them—the Essay is not open, either in tone or in matter, to the imputations justly made against one or other of its companions. It does not offend good taste, nor violate the common principles of honesty, nor indulge in wanton profanity. It does not formally propound or indirectly imply any of the now current forms of unbelief, which disfigure the pages of some of the remaining Essays:—the ideology, for instance, which dissolves Scripture into a subjective reflection of the Oriental mind, and exhibits it as the merely human product of a peculiar national literature,—or the metaphysical scepticism, which denies the possibility of revelation or of any dispensation of God to man as inconsistent with the perfection of the Divine attributes,—or that perversion, again, of the Baconian spirit, which is striving to confound both the animate with the inanimate, and the moral with the physical, and having frozen the whole into a like mechanic slavery to law, to crown the absurdity by substituting an abstraction of the human mind for a personal God. Even that which is more akin to the speculations of the Essay, and which forms the staple of those of one of its companions,—the tracing up the battle of human opinion into the substance of the New Testament itself, and the assertion of an unauthorized development, not only as between Scripture and the Creeds, but as between our Lord and His Apostles, or as between our Lord in Himself and the representation of Him and of His words which is described as reflected to us through the mirror of the minds of early disciples, who were of course fallible men,—these have no place here. Neither does it tamper with texts of Scripture, or affirm the honesty of subscribing theological propositions which the writer does not believe, or assert any special point of false doctrine. The whole field, again, of Biblical criticism is out of its way. One text of Scripture alone claims a mention of its various interpretations, but is not interpreted by the Essay itself. And had its writer only refrained from some cursory remarks at the beginning of his paper, which seem to imbed his special subject in a naturalistic theory of Church history in general and form a neat and compact formula of successive "theories of belief" current from time to time in the Church, which seems to land us in the position that the Church has not yet found a trustworthy "theory of belief" at all, little would have been said theologically of his Essay. It would have given offence to the holders of some popular opinions. It would have left an uncomfortable impression respecting the extent to which ambiguous phrases were intended to reach. It would *not* have done,—what the writer might have well done,—aided the good cause by his shrewd insight and great analytical powers. But neither would it have drawn down the severe censure which has now swept over it. The one or two sentences,* singled out

* Two passages are cited in the Report of the Committee of the Lower House of Convocation from Mr. Pattison's Essay. One, we must take leave to affirm, is capable of a better interpretation, while the other is incapable of the bad one affixed to it.

1. From pp. 327, 328 of the volume:—"If reason be liable to an in-

to justify its inclusion in that censure, would have been interpreted in the better instead of in the worse meaning. And nothing would have involved the writer then,—as indeed there is little now, generosity apart, which need continue to involve him,—in the general

fluence which warps it, then there is required some force which shall keep this influence under, and reason alone is no longer the all-sufficient judge of truth. In this way we should be forced back to the old orthodox doctrine of the chronic impotence of reason, superinduced upon it by the Fall; a doctrine which the reigning orthodoxy had tacitly renounced."

The previous sentence in Mr. Pattison's text shews that he is here pointing out the inconsistencies of the evidential school of divines upon their own (imputed) principles. It is they, not himself, who would be "forced back" upon the orthodox doctrine of the Fall by the conditions of their own hypothesis: whereas, according to Mr. Pattison, they had implicitly renounced that doctrine by their assumption of the supremacy of reason. It is impossible, he says in effect, at one and the same time to rest the claims of religion upon the paramount authority of reason, and to impute to all who deny those claims, an incapacity in point of reason to apprehend them. Mr. Pattison seems to have exaggerated his case, in point of fact, in both parts of this argument. Divines of those days were neither rationalists, nor deniers of the feebleness produced in the reason by means of the Fall, to the extent to which he alleges they were. Neither is the tone of the allusion to such a subject such as one is disposed to defend. But assuredly the paragraph implies nothing whatever of Mr. Pattison's own belief or disbelief in the doctrine of Original Sin or its consequences.

2. From p. 297:—"In the present day, when a godless orthodoxy threatens, as in the fifteenth century, to extinguish religious thought altogether, and nothing is allowed in the Church of England but the formulæ of past thinkings, which have long lost all sense of any kind, it may seem out of season to be bringing forward a misapplication of common sense in a bygone age."

Unhappy words, no doubt, on any shewing; and if they *did* apply to the Creeds, (as the Convocation Committee suppose,) then worse than unhappy. But surely the very turn of the language excludes the alleged reference. The common sceptical objection to the Creeds lies, not against the obsoleteness, but against the precision of their meaning. Neither was it the Creeds, but the overgrowth of theological systems, which did the mischief in the fifteenth century. It is at least far more probable, that the writer was thinking of those relics of the phraseology of mediæval or of still later controversies which have been embalmed, not only in our formularies, but also in the established orthodoxy of predominant schools, or of what is commonly acknowledged as standard divinity: to some of which he elsewhere alludes, and upon which a good deal of the Atonement controversy undeniably turns. And the question then must be, 1. To what extent he intends to carry his censure? Are *all* parties alike, or is the prevailing party really imposing upon us, by the help of bigoted public opinion, unauthorized terms of communion, which after all will not bear sifting by the light of reason and sound knowledge? There *is* something of such a spirit. There *are* party formulæ which very many would en-

and deserved condemnation of the volume as a whole. For if rationalism is imputed in the Essay to any, that rationalism, be it remembered, is condemned. If a particular theological school is accused of failure, it is because that school assumed the supremacy of—not the reason only, but—the common reason of man over

force, in spite of the reclamations of a sounder divinity, by the silent martyrdom of social persecution. Yet one would be sorry to say of even the fautors of these, that they were "godless." They are only narrow-minded and in earnest, determined to support truth, but not exactly qualified to know what is truth. And are they the Church of England? And if the Church as a whole is meant, then, 2, one must ask, What *is* included under this term of "past thinkings"? Mr. Pattison probably means only that there are many narrow views to which religious people generally cling as to essential truth, although advanced knowledge has shewn them to be untenable. There certainly *are* such views. But under the circumstances it is not unreasonable to ask a direct disclaimer of including under them more than the mere relics of Evidential, or Puritanical, or other older schools, and not what other Essayists appear to intend, the current unquestioning belief in Scripture and the Creeds, which is undoubtedly cherished with a jealous care by a *not* godless orthodoxy. That Mr. Pattison means this, I see nothing in his words to shew. I wish there was more in those words to render it impossible. Surely, too, it is the hastiest of historical paradoxes to parallel the present time with that horrible Pharisaism of self-complacent orthodoxy (so called) combined with outward pomp and inward corruption which ushered in the Reformation. But it is one thing to protest against the exaggeration of the passage historically considered, or against the unsoundness of the principle involved in it, or against the imputation it contains upon the Church of the present day: another to condemn a writer of fundamental denial of Christianity, because he demurs to the retention and (alleged) unintelligent and bigoted use of past controversial language. Nor does it follow, that Mr. Pattison denies the truth of these formulæ,—rather it seems implied that he believes in them,—as referred to their original historical place and circumstances. That the present Church of England is indeed so intolerant of "religious thought," as the passage asserts, is at least not the common opinion. Legally, she is held by most people to be more tolerant than she ought to be, and at least as tolerant as is consistent with holding any dogmas at all. That there are narrow and intolerant men within her, is perhaps rendered more prominent in proportion to her own laxity and their consequently louder reclamations. And undoubtedly there are kinds of "free-handling" of religious subjects, against which the faith of Church-people generally rises in protest. But with respect to these the only question is one of degree. The most liberal thinker would allow that *some* scepticism ought to be met by the moral coercion of an earnest counter-belief in the Church. The point is, whether the line is drawn at present too narrowly, and whether that counter-belief is really a sound and earnest one; and this, not as regards particular coteries or parties, but prevailing public Church opinion. Are people really disabled too *much* from preaching or printing what they please?

divine truth. If the transcendental reason, in the judgment of the Essayist, cannot solve clearly, and the common reason cannot solve at all, the popular objections against Scripture morality, it is the rationalist hypothesis which is in fault, for assuming as a principle that such objections have a right to a clear solution. If the Deistical and the Christian arguments are represented as almost evenly balanced, the reason lies, not in any denial of the superiority of the latter cause in itself, but in the mistaken principles upon which both alike are alleged to have proceeded. And although the various theories are found fault with into which men have hitherto analysed the grounds of their belief, yet the "eternal verities" of the faith itself, and the revelation of them, are throughout assumed.

The Essay is a chapter, or part of one, in Church history, written with a professedly practical object, and upon certain principles. What lesson, then, does the writer intend us to draw from the facts he analyzes? And are those facts correctly represented? And, lastly, what principles are implied in the sketch given of them?

To "guide us through the maze of religious pretence by which we are now surrounded," is the practical use suggested of the picture here drawn of our antecedents. We are to learn our present bearings by tracing the mental route that has actually brought us where we are. No doubt the true use, or one of them, of the study of Church history. But the Essay leaves us, nevertheless, to frame our conclusion for ourselves.

Now there does indeed appear to be one unmistakeable lesson impressed upon us by the history of religious thought in England during the last century; and that is, the untold value of the Church movement of thirty years ago. The obvious remedy for the patent defects of eighteenth-century divinity in England lay in Church principles, to the revival of which indeed these defects did, historically, lead. A sceptical spirit of toleration, based upon indifferentism,—and as a reaction from this, an unregulated and individualizing Methodism,—and throughout, an attempt to deal with religious truth through the instrumentality of reason in its shallowest form,—are the "agencies" specified in the Essay as marking that period; and they are also the "agencies," against which a deeper reason, and a more chastened spiritualism, and the craving of men's minds for truth out of and above themselves, have in this present century risen in a most righteous rebellion. Other and collateral causes co-operated; political circumstances, the revival of learning, a corresponding revolution in mental philosophy, wider social sympathies, improved taste, the wonderfully increased intercourse between the various portions of the Church throughout the world. But the results of the misuse of private judgment, which Methodism, and afterwards Evangelicalism, had only transferred from the tribunal of the common reason to that of the spiritual emotions, underlay the whole. That sincerity is a legitimate substitute for truth, that the inward emotions of the individual believer supply the basis of faith, that belief is to be limited to the boundaries of the understanding,—these and the like propositions, held under various forms and by different schools, indicate the tone of thought, originating in the period which this Essay delineates, and continuing even now, against which a profounder religious movement has in good time protested.

But the Essay itself may be thought perhaps to suggest another conclusion, and to point to a different sort of religious movement. The failure of common sense as an organ of religious inquiry is the main result which it (most truly) signalizes. The merit which counterbalanced the failure was the practical application of religion, such as common sense had made it, to the real wants of the time. And the use of reviving the remembrance of that failure is hinted to be the necessity of a similar effort now to render religion truly practical, only with a higher and better instrument. The fuller language of other Essays lends to the suggestion a more decided meaning, for which the words of the particular Essay merely leave room. The thoughts and language of a past generation do not meet the religious wants of the present, and religion, it is assumed, is becoming in consequence unreal. But while the present Essay merely indicates the want, the others claim, as belonging to their own school, the only true and efficient way of meeting it. Now about the facts, it is to be supposed, the whole world unhappily are agreed. From various causes there is an infidelity among us of a new kind, to which older writers supply no answer. To put the apologists or the divines of the last or any preceding generation into the hands of assailants of the truth now, or into those of persons who really desire to believe, is no doubt a mockery. Their mode of reasoning, their very principles, their range of knowledge, however grounded upon substantial truth, are out of date. The Paleys or the Lardners supply no answer to the Strausses or the Hennells. And we must needs come to the modern pages of Rogers or of Mansel to find the appropriate reply to Francis Newman or to Theodore Parker. That there is need, then, of a new "Rationalism," and specially of an application to the altered difficulties of the time of a profounder and more critical knowledge and of the higher reason, is a statement in which all must agree. And though it may be hard to see the sincerity of an attempt which, as a whole, seeks to conquer infidelity by admitting its principles and adopting its conclusions, yet one is bound to give even the extremest of the Essayists credit for at least the intention of making it. But the real thing wanted is not new Creeds, but to bring the new modes of thought into subjection to the old ones. And which have laboured most successfully at this task, Mr. Maurice and Professor Jowett, or Mr. Rogers and Professor Mansel? The Church does indeed want a new "Rationalism," that shall employ a higher range of faculties than the common sense of the older rationalists (if they may be truly so called), and shall base itself upon a wider and more intelligent knowledge than theirs, and shall aim at a higher and more spiritual and distinterested morality than the prudential bargaining with

God and with the world which satisfied them. But she must find it,—and whatever might be feared, there is nothing in the Rector of Lincoln's own pages to prevent his finding it also,—in a school *toto cœlo* opposed to that, which first of all has specially distinguished itself by denouncing the higher reason as no reason at all, and as leading to atheism; and secondly has adopted the unsound history and crude theology of such as Bunsen; * and thirdly, while shrinking honourably from the ethical fatalism under which the Mills and the Buckles have revived the old "sufficient-cause" quibble of Hobbes, has itself become the apostle of a half-pagan type of physical morality, too self-reliant and too much wrapped up in the world we live in to be wholly Christian, to say nothing of the omission from its leading idea of manliness of most of the gentler, and many of the nobler, meanings of "humanity." We do want, indeed, a new "Rationalism," but it must be far other than this. It must be a rationalism that shall not seek to defend the Creeds by giving them up; shall not mutilate them of obnoxious doctrines in order to purchase from man's reason a hollow and patronizing acquiescence in the remainder; shall not leave us to the alternative of Romanism or Socinianism by assuming the Catholic faith of the first centuries to have been a human development of a primitive undoctrinal morality; shall not, in a word, make a peace with human reason by acknowledging its supremacy in order to retain at its mercy the relics of a pseudo-Christianity. It

* The historical critic who can postpone the Bible to Manetho, surely puts himself out of court on purely literary grounds. And if any one wishes the measure of Bunsen's theology, let him read his speculations on the doctrine of the Trinity in his "Christianity and Mankind," vol. iv. part ii. sect. iii. cc. 2, 3, ed. 1854. Really one ought to speak out about a writer whom persons of such opposite schools in England have at different times so strangely combined to idolize. If any religious and sensible man, no matter what his views so that he be a Christian, can read the passage just referred to without an involuntary thrill of mingled horror, pity, and contempt, I am sadly mistaken. It may sound arrogant, but the truth is greater than great men. And I do say advisedly, that such ravings have seldom darkened counsel by words without knowledge since the days of the Gnostics.

must be one, on the contrary, that shall so use the deeper philosophy and wider knowledge of the day, as to add one more link to the ever-lengthening chain of proof, that the truths of revelation overmaster all phases of human reason, and that each new development in man's mental history has ever found itself constrained to submit to the conditions of thought laid down once for all in the faith of Christ. Would that the Rector of Lincoln may turn his own great powers to the task, of which he so vividly sees the need, and the lines of which he has so truly laid down by contrast in the masterly picture he has drawn of an unsuccessful rationalism.

But we turn from the object of the Essay to its contents; from the lesson it designs us to draw, to the facts upon which the lesson is based.

I. Its main subject is the anti-deistical writers of 1720—1750. It imputes to them rationalism. The acceptance of reason as the supreme judge of the matter as well as the evidence of revelation, is the main feature in the picture drawn of them. Without attempting to settle the true bounds of the functions of reason in religious subjects, or to define differing degrees of excess in the matter, an extreme view of the subject is laid to the charge of the school of writers above named as a whole, including names eminent not only then but for all time. Is this charge well grounded?

There can be no doubt that the eighteeenth century was a rationalistic age. Reason was its cry. And the tone of the time infected the Church as well as its opponents. But then rationalism appears in Church writers in the form of a concession, under continual protest, and carefully shackled by all possible limitations. Of the writers named in the Essay, even Rogers talks of "inevident" propositions in religion. And Tillotson denies that "the finite can comprehend the infinite," or that human similitudes can fully explain divine mysteries. And Prideaux qualifies his own broad principle, in the end of the Tract from which the Essay quotes. And of others we shall see below, that a denial of the supremacy of reason is really more their object than an assertion of it. Conceding then (as we must) the name, and the fact, so far as they indicate a difference betweeen particular schools of English theology, it is clearly unfair to reckon these divines and their opponents as alike rationalists. And the result of so indiscriminate a statement is simply to leave the impression that the Christian reasoners in that controversy did precisely the opposite of what they really did. It is equivalent to saying that their chief occupation was to maintain the supremacy of reason; whereas they rather accept the principle at their opponents' hands as containing a basis of truth, while their own works were mainly written in order to limit and control it.

Indisputably, however, the school was unduly rationalistic. And every one familiar with their writings must admit the general truth of the masterly analysis given in the Essay, of their line of argument. In many things the age was too much for them. They treated reason, to use Butler's phrase, with far too much of "consideration."

1. That religious faith ought to be the issue of a purely intellectual process, is maintained by them in a far too unguarded way. While admitting that in point of fact it can hardly be the actual case with any, their ideal of a Christian belief was yet that of a state of mind which, starting from pure impartiality, had admitted no influences to build it up save those which reach the heart through the understanding. So far the Essayist has not done them injustice, and has supplied to ourselves a powerful and profound criticism upon a position too common still to render that criticism unpractical, and too much mixed up with truth to allow it to be useless.

2. Again, that the truths of revelation, on that side of them which relates to the nature and attributes of God, belong to a different order of truths from those which come within the range of human experience; that the causes of our inability to fathom religious mysteries, do not lie simply in the partial and limited extent of

our knowledge, but in the necessary texture of that knowledge in itself; that the infinite is not simply an indefinite extension of the finite, but belongs to a different range of intellectual powers, and appeals to faculties which man has not, although he can perceive the limitations of those which he has, and can recognise accordingly the existence of truths which he cannot master,—these and the like familiar results of later philosophy were mainly wanting to philosophers and divines alike of a century since. And the Essayist has justly noted the defect. It is one prominent in the unmetaphysical pages of Bishop Butler. And though intimations may be found of the deeper view in the writings of eighteenth century divines,—and the celebrated work of Bishop Browne is a proof that the formal speculations of even theologians tended sometimes, wisely or unwisely, in a like direction,—yet the general tone of speculation on the subject tended to the encouragement of undue rationalism, by omitting to mark distinctly the existence of those deeper truths before which reason fails in its own intrinsic powers.

3. Further still, the Hanoverian divines of the last age, though the Essayist only notes this incidentally, paid little attention to the authority of the Church, in any sense of the phrase. It was no age, so far as they were concerned, for Catenas, except as an *argumentum ad homines* against Rome. Nor do we find in them patristic quotations, as a rule, and hardly at all. Nor do they make more than passing references, more for completeness' sake than anything else, to the views of the primitive church or of Œcumenical Councils upon religious truths. So far from going into any excess in this direction by way of counterbalance to reason, the leading divines of that time did not lay even due stress upon that historical and external system of belief which offers an authoritative interpretation of Scripture upon essential doctrinal points. They threw individuals too nakedly upon their own bare reason, and bade them make a creed for themselves with too little of safeguard in respect to the Creeds of the Church. Yet even this

must be qualified. For to talk of Church authority to deistical opponents would have been waste of words. And the theory at least of "the use and value of ecclesiastical antiquity" cannot be said to have been wholly forgotten or denied in the age that produced Cave and Waterland.

4. Again, there is of course a sense in which reason *is* supreme. Just as the most vacillating will practically decides; just as it is his eyes with which a man must see, although he may see very badly: so the reason of each man necessarily rules the judgments which he forms. It is a common fallacy which shifts the real burden of the private judgment question to an irrelevant issue. That question is not, by what faculty a man must shape his religious faith, but by what rules and with what auxiliaries he must govern that faculty in the process; to what limits and to what conditions reason itself says that reason ought to submit in the matter. Locke's dictum, then, is self-evident—that to extinguish reason in order to exalt faith is the same as to put out our eyes in order to see better with a telescope. The information supplied by faith must perforce be cast in the mould of the human reason in order to obtain access to the human mind at all. The supremacy of reason in this sense is a truism. The real question is, how far the forms of the reason are discovered by the reason itself, whether upon internal or upon external grounds, to be adequate or inadequate to present truly the truths which they convey; how far it is reasonable to believe that the subjective representation corresponds to the objective truth. We must perforce argue on the assumption of the forms of the reason. And reason itself must settle, for us, how far these forms are to be trusted as sufficient equivalents for the ideas represented under them. It must be admitted, then, that large general statements about the power of reason in any school of divinity prove little; but that the gist of the question lies in the explanations and qualifications by which these statements are reduced from bare truisms to a special theological view.

5. And in particular of the primary axioms of the moral reason. Surely nothing can be made out respecting the doctrines of a particular school from admissions of the independence and supremacy of the simplest moral ideas. The Occham doctrine (if it was Occham's) which resolves morality into the arbitrary Divine will, can be nakedly held by none who understand their own words. When Waterland maintains something like it as against the free-thinkers, his argument is perforce a heap of confused self-contradictions. I do not mean that human reason can theoretically combine religion and morality into a single idea, so as to obviate all cavil, or even all reasonable difficulty; or that there is not a truth at the bottom of the perversion which goes by Occham's name, and which must not be got rid of by a simple assertion of the contradictory of it. Morality must not be set up as something overruling God from without Him. But if we are to have any real meaning in our words, the proposition that God is good must needs contain something more than that He is anything whatsoever that He has pleased to be. And every one who would argue on moral subjects, must needs have distinct and substantive principles on which to argue. It is no "rationalism," then, in any specific sense, to maintain that elementary moral truth is as axiomatic as the bare forms of the reason themselves. The real questions are, to what extent we know the facts and are capable therefore of applying the axioms; and how far these elementary truths are adequate representations of absolute morality, and capable therefore of bearing the inferences which, on the assumption of such adequacy, seem to follow from them. Such statements, then, as those of Butler, of which the Essayist, by the way, has not quoted the strongest, prove nothing of Butler's "rationalism." For they are the common "rationalism" of all reasoners, the essential prerequisites to any reasoning, or to any reasoning on moral subjects, at all. Every one must say with him, that "reason is indeed the only faculty we have wherewith to judge concerning anything, even revelation

itself;" and that he must not "be misunderstood to assert that a supposed revelation cannot be proved false from internal characters: for it may contain clear immoralities or contradictions; and either of these may prove it false." Still more, in the words quoted in the Essay, must it be maintained, that there is a "moral fitness and unfitness of actions, prior to all will whatever:" and further still (what is necessary to make this passage relevant) that this moral fitness or unfitness is discernible to some real extent by human reason, even as weakened by the Fall.

So far, then, the imputation of rationalism to the eighteenth century is very far from being an untrue imputation. Not only were the divines of the ruling party of that time rationalists in the sense in which every reasoner and every moral reasoner must be so; but beyond this, they must be admitted to have laid too exclusive a stress upon the reason, to have ignored too much, if not in many instances altogether, the higher faculties of the reason, and to have unduly left out the counterpoises provided against unwise private judgment. But the Essay imputes to them a much more extreme rationalism than this. It represents them as claiming or admitting a "verifying faculty" in the largest sense. Reason, in their use of it, is described as "proving instead of evolving, arguing upon instead of appropriating, the eternal verities." And the "supremacy of reason" appears to mean, that although Christian mysteries could not have been discovered by reason, yet when made known they must be capable of rational proof, must harmonize with rational presumptions, must be such that reason distinctly recognises their necessary truth upon its own principles. It is a legitimate result of such a view, for instance, that the doctrine of the Holy Trinity could not indeed have been discovered by man uninformed from God; but that, being thus made known to him, he can perceive by reason, that the case could not have been otherwise; and that if he could not perceive this, the doctrine must be false. The comparison of the early anti-deistical writers to Coleridge sufficiently shews that this is the meaning here attributed to the word Rationalism. It is not simply that nothing is to be allowed which is contradictory to reason, but that "the mysteries of Christianity *are* reason in its highest form;" i. e. necessarily, reason as man now possesses that faculty, only, as Coleridge meant it, in respect to its transcendental and not its common-sense powers. "Human reason as strengthened by Christianity"—so his view has been expressed—"can evolve all the Christian doctrines from its own sources." Still more, in the words quoted in the Essay itself, must "the compatibility of a document with the conclusions of self-evident reason, and with the laws of conscience," be "a condition *à priori* of any evidence adequate to the proof of its having been revealed by God." And so also, in the language of the Essay, the earlier eighteenth-century divines are described to us as holding, that the truths revealed by Christianity, over and above those previously known by the light of natural religion, "could not have been thought out by reason, but when Divinely communicated, approve themselves to the same reason which has already put us in possession" of those previous truths. Or in other words, the "supremacy of reason" is alleged to have been maintained by these divines, not simply as judging of evidence, but as judging also, and as by an adequate instrument for the purpose, of the possibility and of the rightness of the thing evidenced; and again, not simply as understanding the meaning of terms so far as to attach a real and precise sense to them, and as deciding upon the compatibility of those terms with one another in a proposition to the extent of rejecting simple contradictions, and as drawing immediate inferences, as e. g. from moral or other axioms, within the limits of its own experience and of its own comprehension of those terms, but as thoroughly master of religious ideas, so that no doctrine can be accepted as true unless its terms in their full meaning, and the entire relations of those terms to one another, and not their compatibility only with self-evident principles of reason but their dependence upon such principles, be patent to the human reason itself. Now nothing is easier than to shew that the leading divines of that age were so far from accepting, that they distinctly rejected, the supremacy of reason in this sense and to this extent. That as a rule they did not appeal simply to authority, whether of the Church or of the Fathers or of primitive tradition, but to reason, and to authority, if at all, only as entirely subordinate to reason, is perfectly true. Partly it did not harmonize with their own tone of thought or doctrine to do otherwise. Partly they were compelled by the necessities of argument to take ground which their opponents would admit. It is true, also, that the line was by no means sharply drawn, in the philosophy of the time, between the sensuous and the transcendental, between the world of experience and of phenomena, and that of intuitions and of things as they are in themselves, between the common and the higher reason. And divines did not anticipate the philosophical speculations of a later date. The Tertullianistic paradox, 'The harder a doctrine the better for faith,' was the opposite to their line of thought. But assuredly the divines of those days neither asserted the comprehensibility, still less the capability of being rationally proved,—nor alleged that comprehensibility or capability as conditions of the truth,—of religious mysteries. They did not hold that mysteries must have ceased to be such, if they are to be reckoned in the list of Gospel doctrines. They seem, on the contrary, to have drawn the line between reason and faith, practically and substantially, although in language of very different aspect and approaching the subject from an entirely different side, pretty much where the philosophical defenders of the Christian faith at this very day would draw it. Their main object is to depress reason. They treat it tenderly, but from argumentative considerations. It was their opponents' main theme, and that on which they relied: and controversialists must needs make all possible concessions to the main strength of an opponent's argument, in order at once to shield themselves from sound objections, and to obtain the greater vantage-ground for their own assault. But the whole drift of their reasoning is to put limits upon reason, although they certainly draw those limits far too laxly. One might almost say, that the Essay, unintentionally and for want of sufficient discrimination, but really, represents the greater Christian defenders as yielding the precise points upon which they most insisted. The whole of Butler's "Analogy," for instance, is an elaborate depreciation of the supremacy of reason. It seems to imply, indeed, too strongly, that if we knew all the facts, we *could* judge, even with our present faculties. But then we *cannot* know all the facts, or more than the very least portion of them. And its main principle is, that reason must accordingly be content with being irrational,—that it is the height of reason to discern, that reason cannot judge, because it has not the principles on which to judge, but must expect to continue always in this world baffled by difficulties that it cannot solve, and compelled to accept as truths positions that it can neither reconcile nor comprehend, much less prove. And if we turn from Butler to other and inferior writers, who yet were among the leading writers of the Church side of the controversy, we find generally the same character in their speculations also. With some exceptions certainly, and above others that of Tillotson, (and even he, here and there, largely qualifies his generally over-strong statements,) they are truly described in the words which Waterland uses of one of them, when he tells us "that the *insufficiency* of reason to be a guide in such matters," viz. of religion, "hath been very lately set forth" (viz. in Bishop Gibson's second Pastoral Letter) "in the clearest and strongest manner for the conviction of infidels."

Take, for instance, the following passages from the writers selected by a Regius Professor of Divinity in the latter part of last century as leading defenders of the faith, those writers themselves belonging to the earlier period with which the Essay is directly concerned, and one of them indeed, viz. Gibson, being quoted in the Essay itself.

1. Bishop Stillingfleet, "On Scripture Mysteries," from the *Enchiridion Theologicum*, vol. i. p. 383, 3rd edition:—

"Truly no men (by their own authority) can pretend to a right to impose on others any mysteries of faith, or any such things which are above their capacity to understand. But that is not our case; for we all profess to believe and receive Christianity as a divine revelation; and God (we say) may require from us the belief of what we may not be able to comprehend, especially if it relates to Himself, or such things as are consequent upon the union of the divine and human nature. Therefore our business is to consider, whether any such things be contained in that revelation which we all own; and if they be, we are bound to believe them, although we are not able to comprehend them."

2. Id. ibid., pp. 389, sq.:—

"Although in the language of Scripture it be granted, that the word *mystery* is most frequently applied to things before hidden but now revealed, yet there is no incongruity in calling that a mystery, which being revealed, hath yet something in it which our understandings cannot reach to. But it is mere cavilling to insist on a word, if the thing itself be granted. The chief thing therefore to be done is, to shew that God may require from us the belief of such things which are incomprehensible by us. For, God may require anything from us, which it is reasonable for us to do; if it be thus reasonable for us to give assent where the manner of what God hath revealed is not comprehended, then God may certainly require it from us. Hath not God revealed to us, that 'in six days He made heaven and earth and all that is therein?' But is it not reasonable to believe this unless we are able to comprehend the manner of God's production of things? Here we have something revealed, and that plainly enough, viz. that God 'created all things;' and yet, here is a mystery remaining as to the manner of doing it. Hath not God plainly revealed that there shall be a resurrection of the dead? And must we think it unreasonable to believe it, till we are able to comprehend all the changes of the particles of matter from the Creation to the general Resurrection? But it is said, that there is no contradiction in this, but there is in the mystery of the Trinity and Incarnation. It is strange boldness in men to talk thus of monstrous contradictions in things above their reach. The atheists may as well say, Infinite power is a monstrous contradiction, and God's immensity and His other unsearchable perfections are monstrous paradoxes and contradictions. Will men never learn to distinguish between numbers and the nature of things? For three to be one is a contradiction in numbers; but whether an Infinite Nature can communicate itself to three different Subsistences without such a division as is among created beings, must not be determined by bare numbers, but by the absolute perfections of the Divine Nature; which must be owned to be above our comprehension. For let us examine some of those perfections which are most clearly revealed, and we shall find this true. The Scripture plainly reveals, that 'God is from everlasting to everlasting;' that 'He was and is and is to come;' but shall we not believe the truth of this till we are able to fathom the abyss of God's eternity? I am apt to think (and I have some thoughtful men concurring with me) that there is no greater difficulty in the conception of the Trinity and Incarnation, than there is of eternity. Not but that there is great reason to believe it; but from hence it appears that our reason may oblige us to believe some things which it is not possible for us to comprehend. We know that God must have been for ever, or it is impossible He ever should be; for if He should come into being when He was not, He must have some cause of His being; and that which was the first cause would be God. But if he were for ever, He must be from Himself; and what notion or conception can we have in our minds concerning it? And yet, atheistical men can take no advantage from hence; because their own most absurd hypothesis hath the very same difficulty in it. For something must have been for ever. And it is far more reasonable to suppose it of an infinite and eternal Mind, which hath power and wisdom and goodness to give being to other things, than of dull, stupid, and senseless matter, which could never move itself, nor give being to anything besides. Here we have therefore a thing which must be owned by all; and yet such a thing which can be conceived by none; which shews the narrowness and shortness of our understandings, and how unfit they are to be the measurers of the possibilities of things."

(Stillingfleet pursues the like argument through others of the divine attributes, such as the spiritual nature of God, His foreknowledge, His infiniteness; following out a train of thought in substance identical with that of Mr. Mansel in his sixth Bampton Lecture, however differing from that lecture, as of course is the case, in context and immediate purpose, in style of thought and terminology. The same line of reasoning is also followed, to the extent of—not "hewing" Athanasianism down to "an intelligible human system," but —maintaining the doctrine of the Trinity as set forth in the Athanasian Creed, in Stillingfleet's "Doctrine of the Trinity and Transubstantiation Compared," ib., pp. 427, sq.; of which treatise one main object is, to maintain such a difference between the relation of the two doctrines respectively to reason as to support a rejection of the latter consistently with an acceptance of the former; and this is done, not by affirming the former to be comprehensible, still less proveable by reason, but only not contradictory to it, whereas the latter is alleged to be so.)

Taking Stillingfleet for the beginning of the period, we may turn now to a writer at the close of it.

Bishop Conybeare, (Bishop of Bristol 1750--1755,) "On Mysteries," ib., vol. ii. p. 32:—

"The point therefore in which they [the Socinians] differ from us, is this: we affirm that there are several doctrines above our reason; and which we are still incapable of comprehending, notwithstanding the revelation which hath been made to us concerning them: they affirm, on the contrary, that there is nothing in the Christian religion above our reason; nothing but what, by a due use of our faculties, we are able to comprehend: and in consequence of this they reject such interpretations of Scripture as carry with them anything incomprehensible."

Ibid., p. 34, sq.:—

"This account supposes that of these mysterious doctrines we have some ideas; we have ideas, though such as are either partial or indeterminate. Indeed, where we can frame no ideas we can, strictly speaking, give no assent. For what is assent, but a perception, or at least a firm persuasion, that the extremes in a proposition do agree or disagree? But where we have no manner of ideas of these extremes, we can have no such perception or persuasion. And as no combination of terms really significant can make a real proposition; so no combination of terms to us perfectly unintelligible, can, with respect to us, be accounted propositions. We do maintain, therefore, that we have some ideas even of mysterious doctrines. And thus, I conceive, we are sufficiently guarded against an objection sometimes made against us as contending for unintelligible doctrines. There is a vast difference between unintelligible and incomprehensible. That is, strictly speaking, unintelligible, concerning which we can frame no ideas; and that only incomprehensible, concerning which our ideas are imperfect. It is plain, therefore, that a doctrine may be intelligible, and yet incomprehensible. Nay, I shall adventure to maintain, that there are several propositions of whose extremes we have ideas, but are yet incapable of discerning how far these extremes do agree or disagree. For since this agreement or disagreement is, in most cases, to be proved by the use of several intermediate ideas, we are incapable of discerning whether they do agree or disagree. In all such instances the propositions are intelligible, and yet incomprehensible. The incomprehensibility therefore of certain doctrines in our religion does not arise from our having no ideas of them; but from hence, that our ideas are either inadequate or indeterminate. I conceive it is very evident, that there may be infinite relations of one thing to another, which for want of adequate ideas will be to us undiscernible; but any propositions with respect to such undiscernible relations will, when proposed, be to us mysterious: and consequently, those who explode all mysteries, can maintain their ground only by asserting that all their ideas are adequate; a perfection which the sober part of mankind will be very backward in allowing them. Besides this, there are other things concerning which our ideas are indeterminate. The importance of the observation will best appear by considering that in those revelations which God is pleased to make, He deals with us as men, and does not produce in us any new faculties different from what we had before. If the doctrines revealed are made up of such ideas as we are capable of receiving in the ordinary methods of knowledge, then the revelation is either a farther enforcement of such truths as might naturally be known, or a discovery of such truths as (for want or adequate ideas) could not naturally be known. But it hath happened in some instances, that the doctrines revealed are made up of such ideas as we are incapable of receiving in an ordinary way: such as the doctrines concerning the generation of the Son of God, the distinction between the Persons in the ever-blessed Trinity, and the like. In these cases the ideas are themselves revealed;—revealed, I say, not by producing in us any new faculties of receiving them, but by representing them by some other ideas, with which they have a remote resemblance and analogy."

Id. ib., p. 39:—

"As creatures we must be dependent and finite; and whatever is finite in its nature must be finite in its attributes. The consequence will be, that every creature must be bounded in its capacity of knowledge. Or thus; no being can be endued with absolute knowledge, unless it be endued with absolute pefection; and no being can be endued with absolute perfection, but the supreme self-existent Being. From hence it follows, that there must be an infinite number of truths actually comprehended by the self-existent Being, and yet incomprehensible by the most perfect creature: i. e. there must be an infinite number of truths to us mysterious."

Again:—

"I do maintain, that . . . we may have in some cases demonstrative evidence of doctrines mysterious."

Id., "On Scripture Difficulties," ib., p. 108, sq.:—

"Mysteries are points in which the Supreme Being hath imparted some knowledge to us;—but the revelation stopping there, several questions to be raised about them are obscure. Difficult, therefore, they must be, unless our notions concerning these things were more full and determinate;—unless our capacities were greater and the revelation itself more complete. . . . Words are the immediate representatives of our thoughts; and consequently can reach no farther than our thoughts themselves. The things, therefore, of which we have hitherto had no manner of notion, cannot be perfectly represented in our words: from whence it follows, that to clear up some things in reference to Divine doctrines, an immediate inspiration to each particular person would be necessary;—a new language to express such matters, and new ideas to understand the language. And after all that can be supposed this way, as ours is a finite nature, it is impossible but some things must exceed our knowledge."

Turn from these to a writer of intermediate date.

Bishop Gibson, "First Pastoral Letter," ib., pp. 132, sq.:—

"When a revelation is sufficiently attested to come from God, let it not weaken your faith if you cannot clearly see the fitness and expedience of every part of it. This would be to make yourselves as knowing as God; whose wisdom is infinite, and the depth of whose dispensations, with the reasons and ends of them, are not to be fathomed by our short and narrow comprehensions. God has given us sufficient capacity to know Him and to learn our duty, and to judge when a revelation comes from Him: which is all the knowledge that is needful to us in our present state. And it is the greatest folly as well as presumption in any man, to enter into the counsels of God, and to make himself a judge of the wisdom of His dispensations to such a degree, as to conclude that this or that revelation cannot come from God, because he cannot see in every respect the fitness and reasonableness of it: to say, for instance, that either we had no need of a Redeemer, or that a better method might have been contrived for our redemption: and upon the whole, not to give God leave to save us in His own way. In these cases the true inference is, that the revelation is therefore wise, and good, and just, and fit to be received and submitted to by us, because we have sufficient reason to believe that it comes from God. For so far He has made us competent judges, inasmuch as natural reason informs us what are the proper evidences of a Divine revelation; but He has not let us into the springs of His administration, nor shewn us the whole compass of it, nor the connection of the several parts with one another; nor, by consequence, can we be capable to judge adequately of the fitness of the means which He makes use of to attain the ends. On the contrary, the attempting to make such a judgment is to set ourselves in the place of God, and to forget that we are frail men; that is, short-sighted and ignorant creatures, who know very little of Divine matters further than it has pleased God to reveal them to us."

To which let me add the whole of another passage of the same Bishop, where the writer of the Essay, quoting the first sentences, has surely not looked to the next page;* and which will also clear two writers at once from the charge—not of rationalism, but of the extreme rationalism we are here considering, viz. Gibson himself, and Locke whom he quotes. It is part, too, of a set of treatises written expressly to confute those who claim to assent or dissent from Scripture, "just as they judge it agrees or disagrees with the light of nature and the reason of things."

Id., "Second Pastoral Letter," ib., p. 167:—

"Those among us who have laboured of late years to set up reason against revelation, would make it pass for an established truth, that if you will embrace revelation, you must of course quit your reason; which if it were true, would doubtless be a strong prejudice against revelation. But so far is this from being true, that it is universally acknowledged that revelation itself is to stand or fall by the test of reason; or, in other words, according as reason finds the evidences of its coming from God to be or not to be sufficient and conclusive, and the matter of it to contradict, or not contradict, the natural notion which reason gives us of the being and attributes of God, and of the essential differences between good and evil."

So far, save the last clause, the quotation in the Essay. But Bishop Gibson adds some most important qualifications of his statement. He continues:—

"And when reason upon an impartial examination finds the evidences to be full and sufficient, it pronounces that the revelation ought to be received, and as a necessary consequence thereof, directs us to give ourselves up to the guidance of it. But here reason stops; not as set aside by revelation, but as taking revelation for its guide, and not thinking itself at liberty to call in question the wisdom and expedience of any part after it is satisfied that the whole comes from God; any more than to object against it as containing some things, the manner, end, and design of which it cannot fully comprehend."

And then, quoting Locke, he adds further:—

"These were the wise and pious sentiments of an ingenious

* This is noticed in a pamphlet in reply to the Essay by Mr. Candy.

writer of our own time; 'I gratefully receive and rejoice in the light of revelation, which sets me at rest in many things, the manner whereof my poor reason can by no means make out to me.' And elsewhere, having laid it down for a general maxim, that 'reason must be our last judge and guide in everything,' he immediately adds, 'I do not mean, that we must consult reason, and examine whether a proposition revealed from God can be made out by natural principles, and if it cannot, that then we may reject it. But consult it we must, and by it examine whether it be a revelation from God or no. And if reason finds it to be revealed from God, reason then declares for it as much as for any other truth, and makes it one of her dictates.'"

Lastly, let the following passage of Butler be considered, which is one of the strongest of his statements. And let it be asked whether, after all, it does not qualify as much as it affirms the power of reason: and whether it in any degree bears out the extreme imputation hazarded in the Essay.

Butler, "Analogy," Pt. I. c. 3:—

"Reason can, and it ought to judge, not only of the meaning but also of the morality of the evidence of revelation. First, it is the province of reason to judge of the morality of Scripture; i. e. not whether it contains things different from what we should have expected from a wise, just, and good Being; for objections from hence have been now obviated: but whether it contains things plainly contradictory to wisdom, justice, or goodness; to what the light of nature teaches us of God."

An admission this, let it be observed: a concession to opponents, made as strong as the temper of the arguer, candid and discreet to a degree, could fairly make it, yet qualified in itself to a sense not only allowable but necessary, if we are to retain any meaning in the names of moral attributes at all, and to be taken also with the fuller qualifications which the work as a whole is expressly intended to supply.

Of the other points in the Essayist's masterly analysis of the general argument of the anti-deistical divines, I have only to say that they form a contribution of no small value to a yet unwritten chapter of English Church history. That analysis as a whole no one can doubt to be a true one: unless so far as this, that as in the general imputation of rationalism, so in the other lines of the picture,—e. g. in the doctrinal, ethical, and social aspects of it,—there is sometimes a breadth of statement which omits the qualifications necessary to exactness. The powerful microscope has occasionally intensified the lights and shades into lines so marked as to be practically beyond the truth. It is true, for example, that the doctrine of the fallibility of human reason arising from the Fall, as of any other portion of the results of original sin, was not prominent in the writings of that school. But it is not true that such a doctrine was, even "tacitly, renounced" by them. It occurs in terms even in Rogers. And Bishop Gibson, e. g., expressly cautions us against the "fallacious" method of "arguing from the powers of reason in a state of innocence, in which the understanding is supposed to be clear and strong, and the judgment unbiassed and free from the influences of inordinate appetites and inclinations, to the powers and abilities of reason under the present corrupt state of human nature, in which we find by experience how apt we are to be deceived; . . . and more particularly in the case of religion, how apt our judgment would be to follow the bent of our passions and appetites, and to model our duty according to their motives and desires, if God had left this wholly to every one's reason, and not given us a more plain and express revelation of His will, to check and balance that influence which our passions and appetites are found to have on our reason and judgment." Again, it is quite true that the prudential view of morality, which subordinated religion to police, the next world to the present, was not only prevalent, but was pushed by some of the divines in question to a degree quite as extravagant as that imputed to them by the Essayist in his comparison of their view with the sceptical saying of the deist

Collins. Archbishop Tillotson,* whom the Essayist selects, has actually gone so far as to demand, "What religion is good for, but to reform the manners and dispositions of men, to restrain human nature from violence and cruelty, from falsehood and treachery, from sedition and rebellion?"—a doctrine to which its propounder himself would perhaps hardly have stood if drawn out into its consequences, but which fully deserves the extremest of the condemnation which the Essayist bestows upon that writer, though without quoting this emphatic passage. Yet in depicting the theology of the period it would only have been fair to add, that Waterland pointedly and at length confutes and censures the statement. Further, although, after making allowances for the style of controversy prevalent in the age, there was still too much of polemical violence, and although it is true also that Bishops, writing gravely and calmly, e. g. Gibson and Berkeley, do impute directly or by implication to freethinkers as a body a generally lax morality, yet surely it is unreasonable to accuse divines, whose usual tone is that of candour and calm reasoning, of malignantly imputing evil to opponents, on the *à priori* assumption that freethinking opinions and defect of morals must needs go together, while omitting inquiry into the fact whether or no they actually did so. Bishops would not have ventured on the assertion if it could have been refuted by notorious facts, nay, if it had not been supported by them. And the Essayist's own account of the period harmonizes but too well with the truth of the accusation.

On the whole, agreeing in the main with the Essayist's estimate both of evidential schools as such, and of the particular school of internal and *à priori* evidence here described;—admitting fully, that the common reason of men, if assumed to be capable of measuring divine truth, will inevitably mutilate and attenuate it in order to bring it within its own grasp, and that religious views, if exhausted of all spiritual depth by being reduced to a merely intellectual perception of

* I take the quotation from Waterland.

moral obligation, will undoubtedly be degraded into a worldly and utilitarian code of cold prudential precepts and nothing more,—acknowledging also, that the tone of religious thought in the ruling divines of the eighteenth century certainly was thrown into the line of undue appeal to plain common sense, by the over reaction of a very reasonable disgust against the theological excesses of predestinarian controversy,* and into that of a suppression of the spiritual and mystical element through horror of such hideous perversions of truth and morality by the "fanatics" as may be found recorded at length in, e. g., Edwards's *Gangræna*, or the like books;—I think it must be said, 1. that the present sketch of these divines, masterly and in the main true, does nevertheless bring out the dark lines of the picture without sufficient qualification from those counter views which still held their ground; and 2. that it swamps in particular such men as Butler, too indiscriminately in the general condemnation; and 3. that it overlooks the decisive evidence to the real ability of the school, afforded by its undeniable success. Both combatants it is true were fighting, so to say, with their right hand tied and their right eye bandaged. Yet even so, the Christian defenders, as a matter of fact, maintained their ground, and defeated their opponents. The deistical school, as a fact, died out. And its line of thought and moral tone are as dead and repulsive, even to sceptics of the present day, and its powers of argument and knowledge as contemptible, as the sharpest satire could ever represent those of the Christian apologists to have been. And though the awakened earnestness and deeper spiritualism of the Methodist movement claims a large share in the victory, yet some portion of the credit is plainly due to the unanswerable,

* Certainly the origin of the Latitudinarian school, and of its legitimate development in the eighteenth century divines, was, historically, not any reaction from undue authority claimed for the English Church by the Laudian divines or any other, but distinctly a reaction from Puritan excesses, both of theology and of a persecuting spirit. The history of Whichcote and his friends at Cambridge is sufficient proof of this.

however limited, arguments of a Leslie on the one hand, and a Butler on the other.

II. The Essay however is, I think, harder upon other schools of divines than upon that which is its main subject. An incidential notice is bestowed by it in passing upon the school of external evidences represented by Paley, upon the Laudian divines, upon the religious tone and temper of the present day in England. But the brevity of the notice only aggravates the severity of the censure in each case, by leaving it in the form of a sharply expressed general condemnation, unlimited and unapplied.

A "factitious thesis," for instance, and "unreal matter," and a "conventional case," are the words flung at the head of Paley's great argument for Christianity; or again, that it combines a large breadth of assumption with a narrow result of proof. And it is compared disadvantageously with the "only honest critical enquiry into the origin and composition of the canonical writings," in the last century, Bishop Marsh's Germanizing lectures on the document-hypothesis of the origin of the Gospels.

Surely the comparison is hardly fair. It implies that the two lines of enquiry are divergent modes of investigating one and the same subject,—the one honest, and the other not so. They are really distinct and parallel enquiries, proceeding from a like evidence-seeking temper, upon different subjects, and neither of them, so far as I can see, blinking evidence or facts dishonestly. Each would have welcomed the other as a fellow-labourer in different compartments of the same field. Further, while refusing to interpret the unexplained praise of this Essay by the elaborate dissolution of the first three Gospels into an uncertified and inconsistent tradition, which is built upon a like eulogy of Marsh in another part of the volume, it must be said that this whole inclination towards such enquiries as Marsh's proceeds very much upon an ignoring of the external testimony of the Church from the beginning to the Scriptures. The Gospels claim to be inspired

Scripture, primarily, upon the historical evidence which proves them to have been received as such,—as the inspired writings of certain inspired men,—from Apostolic times. Into what earlier sources they were resolvable in the process of composition, is to believers a question of curiosity only, except so far as the answer to it may, 1. remove cavils against the alleged account of their inspired origin, and 2. throw light upon their meaning. To unbelievers such a line of inquiry can do little more than establish the groundlessness of the cavils in question. I cannot see then how an enquirer is otherwise than honest who accepts external testimony on such a subject. The one question in the point for such an enquirer is, whether there be indeed such difficulties in the mutual relations of the language, and of the meaning, of the first three Gospels one to the other, as to overpower the external testimony. And the one value of works like Marsh's seems to be, not the discovery by them of the real account of the materials from which the Evangelists wrote,—the building has been raised and the scaffolding knocked down, and no divination can now conjecture whence each particular stone was hewn,—but simply to establish that there is a *possible* account to be given of the existing phenomena, which shall remove all difficulty from the path of that external evidence into which the arguments for belief must be really resolved. The particular account given by Marsh in the volume in question is indeed futile enough. And like the similar hypothesis respecting the Pentateuch, one serpent of the kind has swallowed up another so rapidly in German speculation on the subject, as to shew that all solid discovery about it is as impossible as it is indeed superfluous. And surely it was from this feeling of the inutility of an enquiry which is to a large extent surpeseded by evidence of another sort, coupled no doubt with a considerable ignorance of German theology, and with a pre-occupation by nobler and more profitable themes, and not from any such dishonest fear of results as the Essayist speaks of, that so few English divines have been found to tread in Dr. Marsh's steps. However, there is a ground of comparison between the historical argument of Paley and the critical analysis of Marsh, apart from the merits of the particular writers. Undoubtedly exegetical enquiries, assuming them to be rightly conducted, tend to establish a more profound knowledge and a more convincing proof than the external and historical. The light thrown upon Scriptural studies by the complete living reproduction of the actual circumstances under which each book was written, at which modern criticism aims, has its undoubted advantages. It breathes life and motion into what was before like an object seen in the mass under shade. And so far, I freely own, that the laboured result of Paley's lengthy argument is jejune and narrow compared with the results of a study of the sacred text itself. The very boast of that writer, —that his book will be serviceable to all denominations of Christians, because the rent between sects does not go down to the foundation, which it is his work to lay,—shews plainly enough how vague that foundation is, which is the extent of his results. Setting aside, then, all question respecting the exceedingly imperfect historical and patristic knowledge of the time and of the school, (although Lardner, at any rate, cannot be called ignorant of the latter subject,) it is plain that a living knowledge of the meaning of Scripture, though considered only in its literal and direct sense, will present to the mind a far more profound and exact conception of the Gospel and of its origin, whether for the purpose of evidence or of devout thought, than any amount of bare outward proof of the barren general proposition that "Christianity," a word connoting many complex and disputed ideas, rests upon the testimony of witnesses who could be "neither deceivers nor deceived." Moreover, one cannot but sympathize with the general remarks, which stigmatize the direct study of merely external evidence, however necessary with respect to the unbeliever, as nevertheless injurious to that temper of belief in the student of which it necessitates the temporary suspension. Apart from the profanity which seems almost inseparable from the bare argumentative statement of the case, the mind is taken off for the time from religious thinking itself to the mere historical proof of the facts upon which religious thought may be exercised, which is of course in no sense religious thinking at all. A rational mind must indeed have reasonable ground for believing. There is a legitimate function to be discharged by evidential reasoning. There is a strength in such evidence which occasionally may be useful to confirm the faith even of a believing mind. But it is not the task on which a Christian temper would choose habitually to employ itself.

But allowing all this,—allowing that the study of the text of Scripture is more remunerating than that of external evidences; and that, even as an evidence-writer, Paley is certainly narrow in the result of his laboured proof;—does he prove nothing because he proves little? A "conventional case," and "unreal matter," and a "factitious thesis," imply that the argument thus stigmatized falls to the ground altogether, unless upon some one or more groundless assumptions. And in Paley's great argument,—to say nothing of Leslie's before, and of Lardner's after him,—what are these groundless assumptions? It is perfectly true that the historical fact of certain miracles, which became almost the ground of a new religious body among men, is the sum total of Paley's results. The theory of miracles in themselves, the value of miracles as evidence, the exclusion of the possibility of any conversion of subjective belief into supposed objective testimony, the value of historical evidence as set over against *à priori* reasonings on the subject, the application of the argument to the special and cardinal doctrines of the faith, —in a word, the entire subject of the argumentative bearings and value of the naked skeleton of an argument put forward, are not touched. The book is no answer to modern infidelity, no basis for a complete faith in Christian doctrine; only a very small portion of the materials for either. But it is one thing to say that an argument is incomplete, or that it did not anticipate, and so did not notice, modes of thought and reasoning posterior in date to itself; another to stigmatize it as founded on mistakes. And if the Essay, as I believe, means simply the former of the two, then one cannot but feel it unwise to fling out harsh-sounding words upon the sensitive mind of the religious public, all alert as it is at the present moment, and with considerable provocation, to find heresy wherever it can.

III. But the Laudian divines come off far worse. Two or three hard words, which find in the facts a partial justification, are bestowed, in passing, upon Paley: has not the Dalilah of a neat historical formula tempted the Essayist to sacrifice Laud and his school to an antithesis? In a brief sketch of the successive "theories of belief" which have prevailed among Christians, it was needful so to describe each as to bring out the link of connection which led to its successor. And the Caroline divines are summarily characterized as having substituted the authority of the National Church for that of the discarded Church Universal of pre-Reformation times: and this in such a way as to render it "impossible to justify the Reformation and the breach with Rome."

Now, the only supposition that will justify the first statement is, that those divines resolved the ultimate intellectual ground of religious faith into the decree of the existing and national Church of England. The only supposition that will justify the second is, that they resolved it into the decree of the existing Catholic Church assumed to be represented by the Pope, or at the outside by the Churches in communion with the Pope. And surely the Caroline divines were so far from assuming either of these suppositions, that they unhesitatingly deny both. Nay, did any man ever assert for any national Church, as such, the attribute of infallibility, or the right of concluding the faith of its own members by its own simple testimony, which implies infallibility? Or did any English divine of the

Church school ever so give up his own cause, as to allow the identification of the Church Catholic with any of the half-dozen forms under which the Roman Catholic controversialist claims infallibility for his own part of the Church? It is absolutely certain that Laud did neither; nor, I think, any of those divines who are roughly classed together as forming the Laudian school. The Church, according to their view,—no doubt to each individual his own branch of it,—proposes to each the doctrines of the faith as the doctrines of the Church in its entirety and from the beginning, gives him there-with also the Holy Scriptures as God's inspired Word, refers him to the traditional and historical faith of the Church Universal, reaching up to and including Apostolic times, as presenting an authoritative interpretation of Scripture in fundamentals, and bids him then see for himself that the doctrines she thus lays before him are in Scripture. If he in a teachable and earnest spirit endeavours with both heart and reason to embrace the truth thus proposed, she tells him that he will be led on by God's grace to recognize the doctrines, thus pointed out to him in Scripture, to be in themselves divine. An experimental Christian life will give him an internal evidence of that which first comes to him on external and historical grounds. And then according to his measure he will have true faith. He will at length know his Saviour, not because others have told him, but for himself. The case of the Samaritans in the fourth chapter of St. John was the favourite type, taken from older divines, and employed to enforce the view thus laid down. The woman was as the present and national Church. She proclaimed Christ to the people of her village, and announced to them His supernatural knowledge, and His claim to be the Messiah; and she bade them come and see for themselves. Her office was external, introductory, evidential, needing their own act to bring it to a completion. She could only repeat what she had been told, and testify to her own experience. They accept her invitation, invite the Saviour to dwell with them, and then declare to the woman that their belief corresponds to, and crowns, her declaration; for that they now believe, not because of her saying, but because they have heard Jesus for themselves, and know that he is indeed the Christ, the Saviour of the world. Here is nothing surely of a "substitution of the voice of the national Church for that of the Church universal." So far as the Church of the day, national or universal, claimed a self-terminated authority to impose doctrines upon her members as of herself, so far there is a rejection of all such authority on the part of the Church altogether. So far as the question is of proposing the truth with the moral authority of a witness, referring the disciple to the ultimate and divine authority of Scripture, so far there is no substitution but a retaining of both Church universal and Church national; the latter as necessarily the immediate representative to the individual Christian of the former, but as partaking its authority, and that simply a moral authority, only in the due proportion which the case itself implies. And so stated, there is assuredly no suicidal surrender of the Reformation to Rome in the adoption of the principle. For the Reformation is to be justified on the very ground that it was an appeal from a corrupt part of the present Church to the collective witness of the whole Church yet undivided; and that corrected by the Scriptures themselves as being the witness of the first and inspired Church, to which Scriptures it is the very office of the present uninspired Church to introduce her members as to the final and conclusive Word of God.*

Take Laud's own view, too long to quote, but which any one may find set forth repeatedly in his "Conference with Fisher." We have there, first, as the ultimate objective ground of faith, not the Church in any sense, but the Scriptures: and these subjectively

* A reference to Laud's "Conference with Fisher" would be conclusive on this subject. And quotations to the point may be found ready collected in an "Anglican Catena" ("Tracts for the Times," vol. iv.); which, by the way, beginning with Jewel, does *not* end with Brett or Waterland, but with Jebb and Van Mildert.

apprehended, through the aid of the Holy Spirit, not by the understanding merely, but by the entire complex experience of the mature Christian man. And then we have, next, the Church, the Church Catholic, the Church from the beginning, brought before the believer by the voice of the Church present, but with no claim of formal authority without appeal, even for the former. And the office of the Church so understood is introductory, corrective, educational, regulative, interpretative, possessed of a moral authority proportioned to the universality and antiquity, and other corroborative circumstances, of the testimony given, but not claiming to be the formal and ultimate ground of faith.

And if we look further for express statements of the relative authority of the Church Catholic and the Church national, these are not far to seek; and assuredly negative outright any notion of a desire to substitute the latter for the former. Jeremy Taylor, perhaps, can scarcely claim rank as a Laudian divine, although in his later works he may be mostly so reckoned, and his departures from that school at any time were partial and occasional only, however extravagant. Otherwise, his *Ductor Dubitantium* would supply us with a precise testimony. But none can doubt the right of Archbishop Bramhall, the Irish Laud, to represent that school. And his declaration of faith on the subject (in the Address to the Christian Reader, prefixed to his "Replication to the Bishop of Chalcedon") is as exact as it is instructive. First the "Catholic œcumenical essential Church," to which he "submits himself implicitly" until its testimony be given, and "in the preparation of his heart;" seeing that his "adherence is firmer to the infallible rule of faith, i.e. the Holy Scriptures interpreted by the Catholic Church, than to his own private judgment and opinions." And next, and in a distinct line from this, a simple "submission" to "the representative Church, i. e. a free General Council," and "until then to the Church of England, or to a national English synod, to the determination of all which, and of each of them respectively, according to the distinct degrees of their authority, I yield," he says, "a conformity and compliance, or at the least, and to the lowest of them," (i. e. the English national synod,) "an acquiescence." Assuredly there is no substitution here of the particular for the universal. As well might the Archbishop be called a "rationalist," because he concludes this very declaration of his "theory of belief," by bidding his opponent in the end to "follow the dictates of right reason." And his more expanded statement of the nature of the authority which he assigns to the national Church, in his "Answer to La Milletière," shews plainly that the "authoritative" judgment which he there claims for it, the "judgment of jurisdiction," is one to which obedience, and not faith, is the correlative, and which is therefore in no sense a substitute for the formal infallibility claimed by the Romanist for the Church Universal as in communion with the Pope, or even for the practical infallibility claimed by the Anglican for the Church, as a whole and from the beginning, irrespective of the Pope altogether.

IV. The condition of religious feeling in the present English Church is a more delicate subject. The religious world in England at present is described, in different parts of the Essay, as being in the unsound and unhealthy state of holding views of which it is afraid to "allow the proofs to be sifted in open court;"—views which have become mere formulæ, once but no longer the living expression of earnest belief, now a "godless orthodoxy," which "extinguishes religious thought," and shrinks from honest enquiry lest it should prove fertile "in unpleasant results." That orthodoxy has "ceased to be a social influence,"—so it is hinted—and is growing into an artificial system, where theological virtues are no longer moral ones, and theological doctrines have "stiffened into phrases," and "bear no relation to the actual history of man;" while a "factitious phraseology," or the "passwords of the modern pulpit," are "substituted for the simple facts of life." Severe language, surely, to be applied either expressly or by implication to the existing tone of religious thought among us, or to its tendency; language strangely at variance with the more common and cheering belief, finding both utterance and evidence in ways so numerous, of an unprecedented revival within the past generation of a living and chastened faith. But when we come to interpret and criticise this language, the question must be first answered, to what extent is it intended to reach? Is it the whole belief of the Church as such that is thus dissevered from the faith and the wants of the age? Or is it merely that such moral defects exist in a particular party, or extend to only the manner in which the truth is taught? It is quite possible,—and in an age of thought and of discovery must needs be the case,—that a large amount of unreasoning, unsifted belief in the bulk of mankind will enshrine the particular opinions of a previous generation, and its errors among them, in a religious reverence, long after the more learned of individual enquirers have renounced these errors. The various readings of Kennicott's Hebrew text, and the critical emendations of Mill's New Testament and the very Polyglott of Walton, were each of them heresy in their day and for a while to some people. And probably we are as our forefathers were; not less, yet not more likely to be obstinate in retaining exploded errors. Dean Ellicott, for instance, runs no particular risk of being called hard names for giving up the θς, in the 1st of Timothy. Again, it is very possible, that when the life of a religious movement is pretty nigh exhausted, and its existence has become rather one of opposition to more living movements of a later date,—when a theological school has outgrown the conditions which called it into existence and made it the real supply to a true want,—the peculiar forms of speech that once had, but now have lost, a real meaning, shall nevertheless retain a traditional and customary acceptance, and be defended with a bigotry and acrimony proportioned to the loss of a living faith in them and of an honest appreciation of their evidence. Something of a "godless orthodoxy" is almost a necessary incident of a declining theological movement. It is possible, yet once more, that a true Scriptural theology may be preached in a conventional and unreal tone, and that men who have confounded their own stiff modes of handling the truth with the truth itself, may be apt to "stifle thought" to the best of their power by condemning those who throw themselves into a heartier way of teaching it. These suppositions taken together—and I believe each of them has, or has had, a real application to ourselves—give an innocent, and I believe the actual, meaning of the Essayist's language. Unhappily, however, other Essays, for which the Rector of Lincoln is not responsible, attach a much wider sense to similar censures of the present time. The factitious phraseology, the positions which will not bear the light of day, the formulæ which are unreal, and yet from which an irrational bigotry will tolerate no departure,—are interpreted elsewhere to be questions of Biblical interpretation, of the construction of creeds, of the Church of the future. And the unquestioning belief in an inspired Book, the absolute acceptance of the doctrines of the Creeds, the customary theology to be found in Prayer-book and Catechism, preached in the old letter and not in the new spirit,—these are proclaimed to be in opposition so diametrical to the intellect, and knowledge, and moral instincts of the age, as to render it impossible for many honest enquirers to continue to accept them. If so, then let the real issue be raised openly: only let it be remembered, that it is not raised by the words of this Essay, but by the piecing out of the indefiniteness of those words through the language of others. Then it is indeed Christianity itself which is assailed. The Christianity of 1,800 years is held to have done its work, and lived its life, and to be now effete. And the difference between Comte, for instance, or any other open assailant of the Gospel, and the extremest of the school that is now rising among us, will be simply the difference between an open substitution of a human system for Christianity, and an attempt to alter the latter into conformity with a human system—the difference, in a word, between rejecting or retaining the mere name of the Gospel, while equally giving up the thing. Only let it be repeated, while thus in all sadness insisting upon the real issue at the bottom of this conflict, that the deliberate intention of raising that issue is not to be imputed to men who profess, however (we may think) groundlessly, to be only recalling the Christianity of the day to a truer, and therefore more effective condition; and who do beyond a doubt intend, in their own purpose, however unhappily, to reconcile intellect with revelation. And, at any rate, the words of the present Essay are responsible for no question of the kind. Meanwhile, it certainly does seem to meet the facts of the case more truly, that we should recognise rather an improvement than a deterioration in the present tone of English theology. English preaching has surely thrown off the pompous conventionalities and rounded Latinisms that sent our fathers to sleep, and has become more of a living and flexible instrument, fitting into men's hearts and speaking to their real wants; while, at the same time, and with the very reverse of a diminution of acceptableness, it has learned a deeper theology and preaches more thoroughly and more livingly the "terminology of the Creeds." And English exegesis has been so far from refusing to face the extremest researches of German criticism, that it has been learning of late to rifle them of their solid and minute learning without being tainted by their generally crude and unpractical spirit. And without denying that there is much among us of narrowness and of bigotry, or that the Church has been well-nigh rent in half by a bitter and unreasoning party spirit, it is surely plain, that a large part at least of the polemical ferment which has arisen now, means only—what is both right and reasonable—that earnest men are shocked at what they hold to be a tampering with fundamental truth, and a wanton assault upon Scripture; that they expect that clergymen shall believe what they subscribe, instead of spending their labour in determining the minimum of belief that is unavoidable; and that Christians shall submit their judgments to the faith of Christ, instead of altering that faith to suit their own narrow conceptions. This is assuredly the impression under which the whole Church, so to say, has undoubtedly acted; and the very strength of which shews, at any rate, no unreality of feeling, while the breadth of the provocation excludes any charge of narrow bigotry.

It yet remains to notice one further topic, of deeper interest and wider reach than any mere question of matter of fact respecting the doctrines or temper of particular periods of the Church. Having spoken hitherto of facts, let us now turn to principles. There are two ways of writing the history of religious, as of any other class of opinion. Either an historian may trace the course of that opinion with continual reference to a standard of truth, by which he measures his judgments of each passing phase of belief; or, waiving this, he may trace the successive shades and schools of belief on the hypothesis of a merely natural succession of ideas, developed according to "a law of necessary continuity" by the simple operation of the laws of thought. He may either write, as a Christian, a history of his own religion, discriminating the mingled truth and falsehood of successive schools of doctrine; or as a spectator, placed externally, he may analyze the growth and variations of a philosophy, irrespective of truth or falsehood altogether. In the first case, he will run the risk, no doubt, of colouring his statements, unconsciously if not intentionally, by the particular views of his own school and time. His book, if he is not on his guard, may degenerate into the special pleading of a partizan. In the second, he must of necessity deprive himself of that sympathy with his subject, which alone can enable an historian to depict aright a history of religion. He will become a mere dry analyzer of facts, to the true life of which he has voluntarily blinded himself.* The philosophical spirit, which realizes to the life the en-

* There are some good remarks on this subject in the beginning of Neander's "History of the Church."

tire atmosphere of thought and fact under which any view of doctrine came into existence, seems impossible in matters of religion, unless to a religious thinker. Truth, in such subjects, hides itself from those who deliberately write without any thought of truth at all. So far, however, the question is only one between two opposite extremes; both of which, indeed, must be blended together, in order to produce a perfect history. A history of truth will be unreal and technical, unless it be also clothed in the flesh and blood of the successive phases of opinion. And a history of opinion, independent of the moral certainty that it will in such a case lean towards falsehood, will be destitute of insight into the deeper springs of human action, much more into the dispensations of God, unless it be referred throughout to the standard of truth. But the case is materially altered, if the natural connection of successive theological views be assumed to be inconsistent with any "theory of belief," by which objective truth is held to be attainable. If the value of ecclesiastical history be asserted to be, that it eliminates the subjectivity of one age by the neutralizing effect of comparing also those of other ages, the assertion no doubt is to the point, and true. But if it is also implied, that no more present and immediate instrument exists for ascertaining fundamental religious truth than the tracing back the opinion of the present day to its antecedents, and that men are in the midst of a kind of mesmeric chain of external influences through which no hand is stretched to lift them up to the truth itself, such a view claims to be otherwise characterized. It seems to ignore the provisions made under the Gospel for perpetuating truth, the external teaching of Church and Bible, and the internal powers of the reason as guided by the Holy Spirit; and to substitute accordingly, for truth belief, for dogma opinion, for the Creeds a mere philosophy. And the ultimate result of such a view must be a very sad alternative, yet one which the events of the last few years have shewn too plainly to be a real one. For men will not rest content with a faith held to depend upon grounds that are illusory. And they who are so placed, must needs end either in believing nothing, or in arbitrarily choosing and blindly accepting some external and self-constituted standard of belief for themselves.

Now the undeveloped and cursory remarks at the beginning of the Essay here considered, leave undeniably the impression of favouring such a view. They seem to exhibit as the grounds of the faith, what are in truth the causes of its corruption, the character and mental condition of each successive age. They appear to speak of "the external verities" of the original revelation, as though they were visible to us only through the vista,—the tortuous windings and hazy atmosphere,—of the past world of thought that intervenes between them and ourselves; and as though they owed their present form, less to the unchangeable Divine informant, than to the minds of the men who teach and the men who are taught. And they do distinctly include within the influence and sphere of variable opinion, all theories of objective standards of religious truth; ranking, under a trenchant though surely a rather strained alternative, as alike untenable, the outward and the inward, the Roman Catholic and Anglican, and the Protestant, theoies; or, in other words, the assertion of an external and living instructor, whether single or corporate, immediate or traditional, or of an inspired book, capable of being interpreted whether by Church or individual, or of both combined, if assumed to be channels of a truth above opinion, and able, therefore, to overrule and inform it. Of course there may be theories, on the one hand, of a continuous external source of Divine teaching, which yet recognise "the laws of human thought;" and on the other, of individual enquiry, which do "take account of the influences of education:" either of which, therefore, escape the rather verbal antithesis of the Essayist's dilemma—a dilemma, however, professing by its terms to be an exhaustive one. But while, if pressed to their most precise meaning, room is thus left by the words for the loftier view, it is impossible to help feeling that the tone of the remarks in question does tend to include the whole body of religious truth within the shifting mass of current human opinion, and to deny to ourselves the possession of any competent instrument for ascertaining that truth, in its purity objectively as truth.

And what, then, is the question, suggested rather than distinctly put, still less formally answered in either direction, by the remarks of the Essay—an old question that has underlain much of the controversy between England and Rome as well as between Christian and Deist, and that has come to the surface again now in more places than in the volume of Essays? It is the question whether or no the Church has yet succeeded in propounding a true "theory of belief." Faith is correlative to a Divine informant; yet here is, directly and to ourselves, only man, one man commonly against another. Truth must rest upon absolute grounds; yet religious belief, as a matter of fact, is what it is mainly because men are born in this or that school of theology, in Italy or in England, in a cottage or in a palace. The interpretation, again, of the Bible must needs vary with the opinions, and temper, and knowledge of the age. And the present Church, under whatever form represented, must needs consist of men, who do not by reason of their Church position rise above humanity, and who therefore see with the eyes of their age, and judge according to the *idola* with which that age surrounds them. Does it not follow, either that there must be, besides these, some visible and continuous present Divine informant, if we are to have a truth in religion at all above opinion, or that we cannot attain to such truth? Neither a living Pope nor an open Bible are an adequate answer to this question. The former leaves us still to mere moral evidence, even granting that there was such evidence, to establish his right to be the required oracle. Nor does the present Church at large, even omitting the divisions that impair its authority and silence its voice, claim more certainly, although more plausibly, the privilege of formal infallibility. And although, granting the conditions of an accessible Bible, and a belief in its inspiration, and a fair average of education, I do not believe that broad or fundamental error in religion could in the long run hold its ground; yet, doubtless, the very text of the Bible, and the canonicity of it, and its inspiration, and the body of doctrine to be deduced from it, depend to us upon human reasoning. But if there be thus no living Divine informant, is there, for that reason, no philosophically tenable ground for religious faith at all? Is the voice of God not brought to our ears, becuse there are no audible accents of that voice speaking to our physical sense of hearing from a visible Sinai? Because moral evidence is not in itself formally infallible, is it impossible that *some* moral evidence shall bring within the reach of men truths which *are* formally infallible? And there is abundant moral evidence to a past infallible revelation, and to the embodiment of the words of infallible men in a still existing book; and to the continuous existence of a certain Creed from the beginning, taught by those infallible men, and held by the Church at all times, although mixed up with a mass of error at this or that time; and held from the beginning to have been the Creed, upon belief in which that book was founded, and which its text therefore implies, and which may be read and re-read, in that text, from time to time. In a word, there is that which does seem, as it has seemed, surely, to the Reformed Church of England, to be a philosophically sound "theory of belief," in fundamentals, viz. Scripture interpreted by Catholic consent. Here is the sufficient foundation for a belief, that shall rest upon a truth above opinion, and be correlative to a Creed and not to a mere philosophy. It is unreasonable and presumptuous to refuse to believe unless a present and living voice speaks to ourselves with a Divine power; and if men cannot find such a voice, to declare belief impossible. The evidence of the Christian Church of all times and places,—omitting all question of Divine aid or appointment,—constitutes a collective witness to the facts of the original revelation,—to the written records left behind by its inspired teachers,—to the main lines of their teaching itself,—such as at least rises to a level above the fluctuations of opinion or the subjective conditions of particular periods. Ritual, liturgies, an ordained clergy, a traditional orthodox faith, the counterpoise of opposite influences in different peoples neutralized by combination, the views of one age corrected by those of another, in a word, the collective evidence of the Church of all times and ages,—and this corrected, checked, enlightened, gifted as it were with a living and human power, by the volume of Scripture, by the written words in which are embodied the living teachings of prophets and apostles, and of Christ Himself,—and vitalized, again, and applied by the spiritual experience and spiritually guided reasons of individual Christians,—constitutes together a complex but wonderful machinery for the preservation of truth; which cannot be got rid of by pointing out that its operation is modified, as no doubt it is, by the nature of the subject on which it is brought to bear. A floating mass of uncertified and confused opinion will, of course, always exist; and the tone of thought will vary; and the aspect of the truth, and the stress laid upon particular portions of it, and the inferences drawn from it, and the amount of error mingled with it, will fluctuate with the knowledge, and the philosophy, and the moral tone of the time. Difficulties again, transformed by the solution of them into evidences, will arise on the side of metaphysics, physics, criticism, morals, history; yet each passing away, as a matter of fact, with the conditions of the time to which it belonged, and out of which it arose, and all together dwarfed into insignificance by the side of the counter-difficulty of explaining the historical fact of Christianity on any other supposition than that of its truth. But, old-fashioned as the words may sound in the ears of modern intellect, the Bible, as interpreted by Catholic consent, does appear, nevertheless, to be the very instrument fitted to the very need with which we are here concerned. Moral evidence of course it is, and not demonstrative. But it is moral evidence which, practically, and to a temper not blinded by moral defects, precisely performs the office of lifting the mind above the conditions of the time, and of bringing it in contact with the uncoloured truth. It is moral evidence which rests upon an ultimate Divine informant, and checks itself by a continued reference to recorded Divine words. And a large view of Church history will shew, that on the whole, and for its main purpose, it has actually answered the end for which God gave it. The fundamental truths of the Gospel have been overlaid, but not forgotten; have been distorted, but not blotted out; have "progressed by the antagonism" of opposing tendencies, yet have ever oscillated again to their true balance; have been preserved, in a word, as it has pleased God to preserve all truth for man, by the instrumentality of man himself; not with mathematical demonstration or rigorous precision, but with moral certainty and with substantial truth; not by abolishing the atmosphere of human thought and feeling, but by penetrating that atmosphere with the rays of a distant but unmistakeable and glorious sun.

ON THE INTERPRETATION OF SCRIPTURE.*

WHEN the gallant Percy was smarting under his wounds on the field of Holmedon, where he had fought nobly for his king and country, he was accosted by a courtier who had taken no part in the fray, and who discoursed to the faint and weary soldier on the calamities of war. It was a strange thing, he said, that men should risk their lives in battle :—

"... . It was great pity,
So it was, that villainous saltpetre should be digged
Out of the bowels of the harmless earth,
Which many a good tall fellow had destroyed
So cowardly."†

He also informed the bleeding man that there was an excellent recipe for the healing of his wounds :—

"... The sovereign'st thing on earth
Was parmaceti for an inward bruise."

The temper of the brave soldier was nettled by this

* *Note.*—In the following pages the writer has endeavoured to remove objections, and to shew the result of erroneous principles. This, he is well aware, is only a portion of the work to be done with regard to the subject before him. It is necessary to build up, as well as to pull down; to establish the truth, as well as to refute error. He has therefore attempted to deal with that other part of the argument in "Lectures on the Inspiration, and on the Interpretation, of the Bible, delivered at Westminster Abbey." (Rivingtons, 1861. 2 vols., 7s.)

† Shakespeare, Henry IV., Pt. I. Act. i. sc. 3.

impertinent talk, and he answered it in good plain downright English, for he says "it made him mad."

Hotspur knew by experience that war was not a pleasant trade, and he felt some of its evils at that time. But, human nature being what it is, it did not seem to him a strange or surprising thing that men should fight. He knew that they have passions and lusts, and if he had read the Epistle of St. James in the Latin Vulgate, or in Wickliffe's Version,—for he probably did not know Greek,—he had learnt the cause of war,—"Whence come wars and fightings among you? Come they not hence, even of your lusts that war in your members?" *

He felt also an instinct within him, prompting him, when called by the voice of his sovereign, to fight valiantly for his king, his country, and his God.

The author of the Essay before us will not, it is hoped, resent the comparison of the first six pages of his Essay to the discourse of the courtier at Holmedon.

The Essay opens thus:—"It is a strange though familiar fact, that great differences of opinion exist respecting the Interpretation of Scripture." † It is a wonderful thing, that men are not all agreed as to its meaning, and that they should engage in conflicts and controversies upon it. "It is so extraordinary a phenomenon," he tells us, "that it requires an *effort of thought* to appreciate *its true nature*." ‡ What a wonderful prodigy it must be, to demand such a distressing strain of our mind that we should absolutely be obliged to *think!*

Is not this very like the lack-a-daisical languor of the courtier in the play? It required of him an effort of courage to look the enemy in the face, and buckle on his armour and fight; and "it requires an effort of thought to appreciate" the true nature of differences of Interpretation of Scripture. It is a sad thing that such differences should exist. Pity it is, that the salt-

* James iv. 1. † Essay, p. 330. ‡ P. 334.

petre should be dug out of the earth which has supplied the material for this controversial warfare.

Yes; but in sober seriousness, are not all the plaintive notes which compose the dolorous dirge of these first six pages of our Essay like the effeminate effusions of a maudlin sentimentalism? True, very true it is, that there are differences, and have been differences, and ever will be differences in the Interpretation of Holy Scripture. But let us look them honestly and courageously in the face. Is it "a strange thing," is it "an extraordinary phenomenon," that there should be such differences? No, certainly not; at least in the estimate of those who acknowledge the divine origin of Scripture, and who consider the corruptions of the human heart and the operations of our spiritual Enemy. It is not more strange and extraordinary that there should be controversies concerning the meaning of Scripture, than that there should be wars and fightings among us. Scripture is God's word. And the Evil Spirit is the enemy of Scripture, and he has been ever eager to take the seed of God's word out of men's hearts;* and our hearts are often bad soil, and do not retain the Word. He stirs up some men to deny the Inspiration of Scripture; and to treat the Bible as a common book. He excites others to pervert its meaning and to bend it in various directions, as a mere "*regula plumbea*, a leaden rule," to suit their own wayward imaginations, which they call their "verifying faculty;" and to twist it about as a "*cereus nasus*, a nose of wax," to be moulded with easy pliancy so as to accommodate itself to their "inner consciousness;" and to set at naught all the guidance which the Holy Spirit affords for the true Interpretation of Scripture, both in Scripture itself, and in the primitive consent and practice of the Christian Church.

All these machinations of the Enemy of Scripture are perfectly familiar to every student of Church history, and will not seem strange to any child who reads

* Luke viii. 12.

Scripture itself. At the Temptation in the wilderness, the Devil quoted Scripture against the Divine Author of Scripture.* And St. Peter tells us that even in his own days there were "differences in the interpretation of Scripture," and that "unlearned and unstable men" wrested some things in St. Paul's Epistles, as they did "the other Scriptures, unto their own destruction." †

From the times of the Apostles, and after them in the days of St. Ignatius and St. Polycarp and St. Irenæus and Tertullian, even to the present age, the same Evil Spirit which stirred up the first false teachers to corrupt the sense of Scripture, has been always at work in prosecuting the same design. Therefore no one need be surprised or staggered by the fact, that there are great differences in the interpretation of Scripture. No one ought to consider it a "strange and extraordinary phenomenon," but he ought to recognise in it a proof of the divine truth of Scripture warning us that so it would be; and he ought to see here an evidence of the divine worth of Scripture, which the Evil Spirit desires to destroy; and he ought also to derive from it a strong motive to hold fast the *true sense* of Holy Scripture, which the Divine Author of Scripture declares to us by the witness of His Church universal, "the Church of the living God, the pillar and ground of the truth."

The Essayist, having expressed his surprise "that differences of opinion should exist respecting the Interpretation of Scripture," and having said that "it requires an effort of thought to appreciate the nature of so extraordinary a phenomenon," proceeds to prescribe a remedy for the evil. If we will follow his advice, our differences respecting the Interpretation of Scripture may, he says, be abated, and eventually disappear. He has discovered an excellent medicine which will cure the malady. He has found out a spiritual panacea, he has invented a soothing balm more potent than that

* Matt. iv. 6; Luke iv. 10. † 2 Pet. iii. 16. ‡ 1 Tim. iii. 15.

"Nepenthes which the wife of Thon
In Egypt gave to Jove-born Helena."*

He has compounded a wonderful diallacticon, to reconcile the divided members of Christendom, and assuage their aches and pains, and make them move in harmony and peace.

It is much to be regretted, that, when we come to examine this marvellous recipe, we do not find that it answers our expectations; we shall see what it is when we proceed a little further.

In the meantime we must be permitted to say with all due respect to the inventor of this new medicine, that here also we recognise a resemblance to the courtier at Holmedon. He lamented the differences and strifes of frail humanity; and he then proceeded to recommend his own remedy. He told Hotspur that

"The sovereign'st thing on earth
Was parmaceti for an inward bruise."

It is much to be feared that the Essayist's panacea may prove very like the courtier's parmaceti. But we must pass on.

§ 2. The Essayist complains that there is great reluctance among Christians to profit by recent researches of Biblical criticism. Hence, in part, he would account for the differences which he deplores in the interpretation of Scripture. He says that the Elzevir edition of the Greek New Testament, published in the year 1624, "has been invested with authority, and is made a *pièce de résistance* against innovation." † This is a marvellous assertion; and if the writer's name had not been prefixed to this Essay—if the title-page had not told us that it was produced by one who occupies the chair of Regius Professor of Greek in the University of Oxford, which was lately filled by one of the most learned critics in Christendom, the late Dean of Christ Church, we should rather have imagined that it was put forth by some of those benighted persons whose blindness he deplores.

* Milton's Comus. † Essay, p. 335.

The Essayist of course is speaking of England when he uses this language. Germany, it is certain, does not need his pity. Tischendorf cannot be charged with bigoted adherence to the edition of 1624. Nor can *Lachman*, as the Essayist calls him; * nor can *Meier*, as our author writes his name.† And as far as England is concerned,—enveloped in darkness as she is, in the Essayist's estimation, like a land of critical Cimmerians,—there is scarcely a single Biblical scholar in this country, among those who have put forth annotated editions of the whole or portions of the Greek Testament in the last half-century, who has made a stand for the text of 1624, and has regarded it as a "*pièce de résistance* against innovation." Dean Alford, Dean Ellicott, Dr. Bloomfield, Dr. Tregelles, and others, have shewn themselves free from the trammels of a superstitious reverence for that edition. We had even supposed that Professsor Jowett himself had resisted the claims of the *Textus Receptus*, and had adopted the text of Lachmann in his edition of four of the Epistles of St. Paul: and, as a learned writer has observed,‡ he seems to cling with great tenacity to that text,—which in very many instances is less correct than that of the *Textus Receptus*,—and to make *it* a "*pièce de résistance* against innovation."

It is indeed a "strange fact," an "extraordinary phenomenon," that a writer who expresses a desire to see a history of Biblical Interpretation, § and who proposes to inaugurate a new era in Scriptural criticism, should exhibit so much forgetfulness of what has been done in that department in his own country and in his own age. Did it require "an effort of thought" to appreciate the true nature of the case? and was that effort too great to be made?

§ 3. The Essayist next states his opinion on the duties of an Interpreter of Scripture. "The office of an Interpreter of Scripture," he says, "is to transfer him-

* P. 352. † P. 339.

‡ The Rev. J. B. Lightfoot, in the "Journal of Classical and Sacred Philology," No. VII. p. 88. § Essay, p. 338.

self to another age," to "recover the meaning of the words as they struck on the ears or flashed before the eyes of those who first heard and read them." *

We must here again, with great reluctance, crave leave to dissent. We venture respectfully, but confidently, to assert that here is a great mistake; and it does not seem to be improved by what immediately succeeds it. "The Interpreter," we are told, "is to disengage himself from all that follows" the age in which the words of Scripture were first spoken. He is "to know nothing" of all subsequent history, ecclesiastical and civil. Armed *cap-à-pie* in this panoply of ignorance he is to set forth as knight-errant to do battle against all comers, for the truth of his own interpretations of Scripture. Cervantes himself could not have imagined a more portentous form of self-deception than is displayed in this exegetical Quixotism. Let us observe what it involves. It supposes that the first hearers of the words recorded in Scripture were fully conscious of their meaning. Surely a greater delusion than this never entered the mind of the chivalrous knight of La Mancha.

We know that the ancient Hebrews had only dim visions of the meaning of the prophecies which they heard, and even the Prophets themselves did not fully understand the meaning of their own prophecies; † but, as St. Peter tells us, "they *searched diligently* what the Spirit of Christ that was in them did signify." ‡

We know also from the Apostles and Evangelists, that they themselves did not understand the meaning of many of their Divine Master's words when they were first uttered. How often do they confess this! how often do we read in the Gospels that "they understood not this saying, and it was hid from them, and they perceived it not!" §

Many of our Lord's *sayings* were hard sayings at first, but were afterwards made easy; many of His say-

* Essay, p. 338. † See, for instance, Dan. xii. 4—9.
‡ 1 Pet. i. 11. § Mark ix. 32: cf. Luke ii. 50, ix. 45, xviii. 34.

ings were at first dark, but were made clear by His subsequent *acts*. Nicodemus could have had little notion of our Lord's meaning when He said, "Except a man be born of *water* and of the Spirit, he cannot enter into the kingdom of God." * But this saying of our Divine Teacher was afterwards explained, when our Lord gave a general commission to His apostles, "Go teach all nations, *baptizing* them:" † *that* saying also itself must in another respect have seemed a hard one to those unlettered Galilæans, until they received the gift of the Holy Ghost, empowering them to speak in new tongues.‡ And our Lord's assertion of the general obligation to "eat His Flesh and drink His Blood" was, we know, "a hard saying" § to those who first heard it. But its meaning was afterwards explained, when the same Divine Speaker said, "Take, eat, this is My Body. Drink ye all of this." ‖

If the Scriptures of the Old Testament had been clear to those who *first heard or read* them, or even to those by whose instrumentality they were *written*, there would have been little need of the work which our Blessed Lord wrought in the hearts of the two disciples going to Emmaus, and of the assembled apostles at Jerusalem. "Beginning at Moses and all the Prophets, He *expounded to* them in *all the Scriptures* the things concerning Himself." ¶ And again we read, "Then *opened He* their *understanding*, that they might understand the Scriptures." ** *If* the *true* meaning of the words of our Lord had "struck on the ears of those who first heard them," there would have been comparatively little reason for the miracle of Pentecost, and for the effusion of the glorious light of the Holy Ghost then shed on the minds of the apostles and first disciples, and on the words which they had heard from Christ. Then it was, but not till then, that the true meaning "flashed before their eyes."

"Every prophecy," says St. Irenæus, "is an enigma

* John iii. 5. † Matt. xxviii. 19. ‡ Acts ii. 7, 8.
§ John vi. 60. ‖ Matt. xxvi. 26, 27. ¶ Luke xxiv. 27.
** Luke xxiv. 45.

before its fulfilment." * How different is this language from that of the Essayist! He would have us place ourselves in the age of those who first heard or read the words of Holy Scripture. He would have us abandon our Christian privileges, and go back from the noonday splendour of the Gospel to the dim twilight of the Law. How many degrees would the sun go down on our spiritual dial if the Essayist had his will! When it was rising on our horizon, he would send us to the antipodes. In reading the Old Testament, he would have us see with the eyes and hear with the ears of those who lived before the first Advent of Christ!

Consider also the prophecies of Christ.

His predictions concerning His sufferings and death were like inexplicable riddles to those who first heard them.† The Evangelist declares that "they understood none of these things, neither knew they the things which were spoken." Does the Essayist desire that his pupils should relinquish all the helps which were furnished by subsequent events for the interpretation of those things? And to take another example, when our Lord prophesied concerning St. John, "If I will that he tarry till I come, what is that to thee?" then the meaning which "flashed before the eyes" of the brethren who first heard those words was, that "that disciple should not die." ‡ Will the Essayist maintain, that, as "the history of Christendom is nothing to him," and that he must take the sense of Scripture as it "first sounded on the ears of those who heard it," therefore the Evangelist St. John is still alive?

What also shall we say of our Lord's prophecies concerning the destruction of Jerusalem? Eusebius § and other ancient Christian writers were rightly of opinion, that the comparison of those prophecies with the history of the siege of Jerusalem is very conducive

* St. Irenæus, iv. 26, 1. † See Luke ix. 44, 45, xviii. 32—34.

‡ John xxi. 23.

§ See Eusebius, Eccl. Hist. iii. 6—9. Cf. St. Jerome in Isa. lxiv. and Zech. i., where he infers from Josephus the truth of other prophecies of Scripture concerning Jerusalem.

to the correct interpretation of them, and affords clear evidence of Christ's divine foreknowledge, and supplies a strong argument for the truth of our holy religion. But the Essayist tells us that his ideal interpreter of Scripture shall know "nothing of history." "The greatness of the Roman empire is nothing to him; it is an inner and not an outer world that he is striving to restore. All the after-thoughts of theology are nothing to him." *

Happy expositor! thrice happy interpreter! dwelling in the Epicurean ease of his own serene self-sufficiency. He has no need to take down any ponderous folios from his shelves. He need not have any on his table. He need not invest any of his income in the purchase of a theological library. He may live in a room with four bare walls. He need not pore over the pages of Polyglotts. No Chrysostoms or Augustines shall darken his doors. Perhaps he will admit a Lexicon and a Grammar; "a few rules guarding against common errors are enough for him." † But "no voluminous literature" shall obscure the cloudless calm of his solitary speculations. He will dwell a visionary æon in the pure pleroma of his own imagination, and thence come forth as a spiritual emanation to create a world. He will read the prophecies of our Lord concerning the siege of Jerusalem without troubling himself about the evidence of their fulfilment. "All this is nothing to him." No; he is determined to live in the time when these prophecies were first spoken; he has taken his seat on the Mount of Olives and looks down on Jerusalem as it then was; and no power on earth shall disturb him from his place. There he remains firmly seated like a gray lichen-covered rock upon the mountain in the first century of the Christian era; "sedet æternumque sedebit." From that prophetic tripod on which he has placed himself he will deliver oracular responses to all future generations.

When the Puritan Divines of the Westminster As-

* Essay, p. 338. † Ibid.

sembly had seated themselves comfortably in their arm-chairs, and held their little gilt-leaved Bibles with metal clasps in their hands, they imagined themselves wiser than all the Fathers who ever wrote, and than all the Councils which ever sat.

The learned John Selden ventured sometimes to ruffle their self-complacent equanimity by a few importunate questions; but it was not easily perturbed. Every one of that august body had more wisdom, in his own conceit, than if he had all the contents of the *Bibliotheca Patrum Maxima* in his mind.

The Essayist seems to have earned a place in that venerable conclave. "*Unus Bibliotheca liber.*" One book is his library. "When the meaning of *Greek words*" (of the Bible, why not also of the *Hebrew?*) "is once known, the young student has almost all the real materials which are possessed by the greatest biblical scholar—in the Book itself." * And he is determined to live in the age in which it was written. "All the after-thoughts of theology are nothing to him; the history of Christendom is nothing to him." No; all these things are nothing to him. Indeed, we might almost say that his stock in trade is "*totum nil.*" And having set up himself in the business of interpreter, he proceeds to deal out his wares, and to assure his customers that "he has no connexion with any other house," and that genuine articles, unadulterate viands, are only to be procured at his depôt and at that of others who imitate his example of embarking in the trade of interpreter without any capital for carrying it on.

Gentle reader, pardon this raillery. The subject is indeed a very serious one. But our Essayist's new mode of forming an Interpreter of Holy Scripture is really—excuse the word—so ludicrous, that it could hardly be treated with gravity. Elijah himself could not refrain from irony when he saw the miserable infatuation to which the worship of Baal reduced its votaries.† And the self-idolizing worship of the Essayist is scarcely less

* Essay, p. 384.

† 1 Kings xviii. 27.

fanatical. Indeed, in reading the pages of this Essay, we may be sometimes disposed to doubt whether the author himself is not in jest, and whether he is not amusing himself with speculating on the credulity of his readers, and with trying how large an amount of paradox they are ready to receive at his hands.

But if he is really in earnest, then let us be permitted to say, that in the interpretation of Holy Scripture the history of Christendom is *not* "nothing to" us; the "after-thoughts of theology," as he is pleased to call the workings of the Holy Spirit in the Church, "are" *not* "nothing to" us. No: they are *something;* they are *a very great deal to us;* and are designed by Almighty God to be so; and he who shuts his eyes to their light, and desires that others should listen to the dictatorial dogmatism of his own arbitrary conceit, and fall down and worship the image which he sets up of himself, is not only wilfully blind, but is "a blind leader of the blind; and if the blind lead the blind, both shall fall into the ditch." *

A diligent study of "the history of Christendom" has ever been regarded by sober-minded and pious men as one of the best aids to the right understanding of Holy Scripture.

In reading the history of Christendom we see the record of the successive attempts which have been made by the Evil One, who is the enemy of Scripture, to pervert or obscure the true meaning of Scripture. We see also the means by which the Holy Spirit has been pleased to use, by the agency of holy men whom He has raised up from time to time in the Church; and whom He has enabled to resist those efforts of the Adversary, and to refute error, and to vindicate the true meaning of Holy Scripture, † and to declare that meaning to the world in Creeds and Confessions of faith.

By examining those records, we learn to admire and adore God's goodness in eliciting truth from error, and in overcoming evil with good, and in making heresy

* Matt. xv. 14.

† Cf. St. Augustine in Ps. liv., and in Ps. lxvii.; Hooker, V. xliii. 6.

itself to be subservient to the clearer manifestation and to the firmer establishment of the faith. Here also we see the fulfilment of Christ's prophecy, that "the gates of hell shall not prevail against His Church;"* and we derive from this contemplation the cheering assurance, that He will be ever with her "even to the end of the world."†

Well therefore did Lord Bacon say, that "Church-history thoroughly read and observed" is of great virtue in "making a wise divine."‡ Well did he also say that inasmuch as "the Scriptures are written to the *thoughts* of men, and to the succession of *all ages*, with a *foresight* of *all heresies*, and of all contradictions and differing estates of the Church, they are *not to be interpreted* only according to the latitude of the proper sense of the place, and respectively towards the *present occasion* whereupon the words were uttered."§ No; but the full explication of them is often to be derived from *subsequent events*, which were within the scope and range of the divine eye of Him who uttered them, and to whom all things are present; but which were not visible to those who first heard those words, nor indeed were fully revealed to the eyes of those holy men by whose agency they were written, but were afterwards explained by God's Providence in the government of the world and of His church.

In page 361 the Essayist thus speaks:—

> "To avoid misconception, it may be remarked that .... *Infant Baptism*, or (qu. and) the *Episcopal Form* of Church Government, have sufficient grounds; *the weakness* is *the attempt to derive them from Scripture.*"

Here is a striking example of the character and tendency of his system of Interpretation. If we are to treat Scripture as he would have us do, then we must allow that this assertion is true. There is *no express* command in Scripture that *infants* should be baptized, or that the Church should be governed by *bishops;* but

* Matt. xvi. 18. † Matt. xxviii. 20.
‡ Lord Bacon, Advancement of Learning, bk. ii. p. 100.
§ Ibid., p. 267.

it has been generally maintained by the best divines that *Infant Baptism* and *Episcopacy* can and ought to be *derived* by *logical inference* from Holy Scripture.

With regard to *Infant* Baptism, even the theologians of the Church of Rome have asserted this: Bellarmine,* Gregory of Valentia,† and Suarez,‡ and even Pope Innocent III., in one of his Decretals.§ And the ancient Church with one consent applied to the sacrament of Baptism ‖ the words of our Blessed Lord, "Except a man be born again"—or, more correctly, "Whosoever is not born again"—"of *water* and the Holy Ghost, he cannot enter into the kingdom of God;" and therefore the Church of England begins her office for the Public Baptism of *Infants* with rehearsing those words of *Holy Scripture.* She also rightly considers that *infants* are a part of *nations*, and she therefore cites in the same office the words of *Scripture* in which our Lord gave a commission to His disciples to "go and teach all nations, *baptizing* them." ¶

The *true sense* of Scripture *is* Scripture, and *that* sense is to be ascertained by rational inference, and by comparison of one passage of Scripture with another; and the Church rightly accepts whatever "is read in Scripture *or* may be *proved* thereby;" ** and on this principle it may surely be asserted, that it is *not* a "*weakness* to attempt to *derive Infant Baptism* from *Scripture*."

Precisely the same reasoning may be applied to Episcopacy. It may be, and ought to be, *deduced* by logical inference from *Scripture.*†† The best *interpretation* of a law is the *practice* of those who lived at the time when the law was delivered. And when we find

* See Bellarmine, De Bapt., lib. i. c. viii.

† De Bapt. Parvul., § 2.

‡ In Thom. Disput. xxv. p. 3.

§ Decret., lib. iii. tit. xlii. c. 3.

‖ St. John iii. 5; cf. Hooker, V. lix. 2. See also the testimony of St. Cyprian and the sixty-six bishops of Africa, A.D. 253, Epist. ad Fidum.

¶ Matt. xxviii. 19.

** Thirty-Nine Articles, Art. VI.

†† The author will not repeat what has been said by him on this subject in an introductory note to the third chapter of St. Paul's first Epistle to Timothy.

not only a contemporaneous and uniform practice immediately after the delivery of the law, but also a continuous and uninterrupted usage for many centuries after the law was given, we may accept that usage as affording the clearest exposition of the meaning of the law. From the time of the Apostles for fifteen hundred years there was no Church in Christendom without a Bishop.*

The Essayist says that in the Interpretation of Scripture he has nothing to do with "subsequent history." Thus he shuts the windows which let light in upon Scripture, and darkens the house in which he dwells. If he likes to close his own casements, and prefers a dark house to a light one, we need not quarrel with his taste; but let him not induce others to come and live with him under the same roof; let him not censure them as bigots if they do *not* "love darkness rather than light."

§ 4. The Essayist seems to have felt that his readers would naturally ask,—

What have been the fruits of his method of interpretation? Has it been adopted? Has it produced any results? What are they?

He answers these questions with the following assertion:—The science of Biblical Criticism, he informs us, has made some progress in our own day. In England, it is true, in his opinion, we have not done much. We are too timid and cautious. Among ourselves "the Interpretation of Scripture has assumed an apologetic character, as though making an effort to defend itself against some supposed inroad of science and criticism." †

But our continental friends, it seems, are more adventurous, and therefore more prosperous. The Essayist tells us that "among German commentators there

* Cf. Hooker's Preface, IV.:—"We require you to find out one Church upon the face of the whole earth that hath not been ordained by episcopal regiment since the time that the blessed apostles were here conversant;" and see VII. V. 2—8; and cf. Barrow, vol. iii. serm. xxiv.

† Essay, p. 340.

is, *for the first time in the history of the world, an approach to agreement and certainty.*" *

And again, "The diversity among German writers on prophecy is far less than among English ones. That is a new phenomenon which has to be *acknowledged.*"

Acknowledged! By whom? Certainly not by Germans themselves. They make no such professions of "agreement and certainty," as the Essayist claims for them. We have already seen, that in his disdain for "the voluminous literature which has overgrown the text" of Scripture, he has hazarded some extraordinary assertions with regard to that literature; † and we are constrained to say that his statements concerning the condition of Biblical Interpretation in Germany are not more accurate than those which this Essay presents to our notice in reference to the critical labours of scholars in our own country.

Most Biblical critics are aware, that at the close of the last century, and in the earlier part of the present, Rationalism was dominant in the theological schools of Germany. The booksellers' shops were filled with the critical works of Paulus, Wegscheider, Bretschneider, Gabler, and others. "Hic meret æra liber Sosiis," was then the word current concerning the newest rationalistic volume that appeared in the spring at the Leipsic book-fair. But no one now ever reads their writings, or cares one jot for their theories. They are exploded.‡ The books which contain them are waste paper, and are wrapping up

"... thus et odores,
Et piper, et quicquid chartis amicitur ineptis"§

in the grocers' shops. Paulus and Wegscheider, and Gabler, have shared the fate which, as Burke says, had overtaken the English free-thinkers of the sixteenth and

* Essay, p. 340. † See above, p. 354.

‡ See the recent histories of Biblical Interpretation in Germany, especially Dr. Kahnis, *Der innere Gang des deutschen Protestantismus*, Leipzig, 1860; and Karl Schwartz, *Zur Geschichte der neuesten Theologie*, Leipzig, 1856; and Hagenbach, *Dogmengeschichte*, Leipzig, 1857.

§ Horat., Epist. II. i. 269.

seventeenth centuries, Chubb, Collins, Morgan, and Tindal,—"They are gone to the tomb of all the Capulets."* The pantheistic speculations of Strauss and others who followed them have fared little better, and a struggle has ensued between more orthodox interpreters, such as Hengstenberg, Hävernick, Delitzsch, Oehler, Stier, on the one side, and a sceptical and destructive school of expositors on the other. But to say that German exegesis has found a safe mooring and anchorage in the calm and quiet harbour of "agreement and certainty," is to venture upon an assertion which any one who has dipped into the first pages of any German *Einleitung*, is able to refute. Any of the Essayist's pupils who may spend a few weeks of a long vacation in Berlin, Heidelberg, or Bonn, will supply him with abundant proofs to the contrary.

Let us read on:—"The diversity among German writers on *prophecy* is far less than among English ones."

Before the publication of the "Essays and Reviews," it might have been truly affirmed that there was almost an *universal consent* in *England* with regard to the interpretation of prophecy in the most important respect of all, namely, in its relation to the actions and sufferings of Christ. It was this *universal consent* which caused an almost universal horror, when we heard from one of the Essayist's fellow-labourers that hardly any of the prophecies which have hitherto been connected with Christ by Christian interpreters in England "are capable of being made directly Messianic." †

The "agreement and certainty" which prevailed in England in this respect has been disturbed by that announcement; but that disturbance, it is to be hoped, will only be like a temporary ripple on the surface. The "agreement and certainty" in England have been produced by firm faith in the teaching of Christ and His Apostles, who have instructed us how to interpret those prophecies,‡ and we shall not forsake their interpreta-

* Burke's Works, v. 171. † Essays and Reviews, pp. 69, 70.

‡ Luke xxiv. 25—27, 44—48, and Acts ii. 25—32, iii. 15—25, viii. 32—35.

tion for those of our Essayist's companions, and, I regret to add, of our Essayist himself; * even though they should be leagued with all the critics of German,—which happily is not the case.

With regard to the prophecies of the New Testament, the claim set up on behalf of German interpreters is not much more tenable. There is no "certainty and agreement" among them. Let us turn to one of the most recent German expositions of the Apocalypse, that of Düsterdieck, published at Göttingen in 1859, and forming the last volume of Meyer's series of Commentaries on the New Testament. If the reader will have the goodness to look at the Introduction to that volume, he will see that not only is there great diversity among German writers with regard to the plan of that prophetical book,—the only prophetical book of the New Testament,—but also with respect to its date, and even the person of its author, and he will be satisfied that "the new phenomenon," of which the Essayist speaks, is in fact, in the proper sense of the word, no phenomenon at all, for it is not yet visible, nor seems likely to appear on the horizon for some time to come.

§ 5. How can we account for the celebrity of the volume entitled "Essays and Reviews"?

Not, certainly, from any intrinsic merit, but from the position of its writers.

The stations which they occupy in the Church, and in one of our Universities, have given to this volume an importance which it would not otherwise have acquired. If it had been produced by authors who had no such adscititious advantages, it would long since have slept in oblivion. But, when Trojans wear the armour of Greeks they become more dangerous, and make more havoc in the camp,—

> "Mutemus clypeos, Danaûmque insignia nobis
> Aptemus."†

* Essay, p. 406. "There are many quotations from the Psalms and Prophets in the Epistles, but hardly any—probably none—which is based on the original sense or context."

† Virgil, Æn. ii. 389.

When six persons dressed in academic hoods, cassocks, and surplices, come forth and preach scepticism, they do more mischief than six hundred sceptics clad in their own clothes. They wear the uniform of the Church, and are mingled in her ranks, and fight against her, and therefore they may well say—

> "Vadimus immixti Danais *haud numine nostro*,
> Multaque per cæcam congressi prœlia noctem
> Conserimus, *multos Danaûm demittimus Orco*."

Among many evidences of this, we may refer to one which now meets us. The Essayist is charging the Biblical critics of his own age with disingenuousness. They will not allow, he says, that there "is any error in the Word of God.* The failure of prophecy is never admitted" by them, "in spite of Scripture and of history, (Jer. xxxvi. 30, Isaiah xxiii., Amos vii. 10—17.")† And in a later passage of the Essay he does not hesitate to say that "the majority of the clergy"‡ are leagued in a cowardly conspiracy to "withhold the truth" on these and similar matters; and he ventures to insinuate that he and his friends are the only people in England who hold the truth and have the courage to speak it.§

But to return to the specific charge concerning the supposed failure of prophecy.

On this, and similar allegations in this Essay, let us offer one general remark. They are not original; they have no charm of novelty; they have been already urged in *other* publications, and they have been advocated there with not less ability, and, we are constrained to add, with more openness and honesty than in the present Essay; they have been adduced in sceptical books, and those sceptical books have attracted little notice. A few copies of a single edition of them have been sold. But mark the difference! When these same sceptical objections are urged, with less intellectual vigour and logical acumen, by Professors and

* Essay, 342.
† P. 343.
‡ P. 372.
§ Pp. 374, 375.

Tutors of a famous University, then these obscure and feeble objections assume an importance which they never before possessed; then the book in which they are contained runs with the rapidity of electric fluid through nine or ten editions. Then the intelligence contained in them is devoured with eager appetite by many thousand readers, like the most interesting news in the columns of the daily press.

The allegation just quoted may serve as a specimen. It is only a *repetition* of an objection which appeared ten years ago in a sceptical book called "The Creed of Christendom,"* which is certainly not inferior in literary merit to the Essay now before us, and yet attracted little or no observation. Let us place the passages from the two volumes side by side:—

Creed of Christendom, p. 55.	*Essays and Reviews*, pp. 342—3.
"It is now clearly ascertained, and generally admitted among critics, that several of the most remarkable prophecies were never fulfilled at all, or only very partially and loosely fulfilled. Among these may be specified the denunciation of *Jeremiah* (xxii. 18, 19, xxxvi. 30) against Jehoiakim; as may be seen by comparing 2 Kings xxiv. 6, and the denunciation of *Amos* against Jeroboam (vii. 11); as may be seen by comparing 2 Kings xiv. 23—29."	"*The failure of a prophecy* is *never admitted*, in spite of Scripture and history, (*Jer.* xxxvi. 30; Isaiah xxiii.; *Amos* vii. 10—17.")

I will not affirm that the Essayist copied from the Sceptic, but the coincidence is certainly remarkable. The Essayist says that "a failure of prophecy is *never admitted*," i. e. by orthodox critics: the Sceptic says that "it is *generally admitted* by critics," i. e. those who agree with him in his sceptical opinions. The Sceptic cites two instances of alleged failure: *both* these instances are also cited by the Essayist. And the Es-

* By W. R. Greg. (London, Chapman, 1851.)

sayist must not be surprised to hear that on the score of ingenuousness the balance is in favour of the Sceptic. And why? Because the Sceptic tells us honestly *in what* the *alleged failure consists:* he cites chapter and verse of the passage of history which he asserts to be at variance with the prophecy. The Essayist does no such thing; but in a mode of dealing which is too common with him, and which cannot be too strongly reprobated, especially when it affects the characters of the writers of Scripture, he wraps up his charge in indefinite terms, which make it appear more formidable. The failure of a prophecy "is never admitted, in spite of *Scripture and history.*" What! "in spite of Scripture and history" generally? Is this a specimen of the new school of Biblical criticism which the Essayist would establish? No: surely this insidious language of insinuation and inuendo can never become current in an English University. It is utterly un-English, and, we must needs add, utterly un-Christian. It is not fit for the Romish Inquisition. Fortunately the Sceptic enables us to fill up the gap left by the Essayist. The prophecy in Jeremiah xxxvi. 30 is alleged to have failed *because* it is not consistent with the history in 2 Kings xxiv. 6. There the sacred historian relates that "Jehoiakim slept with his fathers, and Jehoiachin his son reigned in his stead." *Therefore*, it is said, the prophecy of Jeremiah concerning Jehoiakim failed:—" He shall have none to sit upon the throne of David, and his dead body shall be cast out, in the day to the heat, and in the night to the frost."

Here is a *seeming* discrepancy, and it is of very great service, for it shews the futility of allegations such as meet us in this Essay, and in others of the same volume, that the *prophecies* of the Old Testament have been *tampered with*, in order that they may fit the history. And this seeming discrepancy may easily be reconciled. I will not quote any English critic in behalf of this assertion. But an eminent German writer, who has never been supposed to be credulous, thus speaks:—" Jehoiakim is said to have died in peace (2 Kings xxiv. 6), but Jeremiah (xxxvi. 30) speaks of his dead body as cast out in contempt; but this may easily be reconciled with the history by the consideration that this might have happened as a consequence of the capture of Jerusalem under his successor, Jehoiachin, when his enemies, or even his own subjects, may have vented their rage on the remains of the hated king."*

Still further: if the Essayist who has written a dissertation on the Interpretation of Scripture was really desirous of enlightening his readers on that subject, he might have here taken occasion to remind them of the remarkable fact, that whereas the historical books of the Bible inform us that some of the kings of *Israel* were not buried at all, or omit to mention their burial, they record in every single case of the kings of *Judah*, whose *death* they relate, that they *were also buried*, except only in the one case of *Jehoiakim*.† This circumstance ought never to be forgotten by those who comment on the prophecy of Jeremiah.

As for the succession of his son, Jehoiachin, in his father's stead, when it is remembered that the sovereignty of Jehoiachin was subject to his mother's tutelage,‡ and that it only lasted about a quarter of a year, and that he was then taken captive to Babylon, and that his uncle was made king in his stead,§ and that the Hebrew term to *sit* ‖ signifies *permanence*,—it may surely be affirmed that the prophecy of Jeremiah did *not fail;* and it is well worthy of remark that Jeremiah predicted that some of Jehoiakim's seed should survive him, for he says, "I will punish him and his *seed* and his servants for their iniquity, and I will bring upon *them* and upon the inhabitants of *Jerusalem* all the evil that I have pronounced upon

* Winer, *Biblisches Real-Wörterbuch*, i. p. 395, art. *Jojakim.*

† Cf. Rev. J. Fendall, "On the Authority of Scripture," p. 39.

‡ Cf. Winer, art. *Jojachin*, referring to Jer. xiii. 18.

§ 2 Kings xxiv. 8; 2 Chron. xxxvi. 9.

‖ יֹשֵׁב: cf. Bp. Pearson on the Creed, Art. vi. p. 279, note, ed. 1669. The LXX. well render the word by a participle, *οὐκ ἔσται αὐτῷ καθήμενος ἐπὶ θρόνον Δαβίδ.*

them." * This prophecy was fulfilled by the capture of Jerusalem in the days of the son of Jehoiakim, very soon after his father's death.

Let us now turn to another prophecy quoted by the Essayist as presenting an instance of *failure*, Amos vii. 10—17.

Two able writers in two periodicals† have justly expressed their surprise that the Essayist should have referred to this prophecy; for when we examine it we find that it is not a prophecy of Amos at all! It is a message of Amaziah the priest of Bethel, in which he falsely attributes to Amos words he had not spoken. How are we to account for such a blunder as this? Our answer is, We have seen that the sceptical writer to whom we have referred quotes precisely the same prophecy of Amos, and also asserts that it failed. It seems most probable that our Essayist borrowed his examples of supposed failure from that or some other similar work, but did *not stop to examine them.* And thus it has come to pass, that he has confounded an idolatrous priest of a golden calf with a true prophet of Jehovah! Here is another specimen of enlightened Biblical criticism, or rather, let us say with sorrow, here is another evidence of the character of the materials from which this Essay is derived, and here is a proof of the righteous retribution which overtakes those who fight with "fiery darts of the wicked one," ‡ against the Holy Spirit of God.

With regard to the predictions in Isaiah xxiii., which relate to the destruction of Tyre, any one who has access to such a common book as Bishop Newton's work on the Prophecies,§ will need no other reply to the Essayist's objections.

In the instances recited above, the Essayist alleges

* Jer. xxxvi. 31.

† "Quarterly Review," No. ccxvii. p. 299, for Jan. 1861, and the "Christian Remembrancer" for the same month. The article in the latter has been reprinted by the author, the Rev. J. G. Cazenove: see there, p. 25.

‡ Eph. vi. 16.

§ Dissertation xi., On the Prophecies concerning Tyre, pp. 145—162.

that prophecies have *not been fulfilled;* and now mark his inconsistency. He suddenly shifts his ground, and rejects a prophecy *because it has been fulfilled!* He thus writes:*—"The mention of a name† later than the supposed age of the prophet is not allowed, as in other writings, to be taken in evidence of the date, (Isaiah xlv. 1.)" Wonderful indeed! Because God, who sees all things from the beginning, enabled Isaiah the prophet to do what uninspired writers cannot do, and to foretell the future, and to name beforehand the deliverer of His people, therefore the prophecy of Isaiah is to be rejected! it was composed after the event! How difficult to please is such a critic as this! He complains of some prophecies because they have failed, and of others because they have been fulfilled! Might he not go and take a seat with the Jewish children in the market-place, who in their wayward humour could neither be pleased with piping nor with mourning?‡ How is this to be explained? Is not this the true account of the matter,—that he will have no prophecies at all? that the Bible is like any "other writing?" that it is to be treated as "any other book?"

§ 6. This supposition is confirmed by what follows. We come now to the root of the evil.

The Essayist does not believe in the Inspiration of Holy Scripture, according to the ordinary acceptation of the term.

He asserts that there is no "foundation in the Gospels or Epistles for any of the higher or supernatural views of inspiration." The Evangelists and Apostles do not "anywhere lead us to suppose that they were *free from error or infirmity.*" §

Here is an example of that strange confusion of thought and expression which prevails throughout this dissertation. It is perfectly true that the Apostles do not lead us to suppose that "they were free from error

* Essay, p. 343.

† The name of *Cyrus.* On the same grounds the Essayist must reject 1 Kings xiii. 2, because it mentions the name of *Josiah.*

‡ Luke vii. 32.

§ Essay, p. 345.

or infirmity." Indeed, they plainly declare that they were liable to human frailty. "We are men of like passions with you," they say.* "In many things we offend all." † Holy Scripture itself records their failings. It relates that St. Mark faltered for a time, and that St. Paul and St. Barnabas strove together concerning him. ‡ It narrates that St. Peter was openly rebuked by St. Paul because he walked not uprightly. § But what is all this to the purpose? Nothing, absolutely nothing; except, as we shall presently see, to afford a more striking proof of what the Essayist gainsays, namely, of the *Inspiration* of *Holy Scripture*.

But, first, what are we to say to the Essayist's assertion that "there is not any foundation in the Gospels for any of the higher or supernatural view of inspiration?" We flatly deny it. Holy Scripture *does* assert its own Inspiration. The word *Scripture* ‖ is used in about fifty places of the New Testament, and though that word in its *ordinary sense* simply means *writing*, yet in the New Testament it is *limited* to those particular writings which the Church calls *Scripture*; and thus it shews that those writings *are distinguished* from all *other writings* in the world. Now Scripture itself declares, by St. Paul, that "*every* Scripture is θεόπνευστος, or divinely inspired,"¶ or rather, inbreathed by God, filled with the Divine breath.

Now when we recollect *by whom* this assertion was made, namely by St. Paul, a Hebrew of the Hebrews,** and *to whom* it was addressed, namely to Timothy, the son of a Jewess,†† and that he had been familiar with the Hebrew Scriptures from a child; ‡‡ and when we bear in mind also that this sentence occurs in the *last* of St. Paul's Epistles; and when we remember also the religious reverence and awe with which the Hebrews treated those writings which they called Scriptures,§§ and which they regarded as wholly distinct from all other writings in the world, and as no other than the

* Acts xiv. 15. † James iii. 2. ‡ Acts xv. 37—39. § Gal. ii. 11—14.
‖ γραφή. ¶ 2 Tim. iii. 16. ** Phil. iii. 5. †† Acts xvi. 1.
‡‡ 2 Tim. iii. 15. §§ See Josephus, c. Apion, i. § 8.

unerring words, the living oracles, of God; and when we also reflect that St. Paul's Divine Master, Jesus Christ, the Everlasting Son of God, sanctioned that belief and awe; and when we also consider that the books of the *New* Testament were delivered by the Apostles and Evangelists to the Church, and were received by the Church, as of *equal authority* with the books of the *Old* Testament, which had been recognised as Divine writings by Jesus Christ Himself, and that they are equally called "*Scripture*," by the Apostles * and by the Church, we could not have a clearer assertion of the supernatural origin and Divine authority of all those writings which the Christian Church Universal receives as Scripture, than is contained in the declaration of St. Paul to Timothy, that "Every Scripture is given by inspiration of God." †

But to proceed. The Essayist tells us that the Apostles and Evangelists were not free "from error or infirmity." What is this to the purpose? Who ever supposed that they were? But how does this affect the question of *Inspiration?* Here is another characteristic of this Essay, which makes it the more dangerous. The author begins with asserting a truth, and then he joins an error with it, which, if the reader is not on his guard, he may be tempted to receive together with the truth which introduces it.

The Essayist confounds two things which ought to be kept separate. But let him distinguish the *writings* dictated by the Holy Spirit inspiring the Apostles and Evangelists to write Scripture, from the *practice* of those by whose instrumentality Scripture was written. The *men* were liable to *human* infirmities, but the *writings* are *divine.*‡ The writers assure us that they do not speak by words "which man's wisdom teacheth, but words which the Holy Ghost teacheth." § There-

* Cf. 2 Pet. iii. 16.

† On the claims which Holy Scripture itself makes to Inspiration, the reader may see the additional evidence clearly stated by the Rev. J. W. Burgon on Inspiration, pp. 53—57, and pp. cxcvii.

‡ See Augustine, Epist. ad Hieron., xxviii., xl., lxxii.

§ 1 Cor. ii. 13.

fore, when we say that Holy Scripture is inspired, we mean that the Holy Ghost is its *Author.** We mean that it was written by His inspiration, "for our learning," and "to make us wise unto salvation," and that it is worthy of its Divine Author, and is the word of the living God. We mean, that in writing the Scriptures, the Holy Spirit, who cannot err, used the instrumentality of fallible men, in order that the excellency of the power of the Gospel might not be of man, but of God; † and in order that the perfection of the work done by means of imperfect instruments might prove that the work is not due to the instruments which were used, but to HIM who wrought by them.

We have adverted to the confusion of ideas which is observable in the Essayist's allegation against the writers of Scripture. This confusion of ideas, which is too frequent in the work, has produced a confusion of writing. There is an ambiguity of language—may we not call it an amphibiousness of style—in this Essay, which is very embarrassing to the reader. In perusing it we hardly know sometimes whether we are treading on a solid, or floating in a fluid. We cannot tell whether we are on *terra firma*, or at sea. For instance, in one place the Essayist expresses a hope that after "*sweeping the house*" he may have "found *the pearl of great price*." ‡ To say nothing of the confusion here made in two divine parables, we have in the former part of the sentence the writer comparing himself to a woman sweeping the house, and in the latter he has suddenly become a merchantman, trading for pearls at sea. In another place he speaks of persons who, having chosen "the *path* of practical usefulness, should acknowledge that it is a narrow *path;* for any but a strong *swimmer* will be insensibly drawn out of it by the *tide* of public opinion." § He proposes to make a new world of harmony and order, but it seems more probable that he may bring back the state of confusion,—

* Lectures on Inspiration, p. 14.

† 2 Cor. iv. 7.

‡ Essay, p. 414.

§ Ibid., p. 431.

"Quem dixere choas, rudis indigestaque moles,"

in which

"Frigida pugnabant calidis, humentia siccis,
Mollia cum duris, sine pondere habentia pondus."*

§ 7. The Essayist says that St. Paul "was corrected by the course of events in his expectation of the coming of Christ." † St. Paul, therefore, was in error when he wrote his first Epistle to the Thessalonians, ‡—for to that doubtless the Essayist alludes,—in which the Apostle says that "*we*, who are alive and remain till the Coming of the Lord, shall not prevent them that are asleep."

This also is no new objection: it has been urged by the same sceptical writer already cited, § and unhappily it has derived undue importance from the name of a celebrated person,‖ who, if his life had been spared, would probably have regretted and retracted some of his rash and unsound assertions on such matters as these. May God in His mercy grant that this may be the case with the author of the present Essay!

But what is the fact? St. Paul is here speaking in very solemn terms. He declares that he writes by the inspiration of God. "This we say unto you by the *Word of the Lord*." ¶ If, therefore, he is in error here, the error is a grave one indeed. But what, we repeat, is the fact? Does St. Paul here assert that *he himself* will *be alive* when Christ comes again? The Essayist says that he does, and that his error in this respect was "corrected by the course of events."

No one who is familiar with the chronology of St. Paul's Epistles could have written as the Essayist does here. But he seems to have little respect for such matters as these. "Discussions respecting the *chronology of St. Paul's life*," he says, "have gone far beyond the

* Ovid. Met. i. 7, 19, 20. † Essay, p. 346. ‡ 1 Thess. iv. 15.

§ Creed of Christendom, p. 18, where it is said that "St. Paul is manifestly and admittedly in error in 1 Thess. iv. 15." And again, ibid., p. 25.

‖ Dr. Arnold, Christian Life and Character, p. 490:—"We may safely and reverently say, that St. Paul, in this instance, entertained and expressed a belief which the event did not justify." ¶ 1 Thess. iv. 15.

line of utility." * And he is only applying his own principle of Interpretation; "the history of Christendom is nothing to him;" his "office is to recover the meaning of the words as they struck on *the ears of those who first read them;*" † and here is a signal proof of the utter worthlessness of such a principle of interpretation. Be it so, that the *Thessalonians imagined*, when the words of that Epistle "first struck on their ears," that the Day of the Lord was close at hand. But our enquiry is, not *what they thought*, but *what St. Paul meant.* Most readers of St. Paul's Epistles know that the first Epistle of St. Paul to the Thessalonians was the *first written* of all his Epistles, and that the *second* Epistle of the Thessalonians was written at the same place as the first,‡ and very soon after it. Turn, therefore, to the *second* Epistle. In that second Epistle we read a solemn caution from St. Paul, guarding them *against* the notion that the "Day of Christ was at hand." § *If* St. Paul had believed, when he wrote his *first* Epistle, that he would be alive at Christ's coming, he believed the same thing when he wrote the second. Indeed, he would have had a stronger belief then. No "course of events" had intervened to affect that belief, *if* he had entertained it. But we see that he did *not* entertain it when he wrote the second Epistle. He cautions the Thessalonians against it. Nor had he any such belief when he wrote his first Epistle, and he was not "corrected in his expectation by the course of events."

Few persons who have formed any acquaintance with St. Paul's style can be perplexed by his use of the pronoun *we* in this passage,—"*We* which are alive and remain." It is the habit of the great Apostle to put *himself* in the place of *others*, and to speak, as it were, *from* them; and even to do this when they whom he identifies with himself are very different from him, and even opposed to him. ‖ St. Paul's "*we*" is an uni-

* Essay, p. 393. † P. 338.
‡ Corinth. § 2 Thess. ii. 2.
‖ See, for instance, Rom. iii. 7, and the numerous authorities cited in a note on 1 Thess. iv. 17, and 1 Cor. iv. 6, vi. 12.

versal *we*, and is applicable to every age. Indeed, this is the genuine language of inspiration, and if the Essayist had not been resolved to interpret this passage as one "in any other book," he would not have missed the sense; but his error is like a judicial retribution for unworthy notions of Holy Scripture.

The simple truth is, that the Holy Spirit is speaking by St. Paul, who utters "by the Word of the Lord" what is here revealed. He is writing an Epistle, not merely for one Church or one age, but to be read in the Church of Christ in every country, in every age, even till the coming of Christ. By St. Paul the Holy Spirit delivers a solemn warning, which every age must apply to itself. No age knows when Christ will come, but every age ought to be prepared for Christ's Coming to judgment. Every one ought so to believe and live as if Christ would come in his own day. Therefore with great wisdom has the Holy Spirit spoken by St. Paul on this subject in such a language as that which represents him as contemporaneous with every age. This is genuine Inspiration. It is the language of the Eternal Himself.

Once more. We have seen that in the second Epistle to the Thessalonians St. Paul warns his readers *against* the supposition that "the day of Christ was at hand." Therefore when he wrote that Epistle, the Apostle, who was in frequent peril of death,* did not expect that he himself would be alive when Christ came.

About three years after the date of that second Epistle he wrote his first Epistle to the Corinthians, and in that Epistle he uses the pronoun "*we*" in the same manner as he had done in the *first* Epistle to the Thessalonians. He says, "*We* shall not all sleep," that is, we shall not all die, "but we shall all be changed." † Will the Essayist say, after the emphatic words in which St. Paul himself had disclaimed any such notion

* "We stand in jeopardy every hour. I die daily." 1 Cor. xv. 30, 31; cf. 2 Cor. xi. 26.

† 1 Cor. xv. 51.

in the second Epistle to the Thessalonians, that St Paul expected to be alive at Christ's coming, and that "he was *corrected* in that expectation by the course of events?" No; he cannot say it in this case. Nor ought he to do so in the other. And if he would follow St. Paul's rule for interpreting Scripture, by comparing* one portion of it with another, he would have been saved from the presumption of attributing an error to St. Paul,—or rather to the Holy Spirit, who spake by St. Paul's mouth.

§ 8. Having charged an Apostle with error the Essayist becomes more bold, and brings a similar accusation against two Evangelists at once:—

> "One" Evangelist, he says, "supposes the original dwelling-place of our Lord's parents to have been Bethlehem (Matt. ii. 1, 22), another Nazareth (Luke ii. 4), and they trace his Genealogy in different ways; one mentions the thieves blaspheming, another has preserved to after-ages the record of the penitent thief; they appear to differ about the day and hour of the Crucifixion."*

At the same time the Essayist says "that there is no appearance of *insincerity* in them, or *want of faith*." No appearance of "*insincerity* or *want of faith*" in those holy men whose writings are received by the Christian Church universal as "given by inspiration of God!" Admirable candour, most Christian condescension! But let us see whether there may not be here some appearance of inaccuracy and want of learning and ability, as well as of modesty and humility, on the part of a writer who deals thus freely with the Gospels. The Essayist would quiet our alarms by assuring us that though there are, as he alleges, "discrepancies of fact" ‡ in Scripture, yet that "when we become familiar with them they will seem of little consequence in comparison with the *truths* which it unfolds."

We cannot accept the proffered consolation. For, surely the answer must be, "If the documents are in error, what will become of the doctrines?" It is rightly

* 1 Cor. ii. 13. † Essay, p. 346. ‡ P. 425.

urged, in a recent sceptical publication, against all such low notions of the Bible as this:—"A book cannot be said to carry with it the authority of being God's Word, if the same writer may give us in one verse a revelation from the Most High, and in another a blunder of his own. How can we be certain that the very texts upon which we rest our doctrines and our hopes may not be the uninspired portion of it?" *

In the passage above quoted, the Essayist, as most scholars know, is only reviving the objections which have been often refuted already.

Schleiermacher, De Wette, Strauss, Bruno Bauer, and others,—especially the English Sceptic already quoted,† who has anticipated the Essayist in almost all his allegations against the writers of Holy Scripture,—have made the same objections before him.

If the Essayist had been disposed to treat this important subject aright, he would have reminded his younger readers that St. Matthew and St. Luke wrote their Gospels with *different designs;* the former for the special benefit of the Jews, and the latter for the Gentile world. This consideration alone would have saved him from two of his errors in this place. The Holy Spirit, writing by St. Matthew dwells therefore particularly on the birth of Jesus at *Bethlehem*, the *city of David*, the city pre-announced by the Hebrew prophet Micah ‡ as the birth-place of the Messiah. St. Matthew thus leads the Jews to acknowledge that Jesus is the Christ. He lays stress on the birth at *Bethlehem*, and with divine wisdom *omits* what is not relevant to his argument in that Gospel, the previous residence of

* Creed of Christendom, p. 25.

† Ibid., p. 101:—"In this place we must notice the marked discrepancy between Matthew and Luke as to the original residence of Jesus. Luke speaks of them as living at Nazareth before the birth of Jesus, Matthew as having left their former residence to go to Nazareth only after that event, and from peculiar considerations. Critics, however, are disposed to think Matthew right on this occasion." And ibid., p. 97:—"The genealogy of Jesus given by Luke is wholly different from that given by Matthew. They trace the descent through an entirely different line of ancestry."

‡ Micah v. 2.

the parents at *Nazareth*. The Holy Spirit, writing by St. Matthew, *omits* that incident, but He does not *deny* it; no, with divine foresight He reserves it to be communicated afterwards, in *its proper place*, by a later Evangelist, St. Luke, in his Gospel, the Gospel of the *Gentile* world, to whom it would be welcome intelligence that the Saviour of mankind was conceived in *Nazareth*, in *Galilee of the Gentiles*. Thus the Holy Spirit shews to all who are willing to learn, that He knows when to speak and when to be silent. Thus He dispenses suitable food to all in due season.*

The Evangelists, (i. e. St. Matthew and St. Luke,) says the Essayist, trace our Lord's "genealogies in different ways." He means to imply that they contradict one another.

They trace "His genealogies in different ways." Certainly they do: and why? Because they had *two different designs*. The one, St. Matthew, designed to shew his readers, especially his Hebrew readers, that Jesus of Nazareth was the promised seed of Abraham through Isaac and Jacob, and that He was the King of the Jews, and came of the royal tribe of Judah, and inherited the royalties of David and Solomon, and of the other kings of Judah in succession; and therefore he traces His genealogies from Abraham through David, Solomon, and Rehoboam, and others, who either were kings of Judah *de facto*, or *de jure* after the captivity, and thus proves that the royal prerogatives of the house of David were inherited by Him, and that He was the representative of the kings of Judah by right of His birth, as the only-begotten son of Mary the wife of Joseph, the heir of the royal race. This is

* If the reader desires further information on this point, he will find that the objections reproduced by the Essayist had been already well refuted by Dr. Davidson, (formerly Professor in the Lancashire Independent College,) "Introduction to the Gospels," pp. 116—118. It may well excite the shame and sorrow of all friends of the Church and Universities, that sceptical allegations, exploded in Dissenting Colleges, should be revived by clergymen of the English Church, Professors and Tutors in an English University.

what the Holy Spirit has done by means of the genealogy in the Gospel of *St. Matthew*.

Are we to murmur against Him because He has been pleased to do *something more* than this? Are we to complain, because by the genealogy in *St. Luke's* Gospel He has traced our Lord's relationship to David by a line of personal connection, and has thus shewn that by natural descent,* as well as by royal succession, He is the Son of David; and further, has carried up His lineage through Abraham even to Adam and to God, and thus reminds the readers of that Gospel that *all men*, whether Jews or Gentiles, are one family, children of the same Father, and that as they are all by nature in the first Adam, so by grace they are all joined together in the second Adam, Jesus Christ?

Ought we not, on the contrary, to be thankful to the Holy Spirit that He *has* traced our Lord's "genealogy in different ways?" And what sort of interpretation of Scripture is that, which is blind to these benefits, and would teach us to censure and condemn the Gospels for the very abundance of the spiritual light which Almighty God has been graciously pleased to bestow upon us by their means?

The Essayist's next objection is, that one Evangelist "mentions the thieves blaspheming (Matt. xxvii. 44), another has preserved to after ages the record of the penitent thief, (Luke xxiii. 39.)"

The writer is hardly bold enough to accuse either Evangelist of inaccuracy here, and yet he seems desirous of doing so, for otherwise why does he make this observation, "One Evangelist mentions the thieves blaspheming, another has preserved the record of the penitent thief?" Yes; and ought we not to be grateful to both Evangelists for what they have done? But if he really means that they are not consistent with one

* Jacob in St. Matthew i. 16 was supposed by ancient writers to have been the brother of Heli, (Luke iii. 23,) and on the death of the one, the other brother married his widow, from whom Joseph the husband of Mary was born. See on Matt. i. 1; and thus Joseph was accounted the son of the one brother legally, as well as of the other brother naturally.

another, let him be requested to read what St. Augustine has written on this subject,* and he may perhaps change his opinion.

"They (the Evangelists) appear" also "to differ about the dayand hour of the crucifixion."

Appear! to whom?

Certainly not to any who have carefully examined the subject. As to the appearance of discrepancy, it rests only on a misinterpretation of John xviii. 28, where it is said that "the Jews went not into Pilate's judgment-hall lest they should be defiled, but that they might eat the Passover." Now, whatever may be the meaning of the words, "eat the Passover," it is quite certain that *St. John* places the crucifixion on the *same day* as *the other three* Evangelists.

St. Matthew says that the crucifixion took place "on *the day of the preparation*,"† (i. e. for the Sabbath;) St. Mark says that "it was *the preparation*, that is, the day before the Sabbath;"‡ St. Luke-says, "*that* day was the *preparation*, and the Sabbath drew on."§

What now does St. John say?—"The Jews therefore, because it was *the preparation*, that the bodies should not remain on the Sabbath day, for that Sabbath was an high day, besought Pilate that their legs might be broken, and that they might be taken away."‖ And again, St. John says, speaking of our Lord's burial in the garden:—"There laid they Jesus therefore because of *the preparation*."¶

Thus all the four Evangelists place the crucifixion *on the same day*, the day of the preparation, or day before the Sabbath. And yet the Essayist tells us that "they appear to *differ* as to the *day* of the crucifixion!"

He asserts also that they differ as to the *hour*. He does not let us know the *grounds* of this assertion. This is one of the melancholy characteristics of this book. The writer brings grave charges against holy men, and he does not state the *reasons* on which those charges rest; and thus he makes it more difficult to

* De Consensu Evangelistarum, iii. 52. † Matt. xxvii. 62.
‡ Mark xv. 42. § Luke xxiii. 54. ‖ John xix. 31. ¶ Ibid. 42.

deal with those charges. This is a cruel way of proceeding; not only as regards those who are assaulted, but cruel also it is with respect to those who see the wounds after their infliction. They know not why they were inflicted, and perhaps when they consider the character and office of the person who inflicts them, they may think that they were deserved. We shall see more of this by and by.

What was in the Essayist's mind when he wrote these words, "The Evangelists appear to differ as to the *hour* of the crucifixion?" We are left to conjecture on this point. Our surmise is, that as his allegations are usually repetitions of what has been already objected and answered, he is referring to the supposed discrepancy between Mark xv. 25 and John xix. 14. In the former Gospel it is said—according to the Roman mode of reckoning time—that "it was the *third* hour when they crucified him;" that is, He was crucified at nine o'clock in the morning. St. John says, that Pilate took his place upon the judgment-seat when it was "about the *sixth* hour."

Now here was an occasion for a writer on the "Interpretation of Scripture" to remind his younger readers that, in order to understand the Bible, they must know something of the customs of the countries in which its various books were written. The Essayist, however, proceeds on a different principle. He slights such helps as these. "The greater part of his learning is a knowledge of the text itself;" this is his canon of criticism, but he seems quite to forget that a *true* "knowledge of the text itself," in such matters as these, can only be derived from a knowledge of a great *many other things*,—especially of the circumstances under which the text was written.

Let us apply this principle to the question before us. St. John's Gospel, as all Christian Antiquity testifies, was written in Asia, and St. John follows the Asiatic mode of reckoning time.* Therefore we learn

* Perhaps the Author may be permitted to refer to the passages quoted in a note on St. John iv. 6, in support of this assertion.

two things from St. John's and St. Mark's Gospels. We are told by St. John that Pilate took his place on the judgment-seat at *six o'clock in the morning;* and St. Mark informs us, that the sentence of Crucifixion was pronounced and put in execution at *nine o'clock.*

Where is the contradiction here?

§ 9. "What is Inspiration?"

The Essayist asks this question, and his answer to it is:—"That idea of Scripture which we gather from the knowledge of it." "It is a fact which we infer from the study of Scripture."

This assertion, we must take leave to say, is based upon a very erroneous notion of our capacities. It assumes that *we* are competent to pronounce an opinion on what it *befits God to say.* This surely is a very presumptuous view of the case. It is a kind of theological Protagoreanism. "Man is the measure of all things," was the bold dogma of the ancient Greek sophist;* and according to the Essayist's assertion, Scripture is not to be Scripture unless it pleases us! or as the similar notion was described of old by Tertullian,† "Except God pleases man, He is not to be any longer God!" We must also be allowed to observe that the Essayist's method of arguing concerning the Inspiration of Scripture is totally at variance with the plan which Almighty God has been pleased to pursue—ever since any portion of Scripture was written—to assure us of its Inspiration.

The divine Author of Scripture did not make the proof of the Inspiration of the Pentateuch to depend "on the idea which men might gather from the knowledge of it." No! this indeed would have been a most precarious foundation to build on. Some of the Hebrews took little pains to acquaint themselves with the Pentateuch; others openly violated its laws, and set up idols in opposition to its divine Author. But still the Pentateuch was inspired; and all were bound to acknowledge its Inspiration. And why? Because Almighty God had *visibly distinguished the Pentateuch*

* See Plato Cratyl., iii. 234. † Tertullian. Apolog., c. 5.

from all other books, and had avonched it as His own Book, by enshrining it by the side of the Ark in the Holy of Holies.* And when the Son of God Himself came down from heaven and proved His divine authority by the mighty works recorded in the Gospels, (which in course of time were received as true and divine histories by the Roman Empire itself, which at first persecuted the Christians,) Jesus Christ openly acknowledged all the books of the Old Testament to be given by Inspiration of God, and He commanded all men, as they desire to be saved, to receive those books as divine.

This is the method which God has adopted for assuring mankind that the Old Testament is divinely inspired. Doubtless a *well-constituted* mind, full of reverence for God, and for His holy Word, and humbly seeking for the truth, and praying for the light of the Holy Spirit, will see in the Old Testament clear *internal* testimonies of its divine origin; but God has not made the proof of its inspiration to *depend* on the *idea* which *we* may gather from the knowledge of it, He has authenticated it by *external evidences* and *incontrovertible facts*, manifest to all; so that no man in a Christian land has any just excuse if he does not believe the Old Testament to be God's holy Word.

He has followed a similar method with regard to the New Testament.

Jesus Christ established His Church to remain for ever upon earth; † He has constituted her to be a "Witness and Keeper of Holy Writ;" ‡ He promised to be with her "even to the end of the world," § and to give to her the Holy Spirit to teach her all things, and to guide her into all truth,‖ and to abide with her for ever.

We may therefore conclude, that whatever the universal Church of Christ has received as divinely inspired Scripture, *is* the unerring Word of God. Her

* Deut. xxxi. 9, 24—26.

† Matt. xvi. 18.

‡ Thirty-nine Articles, Art. XX.

§ Matt. xxviii. 20.

‖ John xiv. 16, 26; xvi. 13.

testimony in this respect is the witness of Christ who is with her; it is the testimony of the Holy Spirit who is in her, and speaks by her.

Well, therefore, does the Church of England thus speak:*—"In the name of Holy Scripture we do understand those canonical Books of the Old and New Testament, of whose authority was never any doubt in the *Church*. . . . All the Books of the New Testament, as they are *commonly received*, we do receive, and account them Canonical."†

But the Essayist sets at nought this *external* testimony of Christ and His Church to the inspiration of Holy Scripture. He would have every man take the Bible into his hands as a common book, and test it by his own conscience, or feelings, and then pronounce judgment upon it.

This is no new theory. It has been put forth in Germany and in other countries of the world. And what has been the consequence? Some receive one part of the Bible, and some another; some reject one part, some another; and if this theory is adopted, there will be as many different Bibles as there are persons, and the end of it must be that there will be no Bible at all, but only a Babel of tongues.

§ 10. "The question of inspiration," says the Essayist, "though in one sense important, is to the interpreter as if it were not important; he is no way called upon to determine a matter *with which he has nothing to do.*"

In accordance with this proposition, the Essayist lays down the following rules for expounding Scripture:—

"Scripture has *one meaning* to be gathered from itself, without a regard to *à priori* notions abou its nature and *origin.* It is to be interpreted *like other books.*"‡

* In the Thirty-nine Articles, Art. VI.

† The above argument has been stated more in detail in the "Lectures on Inspiration," quoted above, p. 409.

‡ Essay, p. 404.

Again he says :—

"We can only ascertain the meaning of *Scripture* in the same way as we ascertain that of *Sophocles* or of *Plato*."* "And it would be well to carry the theory of interpretation of Scripture no further than in *other works*."†

And he does not hesitate to suggest an opinion that differences of Interpretation of Scripture arise from the fact that Scripture *is* not treated like any other book, and that we should attain to unity and uniformity in interpreting the Bible, if we would agree to lay aside all questions concerning its inspiration, and if we would consent to interpret it as a common book,‡ in the same way as we would interpret a human composition, e. g. the work of some classical author, "Sophocles or Plato."

Let us consider these propositions :—

"The question of *inspiration* is one with which the interpreter of Scripture has nothing to do."

What! nothing to do with the question whether the Bible is the Word of God? Surely this question *is* important to the interpreter of Scripture, it is the *most important* question with which he can have to do. He cannot stir a step in interpreting Scripture without having first settled it.

If Holy Scripture is inspired, then its author is God: and then the Bible must be interpreted as a book written by a Being to whom all things are present, and who contemplates all things at once in the panoramic view of His own Omniscience. Lord Bacon says, "The Scriptures *being given by inspiration*, and not by human reason, do *differ from* all *other books* in the *Author;* which by consequence doth draw on some difference to be used by the *expositor*. For the Inditer of them did know four things, which no man attains to know: which are, the mysteries of the kingdom of glory; the perfection of the laws of nature;

* Essay, p. 377. † P. 378. ‡ Pp. 334, 375—377.

the secrets of the hearts of man; and the future succession of ages."* And again he says, "The Scriptures being written to the *thoughts of man* and to the *succession of all ages*, are *not to be interpreted* only according to the latitude of the proper sense of the place" (or particular passage of Scripture), "and respectively towards that present occasion whereupon the words were uttered; but have infinite springs and streams of doctrine to water the Church in every part, . . . so that I do *much condemn* the interpretation of the Scripture which is only after the manner as men *use to interpret a profane book.*"

In a similar spirit of wise criticism, our great philosophical divine, Bishop Butler,† thus writes:—"The general design of Scripture may be said to be to give an account of the world in this single point of view, as *God's world*, by which it appears *essentially distinguished from all other books.*"

Consequently an expositor of Scripture must fail in his task *if* he *does not do* what the Essayist says that *he need not do*, and *if* he *does* what the Essayist *recommends* him *to do*. *If* the expositor has not first settled the question whether Scripture is divinely inspired, and *if* he handles it as he would "any other book," he will not be disposed to receive with humility such Christian precepts or doctrines, and such supernatural truths, as may be repugnant to his own reason, will, and appetites. But he will measure them, as indeed the Essayist and his fellow-labourers do, by the standard of his own "inner consciousness." He will try them by what they call their "verifying faculty."‡ Therefore those very precepts and doctrines which constitute the essence of the Gospel may serve as occasions and

* Bacon, Advancement of Learning, p. 265. † Analogy, II. vii.

‡ Essays and Reviews, pp. 31, 32—36, 45; cf. pp. 343, 365. The teaching of "Essays and Reviews" on this point has been thus summed up by a French critic, of sceptical opinions, in an article upon that volume in the *Revue des deux Mondes* for May, 1861, p. 418:—"La Bible ne peut conserver sa place dans notre vie réligieuse qu' à une condition, celle de ne plus exercer comme jadis une espèce de despotisme sur l'esprit humain, mais de *s' identifier avec la voix de la conscience en nous.*"

arguments to him for *rejecting* it. If, again, he is in doubt as to the Inspiration of the Bible, he will set aside every interpretation of its words which would not be applied to those words on the supposition that they were uttered by men unaided by the Holy Spirit, and were not dictated by God.

With regard to the Essayist's notion that Scripture can have *only one meaning*, this is manifestly contradicted by Scripture itself. For example, the words of Scripture, "He hath borne our griefs, and carried our sorrows," * are declared in one passage of Scripture to have been fulfilled in Christ's miraculous healing of men's bodily infirmities; † and are asserted in another place‡ to have been accomplished by His bearing our sins in his own body on the cross.

Here are two meanings assigned in Scripture to the same text of Scripture. Will not every humble and devout reader of Scripture thankfully receive *both?*

The Essayist himself has displayed some remarkable specimens of the disastrous consequences of his own theory, as we shall see hereafter.§ Indeed, the present Essay supplies abundant evidence of the unsoundness of that theory, which, while it professes to be conducive to the right understanding of Holy Scripture, would be utterly destructive of its true interpretation.

The Essayist seems almost to forget, that *moral* and *spiritual* qualifications, as well as intellectual endowments are necessary for the right interpretation of Holy Scripture. The Scriptures cannot be understood except through the illumination of the Holy Spirit who wrote them. He must open our eyes, if we are to see the wondrous things of God's law. But the Holy Spirit will not vouchsafe His divine light to those who venture to treat the Scriptures as a common book. No: He will punish them with spiritual blindness. Spiritual blindness is the just retribution which they who

* Isa. liii. 4. † Matt. viii. 17. ‡ 1 Pet. ii. 24.

§ *e. g.* in his comment on St. Matthew's interpretation of Hosea xi. 1. See below, p. 410.

handle Scripture with familiarity bring upon themselves. "Mysteries are revealed unto the meek."* "Those that are meek shall He guide in judgment, and such as are gentle, them shall He learn His way."†

Here is the true explanation of the delusion which seems to have perverted the understanding of the writer of the present Essay. He has acted on his own maxim, "Interpret the Scripture like any other book." He *has* treated the Bible like a common book. He tells us that it is of no importance to him whether the Bible is inspired or no; and that he "has nothing to do with that question."‡ And he defines Inspiration to be "that idea of Scripture which he himself gathers from a knowledge of it."§ Thus he has blinded his own eyes, and he will also extinguish the light of others who listen to him. Nahash the Ammonite said to the people of Jabesh-Gilead, "On this condition will I make a covenant with you, that I may thrust out all your right eyes."‖ The Essayist does the same; if we are to be scholars of this Biblical Nahash, we must allow him to thrust out our right eyes.

As he loves his own intellectual and spiritual health and that of others committed to his care, let him be earnestly entreated to retrace his steps. Let him not deem it an unworthy thing to sit down as a scholar at the feet of Jesus Christ, and to hearken to that Divine Teacher, who delivers the Holy Scriptures to the world *not* as a common book, but as the Word of the living God, who enabled His Apostles and Evangelists to see and to expound the meaning of the Old Testament, and who promises to give the Holy Spirit to those who meekly receive the Scriptures as the lively oracles of divine truth. Then the scales will fall from his eyes, and he will see the light—but *not till then.*

§ 11. The Essayist has no great veneration for the ancient Fathers of the Church, and yet he endeavours to enlist them in his service. And how? In a man-

* Ecclus. iii. 19. † Ps. xxv. 8. ‡ Essay, pp. 350, 377. § P. 347. ‖ 1 Sam. xi. 2.

ner which could hardly have been expected, and would have greatly surprised them. The question of the Inspiration of Scripture, he says, "was not determined by the Fathers of the Church." *

Here it seems to be silently insinuated that the Fathers had no clear view of Inspiration. This must be the meaning of this sentence, or else it is wholly irrelevant to the place where it stands.

Let us grant now—what is quite true—that no ancient Council ever met to *determine* the question of inspiration, and that no ancient Father has left a treatise on inspiration. Why was this? Was it because that question was *not* determined? Will the Essayist venture to say this? No. It was because the question was *settled*, and because no one in Christendom had any doubt about it.

We may hope that the Essayist is ignorant of this fact, for if he is not ignorant of it, he has wilfully calumniated the ancient Fathers in a matter of solemn concern; but if he is ignorant of it, let him be requested to read the works of the Fathers, and let him name, if he can, a single Father who had any doubt of the Inspiration of the Bible. Let him mention any ancient Interpreter, who ever said that "the inspiration of Scripture was a matter with which he had nothing to do," or who ever thought of interpreting the Bible "as a common book." He cannot do so. And, as far as positive proof on this subject is concerned, any candid inquirer may satisfy himself upon it by consulting the large collections of testimonies gathered from the works of the ancient Fathers of the Church, by the late venerable President of St. Mary Magdalene College, Oxford, Dr. Routh,† and after him by Dr. William Lee, of Trinity College, Dublin,‡ and by the Rev. B. F. Westcott, of Trinity College, Cambridge, in his excellent volume "An Introduction to the Study of the Gospels." §

* Essay, p. 351. † Routh, *Reliquiæ Sacræ*, vol. v.

‡ Dr. William Lee on Inspiration, Appendix G, pp. 470—501. Lond. 1854.

§ Westcott's Introduction, Appendix B, pp. 383—422. Lond. 1860.

The testimony of Christian Antiquity may be summed up in the words of the three hundred and eighteen Nicene Fathers, which have been received by the universal Church for fifteen hundred years,—"I believe in the Holy Ghost, who spake by the prophets."

§ 12. The Reformers also are cited by the Essayist as favouring his own opinions. "The word (inspiration)," he says, "is but of yesterday, not found in the earlier confessions of the reformed faith."

The writer lays a heavy tax on the credulity of his readers,—"The word inspiration is but of yesterday!" Have we not the word "*inspiration*" in our own Authorized Version of the Bible,* and has it not stood there for two hundred and fifty years? Is not the word *inspiration* to be found in that place in the Genevan version of 1557, and in Cranmer's version of 1539, and in Tyndale's version of 1534? Is it not as old as the age of St. Cyprian, who wrote in the third century? Does he not say that the Apostles teach us what they learnt from the precepts of the Lord, being full of the grace of the *inspiration* of their Lord?† Does not Origen say that "the Holy Ghost *inspired* every one of the holy prophets and apostles in the Old and New Testament?"‡ Nay, is not the word used by St. Justin Martyr in the second century, who says that the prophets taught us by *divine inspiration?*§ Does not St. Irenæus, the scholar of Polycarp, the disciple of St. John, say that the Prophets received divine inspiration,‖ and does not all Christian Antiquity testify that the Scriptures are *θεόπνευστοι*, given by *inspiration*¶ of God? And if the ancient Fathers witnessed to the *thing*, why should we dispute about the *word?*

* 2 Tim. iii. 16, where the Vulgate has "divinitus inspiratum."

† "Dominicæ *inspirationis* pleni."—S. Cyprian, De Oper. et Eleemosyn., § 9.

‡ Origen De Principiis, i. § 4.

§ S. Justin M. Cohort. ad Græc., § 38:—*διὰ τῆς θείας ἐπιπνοίας*.

‖ S. Irenæus c. Hær. iv. 34.

¶ In addition to the authorities cited above, the reader may find similar testimonies in Suicer's Thesaurus on *v. γραφή*, and on *v. λόγος*.

With regard also to the *Reformers*, it is equally certain that they asserted the inspiration of Scripture in the strongest terms in their public confessions of faith. Let the Essayist be requested to look again at the "earlier confessions of the reformed faith."

The Bohemian Confession of 1535* thus begins:—"First of all, we all receive with unanimous consent the Holy Scriptures which are contained in the Bible, and were received by our fathers and accounted canonical, as immovably true and most certain, and to be preferred in all things *to all other books*, as sacred books ought to be preferred to profane, and divine books to human;† and to be believed with sincerity and simplicity of mind; and that they were *delivered and inspired* by God Himself, as Peter and Paul and others do affirm.

The Helvetic Confession, published in 1536, declares that they "execrate all who say that the Holy Scriptures are not from the Holy Ghost, or who reject any portion of them;" and that the "Scriptures are the very words of God, who speaks to us by them."

The Gallican Confession, published in 1561, asserts that the "word contained in the books of Holy Scripture," which it enumerates, "proceeded from one God, and are the sum and substance of truth, and that neither men nor angels may add anything to it, or make any change in it."

The Scottish Kirk in her Confession affirms that the "Scriptures were committed to writing through the Holy Spirit of God."

The Belgic Confession says that the Scriptures contain "the holy and divine word, not given by human will, but spoken by men of God, who were inspired by His spirit," and "that they were written by God's command;" and "we believe," say the framers of the Confession, "all things contained therein."

* *Corpus Librorum Symbolicorum Ecclesiæ Reformatæ*, ed. Augusti, Elberfeld, 1827, p. 276; in which volume the other Confessions here cited may be found.

† Art. XVIII.

The doctrine of the old Lutheran divines, at least from the end of the sixteenth century,—for it is readily allowed that some of the earlier Lutherans were less explicit in their expressions,—is stated in these words: *—"*Inspiration* is the act by which God communicated supernaturally to the mind of the writers of Scripture not only the ideas of the things which they were to write, but also the conceptions of the words by which they were to be expressed. The true author of the Holy Scripture is God."

Can any language be more explicit? And yet the Essayist suggests that the Reformers laid little stress on the doctrine of the inspiration of the Bible. What else is the meaning of his language, "the word" inspiration "is but of yesterday, not found in the earlier Confessions of the reformed faith," taken in connexion with his assertion that Scripture is to be interpreted like "any other book," and that "the question of inspiration is one with which the interpreter of Scripture has nothing to do?" Is he ready to adopt the language of those Confessions to which he appeals? If he is not, why did he refer to them? If he is, must he not retract almost all that he has said in this Essay on the subject of Inspiration?

§ 13. When a person comes before a magistrate to bring a charge against a neighbour, he is rightly required to state the particulars of his grievance. He is not allowed to say that the man whom he impeaches is a housebreaker, but he is called upon to specify the circumstances of some act of burglary upon which he grounds his charge. And if he cannot do so, he is justly regarded as guilty of calumny, for injuring his neighbour's reputation, and he will have damaged his own character in the eyes of the whole neighbourhood by such a slanderous imputation.

It is deeply to be regretted that the Essayist is chargeable with this wrong. He brings accusations against others which would not be received by any Justice of the Peace at any Petty Sessions, against the

* See Hase. *Hutterus Redivivus*, 8th edition, Lips. 1855, p. 102.

lowest and least respectable of Her Majesty's subjects. And who are the persons against whom he prefers these charges? The holy Evangelists themselves.

The following example of this mode of dealing now meets us. He tells us that there are "discrepancies in the narrative of the Infancy pointed out by Schleiermacher." * *Tantamne rem tam negligenter!* Is so great matter to be dismissed in this loose way? "Discrepancies in the narrative of the Infancy!" What do these words mean? They look very formidable, and may well inspire the reader with alarm.

Here is the mischief of the Essay. It teems with insinuations. It is a whispering-gallery of indistinct sounds muttering evil.

A young man—one of the writer's own pupils—or an earnest-minded woman looking to the Essayist as a Tutor of a College and a Regius Professor at Oxford, for instruction on the important subject of "the interpretation of Scripture," would be filled with indefinite dread and panic in reading such a statement as this, —"There are discrepancies in the narrative of the Infancy;" that is, in the infancy of our Blessed Lord and Saviour; discrepancies in the narrative of the Gospels which have hitherto been received as the words of the Holy Ghost.

But *what* and *where* are these discrepancies? You bring a charge of discrepancy against the Evangelists. You indict them of error. But where are your witnesses? Come forward boldly, and state the particulars of your charge. Even the heathen populace required this:—

"Quis delator? quibus indiciis, quo teste probavit?"†

But the answer is "Nil horum." Nothing of the kind. The youthful reader is referred to Schleiermacher! To Schleiermacher! Verily, a "verbosa et grandis epistola" is the ground of this terrible accusation, involving a question of life and death. "Discrepancies pointed out by Schleiermacher!" These are to be our reasons for distrusting the Evangelists. Pointed out where?

* Essay, p. 351.

† Juvenal, x. 70.

Dr. Frederick Schleiermacher, as the reader knows, was a German philosopher and divine who published a score of volumes. Is the youthful student to search through them in quest of these "discrepancies in the narrative of the Infancy?" Is he to hunt for the needle in that bundle of hay?

But perhaps he may have heard that one of the learned German's works* was translated into English thirty-six years ago; and if he is fortunate enough to meet with a copy of that translation, now very scarce, he may at length discover † the alleged "discrepancies in the narrative of the Infancy pointed out by Schleiermacher."

Schleiermacher's work, as I have said, was published many years ago, and since that time his allegations have been often refuted.‡ Did the Essayist know this? We can hardly suppose it. If he did, his appeal to those exploded objections becomes more censurable; but if he did not know it, is he well qualified to write a dissertation "on the Interpretation of Holy Scripture?"

Lest, however, the reader should remain in the state of embarrassment into which he has been thrown by this vague charge of discrepancy brought against the holy Evangelists, let us briefly examine what Schleiermacher's objections were, to which the Essayist refers us.

Schleiermacher says that St. Luke's account of the Annunciation cannot be true, because if it were, the Blessed Virgin would certainly have communicated it to Joseph, and then Joseph would not have formed the design of putting her away, as stated by St. Matthew. Schleiermacher, therefore, rejects St. Luke's history of the Annunciation as a poetical embellishment.

This is a specimen of the kind of Interpretation of

* Dr. F. Schleiermacher, *Ueber d. Schriften des Lukas, ein kritischer Versuch.* Berlin, 1817.

† A Critical Essay on the Gospel of St. Luke, by Dr. Frederick Schleiermacher, with an Introduction by the Translator. London, 1825. See there in pp. 44—52.

‡ Particularly, as stated above, by Dr. Davidson, "Introduction to the Gospels," pp. 116—119.

Scripture which the Essayist sanctions with his authority when he directs the attention of his youthful readers to the " discrepancies pointed out by Schleiermacher."

Surely any one of those readers, when he comes to meet this objection face to face, would hardly fail to perceive that it is as hollow and worthless as it is presumptuous and profane.

St. Luke himself supplies an answer to it. He describes the Blessed Virgin Mary as "keeping all" the divine revelations, and "pondering them in her heart." * A beautiful picture of maiden modesty and delicate reserve, and of patient waiting and reverent faith in God. If such was the case *after* her marriage with Joseph, as the Evangelist assures us it was, how much more would it be so before she was united to him, and while she dwelt apart in virgin privacy at Nazareth.

A writer who makes such an objection is not worthy to be recommended to the young. What a poor notion must he have of that quiet meekness and holy piety which are the best ornaments of womanhood!

Let us observe also that St. Matthew does *not* say that Joseph intimated to Mary any intention of renouncing his purpose of a matrimonial alliance with her. No: he was only "*minded*" to do so; and while he "*thought* thereon, the angel of the Lord appeared to him in a dream, saying, Joseph, thou son of David, fear not to take unto thee Mary thy wife, for that which is conceived in her is of the Holy Ghost." †

The Blessed Virgin "was highly favoured" by God, and we may be sure that she was under the heavenly guidance of the Holy Ghost. She was taught by Him even in her *silence*. It was a providential thing that she did *not* mention to Joseph the angelic communication. If she had done so, the assertion would have rested merely on her authority, and he might have been perplexed, and even have been tempted to doubt the

* Luke ii. 19. † Matt. i. 20, 21.

fact. It was a providential thing that she went away from Nazareth soon after the Annunciation, and remained with her cousin Elisabeth * three months; and there she received a testimony to the truth of the vision which had appeared to herself, for she found that it was true which was spoken by the angel, viz., that "her cousin Elisabeth had conceived a son in her old age;" † and the fact of the Annunciation had been revealed to Elisabeth.‡

It was also a providential thing that Joseph did not communicate to Mary his intention of abandoning his design of marriage with her. For thus a fit occasion arose, a *dignus vindice nodus*, for the appearance of the Angel to Joseph in the dream; and he acted upon that appearance, and probably he communicated to Mary the vision vouchsafed to himself. And this act and communication would elicit from her an account of the Annunciation, and would be an independent testimony to it. The dream would confirm the Annunciation, and the Annunciation would confirm the dream. The Angel in the dream who says to Joseph in St. Matthew's Gospel "that which is conceived in her is of the Holy Ghost," shewed that he came from the same divine Lord who revealed to Mary by Gabriel, as St. Luke relates, "the Holy Ghost shall come upon thee, and the power of the Highest shall overshadow thee; therefore that holy thing which shall be born of thee shall be called the Son of God." And so the faith of both Joseph and Mary would be strengthened by God, and they would both receive from Him inexpressible comfort in their union.

This *pairing* of visions, vouchsafed to two several parties, and mutually confirming one another, is characteristic of God's dealings with His saints on great and worthy occasions. We see it in His dispensations to Saul and to Ananias,§ and also to Cornelius and to St. Peter.‖ A writer on the "Interpretation of Scripture" might have done well to bear in mind this char-

* Luke i. 39, 56. † Ibid. i. 36. ‡ Luke i. 45.
§ Acts ix. 12—17. ‖ Acts x. 3—7, 17—19.

acteristic, and to apply it to the illustration of the "narrative of the Infancy."

The other "discrepancies" which Schleiermacher has supposed to exist in the narratives of St. Matthew and St. Luke are disposed of with equal ease. One refers to the two genealogies, and has already been examined.*

He alleges, also, that *if* the wise men came at all to Bethlehem, they must have come to Bethlehem *before* "*the presentation* in the temple," which was forty days after the birth. Schleiermacher adds, St. Luke makes the parents to have returned to *Nazareth* immediately after the Presentation. Consequently if Herod, as represented by St. Matthew, heard from the wise men the fact of the birth of the King of the Jews, and had issued his savage order against the children at Bethlehem, Joseph would never have hazarded the life of the Infant by going to Jerusalem for the Presentation. Schleiermacher, therefore, rejects the narrative of St. Matthew as a poetical fiction, designed "to represent Jesus as immediately recognised by the heathen," "and to establish the right of Christianity to extend beyond the limits of Judaism." †

In the former instance St. Luke was the poet and St. Matthew the historian, but now the tables are turned, and at the bidding of this Berlin necromancer waving his magical wand, St. Matthew is transformed into a poet and St. Luke becomes an historian; St. Matthew has given us a legend which is to be rejected on the authority of St. Luke! To all this gratuitous assumption it may be replied, How does our critic know that the Magi arrived *before* the Presentation? There is no ground in the Gospels for such a supposition, but very much the reverse. The star seems to have appeared at the Nativity. The Magi, led by the star, came from a distance, and would hardly arrive at Bethlehem within forty days after the birth. And if the time between the birth and their arrival had been

* Above, p. 382.

† Schleiermacher, Critical Essay on the Gospel of Luke, pp. 46—50, English translation. London, 1825.

so short, Herod would have hardly extended his sanguinary order to infants of *two years* old.* And if the parents had received the gold of the wise men they would probably not have presented the offerings of the *poor*.†

But it may be objected,—St. Luke tells us that the parents quitted Bethlehem after the Presentation, and returned to Nazareth. Yes; and he also informs us that they were in the habit of coming "to Jerusalem every year for the Passover." ‡ What more probable than that after the birth at Bethlehem, the *city of David*, where the Messiah was to be born,§ and after the glorious revelations at Bethlehem in the angelic vision to the shepherds, Joseph and Mary should have had a strong yearning for Bethlehem, and that in visiting Jerusalem for the Passover they should come to Bethlehem, in its neighbourhood, in order to *settle there?* Perhaps their return to Nazareth after the Presentation was only for the sake of arranging their affairs there, with a view to a migration to Bethlehem, which had such glorious associations and such gracious attractions for them; and when they were there, not any longer in the stable of the *inn*, at the Nativity, ‖ but, as St. Matthew notes, in a *house*,¶ they received the visit and homage from the wise men coming from the East.

This arrangement of incidents is certainly very probable; ** indeed, anything is more probable than that St. Matthew, who wrote his Gospel for the Jews, and published it in Judæa a few years after the Ascension, should have commenced his narrative with a falsehood, which any one almost in that country would have been able to refute. But so far was this from being the case, that Christians of that age and country not only received his Gospel as true, but died cheerfully in defence of its truth; and in course of time the Roman mistress

* Matt. ii. 16.
† Luke ii. 24.
‡ Ibid. ii. 41.
§ Micah v. 2.
‖ Luke ii. 7.
¶ Matt. ii. 11.
** It has already been submitted to the consideration of the student of Scripture in a note on Matt. ii. 9, with some other reasons not repeated here.

of the world, which at first persecuted the Christians, was convinced that St. Matthew's Gospel is true, and placed it on thrones in her imperial council-chambers, and revered it as the Word of God.

Let us now be permitted to put the question,—How would the Essayist's friends bear it, if a writer holding a high place in a learned University were to treat *his* character in the same way as he has treated that of the *Evangelists?* How would they brook it, if a Tutor and Professor had charged the Essayist with putting forth fictions as facts; and if, in support of such imputations, his accusers had appealed to some voluminous writings, without any specification of any particular charge; and if, after much search, the grounds of that accusation had been discovered to be frivolous and nugatory, and to have been already examined and refuted? Would not the Essayist's friends and admirers have resented such dealing as disingenuous and dishonest? Would they not have protested against it as calumnious, cowardly, and base? Surely they would, and they would have done rightly. But this is precisely the manner in which the Essayist himself has treated St. Matthew and St. Luke. And is it not the duty of the *friends and scholars* of the *Evangelists* to vindicate *their* credit? Are we to sympathize with the Essayist, and to have no sympathy with the Evangelists? The Essayist is alive, and is able to vindicate himself; but the Evangelists are dead and cannot speak for themselves. Therefore every lover of truth and justice ought to become their advocate, and to rise up in their defence against such accusations as these.

Again: if a medical practitioner had mixed poison with the diet of his patients, and if he had told them that the poison was wholesome nourishment; if he had put deleterious drugs into a beautiful vessel, and had inscribed upon it the name of some pleasant and healthful potion; if he had thus disarmed their suspicions, and attracted them by his own fair name, and by that of some other person commended by his eulogies, would he not be more censurable than if he had openly endangered their lives? Certainly he would. And what has been done by the writer of this Essay? He has administered poison to the souls of his youthful readers; he has inscribed a fair name upon the poison, he has afforded no test for its detection, he has commended it as a palatable food, he has dispensed it to thousands and tens of thousands as spiritual nourishment, good for their souls' health.

§ 14. The Essayist is ready enough to imagine discrepancies in the Gospels, but he does not seem equally sensitive as to the discrepancies in his own Essay:—

"Non videmus manticæ quod in tergo est."*

But let him shift the wallet from his back and place it before his eyes, and he may perhaps find it amply stored with what he imputes to others.

He has assumed the existence of contradictions in the Gospels; he says that there "is so much disagreement in facts in the Gospels;" † and yet, in another part of his dissertation, he assures us that it is "a *great fact*"—as he terms it—that "the Gospels are for the most part of *common origin;*" ‡ and insisting on this "*great fact*," he assumes it as a necessary inference, that "we can no longer speak of *three independent witnesses* of the Gospel narrative." §

Here he has revived the obsolete theory, of which German scholars have long since been ashamed, that the Gospels are from "some common original." A century ago this notion, which was put forth by Semler and others, was rightly discarded as chimerical and ridiculous by J. G. Rosenmüller. ‖ For who had ever seen that original Gospel? Who among the ancients had ever mentioned it? It was a mere legendary fiction of critics eager to find some support for their own baseless hypotheses. And the Essayist, now in the middle of the nineteenth century, has disinterred that the-

* Catull. xx. 21. † Essay, p. 370. ‡ P. 371. § Ibid.

‖ *Scholia in Matthæum*, 1787; cf. Meyer's *Einleitung* to St. Matthew's Gospel, § 4.

ory from its grave, where it has slept quietly for some time; he would galvanize into new life this crazy skeleton, and set it up for our admiration; and in his affection for it he would have us relinquish our own belief in the living reality of the three synoptical Gospels, "as *independent* witnesses" of our Lord's history! And yet, mark his own discrepancy! he charges those same witnesses with inconsistencies! They are all dependent on one *common* account; and yet they are *at variance* with one another! They do not even agree in the "original dwelling-place of our Lord's parents;" * they "trace His genealogy in different ways;" and besides other differences which he assumes, there are the "discrepancies in the narrative of the Infancy pointed out by Schleiermacher."

Observe, also, the modesty with which this superannuated theory of a common origin of the Gospels is put forth. Ancient writers, from Papias the disciple of St. John and Irenæus the scholar of Polycarp, have agreed in testifying that there was a connection between St. Mark's Gospel and the holy apostle St. Peter, who calls Mark "his son;" † and Biblical critics, and readers of the New Testament generally, have recognised an internal evidence of the truth of that ancient testimony in the interesting fact that *St. Peter's failings* are dwelt upon with particular emphasis in the Gospel of *St. Mark.* But observe the Essayist's diffidence. In spite of all that ancient testimony, confirmed by internal proof, St. Mark is only to be a copyist of an apocryphal original Gospel, which never had any existence except in the Essayist's imagination! And the testimony of Irenæus, Clement of Alexandria, Origen, and a host of other ancient writers, who agree in asserting the connection of St. Mark's Gospel with St. Peter, is summarily dismissed by the Essayist with this contemptuous sentence:—

"It is *evident* that no weight can be given to traditional statements of facts about the authorship [of the Gospels]; as,

* Essay, p. 346.

† 1 Pet. v. 13.

for example, that respecting *St. Mark* being the interpreter of *St. Peter;* because *the Fathers* who have handed down these statements *were ignorant* or unobservant of *the great fact* which is proved by interna l evidence [qu. of their '*discrepancies?*'] that they [the Gospels] are for the most part of *common origin.*"*

Another specimen of our author's modesty and consistency may here be noticed. He says in one place very truly, that "Scripture is to be interpreted from itself," "Non nisi ex Scripturâ Scripturam potes interpretari." † But how does he apply his own rule in *other* parts of his Essay? As we shall see hereafter, he will not accept the interpretations of the *Old* Testament which are given by the Holy Spirit in the *New*. And yet "Scripture is to be interpreted from itself!" He says that there "is hardly any quotation in the Epistles of the New Testament from the Prophets, in which the meaning is based on the original sense;" ‡ and he earnestly warns his pupils against accepting more *than one meaning* § of a prophecy; and he asserts that the only true meaning of Scripture is that which is to be gathered from Scripture interpreted *like any other book;* and *therefore* he rejects those meanings which are assigned by the Evangelists in Scripture themselves to prophecies of the Old Testament! ‖ And yet we are gravely assured by the Essayist that we cannot interpret Scripture *except from Scripture itself!*

It may perhaps be asked by the reader, 'How does the Essayist reconcile his mode of treating the New Testament, with the reverent affection, which is often professed in this Essay, for the person of our Blessed Lord? Our Blessed Lord Himself is the Author of these interpretations of the prophecies of the Old Testament, either directly in His own person, or mediately by His Apostles or Evangelists. How can the Essayist's rejection of the teaching accord with veneration for the Teacher?'

This question has evidently presented itself to his

* Essay, p. 371. † Pp. 382, 384. ‡ P. 406.
§ P. 404; cf. 377, 378. ‖ See p. 358.

mind; and it is answered by means of one of those unhappy expedients, which the Essayist found already made to his hand in the magazine of German theology from which his materials are derived.

All who are familiar with the history of German Protestantism will at once anticipate the reply. It is supplied by the theory of *accommodation*. That theory was propounded about a century ago by Semler * and others.† It is well described by the late revered Hugh James Rose, in one of his Sermons preached before the University of Cambridge in 1825: ‡—"Semler invented an hypothesis to get rid of what offended him in the New Testament. He contended that we are not to take all the declarations of Scripture as addressed to us, but to consider them as in many points *adapted* to the *feelings* and dispositions of *the age when they originated*. This was the origin of that famous theory of *accommodation*, which Semler carried to great lengths, but

* Compare the account in the "Historical Sketch of German Protestantism," by G. H. Dewar, M.A., p. 107:—"Semler, thirty years Professor at Halle, was the founder of what is called the historical method of interpretation. The principal feature of this system is, that every passage of Scripture is to be interpreted with reference to the time and circumstances under which it was delivered. True as this principle in a certain sense may be, it is easy to perceive that in the sense in which it has been used by Semler and his successors, and as a foundation for the so-called doctrine of *accommodation*, it must lead to a total abandonment of the doctrine of the Inspiration of the Holy Scriptures. If in speaking of the expectation of a Messiah, of His own miraculous birth, of the effusion of the Holy Ghost, of a future judgment, of a heaven and a hell, of angels and of evil spirits, Jesus and His Apostles were only *accommodating themselves to the preconceived opinions and errors of the Jews*, in order to gain an influence over them, and thus induce them to submit to the pure and spiritual requirements of the Gospel, which Semler, educated among the Pietists, considered of more importance than a distinctive belief;—if, I say, on such points as these, Jesus and His Apostles were *accommodating* themselves to Jewish prejudices, surely the volume of Holy Scripture would be of a very similar character with the fables of Æsop, which, in order to convey to children some useful lesson, endeavour to excite their attention and please their fancy by absurd and unnatural fictions; and surely then the words of Scripture cannot have emanated from that Holy Spirit with whom is neither falsehood nor deceit; surely it cannot claim our reverence; it cannot be unto us a rule of faith, or an instructor in holiness."

† Eckermann, Van Hemert, Kirsten, Vogel, &c., &c.

‡ On the State of the Protestant Religion in Germany, p. 447.

which, in the hands of his followers, became the most *formidable weapon ever devised against Christianity.* Whatever men were disinclined to receive in the New Testament, and could not with decency reject, while they called themselves Christians and retained the Scripture, they got rid of by this theory." They "maintained that the Apostles, and even Jesus Himself, *had adapted Himself*, not only in His way of teaching, but in His doctrines, to the prejudices of the Jews." . . . "When the prophecies of the Old Testament were cited, then appeal was made to the interpreters on the new plan, who asserted constantly that there were *no prophecies to be found*, or (what was perhaps stranger still) that there was nothing in the Old Testament clear enough to argue from, without danger of arbitrary conclusions."* "I cannot," says the same excellent writer,† "mention this theory (of accommodation) without adding to it an expression of the strongest abhorrence. Strange, indeed, must men's notions be of a divine, or even of a sincere human teacher, when they can believe that He would endeavour to recommend a practical system of the most lofty virtues by a sacrifice of truth."

Yet this is the idea which the Essayist seems to have formed, or rather reproduced, of our Blessed Lord, and His Apostles and Evangelists.

Having said that there is scarcely any prophecy of the Old Testament which is interpreted in the New according to its original sense," ‡ he adds, that we are not to be surprised at this; for we ought to be prepared to see Scripture interpreted according to the "*ideas of the age or country in which it was written*," and therefore we ought not to insist "on the applications which the New Testament makes of passages in the Old, as their original meaning;" § and he puts a question to which he himself has already suggested the answer, "Is the Interpretation of the Old Testament in the New to be regarded as the meaning of the original text, *or* an *accommodation* of it to the thoughts of other times?" ‖

* On the State of the Protestant Religion in Germany. † Ibid., p. 48.

‡ Essay, p. 406. § P. 407. ‖ P. 370.

The Essayist professes a feeling of reverence for the Divine Saviour of the world; but how can this question be reconciled with such a professsion? Christ is "the Way, the Truth, and the Life;"* and "He came to bear witness to the truth;"† and He sternly denounced the sins and errors of the Jews and their teachers; and therefore He suffered death at their hands. And yet we are to entertain the question, whether He was not guilty of equivocation, dissimulation, and cowardice! and whether He did not adapt His language to the prejudices of His hearers; and whether His teaching is any longer to be regarded as of universal application, or only to have a temporary and local significance, *accommodated* with dexterous pliancy to the temper and circumstances of the times in which His language was uttered!

This theory of *accommodation* being once assumed to be true, there is no limit to its application. All the teaching of Christ and His Apostles must eventually disappear under its withering influence. The doctrines of Christianity will soon be treated as merely ephemeral ideas, or floating fashions adapted to the spirit of the age in which they were first published. Indeed, as is well known, these disastrous results *have* already followed from that theory of accommodation. It brought forth an abundant harvest of unbelief. "The lessons of Semler," the author of that theory, "have not been lost," says the writer just quoted. "The evil seed which he committed to the earth produced an hundredfold; and even the sower himself would have contemplated with surprise and horror the evil and poisonous crop which has sprung from the seed he planted . . . . In the works of Semler's followers there is a daringness of disbelief, a wantonness of blasphemy, which in a professed unbeliever we should expect and understand, but when we turn from *the works where it is found to the page which records the name and situation of the writers, and when we find that to many of them is entrusted the solemn charge of educating the younger brethren, and to all*

* John xiv. 6. † Ibid. xviii. 37.

is committed that still more solemn charge of feeding and watching over Christ's flock on earth, there would be no consolation for the Christian heart, were it not persuaded that God has some great end in view, some great lesson to teach, in allowing so dreadful a pest to infest this portion of His vineyard, and to threaten the destruction of all that is dear, sacred, and holy." *

Such were the fruits of Semler's theory of accommodation, in the Universities, schools, and parish churches of Germany. It is now revived in England; and if it is allowed to take root among us, its consequences will be the same here.

§ 15. Having impeached the historical veracity of the Evangelists, the Essayist does not hesitate also to impugn their authority in *interpreting* the *prophecies* of the Old Testament. He discards their interpretations as obsolete. Their expositions might do well enough formerly, but the world is now becoming wiser. Listen to his words: †—

"The time will come, when educated men will be no more able to believe that the words, 'Out of Egypt have I called My Son,'‡ were *intended by the Prophet* to refer to the return of Joseph and Mary out of Egypt, than they are now able to believe the Roman Catholic exposition of Gen. iii. 15, 'Ipsa conteret caput tuum.'"

The reader is aware that "the Roman Catholic expostion" of that passage in the Book of Genesis is grounded upon a perversion of the Hebrew original. According to that exposition, the words of God to the serpent are interpreted as if they signified "*She* shall bruise thy head," and those words are applied by the Church of Rome to the Virgin Mary; whereas the words clearly mean "*It* shall bruise thy head," and, as all Christian antiquity testifies,§ they refer to the Seed of the woman, which is *Christ.*

* Hugh James Rose's Discourses, preached before the University of Cambridge, on the "State of the Protestant Religion in Germany," p. 58.

† Essay, p. 418. ‡ Hosea xi. 1; Matt. ii. 15.

§ See Rom. xv. 20; St. Leo Magn. Serm. de Nativ. ii.; St. Jerome, Quæstion. Hebr. in Gen., tom. ii. p. 110; and the Benedictine note on Gen. iii. 15.

Here, therefore, is a glaring misrepresentation of a most important text of the Old Testament; and yet the Essayist tells us "the time is coming, when educated men" will acknowledge that the interpretation which the *holy Evangelist St. Matthew* gives of the words of the Prophet, Hosea xi. 2, "Out of Egypt have I called My Son," is not more credible than that glaring misrepresentation!

The Essayist has not much respect for the early Fathers; he "has no delight in the voluminous literature which has overgrown the text"* of the Gospels. If he had been more conversant with it, perhaps he might have been preserved from raising this objection to St. Matthew, by which he has brought himself into the company of Julian the Apostate, who made the same accusation against the Evangelist † fifteen centuries ago.

Let us consider the allegation.

The Essayist says:—

> "The time is coming, when educated men will no more be able to believe that the words, 'Out of Egypt have I called My Son, were intended by the Prophet (Hosea) to refer to the return of Joseph and Mary from Egypt, than they are now able to believe the Roman Catholic exposition of Gen. iii. 15."

On the other hand, an Evangelist, St. Matthew, assures us, that those words of Hosea *were fulfilled in that return.* St. Matthew thus writes, ‡—"When he (Joseph) arose, he took the young child and His mother by night, and departed into Egypt, and was there until the death of Herod, that it *might be fulfilled* which was spoken of (or *by*) the Lord, by (or *through*§) the Prophet (Hosea), Out of Egypt have I called My Son."

The Essayist intimates that the Evangelist has made a mistake here; otherwise his remark is wholly unmeaning. The Evangelist is wrong; and "the time is coming when educated men" will discover his error, and correct it, and discard the interpretation of Hosea which St. Matthew would impose upon them.

* Essay, p. 338. † See St. Jerome on Hosea xi.
‡ Matt. ii. 15. § διὰ.

But what is the fact? Has St. Matthew misinterpreted Hosea?

Assuredly not. The truth is, that the Essayist has been caught in the snare which he has laid for others. He had advised us to "interpret Scripture as any other book," * that is, as a human composition. He also assures us that no passage of Scripture can have any more *than one meaning*, † and *that one meaning* "is to be gathered from (Scripture) itself" without regard to its nature or origin; and again, "Scripture has *one* meaning,—the meaning which it had to the mind of the *Prophet* or Evangelist . . . who first uttered it." And again, "We have no reason to attribute to *the Prophet any second* or hidden sense, different from that which appears on the *surface*." ‡

These are his famous canons of Interpretation. Unfortunately for himself he has applied them here. He tries the prophecy of Hosea by his own critical standard, and finds that Hosea is speaking of *Israel* coming forth *from Egypt*. And Hosea is to have but "*one* meaning;" and *that* meaning is "the meaning which is *on the surface*," the meaning which may be gathered from Hosea's writings, treated "like any other book." Hosea meant to refer to Israel's coming out of Egypt. His prophecy refers to *that* coming, and *therefore*, argues the Essayist, it cannot refer to anything else. Consequently St. Matthew is wrong in saying that "Joseph took the young child and His mother by night, and departed into Egypt; and was there until the death of Herod, that it might *be fulfilled* which was spoken by the Lord through the Prophet, Out of Egypt have I called My Son;" and "the time is coming when educated men" will reject this interpretation.

In contemplating such reasoning we are lost in astonishment. The vanity and self-conceit of the human heart is indeed great, and scarcely any common exhibition of it ought to cause much surprise. But surely this is a phenomenon almost unparalleled. The Essayist correcting the Evangelist! The Essayist in the

* Essay, pp. 350, 377. † Pp. 404, 378. ‡ P. 380.

nineteenth century correcting St. Matthew—a Hebrew by birth, a companion and apostle of Jesus Christ, and writing a Gospel for Hebrew Christians which was received by them as a divine work! The Essayist correcting St. Matthew in the interpretation of Hebrew prophecy! This is something almost beyond the powers of all human conception.

Consider also, *if* haply it be true, that the Scriptures are *not* "like any other book," and *if* St. Matthew wrote under the guidance of the Holy Spirit of God, and *if* his Gospel *is* indeed, what all Christendom for eighteen hundred years has believed it to be, a divinely inspired work, then we have this fearful phenomenon—the Essayist correcting the Holy Ghost!

When, however, we come to analyze this strange prodigy, it is not altogether inexplicable. Holy Scripture enables us to explain it. The first requisite for "the Interpretation of Scripture" is humility. The second is reverence for Scripture. If we rely on ourselves and our own intelligence, and if we disparage Scripture and treat it "as any other book," then Almighty God, Who is the Author of Scripture, will punish us by our own devices. He will "choose our delusions." * He will "chastise us by our wickedness," and "reprove us by our backslidings," † and "give us the reward of our own hands." ‡ Our presumption and our irreverence will be the instruments of our punishment; we shall have provoked God to withdraw His Holy Spirit from us and to give us over to spiritual blindness, and then we shall display to the world that most wretched spectacle, the spectacle of men professing themselves wise, and vaunting their own intelligence, and setting themselves up to be censors of the Evangelists, and to enlighten the Holy Spirit Himself! Miserable ignorance! pitiful infatuation! the fruit of arrogance and irreverence. And is not this the spectacle before us? The Essayist comes forward to instruct the world in his new method to be used for the interpretation of Scripture. He puts forth with oracular authority his own canons of Biblical

* Isa. lxvi. 4. † Jer. ii. 19. ‡ Isa. iii. 11.

criticism. We have seen what those canons are and how he applies them. And yet, after all this show of knowledge, he convicts himself of ignorance concerning the authorship of prophecy; and he deprives himself, and would rob his scholars, of all the beautiful imagery which they may derive from the illumination of the Holy Ghost, teaching them to recognise in Israel a type of Jesus Christ. This is a specimen of the glorious gain which the rising generation is to receive from this new method of Interpretation.

He takes for granted, that because *he himself* cannot see the meaning which St. Matthew assigns to Hosea's prophecy, and because that meaning does not "appear on the surface," and because the Prophet Hosea himself may not have had that meaning fully revealed to him,—*therefore* the prophecy of Hosea has no such meaning! But let us ask one question. Did any educated man, who has reflected seriously on the prophecies, ever imagine that the Prophets themselves were the *original authors* of those prophecies? * Has not the whole Church of Christ always held "that the Holy Ghost spake by the Prophets?" And let us also ask this, Is not the Holy Ghost, speaking by the Evangelist St. Matthew, to be believed, when He tells us what was in His own divine mind when He spake by the Prophet Hosea? Is the Essayist to be permitted to come forward and enlighten the Holy Spirit, and to inform Him that He had no such meaning as that which He Himself assures us that He had?

Can any arrogance in the world be conceived greater than this?

A writer in a celebrated periodical † thus speaks:—"The position of Professor Jowett has a significance

* On this subject the reader may refer to St. Augustine, De Doct. Christ., iii. 39; Bp. Butler, Anal., II. vii.; Bp. Sherlock on Prophecy, ii. p. 21; Bp. Marsh on the Interpretation of the Bible, Lect. x. p. 443, cf. p. 403; Dr. W. Lee on Inspiration, x. p. 198, 199. The passages may be seen quoted in the present writer's Lectures on Interpretation, pp. 80—89.

† Edinburgh Review, No. 230, for April, 1861, p. 476, where this Essay is thus characterized:—"Professor Jowett has furnished what may

of its own. Since the termination of the great movement of the 'Tracts for the Times,' he is the only man in the University of Oxford who has exercised a moral and spiritual influence at all corresponding to that which was once wielded by John Henry Newman."

The parallel here is remarkable, and suggests some ominous forebodings. Dr. Newman has unhappily fallen away from the Church of England, and has led many others into the communion of that Church which has devised the monstrous interpretation, rightly censured by the Essayist, of Gen. iii. 15, which refers that text to the Virgin Mary. He has accepted the teaching of that Church, which, mainly on the groundwork of that text,* has lately put forth a new dogma of faith, and anathematizes all who do not believe that new dogma, namely, the Immaculate Conception of the Blessed Virgin. This is one of the Romish interpretations which Dr. Newman and his followers have now solemnly bound themselves to receive, in opposition to Scripture, Councils, and Fathers of the Church.

Whether the Papal mode of Interpretation is not quite as safe as that propounded by the Essayist, may well admit of a doubt; and whether the consequences of the Essayist's method, if adopted in our schools and colleges, will not be at least as calamitous as those of the Roman, deserves carefully to be considered: especially if it be indeed true, as the Reviewer affirms, that the Essayist exercises so commanding an influence in the University of Oxford, that, to quote the Reviewer's words, "he stands confessedly master of the situation in the eyes of the rising generation of English students and theologians." †

be termed a valuable supplement to his work on St. Paul. It is intended to clear away some of the misconceptions which have prevented Biblical students from deriving the full advantages to be reaped from the sacred records, and to point out what those advantages are." These words of the Reviewer suggest sorrowful reflections; at the same time they will awaken the energies of those who feel a reverent regard for the sacred records, and will excite them to greater vigilance and zeal in their behalf.

* See the Papal Decree promulgating that new Article of the "Immaculate Conception," Dec. 8, 1854, and appealing to that text in its support.

† Edinburgh Review, No. 230, p. 476.

Is this really the case with the University of Oxford,—the University of Jewel, Hooker, Sanderson, and Bull? If it indeed be true, "how are the mighty fallen!"

Surely "the time is coming, when educated men will be no more able to believe" that such notions as these concerning the Interpretation of Scripture were propounded as valuable discoveries in an Essay published by a Tutor in a distinguished College, and a Regius Professor in that University, and that the Author of that Essay exercised the greatest influence among all his contemporaries there, and stood "confessedly master of the situation in the eyes of the rising generation of English students and theologians,"—than they are now able to believe the Roman Catholic exposition of Gen. iii. 15, or any other strange dogma or portentous figment which the Roman Church would impose on a credulous world. And if it be really true that the Author of this Essay does exercise that dominant influence over the "minds of the rising generation of English students and theologians," then it is high time that all who feel a loyal attachment to the Church of England, and who are animated with a generous zeal for the intellectual reputation and for the moral and spiritual character of our ancient Universities, should consider well, whether they are content that the teaching of that Church and of those Universities should be abandoned and discarded as obsolete and erroneous, and that the opinions promulgated in this Essay should henceforth be adopted in their place.

§ 16. Let us now proceed to examine the probable consequences of this system of Interpretation.

In the year 1774 a celebrated German theologian, J. S. Semler, already mentioned, published at Halle his "Plan for the Liberal Teaching of Christian Doctrine."* Semler had been educated among the *Pietists*, as they were called, who thought that outward forms and confessions of faith were not of much use for the maintenance of spiritual life, and who disparaged

* *Institutio ad Doctrinam Christianam liberaliter discendam.*

human learning and theological science as of little benefit to vital devotion. With them religious emotions constituted true spirituality. With them fervour and enthusiasm were almost everything, but ecclesiastical organization and order were of very little account. They professed a laudable zeal for practical piety and moral virtue, but they did not ground them on the principles of Christian doctrine and on the articles of the Christian faith. They regarded the Bible with reverence; but they had no sound foundation of belief in its inspiration, nor any safe guidance for its interpretation. They appealed to their own inner consciousness and spiritual illumination for direction in these two questions,—What is the Bible? and, How is it to be understood? They separated the Scriptures from the Church, to which the Scriptures were delivered by God. They did not regard the Bible as a heavenly message, authenticated, delivered, and interpreted by a divinely appointed messenger, the universal Church of Christ; but they looked on it as like some wondrous aërolite, which had fallen down from heaven they knew not how.

Semler, in course of time, came under the influence of the philosophical divines of the school of Wolff, whose theories developed themselves into Rationalism. From the *Pietists* he had brought with him a sanguine confidence in his own opinions, not restrained by the correctives and controls of the public authority and judgment of the universal Church, as declared in her formularies and practice. To quote the language of an English divine, who has drawn an accurate portrait of his character,*—"He never hesitated to desert sober, substantial truth for striking but partial views, subtle error, and ingenious theory. To this quality he added others, which are very frequent ingredients in such a character,—an *undoubting estimation for all his own speculations*, and a rash boldness in bringing them into

* Hugh James Rose, Discourses, p. 47; referring to the Life of Semler in Eichhorn's *Allgem. Bibl.*, vol. v. part i. A biographical account of Semler has also been given by Tholuck, *Verm. Schriften*, ii. p. 39, &c.

public view." And from his *new rationalistic teachers* he derived that adventurous spirit which he applied in the free handling of Holy Scripture, and which he exerted in endeavouring to emancipate it, as he said, from traditional modes of treatment, and from that conventional language by which its meaning, as he alleged, had hitherto been obscured.

What Semler was at Halle in the middle of the eighteenth century, that the Essayist seems to be at Oxford in the nineteenth. If we might venture to form an opinion from his mode of writing, we might suppose him to have been trained, like Semler, among some who have little reverence for the authority of the Christian Church, and have paid little attention to her principles, her polity, and her history; and not having laid any solid foundation in this necessary knowledge, he appears to have entered boldly into theological speculations, with little guidance but that of a warm imagination and an unhesitating reliance on himself.

The resemblance between Semler's "Free-handling of Christian Doctrine" and the Oxford Professor's Essay is remarkable. Indeed, there is scarcely a single point in the Oxford Essay which was not anticipated by Semler a hundred years ago.

Semler made his own conscience to be a criterion of Inspiration. He tells us that "whatever he found in Scripture to be conducive to his own good, *that* he *held to be divinely inspired.*" * He adds, that "he will not however dispute or contend with any one who maintains the Inspiration of *other* books of Scripture which he finds of no use to himself." In fact, the Inspiration of the Bible was with him purely *subjective.* His only knowledge of the Inspiration of the Scripture was the "idea which he himself formed of it."

This notion, as we have seen, is precisely that of the Essayist.† "Inspiration," he says, "is that *idea* of

* P. 256. "Quicquid in Scripturæ illo corpore invenio *mihi* ὠφέλιμον πρὸς διδασκαλίαν, πρὸς ἔλεγχον, illud est θεόπνευστον, seu ad Deum auctorem a me referendum est."

† See Essay, p. 347.

Scripture which *we gather* from the knowledge of it. It is a fact which we infer from the study of it."

As for the *Interpretation* of Scripture, that, said Semler, must also be left to the private consciousness of each individual; so that every man is at liberty to take the Bible into his hands and to extract the best meaning he can from it, without reference to external aids.

Similarly the Essayist assures us that any one who has a tolerable knowledge of Greek may set up for an interpreter of the New Testament. "When the meaning of Greek words is once known, the young student has almost all the real materials which are possessed by the greatest Biblical scholar in the book itself." *

Semler also alleged that the doctrines now professed by the Christian Church are, in great measure, of recent formation, and are due to the influence of the Creeds on the Interpretation of Scripture. The doctrines of our Lord's Divinity, of Original Sin,† and of Grace

* Essay, p. 384.

† See Semler, ibid., pp. 175, 197, 199, and the following account from Dewar, p. 109:—"The formation of the orthodox doctrine Semler attributes to certain hypotheses, which he supposes to have been framed from time to time, and to have given, as it were, a tone to the Interpretation of Scripture. Among these are, at an early period, the hypothesis of the Divinity of Jesus, and, somewhat later, the Augustinian doctrine of Original Sin, that of Grace, of Predestination, and various others. It is deserving of mention, that Semler introduces this whole subject for the purpose of shewing how injuriously pre-existing theories or ideas, or, as he terms them, hypotheses, operate upon the true Interpretation of Scripture. He is indeed a consistent rationalist. He calls himself a Christian, and lays great stress upon spirituality of feeling. He admits the authority of the Bible; but he meets with certain passages in it, which have been supposed to prove certain doctrines,—doctrines which are not in accordance with the results to which the exercise of *his own reasoning powers* has led him. To these passages he can readily give another interpretation, so as to make them mean something very different, or nothing at all. But the fact that for many ages, aye, even from the time of the Apostles, the interpretation which he rejects had been the one received, he cannot so easily get rid of. He resorts therefore to the ingenious theory of assigning to the opinions or hypotheses of the early Fathers the origin of the articles of our faith, and supposes that in support of the doctrines thus framed, was invented an interpretation of Scripture which is not the true one, and that a new and more liberal method must henceforth be adopted. These hypotheses,—in other words this tradition of the Church,—he, as a rationalist, consistently rejects; but inasmuch as with them he rejects all that we hold to be the

are, he supposed, the results of pre-existing theories and hypotheses applied by expositors to the handling of Scripture.

Here, too, he is imitated by the Essayist,* who speaks of "an attempt to adapt the truths of Scripture to the doctrines of the Creeds;" and asks, "How can the Nicene or Athanasian Creed be a proper instrument for the interpretation of Scripture?" and says that great difficulties would be introduced into the Gospels by the attempt to identify them with the Creeds. How different is the language of our Reformers in our eighth Article, and in the *Reformatio Legum*,† where they say that, "in interpreting Scripture in sermons, the preacher should ever have the Creeds in his view."

The Christian Church builds human *duty* on the foundation of *faith* in the *doctrines* of the Gospel. But Semler laid little stress on the articles of the Christian Creed. He relied on the moral sense of mankind, irrespective of divine revelation of supernatural truths, such as the doctrine of Christ's Divinity, the Incarnation, and Atonement.

The Essayist's system of ethics is framed on the same plan. "In religion," he says,‡ "are two *opposite poles*, of truth and action, of doctrine and practice, of idea and fact;" as if doctrine were not the basis of duty, but were only revealed to supply materials to feed the imagination.

It was a favourite hypothesis with Semler, that there were different schools of Christian doctrine in primitive times, even among the Apostles themselves; and that consequently to maintain any uniform system of teaching, or any fixed formulary of faith, is inconsistent with

most sacred doctrines of the Christian faith,—doctrines which, by his own shewing, not only are contained in the tradition of the Fathers, but which that tradition, if its authority be admitted, proves to be contained in Scripture,—he makes it manifest that the written Word is not sufficient to protect the pure faith from the attacks of human reason; he proves to us that the voice of Catholic consent is a testimony with which the Christian Church cannot afford to dispense."

* See Essays, pp. 353—355. † De Summâ Trinitate, cap. xiii.

‡ Essay, p. 356.

the structure of Scripture, and with the facts of primitive history.*

In a like spirit the Essayist ventures to assert that "the first teachers had a *separate* and *individual mode* of regarding the Gospel;" † as if the Apostle did not teach that there is "one Faith," and did not exhort all to "speak the same thing."

Semler depreciates the use of verbal criticism in the interpretation of Scripture; ‡ and in this respect also he has anticipated the Essayist, who says that "there seem to be reasons for doubting whether any considerable light can be thrown on the New Testament from inquiry into the language." §

Semler also imagined the Gospels to be not independent compositions, but to have been derived from some common document, now lost. So does the Essayist.‖

Semler also treats as of little account the interpretations of the Old Testament which are given in the New.¶ As we have already seen,** he explains away those interpretations by his theory of *accommodation;* according to which, our Lord is assumed to have adapted His language to the circumstances of the age in which He taught. Here also he has preceded the Essayist.

Semler also assures us that there are errors and contradictions in Scripture: †† here likewise he has been followed by the Essayist. ‡‡

Semler taught his scholars to treat Holy Scripture as a common book: here likewise we have a parallel in the Essay before us. §§

Let us now pause, and enquire, What were the practical *results* of Semler's teaching?

Frederick Bahrdt was a young man of great promise.

* Cf. Hugh James Rose, p. 51.

† Essay, p. 426; cf. p. 354.

‡ Semler, p. 222.

§ Essay, p. 393. See also pp. 392, 405.

‖ See above, p. 404.

¶ Semler, p. 223. "Anceps atque incerta regula Veteris Testamenti libros explicandos esse ex Novi Testamenti libris."

** See above, pp. 407, 408.

†† Semler, pp. 249, 251.

‡‡ See above, pp. 380, 397.

§§ See Essay, pp. 350, 377, 378, 404.

He was gifted with a lively temper, a quick fancy, and wonderful versatility. He was an ardent admirer of Semler. The effect of Semler's influence on him is thus described by a learned German author:*—"The study of Semler's critical writings had brought him to the persuasion that Scripture is a mere human book. 'I considered Revelation,' he says, in his autobiography,† 'as a common and natural incident of Providence. I regarded Moses, Jesus, as I did Confucius, Luther, Semler, and myself, as instruments in the hand of Providence. I was convinced that these, and similar men, had drawn only from the source of Reason.' It was in this sense that he treated the Gospel history in his writings. The Gospel narrative was changed by him into a sentimental romance. He had become a disciple of Naturalism."

He taught these doctrines as a Professor at Halle, the University of Semler. Strange to say, Semler himself, who had nurtured Bahrdt by his own teaching, and who was then at the head of the theological faculty at Halle, was constrained to deliver an official protest against the scholar whom he himself had trained!

Semler censured Bahrdt. But, exclaims the German writer from whom I am quoting:—‡

"Quis tulerit Gracchos de seditione querentes?"

Who could endure Semler protesting against Rationalism? "Bahrdt," says he, "had right on his side when he wrote against Semler, whose works had contributed to destroy in him the last vestige of the Church's faith." Semler, whose teaching had made Bahrdt what he was, in vain attempted to restrain the effects of his own teaching. The pupil outran the master. Bahrdt carried Semler's principles to their logical results. He became an unbeliever, a preacher of infidelity; he had married a virtuous woman, but he deserted her for the vicious indulgence of his

* Dr. Kahnis, *Der innere Gang des Protestantismus;* (Leipzig, 1860,) p. 100.

† iv. 119.

‡ Kahnis, p. 99; cf. Bahrdt's *Leben*, iv. p. 61.

appetites in riot and debauchery;* he professed to ground his system on Natural Reason and Morality; he even said that he had a mission from heaven to emancipate mankind from the thraldom of superstition, and he boasted to be the teacher of spiritual illumination; but in practice he was a libertine and a profligate, a victim of sensuality and impurity. At length he died at Halle, a miserable death, broken in mind, and wasted in body with a loathsome disease, in the year 1792.

Such is a specimen of the fruits of Semler's teaching in the last century.

The revival of that teaching in one of our Universities in our own day may well inspire sorrow and alarm. It is probable, that the Essayist himself may soon be constrained to censure the errors and to weep over the miseries of some who have imbibed his opinions, and who may be excited by youthful passions and sanguine self-confidence to develope those opinions in their full dimensions, and to act upon them in their lives: but his efforts will then be in vain. Semler endeavoured to reclaim his pupil Bahrdt; but it was too late.

Therefore in the name of God, and in the name of those for whom Christ died, let the Essayist be solemnly entreated to reconsider the opinions put forth in this Essay; and if he sees reason to believe them to be erroneous, let him be implored to retract them. It will be a noble task, worthy of the high place which he holds in one of the greatest Universities of the world, to set an example of genuine love of truth by a public avowal of error.

In the meantime, we may cherish a hope, that, under God's gracious dispensation, the discussion of the questions revived in this Essay may be made conducive to great good. We are all now called upon to examine the *reason* for which we believe the Scriptures to be the Word of God; and it behoves us to consider well, whether Almighty God, who has given us the Scrip-

* Cf. Kahnis, pp. 92, 93.

tures, has not also given us external as well as internal evidence of their Inspiration; and whether He has not also afforded us sure guidance for their right Interpretation, in the consentient faith and practice of the Universal Church of Christ.

If by means of this examination we attain to clearer views on these essential questions, we shall have great cause to thank Him, whose special prerogative it is to elicit good from evil, and who makes the propagation of error to be a great and glorious occasion for the clearer manifestation of Truth.

APPENDIX.

I.

RADCLIFFE OBSERVATORY, OXFORD,
Dec. 21, 1861.

MY DEAR SIR,

In responding to your request that I would add my name to the list of those who have taken upon themselves the task of defending the cause of revealed truth from the cavils and doubts that have been unhappily raised against it by the publication of the "Essays and Reviews," I do so with great diffidence, as neither competent by my learning or my leisure to enter minutely into the controversies which have been promoted by the work in question.

There are, however, one or two points on which both as a Christian man, as a clergyman, and as a cultivator of science, I am glad of the opportunity of expressing my opinion, and I therefore thank you for the honour you have done me, and which I attribute to my office rather than to myself, in requesting it from me.

In the first place, then, I would say that, in common, I hope, with thousands of my fellow-countrymen, I have been deeply grieved, not only at the nature and spirit of several of the articles of the book in question, but at the circumstances under which it has appeared. That philosophic truth, when it is clearly recognised, should be followed at all hazards and independently of all consequences, I am willing to admit; and I trust I have had too long and severe a training in mathematics and the natural sciences to put me in danger of erring on the side of bigotry in religion, or of the reception of any doctrines on the mere plea of authority or tradition. But when I am introduced to a book, not written by one hand but by many, and containing fragmentary essays, and reviews uncalled for by any particular occasion, whose only unity of purpose seems to be that of a deliberate attack on many of the fundamental principles of our most holy faith, and when I find that, with a single exception, all the writers are men bound by most stringent obligations to defend and to teach religion such as it has been delivered to us by our forefathers in the Liturgy and the articles of the Church of England,—when I see this, I am grieved, I repeat it, at the scandal of the spectacle presented.

If, up to this time, we have been mistaken in our faith, and in the objects of our love and reverence; if at this time it is requisite, for the advancement of abstract truth, that we should sit at the feet of these new Gamaliels and be untaught almost every principle of speculative and of practical religion; if it is really true that with regard to the inspiration and authority of the Old and New Testament we have been mistaken; if prophecy, and miracles, and all the old foundations of our faith, are proved to be the weak props that they are here represented to be,—let us, after deep and mature study, yet with bitter tears of regret and disappointment,—let us, I say, give them up; let us, with our new instructors, ransack the sacred pages for disagreements and contradictions; let us use the knowledge of morality which the sacred Word has given us, to prove that the morality inculcated in that Word is indefensible; let us give up every cheering hope which the sure confidence of the truth of that Word has given us, and be henceforth the converts of that new intellectual religion which has refined away all that was tangible, consolatory, and real in the old. But if we be driven by the necessity of truth and consistency to do this, we may still grieve that it has fallen to the lot of the sworn defenders of orthodox Christianity to be its executioners. Unwelcome it is at any time to a tender heart to be the bearer of intelligence which is painful or grievous, and most unwelcome will we still believe that it has been to the Essayists to follow their convictions of the demands of truth to their consequence, and to proclaim, in a volume which has been read by tens of thousands, that the faith of themselves and of their ancestors is a delusion, and that they must now construct for themselves a new, and for the most part a negative, religion. And, that clergymen should feel compelled (by what necessity we know not) to do this, who are bound by most holy vows to defend the ancient faith, defined as it is and limited by ancient creeds, is of all the grievous circumstances connected with this book the most unfortunate, and that which has given (almost alone) notoriety to the work, and such scandal to the community at large.

But surely when men of deep wisdom and learning, most of them occupying responsible situations in society, unite together for so serious a purpose as to convince us that the ordinary grounds on which we hold our faith are no longer tenable, (for there must have been some settled plan of action in the collection of a series of Essays like those in question, having at least one determinate object,) we might at least expect that each subject would be well argued out. To the Christian, whose fundamental article of faith is the resurrection of our Lord and Saviour Jesus Christ from the dead, the most stupendous of all miracles, there should have been given, not a fragmentary Essay, controverting the evidence deducible from miracles, (if not, by implication, denying their possibility,) but a clear and convincing statement, proving, beyond the possibility of mistake, that the Christian miracles are false. Facts should have been discussed first and theory afterwards; and, in a matter so momentous, if regard for truth imposed upon a *clergyman* the necessity of so painful an office as the disproof of the ordinary belief in the Christian miracles, not only should the writer's convictions be clear, but his facts and his inferences should be incapable of contradiction.

Again, if, in the casual discussion of the prophecies of the Old Testament it became necessary to disavow the pertinency of those which ordinary Christians have, ever since the establishment of Christianity, believed to refer to the Messiah,—if it were necessary to revive in these days, with very little variation, the deistical notions of the last century, for the purpose of proving that our faith, as founded on prophecy, is worthless, —we have a right to expect that such an attempt at disproof would be supported by profound wisdom as well as learning, and on grounds totally different from any which have been familiar—too familiar—to English readers. Bishop Chandler's admirable "Defence of Christianity," and Bishop Kidder's "Demonstration of the Messias against the Jews," if the writer of the article to which I refer had read them, (which seems doubtful from the vague way in which they are quoted to support his own views,) might have taught him better the connection between the old and the new dispensations, and the indispensable need of prophecy in the scheme of salvation.

But I need not tell the readers of the "Essays and Reviews," or you, Sir, that there is nothing worked out. Doubts and difficulties respecting numerous points of our faith are suggested, but rarely proved valid; cruel insinuations against the fundamentals of the Christian faith are sometimes obscurely hinted at and sometimes broadly given, sufficient to shake the faith of the young and the ignorant, but without the solutions which would deprive them of their power to do harm, and without the discussion which would call for an elaborate answer from the learned orthodox divine. When, too, the barriers and safeguards of ordinary Christianity have been sufficiently battered by our author, a new scheme of Christianity is put before us to rebuild our religion; a scheme in which everything is mysticised and spiritualized, and in comparison with which the Christianity of the Neo-Platonists was plain common-sense. And, if the subject were not so awfully important, it would be simply amusing to follow the critic in his fondling admiration of the German philosopher. A mild rebuke here, a dash of unqualified admiration there; here an attempt to render the transcendental language and ideas of the German mind intelligible to English readers on points where the well-trained English mind can see nothing but baseless speculation and a perverse ingenuity in distorting plain facts, bordering on the ludicrous.

I did expect, when I read these Essays, to find something which would have better repaid the labour of reading such a heavy and miscellaneous collection of fragmentary papers. I thought that, if I were forced to disagree with the conclusions of the writers, I should at least have an intellectual treat; that I should at least see indicated the sources of these new discoveries which are to put the evidences of our faith upon so different a footing; and that I should have been benefited by the critical disquisitions of some of our best English scholars. I need not tell you, Sir, that I was disappointed to a great extent in my expectations; though it would be unjust to say that there are not in some of the Essays some things both original and instructive, nor that there are some whose chief fault is that they are in bad company. Still the general impression left on the mind was that of weariness and dissatisfaction, both with the matter and manner of the book as well as with its doctrines.

But enough of this;—my province is not to analyse or to criticise the details of the articles in the "Essays and Reviews." This has probably been done, by far abler hands, in the body of the "Replies." It is sufficient for me to express my opinion that as literary productions the Essays cannot be rated very high. Some have evidently been written hastily, and might in any other case have put in a plea for indulgence, but certainly not in this. As a whole, they have had a tendency to invalidate the evidences of Christianity, and to shake the confidence of Christians; and though the writers could not have foreseen the notoriety or the excitement which they have, from circumstances quite independent of their own merits, produced in the public mind, they are equally answerable for any bad effects which may be produced by them. If they are right in their general statements and deductions, then alas for our holy faith, which, till this time, we have cherished as our greatest treasure! If they are wrong, who can properly estimate the mischief which they have done!

I fear that I have already written you too long a letter before I have come to the point which especially concerns me as a man of science, and on which you desired my opinion; namely, the bearings of astronomical research on the arguments of the "Essays and Reviews."

The only article in which the assumed antagonism of the physical sciences to the Bible record is treated of, is that on the "Mosaic Cosmogony," by Mr. C. W. Goodwin, and the discussion has more to do with geology than with astronomy. This, indeed, might be expected from the nature of the case. The earth is man's dwelling-place, and it concerns him to know its origin and its history, while the hosts of heaven, the sun and the moon, the planets and the stars, though equally the work of the same Divine Creator, and included in the inspired record of His works, are rather the objects of man's study and admiration than of his interested inquiries.

Imagine now for a moment that we were in the condition of the ancient heathen world, without a revelation of God's doings and purposes, and left to our own vague and uncertain guesses about our origin and our destiny. What would be the order of our inquiries and of our cravings after knowledge of ourselves and of the universe of God? Assuming, as the later philosophers did, a great First Cause or Author of all things, would not the first yearnings of our souls be to learn what is the relation of this Almighty Being to ourselves, and to the world which we inhabit? And, imagining all the wants of the soul longing after some direct manifestation from God, some authenticated record bearing the impress, as far as human words can do so of His majesty, could we imagine anything more sublime or more worthy of Him than the commencement of that record which we believe to have come from Him: "In the beginning God created the heaven and the earth." Criticism finds no place, either on physical or philological grounds, for analysing the sublime simplicity of this opening message from the Creator to His creatures. The boasted light of modern science can add nothing to it, and take away nothing from it.

The record does not limit the time, nor the succession of the intervals of time, when the Almighty Architect commenced and added to the works of creation; and the religious necessities of man do not require the knowledge of the infinite past. Let imagination here revel as she will, and she can scarcely go too far; let her imagine past duration so far back as the powers of numbers will allow; let her listen to the fiats of the Almighty, at intervals of enormous length, filling up the skies with glittering orbs, and, as a last work, preparing by successive steps the habitable earth for man's dwelling-place, and she cannot go beyond or misinterpret the opening of the divine record, "In the beginning God created the heaven and the earth."

Quite as little can criticism have to do with the second statement concerning creation, "And the earth was without form and void." The sublime simplicity of this statement of the primeval state of the earth is worthy of the divine inspiration which we claim for it, and its truth is unquestioned by scientific investigation. Imagination here may come again into play, and legitimately exercise her functions, for science can do but little either to substantiate or controvert this record of the origin of our globe. A happy scientific guess of a great astronomer (we can scarcely call it a theory) has shewn that, assuming the matter which now constitutes the solar system to have once been a nebulous mass, intensely heated and extending beyond the distances of the now existing planets, it is consistent with physical laws to suppose that the exterior of this mass would cool by the radiation of heat into the void spaces beyond, and would contract or become condensed in cooling. As the velocity of rotation (originally assumed) would necessarily increase with the decreasing distance from the centre of motion, an exterior zone of vapour might become detached from the rest, the central attraction being no longer able to balance the increased centrifugal force. In general, if this zone were not of uniform density it might break up into detached masses, and these would ultimately coalesce into one mass, having rotation on its axis and revolution round the sun in the same direction and in a nearly circular orbit, and thus the formation of the planetary masses would be accounted for. La Place himself supposes, indeed, that, the sun himself being a solid body originally,* his heated atmosphere would thus produce planets; but this would really explain so little, that such a theory is hardly worth framing or contending for, and it is equally valid to suppose the whole mass of which the sun and planets are composed to have been originally nebulous.

Now we may say of this theory, which has been discussed beyond its merits, that it would probably never have been framed if the constitution of the nebulæ which we see in the heavens had been understood as well as it is now. Many of them which appeared, in telescopes of moderate power, to be mere masses of nebulous light, have been resolved into congeries or aggregations of stars when seen through Lord Rosse's large reflecting telescope; and even in cases wherein this resolution has not taken place, there is observed a curdling, or unequal distribution, of the nebulous matter, which makes it appear probable that a still greater optical power would resolve these masses also. We may also observe of the theory, that even granting it a high probability as explaining more phenomena of the planetary movements than any other, it after all explains very little. We have still to assume that the nebulous mass out of which the sun and the planets were formed was created at some time or other; that it was in a state of most violent heat; that on it were impressed those laws of condensation by which solid worlds were formed out of it; and, finally, that it had an initial velocity round an axis. It removes the Creator one step farther from us than if we were to suppose that the sun and each planet were made by His direct personal agency and interference; and this is all. We have still to account for the innumerable, wonderful, and posterior adaptations by which the earth was accommodated to the physical nature of man—a most complicated set of arrange-

* He afterwards, however, imagines a preceding nebulous condition of the sun, for he says, "Dans cet état, la planète ressemblait parfaitement au soleil à l'état de nébuleuse, où nous venons de le considérer."

ments being necessary not only with regard to the earth itself, but also with regard to the orbit which it describes in space.

As bearing, however, on the verse we are discussing, it is important to observe that the earth was once in a fluid state. This is distinctly proved as any problem in pure mathematics, by comparing the ellipticity which we know it to have by direct measurement, or by the law of the increase of gravity in going from the equator to the poles, with that which calculation proves it ought to have had (with its known time of rotation) on the supposition that it was once a fluid mass. And this harmonizes admirably with the desolate condition which the Scripture asserts that it had while cooling down and becoming solid. "The earth was without form and void," —or rather, "desolate and void,"—"and darkness was upon the face of the deep. And the Spirit of God moved upon the face of the waters." Think as you will, favourably or otherwise, of the nebular theory, substitute for it any other which is consistent with known facts;—nothing can exceed in truth and grandeur these words of the inspired historian. Like the bold touches of a great artist, they create a picture which no after addition or refinement can improve.

The only passage besides these which concerns me as an astronomer is that which describes with equal majesty the works of the Creator beyond the earth:—"And God said, Let there be lights in the firmament of the heaven to divide the day from the night; and let them be for signs, and for seasons, and for days, and years: and let them be for lights in the firmament of the heaven, to give light upon the earth: and it was so.

"And God made two great lights; the greater light to rule the day, and the lesser light to rule the night: He made the stars also. And God set them in the firmament of the heaven to give light upon the earth, and to rule over the day and over the night, and to divide the light from the darkness: and God saw that it was good."

The most keen-eyed hypercriticism should see nothing to object to as unworthy of an inspired pen in this grand assertion of God's creation of the sun and moon and stars, and of the provision which He made by them for the necessities and convenience of His creatures. But our critic, Mr. Goodwin, thinks otherwise. Their office is a poor and unworthy one. "They are set in the firmament of heaven to give light to the earth . . . to serve as the means of measuring time. . . . This is the most prominent office assigned to them. The formation of the stars is mentioned in the most cursory manner." Rarely has it been my lot to see so much bad reasoning and petty criticism in so small a compass. As far as man is concerned, and to man is revelation addressed, what more important or more suitable office could these glorious orbs of heaven answer than to minister to his convenience? It may be that they answer other, but scarcely higher, purposes in the general economy of God's providence. The sun himself, astronomy has already taught us, journeys with wonderful celerity through space and in an orbit whose dimensions we scarcely can conceive: he carries with him in their orderly march the grand array of the planets his satellites; all have a mission known only to the Creator, but utterly beyond the sphere of man's destinies or his wants. To us they are the dividers of our days and nights, and of our summer and winter. They bring to us seed-time and harvest, rain and drought, heat and cold; and when we look with humble and thankful hearts towards the Author of these benefits, the inspired record comes to the aid of our religious thankfulness, and tells us that "God made them."

But "the formation of the stars is mentioned in the most cursory manner." I answer, and so is the formation of light:—"And God said, Let there be light, and there was light." And yet one of the greatest of Greek critics considered this as one of the most remarkable instances of the sublime which he could quote; and critics as well informed as our author may be of the same opinion here. To my own mind the impression from childhood has been that of the sublime brevity of the assertion, "He made the stars also." There are men who measure everything by the carpenter's two-foot rule, who would apply the same canons to every possible variety of circumstances, and who would look to the Book of Job for a treatise on natural philosophy. But does not the rule hold in this case which I propounded just now, only with still greater pertinency? The stars are removed still farther from the sphere of man's destiny. Those glittering orbs are placed in general at distances even yet unmeasured. We have made some good guesses at their number, and at the law of their distribution, and we have measured the distance of one or more from our own globe: but, of the purposes which they answer in the economy of God's creation we know nothing whatever, and quite as little do we know *certainly* of their physical origin.

When we look at them on a fine winter's night traversing

the blue vault of heaven in calm and glorious majesty, the coldest amongst us feels the message sent us by their Creator, "God made the stars also."

Of all the writers in the book of "Essays and Reviews" Mr. Goodwin is the most candid. Other writers contradict the revealed word with at least a semblance of regret. Not thus does our critic contradict the inspired prophet Moses. His mission is to prove him incorrect, and this he attempts to do with the utmost straightforwardness. The old story of Galileo is revived for our edification, but the lesson to be derived from it is very different from that which the great philosopher ever dreamt of. The celebrated text, "The world is established, it cannot be moved," implies "the sacred penman's *ignorance* of the fact that the earth does move." Measured by the two-foot rule this is the unanswerable fact. Yet I cannot but think that a little consideration would teach our critic, as it has taught many others, that we need not assume this. The earth undoubtedly to its inhabitants is immoveable; and if the sacred penman intended, as he manifestly did, to indicate in poetical language the perfect stability of man's dwelling-place and security of God's people, he could not have used a better term.

Again, no palliation can be admitted in favour of Moses. Do we meekly suggest that the Bible was not intended to teach science?—we are met with the reply that the first chapter of Genesis "is intended, in part, to teach and convey at least some physical truth." Undoubtedly it is, but not according to the measurement of the two-foot rule. It teaches, contrary to all Oriental and all Grecian and Roman cosmogonies, that God is the sole Author of all the things of which our senses are cognizant. *He* made the earth, and *He* made the heavens; the earth for man's use, and the heavens partly for his use, and partly, as far as we are concerned, for the satisfaction of his reasonable faculties.

But it is not necessary that I should follow Mr. Goodwin through all the instances of his criticism, or shew more clearly than he himself has done, how earnest he is to destroy the credit of the inspired author of the cosmogony. I would rather conclude this too long letter with a few remarks on the general arrangement of the separate acts of creative power, which may help in some measure to a better understanding of the whole narrative, and which I do not remember to have seen insisted on. The three acts of the great drama are, the formation of the earth; of the orbs of heaven; and of living creatures. This is the natural order of events according to that rule which I have insisted upon for the proper interpretation of all Bible history, namely, the nearness or the remoteness of man's interests, in the narrative; and this rule is adhered to without a single deviation. The first verse having asserted the fact that God is the Creator of all things in heaven and earth, the narrative from the second to the thirteenth verse is occupied exclusively with the preparation of the earth for its inhabitants; there is not a single passage in it which is not most rigorously confined to this. I have nothing to do with the scientific objections and real difficulties which may be met with in detailed passages; they may be safely left to the care of our excellent Geological Professor; but, I repeat, everything has relation to this earth in its various stages of formation: the dreary darkness of the primeval chaos; the introduction of light, (whether by this is meant the introduction of the *property* of light in the formation of the luminiferous ether, or the piercing through of the rays of those luminaries afterwards mentioned,) the separation of the clouds and vapours above from the dry land and the water on the surface of the earth; the fertilization of the ground and the introduction of all plants and vegetables fit for the use of its future inhabitants.

Then follows, from the fourteenth to the nineteenth verse, the creation of the heavenly bodies; and, finally, from the twentieth verse to the end of the chapter, the creation of all the inferior animals, and of man.

I do not trouble myself, nor you, Sir, with discussing the meaning of the days within which the separate acts of creation are included. Mr. Goodwin is quite right in reminding us that some school-books still teach to the ignorant that the earth is six thousand years old, and that *it* (he should have said *all things*) was created in six days. No well-educated person of the present day shares in this delusion; but if any there be, Mr. Goodwin's two little rudimentary treatises on astronomy and geology, which increase the bulk of his Essay, will teach them better. We know that we cannot expand our ideas of God's universe too much, both as to space and time. With Him a thousand years are but as one day; and, if we take a thousand years as the unit of our counting, we shall require still an incalculable number of such units to enumerate the sum of creation-periods, and to fathom the depths of space through which He has scattered the millions of His stars. Whatever be the meaning of the six days, ending with the seventh day's mystical and symbolical rest, indisputably we cannot accept them in their literal meaning. They serve apparently as the divisions of the record of creation, lest the mind may be too much burdened and perplexed by all these wonderful acts; but they as plainly do not denote the order of succession of all the individual creations. Something is symbolized, and the author of the Epistle to the Hebrews uses the symbol; and this, the only mystical fact in the whole narrative, we may surely, in all reverence, leave unexplained, without detracting at all from the credit or the veracity of this wonderful record.

During the writing of this letter I find my own mind cleared and elevated. I see, by this additional study of the record of creation, more clearly than I ever saw before, its lucid order, its divine simplicity, its internal evidence of bearing the impress of that Divine Spirit that dictated the narrative; and I wish that I could make others see with me how harmless are the shafts of ordinary criticism when directed against this, the ost wonderful chapter of God's revealed Word.

I am, my dear Sir,

Yours very faithfully,

ROBERT MAIN.

JAMES PARKER, ESQ.

II.

UNIVERSITY MUSEUM, OXFORD,
June 11, 1861.

MY DEAR SIR,

The question which you have done me the honour to ask, touching the bearing of geological discovery on religious belief, as experienced by myself, is the more agreeable for me to answer, because I know how readily your own mind has received the great truths now established regarding the ancient natural history of the earth, and how constantly you have favoured the free and unrestrained teaching of them from the Chair of Geology in this University.

During the last eight years, in sixteen courses of lectures, embracing geology in every form, involving questions of force and time, of the succession of life and changes of physical condition, there has never been produced in my own mind, nor, so far as I know, in the minds of my hearers, the slightest impression that we are considering facts and laws in any degree opposed to Christian faith, to the inferences from natural theology, or to the deductions from Scripture.

How, indeed, could it be otherwise? Seeing that, in common with all the most experienced geologists of this age and nation, in agreement with the conclusions of Conybeare, and the lectures of Buckland and Sedgwick, I see in the vast geologic record which we are invited, if not compelled, to read, not an anti-Mosaic history of the creation of man, but pre-Mosaic tables of stone, inscribed by the hand of the Divine Master, and bearing indisputable traces of His earlier works, earlier co-ordinations of the appointed powers of nature, earlier terms of the one creative series, whose latest period includes the history of man.

Thus viewed, the two great problems on which we are intent,—the physical history of the earlier world, and the moral and religious history of man,—appear in natural sequence and relationship, not in unfriendly contrast, or perplexed and suspicious alliance. The evidence proper to each inquiry is kept clearly separate: we do not seek our Christianity in the rocks, nor our geology in the Bible; we do not confound two independent records; but, examining each by the appropriate means of interpretation, we adopt the conclusions which fairly spring from each, under the guidance of sound criticism and with the aid of healthy discussion.

There are points of contact between the two histories. The great system of physical causes and effects is ever moving onwards, gathering what is present into what is past, and giving us hints, if not measures, of the lapse of time and the changes of nature. The physical events which happen on the earth in our days are but a continuation of its earlier history; and the ages during which man has existed on the earth, though limited within a few thousand years, are linked with a far longer stretch of earthly time, and serve at least as a unit for computing the vast integral of past duration.

The conclusions reached by this kind of computation are at present quite indeterminate, whether they relate to the whole or any particular part of the periods which have passed away. Equally indeterminate are those inferences concerning the length of time during which man may have existed on the earth, which are based on the few, and as yet insufficiently examined, cases of the discovery of the remains or works of men, in bone-caves, gravel-beds, and other superficial deposits. They belong to the latest period of which geology takes cognizance; they are comparatively modern; but we can apply no sure computation to them, founded on the geological evidence.

If it ever could be a serious question whether a diligent and philosophical study of nature were likely to lead to habits of mind unfitted for dealing with the evidences of the truth and authority of the Gospel, I would venture to reply,—and not for geology only,—that this kind of study is eminently fitted to train the mind in the right methods of estimating the probability of remarkable and unusual occurrences, and to touch the heart with a susceptibility of gratitude for the effects of God's goodness, whether we perceive or not the method and motive of His working. His ways are often past finding out in the physical not less than in the moral world; our notion of the laws by which He regulates the changes of nature is but a feeble copy of the truly divine idea; we must not say to Him, as He to the ocean, "Thus far and no farther;" but rather,—thankful for the knowledge already imparted, and conscious of its imperfection, but hopeful of future progress,—we may look forward, and look higher, even towards the Fountain of life, and thought, and hope, for some further exhibition of His goodness, some clearer manifestation of His designs, than can be had in this stage of our existence.

On the whole, I believe, and am satisfied, that geology has added to the defences of natural theology, established no results hostile to the evidences of revelation, and encouraged no disposition of mind unfavourable to a fair appreciation of those evidences. In this faith I cheerfully abide, and remain, ever,

Yours very truly,

JOHN PHILLIPS.

TO THE REV. DR. COTTON,
PROVOST OF WORCESTER COLLEGE, OXFORD.

Aids to Faith:

A SERIES OF THEOLOGICAL ESSAYS.

By VARIOUS WRITERS.

Being a Reply to "ESSAYS AND REVIEWS."

1 vol., 12mo, cloth, 538 pages, $1.25.

CONTENTS.

I.	*On Miracles as Evidences of Christianity.*	H. L. MANSEL, B. D., Waynflete Professor of Moral and Metaphysical Philosophy, Oxford; late Tutor and Fellow of St. John's Coll.
II.	*On the Study of the Evidences of Christianity.*	WILLIAM FITZGERALD, D. D., Lord Bishop of Killaloe.
III.	*Prophecy*	A. M'CAUL, D.D., Professor of Hebrew and Old Testament Exegesis, King's College, London, and Prebendary of St. Paul's.
IV.	*Ideology and Subscription*	F. C. COOKE, M.A., Chaplain in Ordinary to the Queen, one of H. M. Inspectors of Schools, Prebendary of St. Paul's, and Examining Chaplain to the Bishop of Lincoln.
V.	*The Mosaic Record of Creation*	A. M'CAUL, D.D., Professor of Hebrew and Old Testament Exegesis, King's College, London, and Prebendary of St. Paul's.
VI.	*On the Genuineness and Authenticity of the Pentateuch.*	GEORGE RAWLINSON, M.A., Camden Professor of Ancient History, Oxford; and late Fellow and Tutor of Exeter Coll.
VII.	*Inspiration*	EDWARD HAROLD BROWNE, B. D., Norrisian Professor of Divinity at Cambridge, and Canon Residentiary of Exeter Cathedral.
VIII.	*The Death of Christ*	WILLIAM THOMSON, D. D., Lord Bishop of Gloucester and Bristol.
IX.	*Scripture and its Interpretation*	CHARLES JOHN ELLICOTT, B. D., Dean of Exeter, and Professor of Divinity, King's College, London.

EXTRACT FROM PREFACE.

This volume is humbly offered to the great Head of the Church, as one attempt among many to keep men true to Him in a time of much doubt and trial. Under His protection, His people need not be afraid. The old difficulties and objections are revived, but they will meet in one way or another the old defeat. While the world lasts skeptical books will be written and answered, and the books, perhaps, and the answers alike forgotten. But the Rock of Ages shall stand unchangeable; and men, worn with a sense of sin, shall still find rest under the shadow of a great rock in a weary land.

REVOLUTIONS IN ENGLISH HISTORY.

BY

ROBERT VAUGHAN, D.D.

VOL. I.

REVOLUTIONS OF RACE.

PRICE $2.

In this work, Dr. VAUGHAN, the Editor of the *British Quarterly Review*, intends to group together the leading facts of English History, so as to reveal at a glance the progress of the nation. It is a step towards the simplification of English History. By the term Revolutions, the author intends to denote the great phases of change, through which both the government and people of England have passed, during the historical period of their existence.

"A work of this kind," says *Blackwood's Magazine*, "cannot be superfluous, if it is worthily executed; and the honorable position which Dr. Vaughan has earned for himself in both theology and literature, gives us a guarantee that this will be the case. The specimen before us we have read with interest and improvement. We should particularize the ecclesiastical portion of the history as being executed with special care, and as remarkable for the spirit of justice and liberality he displays. To these pages we may honestly recommend the reader, as the fruit of steady and conscientious labor, directed by a liberal and enlightened spirit."

"This treatise," says the *London Athenæum*, "or rather narrative, is deeply and variously interesting. Written plainly, but with all the characteristics of independent thought and accomplished scholarship, it may be pronounced a masterly survey of English civilization from the remotest epoch to the commencement of the fifteenth century. We have found this volume in every way excellent. It is at once a narrative and a disquisition, learned, genial, critical, and also picturesque. The spirit of English history animates it throughout. Dr. Vaughan, by completing such a work will have done good service to literature."

The *Westminster Review*, the very highest critical authority upon English literature, said of this work, upon its original publication in England—"We can sincerely recommend Dr. Vaughan's Revolutions in English History as a thoughtful, interesting, scholarly presentment of the principal sociological vicissitudes of more than two thousand years of our British existence. Dr. Vaughan's composition is extremely lucid and nervous; not without a certain sedate ornamentation, but quite free from the misleading exaggerations of a seductive rhetoric."

www.ingramcontent.com/pod-product-compliance
Lightning Source LLC
LaVergne TN
LVHW021134110826
845150LV00005B/1031

* 9 7 8 1 4 2 5 5 4 9 4 4 2 *